British External Policy-Making in the 1990s

KEELE
UNIVERSITY

LIBRARY

return by the last date or time show

D1428304

5 040 850 X

The Royal Institute of International Affairs is an independent body which promotes the rigorous study of international questions and does not express opinions of its own. The opinions expressed in this publication are the responsibility of the author.

British External Policy-making in the 1990s

Michael Clarke

M
MACMILLAN **for the Royal Institute of
International Affairs, London**

© Royal Institute of International Affairs 1992

All rights reserved. No reproduction, copy or transmission of
this publication may be made without written permission.

No paragraph of this publication may be reproduced, copied or
transmitted save with written permission or in accordance with
the provisions of the Copyright, Designs and Patents Act 1988,
or under the terms of any licence permitting limited copying
issued by the Copyright Licensing Agency, 90 Tottenham Court
Road, London W1P 9HE.

Any person who does any unauthorised act in relation to this
publication may be liable to criminal prosecution and civil
claims for damages.

First published 1992 for the Royal Institute of
International Affairs by
THE MACMILLAN PRESS LTD
Houndmills, Basingstoke, Hampshire RG21 2XS
and London
Companies and representatives
throughout the world

ISBN 0–333–57055–3 hardcover
ISBN 0–333–57056–1 paperback

A catalogue record for this book is available
from the British Library

Typeset by
Ponting–Green Publishing Services
Sunninghill, Berks

Printed in Hong Kong

KEELE UNIVERSITY
LIBRARY

1 9 JUL 1993

B 25674

To
Leonard
Evelyn
and
Jessica

Contents

Acknowledgments

I should like to express my gratitude to the Nuffield Foundation for the grant that supported the work for this study, and to the staff of the Royal Institute of International Affairs, who have proved helpful in many ways over a long period. I should also like to thank all those officials and other academics who granted interviews and offered their opinions on matters of contemporary policy-making, as well as Sylvia Ellis and Richard Wylie for help with some of the research material. I also owe a considerable debt to Margaret May of Chatham House for some very judicious editing and to the staff of the Historical Branch of the Library and Records Department in the Foreign and Commonwealth Office who read the manuscript for me and commented on its factual content. I am also grateful to Keith Povey for his detailed work on the final text of the manuscript. Above all, I owe a great debt to Dr William Wallace for his help and encouragement throughout this study, and to Professor Peter Nailor and Professor Jack Spence for their helpful comments and careful reading of the initial draft. I have learned a great deal from all three. Needless to say, none of the people to whom I owe such debts can be held responsible for anything that follows.

October 1991   MICHAEL CLARKE

Abbreviations

ANC	African National Congress
ASEAN	Association of South-East Asian Nations
AWACS	Airborne Warning and Control System
BIS	Bank for International Settlements
CBI	Confederation of British Industry
CDC	Commonwealth Development Corporation
CND	Campaign for Nuclear Disarmament
COCOM	Co-ordinating Committee
COI	Central Office of Information
CPRS	Central Policy Review Staff
CSCE	Conference on Security and Co-operation in Europe
DHSS	Department of Health and Social Security
DIB	Defence-Industrial Base
DTI	Department of Trade and Industry
EC	European Community
ECD	European Community Department (in FCO)
ECJ	European Court of Justice
ECOSOC	Economic and Social Committee (of EC)
ECU	European Currency Unit
EDM	Early Day Motion
EFA	European Fighter Aircraft
EFTA	European Free Trade Association
EIPA	European Institute of Public Administration
EMS	European Monetary System
EPC	European Political Co-operation
FCO	Foreign and Commonwealth Office
GATT	General Agreement on Tariffs and Trade
GCHQ	Government Communications Headquarters
GEC	General Electric Company
IAEA	International Atomic Energy Agency
IBA	Independent Broadcasting Authority
IBRD	International Bank for Reconstruction and Development
IEPG	Independent European Programme Group
ILO	International Labour Office
IMF	International Monetary Fund

IPU	Inter-Parliamentary Union
ITV	Independent Television
MAFF	Ministry of Agriculture, Fisheries and Food
MEP	Member of the European Parliament
MINIS	Management and Information System for Ministers and Top Management
MNC	Multinational Corporation
MoD	Ministry of Defence
MP	Member of Parliament
NAO	National Audit Office
NATO	North Atlantic Treaty Organisation
NIE	Newly Industrialising Economy
NOP	National Opinion Poll
ODA	Overseas Development Agency
OECD	Organisation for Economic Co-operation and Development
PAC	Public Accounts Committee
PQ	Parliamentary Question
QUANGO	Quasi-Autonomous Non-Governmental Organisation
TBDF	Transborder Data Flows
TUC	Trades Union Congress
UKDEL	United Kingdom Delegation (to NATO)
UKREP	United Kingdom Representation (to EC)
UN	United Nations
UNCTAD	United Nations Conference on Trade and Development
UNESCO	United Nations Educational, Scientific and Cultural Organisation
UNICE	Union of Industrial and Employers' Confederations of Europe
WEU	Western European Union
WHO	World Health Organisation

1 Introduction

Britain in the 1990s is part of a world that is immensely different from that of the 1970s, let alone from what we casually refer to as the 'post-1945' world. The contemporary world, of course, always appears uniquely confusing and intractable: only when it becomes the past do we perceive in it strong elements of continuity. Indeed, current affairs would simply be incomprehensible were it not for the many consistent strands interwoven with the politics of the past. So many of those strands have been cut or ruptured by the events of recent years, however, that it may now seem commonplace to assert that the 1990s will be a time of great change for British foreign policy.

Nevertheless, in the international context the differences from the immediate past are more radical and far-reaching than even the dramas in Eastern Europe and the Soviet Union, and the 1990–91 Gulf war, might imply. External policy-making in the 1990s is not just 'new' because of inevitable change over the years, but involves political processes and calculations that are of a different *order* to anything experienced in the past. The world has not only changed because the Cold War is over: indeed the dramatic events of 1988–90 were more symptoms than causes of deeper changes in the nature of world politics, and some of the most important changes had already taken place by the time the Berlin Wall was breached in November 1989.

In order to capture this 'newness' and appreciate the way in which it can affect the future of British external relations, it is necessary first to consider, albeit at a very general level, the major empirical trends of the last two decades. Chapter 2 attempts, therefore, to highlight those developments in the international environment which have made different types of demands on British policy-makers, and Chapter 3 reviews Britain's place in the world in this context. Chapter 4 analyses the policy-making process for external relations; Chapters 5 and 6 assess institutional influences (such as Parliament) and non-institutional influences (such as public opinion) upon this process; and Chapter 7 considers the party politics of external relations, focusing particularly on the recent leadership.

This is not a book about theories of the state or international relations; it is an appraisal of external policy-making in contemporary Britain. Nevertheless, in a world changing around us so rapidly, two fundamental conceptual issues run through this study, and affect the conclusions drawn in Chapter 8. These fundamental issues, about the nature of the modern European state and political authority within it, are closely linked with different perspectives on world politics: whether one should see the growing diversity or the growing homogeneity as more significant. In an attempt to place this study in its theoretical context, therefore, this chapter focuses on the debate between realist and behaviouralist views of the world, the notion of state sovereignty, and the problem of putting sovereignty into context.

Realism and behaviouralism

Even the sketchiest outline of major international events since the late 1960s reveals that Britain faces a world both more diverse and more homogeneous than hitherto. The 1970s saw the rapid evolution of great diversity in the political alignments that had hitherto structured the international system, and also witnessed an equally rapid growth, both within and between states, in functional homogeneity – that is, greater integration in the political processes developed for the performance of necessary functions. This is a curious phenomenon and is difficult for many analysts – schooled to look for consistent trends or general theories – to accept. Some draw upon the wisdoms of the Realist tradition and claim that most of its principal characteristics remain valid. For the Realist, the world of the 1990s is still essentially a world of nation states, where sovereign actions, backed up by disposable power, provide the framework within which other political processes are permitted to exist. Viewed in this way, the Realist paradigm, with its emphasis on diversity, applies as well to the 1990s as it did to the 1890s.[1] Other analysts, attempting to understand the growing homogeneity of world politics, adopt a behavioural perspective which stands realism on its head. In this view there are a series of political processes in the world that determine which institutional units shall exist, and which shall have authority. Political behaviour determines the relevant institutional units, rather than the other way round. And the nature of the most prevalent current political processes is frankly incomprehensible in terms of the more distant past. We appreciate that we live in an interdependent world but we do not understand the dynamics of interdependence very well; the task of the analyst is therefore to try to make sense of a confusing network of political processes that cannot even be satisfactorily described by reference to the vocabulary we have inherited from the nation state system.[2] In reality, both schools of analysis are more than half right.

Realism and the notion of state sovereignty

There is good reason to believe that Realism remains a sustainable perspective on contemporary world politics. It has a theoretical elegance since the best exponents of it – latterly known as neo-realists – have made a convincing case for the continued political potency of the state. No other political unit commands the same symbolic power over the people involved in it: very few other political units have the audacity to demand what nation states demand from their peoples, and they have a near monopoly over the ominous powers associated with 'last resorts'. Realists are convinced that states remain the most important political animals in the kingdom of international relations, and as such their views on the nature of sovereignty, even in a highly complex world, are remarkably definite. In essence, *sovereignty is a legal expression of statehood*: an assertion that a state recognises no higher legal authority. States are either sovereign or they are not, insofar as final authority for decisions either resides with the government of the state or it does not. Ultimate authority can only reside in one place. Sovereignty, therefore, is to be distinguished from autonomy, which all states possess in different measure, and it can thus apply to many different types of states. In the present century it so happens that nation states are sovereign, but there is no reason why sovereignty could not apply in future to multinational states, city states, or even theocratic states. In other words, *wherever states exist, they are defined by their possession and exercise of sovereignty.*

There is plenty of empirical evidence to support such a perspective. In the 1990s states do exercise their authority and do not automatically submit to transnational forces. One of the most important reasons for this is that states still define the most prevalent political categories in which we both think and act. Transnational forces, on the other hand, cross many political categories but define very few of their own.[3] The need to co-ordinate civil air traffic may be regarded as one of the more obvious and pervasive of transnational pressures, and for half a century it has been a commonplace observation that air travel would increase exponentially. Yet air traffic control has always been defined by reference to national airspace, and in 1990 Europe was burdened with no fewer than 22 national air traffic control systems operating from 42 different control centres. This is not so much a failure to think about the challenges of the future, more a natural and collective tendency to regard airspace, and the administration of it, as the legal right of every state. Air travel, in itself, does not suggest any alternative and authoritative ways of thinking about airspace.

Even when we consider the complexity of politics within the European Community, it is possible to argue not that the state has been internationalised, but rather that the international world has been 'domesticated'.[4] As Hedley Bull said, it is just as likely that transnationalism is an indication that the state-system has 'extended its tentacles over world politics'.[5]

Clearly, Realism – as an explanation and a theory on which predictions can be based – has a lot to tell us about the nature of the world, and sovereignty – as a legally testable concept – about the nature of the state.

The conceptual dilemma

On the other hand, the fact that Realism has some severe limitations has not in itself produced alternatives with equal explanatory power. Behaviouralists who are interested in political processes as the organising device of International Relations cannot produce an impressive theory in opposition to Realism. 'Interdependence' is not a theory, but rather a collective term for some interesting observations about the nature of systemic relations. 'Integrationism' provided a number of elegant theories of federalism, functionalism, and neo-functionalism, but most of these have been discredited as their explanations as to how political integration could take place were not borne out in a reality where the states of the EC continually reasserted their sovereign rights. 'Transnationalism' or 'internationalism' cannot fill the gap since they are little more than generic terms to encompass different sorts of descriptions of reality: they are not *explanations* of the political units or the way in which they act.

When we try to conceptualise the political situation of Britain in the contemporary world, therefore, we can make out a clear Realist case for the relevance of old insights. Britain behaves as a sovereign state and is exercising, rather than forswearing, its sovereignty when it makes politically convenient arrangements in a complicated world. What takes place outside the government's remit does so because the government allows it. Attempts to analyse British external relations cannot avoid defining them in essentially Realist terms, since our thinking is necessarily governed by the state and state-centric political categories. Transnational phenomena are so-called precisely because they are departures from this state-centric view, rather than independent observations.

Nevertheless, the empirical world also suggests that if Realist insights are true, then they apply to an ever narrower range of the political processes that interest us, and that affect the wellbeing of the British public. In an increasing number of cases Realism can offer only somewhat glib explanations of behaviour which we can see is extraordinarily complex. Britain, and states like it, are caught up in various types of interaction which can be defined and described but not satisfactorily explained, and which appear to bear greatly upon the ability of states to exercise – in some cases even to express – their sovereignty. Thus, as theories, transnationalism and interdependence will not stand up: but as empirical phenomena, they will not lie down. This is the conceptual dilemma that the observer faces.

Putting sovereignty into context

If we tend towards a Realist view then we regard the context of sovereignty as the international system. Sovereign states exist because other sovereign states exist, and sovereignty is an attribute of the state system.[6] On the other hand, if we tend towards a behaviouralist perspective then the more relevant context is Britain itself. British sovereignty exists because of the way the British community has developed. And if we assume that Britain will continue to develop, then we may be able to go some way towards constructing a theory of sovereignty and statehood that has the explanatory power of Realism. On this issue, the study of British external relations is more illuminating than most.

Historical conceptions of sovereignty

Discussions of British sovereignty have always been a mixture of the empirical and the normative. Sovereignty is not only a description of reality in the way that John Austin and Thomas Hobbes presented it. There was also a highly normative strand in its definition, as presented by Bernard Bosanquet, T.H. Green and Harold Laski. Hobbes himself regarded sovereignty as both a logical truth *and* a moral necessity – since it was a moral necessity that such a truth should be recognised and accepted. Sovereignty, in other words, has never been an unambiguously neutral concept, still less a matter of deduction. British sovereignty, for example, developed in a way that was significantly different from that of most of its continental neighbours, and was the outcome of a particular sort of competition for power. The 'sovereignty of Parliament' was an assertion of political authority over the rule of the Crown, and thus arose as a highly normative concept, not quite synonymous with democracy in Britain but certainly a prerequisite for it. By the early eighteenth century, Parliament had emerged as the instrument which limited the power of the King, and particularly the moral absolutism that had

attached to the continental Catholic kings. Parliament thus guaran-
teed not only political, but also economic and religious freedom. It
allowed the state only a minimal role in the economy of the British
people and developed its anti-Catholicism into principles of religious
toleration. 'As a result no other country in Europe, not excepting
even Holland, had more real toleration for differing religious views
than England: in none other had the common man so proud, even
insolent, a conception of his own rights and of his part in deciding on
any matters of public policy that seemed to affect him'. Nor was the
law, such as it was, 'supplemented, as in most other countries, by
irresponsible and undefined claims of the administration against the
legal rights of even the meanest in the community.'[7] Such an
analysis, written in the 1950s, reflects both an authentic sense of
eighteenth century sovereignty and a traditional twentieth century
British view of it.[8]

National conceptions of sovereignty

For the observer of British external relations, two important insights
follow from this. One is that this conception of sovereignty, as
opposed to other peculiarly national conceptions of sovereignty, is
still prevalent in contemporary British thinking. Arguments about
Britain's entry into the European Community were debated very
much in terms of the political sovereignty of *Parliament*. They still
are. Enoch Powell's analysis of the Thatcherite approach to the
Single European Act could have been written by John Locke
himself: 'Britain's new and realistic policy of co-operation between
independent sovereign states has performed the surgical operation of
separating the Siamese twins of free trade and political union. That
they were ever connected at all was always a monstrosity.'[9] Only in
British terms does it seem a monstrosity. The alternative view
derives much more from the continental experience of sovereignty.
For in continental Europe sovereignty frequently developed through
the monarchy itself and was never separated from economic, social
or religious matters: the sovereignty of the *nation* – 'the people' –
was at stake rather than the sovereignty of an institution. In such a
conception, therefore, sovereignty can be more easily shared with
other political units in order to achieve political and democratic
control over those matters – political, *and* economic and social – to
which sovereignty quite properly applies. Where Enoch Powell and
Tony Benn would defend the sovereignty of Parliament as a
guarantee of political freedom in Britain, Jacques Delors or Ralf
Dahrendorf would defend the collective sovereignty of European
Community *governments* to guarantee political control over any of
the forces that affect the nations of Europe.[10]

To most other European ways of thinking it is simply perverse to assume that the free market of 1992 will not make monetary union both a theoretical and a practical necessity: there is no logical reason to want to separate economic and political integrative processes. Paulo Cecchini made the point with an elegant empiricism: the single European market could be worth a 4–6 per cent leap in the combined GDP of the member states and at least 5 million new jobs. But it can only work if the market is genuinely and completely free of trade barriers. It will require all EC governments to adopt faster growth policies and to accept some of the painful economic readjustments that the single market will impose. In other words, there will be a political price to pay – a certain loss of national economic autonomy – for the economic benefits of the single market.[11] Indeed, where there were some real doubts about the implementation of the Single European Act in, say, France or the Federal Republic of Germany – as in the Bundesbank, for example – it was precisely because the doubters had every expectation that economic unity would, of necessity, be inseparable from political unity.

If we approach the sovereignty issue from an overtly Realist perspective, seeing it as a function of the state system, then we will tend to view it from a positivist position, wherein it is a description of reality. As such, there is little more to say about it, other than to observe that sovereignty is exercised in a very complicated world these days. On the other hand, if we view sovereignty as a contingent historical phenomenon, then it is apparent that despite the tenacity with which it has consistently been defined in Britain, it is a concept that has never been static and always responded to its historical circumstances. The development of sovereignty in all of the major European states from the sixteenth to the nineteenth centuries occurred as a result of various types of internal struggle for political authority. The achievement of sovereignty was a recognition that a legitimate political community had emerged from the struggle. In the nineteenth century newly-emergent states claimed sovereignty as an attribute of the statehood to which they aspired, in a sense, imitating the older states around them as a way of bolstering their infant authority. Finally, in the latter half of the twentieth century the relationship between sovereignty and authority has been turned on its head. Newly-independent states in the post-1945 period have been formed and had sovereignty effectively thrust upon them as a political definition within which they would have to try to develop an internal political authority.[12] Instead of being the *outcome* of a struggle for authority, the sovereign state throughout the under-developed world has become a *framework* to define the starting point of the struggle. If sovereignty can mean, and has meant, so many different things, there is no reason to suppose that its definition will not change in response to new historical circumstances.

The role of the state

The second insight is that the British concept of sovereignty, whether or not one agrees with it, accounts to a large extent for the ambiguous view of British governments about the role of the state in so many of the processes that affect external relations. As part of their general ideological commitment, Conservative governments over more than a decade preached deregulation and the minimalist state within the context of a free market economic philosophy. This is conceptually clear and is quite consistent with a Realist view of world politics and a fiercely British view of the nature of sovereignty. But it is almost impossible to implement in the empirical context affecting Britain in the 1990s. Britain's partners and rivals do not necessarily share the same views. The world economy is not over-whelmingly deregulated, it is not a free enough market in which to have much faith, and few other states feel that economic autonomy and political sovereignty can be easily divorced. Throughout this study the question of the state's role in the fabric of external relations arises continuously. This is not an accident, for it is a reflection of the fact that the British government's defence of Parliamentary sovereignty, particularly in relation to the inter-dependence of European affairs, becomes even more an argument about current political ideology. Throughout the 1980s the government defended Britain against centralist and pseudo-socialist ideologies in Europe. The rhetoric of sovereignty in Thatcherite ideology was as prescriptive as that of the eighteenth century Whigs.[13]

The future of sovereignty

In such insights lies the possibility that Realist perspectives on the role and authority of the state, and therefore of its foreign policy, can be modified by theories developed from the nature of world politics in the 1990s. For Britain is in a situation where its particular concept of sovereignty is under enormous challenge. It evolved from a particular ideology – anti-Catholic and essentially secular – in the seventeenth century and is now, in the late twentieth century, defended by reference to another – conservative and anti-centralist, in which sovereignty is only one element. Both ideologies, though different, are related by the force of nationalism. The rationale of this perception of sovereignty is to defend Britain against something the government regards as undesirable. Sovereignty is not meant either to define the British state or to be defined by it. As a politically flexible concept employed by leaders in a given moment of history, it may well evolve and be used to justify a defence of values and interests of the nation that is wider than the boundaries of the state. The next chapter looks at how the new international environment both affects the existence and functions of the state and sets a diverse context for the formulation of external relations.

2 Diversity and Homogeneity in World Politics

The world context

Diversity in world politics

A growing diversity in political alignments was probably the most obvious outcome of the dramatic events which tumbled over each other in the early 1970s, and which seemed to transform the face of international politics. It was as if a series of political time bombs had suddenly been triggered by overlapping events to destroy the bipolarity of the previous era. The Cold War itself did not end during the 1970s, but the world of the Cold War did. The international system was no longer dominated by the dangerous certainties of the 'Superpower era'. Instead, in all the major regions around the world in which the Cold War had previously been fought, unprecedented changes encouraged indigenous and more diverse political forces.

South and East Asia

In South and East Asia – a region that encompasses over a quarter of mankind – the political status quo altered completely between the mid-1970s and mid-1980s. The United States had already acknow-ledged defeat in Vietnam and withdrew from the conflict in 1973. This was both a symbolic and an actual withdrawal of the United States from its post-1945 predominance in world politics. The wisdom of US policies, the level of its commitment to other allies, and its actual capacity to maintain such commitments, were all crucially diminished by the Vietnam experience. Within two years of the US withdrawal the South Vietnamese regime had totally collap-sed, and communist forces had triumphed in Kampuchea, Laos and Vietnam. But this was not a major victory for Moscow, still less for Peking. Rather, it was a prelude to renewed war between different communist forces in Kampuchea, backed respectively by the Soviet Union and China.

The balance of power in South East Asia visibly changed. The influence of the United States on the region has not been directly replaced by that of any other power. Regional communist states found themselves impoverished while their great-power mentors became absorbed with the problems of their own reform. Japan began to play a significant role in the economic development of the region, but was very wary of shouldering more political responsibility. Less than a decade after the height of America's involvement in the Vietnam war, Washington was supplying military equipment to communist China, and Indo-China had become the most sensitive arena of the Sino-Soviet dispute. By 1980, the situation in South and East Asia had become so diverse that it no longer bore much relation to the bipolarity of the late 1960s. During the 1980s this diversity increased considerably: the Soviet Union, the United States, the People's Republic of China and Japan all now play different roles in the politics of smaller states in the region, and have adopted quite new postures in relation to each other. Thus Japan is the major foreign investor in China; China's relations with the United States, notwithstanding the Tiananmen Square massacre in 1989, are driven more than ever before by economic considerations, while its relations with the Soviet Union are dominated by security issues; and so on. During the last 150 years there has never been a time when the international order in South and East Asia has been so different from the international order prevailing in Europe; it is now simply incomprehensible in terms of traditional Cold War thinking.[1]

The Middle East

A similar transformation in the balance of forces occurred in the Middle East. When the Yom Kippur War of October 1973 broke out, the price and supply of Middle Eastern oil was already a political issue. But by 1974 the world was plunged into the first, and most dramatic, oil crisis. This, and the second oil crisis in 1979, gave wealth and new political power to Middle Eastern states just when the United States was discovering that it was unable to maintain alone its security commitments around the world. The Vietnam War had weakened the United States: the Middle East war had weakened Israel and strengthened the oil-producing Gulf states. By the late 1970s the resulting great political diversity had undermined America's position in the region, forcing it to work through strong allies. Iran seemed to be the most reliable, but the increasing dependence of the Shah of Iran on the United States and the social tensions aggravated by the rapid westernisation of Iran became the catalyst for the Islamic fundamentalist revolution of 1978.

The war between Iraq and Iran which broke out in 1980, the Gulf war in 1991, and the continuous tragedy of the Lebanon, all illustrate the extent to which Middle Eastern politics have been driven by indigenous forces. Conflicts in the region are about many different issues but are becoming increasingly defined by the struggles over Islamic fundamentalism. It was Soviet-backed Iraq which launched the war against Iran in 1980, Iraq which began to attack merchant ships in the Gulf, Iraq which managed to launch an accidental attack on an American ship, the *USS Stark*, and Iraq which invaded Kuwait. Yet none of this represented a victory for the Soviet Union, still less a clear challenge to the United States. Both superpowers sat out the Iraq-Iran War without having any clear ideas about what to do. A victory for either of the participants would not be welcome in Moscow or Washington, and yet the mere continuation of the war posed several threats to them both. The West feared for regional stability and ultimately for oil supplies, while the Soviet Union had more to fear from the Iranian revolution in both geographical and cultural terms than any Western power.

By 1988 it had become apparent that both superpowers were being manipulated into Gulf commitments by some of the states in the area, and both were reduced to attempts merely to protect their immediate national interests rather than engineer a regional settlement. Their response to the Iraqi invasion of Kuwait on 2 August 1990 offered the clearest example to date of the degree of common interest the superpowers perceived in their attitudes to the region. Their cooperative actions threatened both of them with the possibilities of a radical Islamic backlash.

A similar phenomenon was evident in relation to Lebanon and the Arab-Israeli conflict. Here too, the issues were no less complex and deeply rooted in historical experience, but they became increasingly defined by the Islamicisation of the region. The fact that Soviet-backed Syria could not be driven out of Lebanon was more of a problem than a victory for Moscow; and Israel's successful defence of the Palestinian territories it had occupied represented a similar dilemma for the United States. Neither superpower has had very much diplomatic leverage over Arab-Israeli events and neither has made much impression on a series of conflicts that are no longer a part of the East-West struggle.

Southern Africa

In 1974, after a coup in Portugal, the former Portuguese colonies of Angola and Mozambique were rapidly relinquished. With that, the political map of Southern Africa altered irrevocably. The 'bulwark against communism' in Southern Africa – a bloc of white-dominated states from Angola to Rhodesia and Mozambique which physically locked weaker black states within its boundaries – was decisively breached by the victory of radical governments seen by the West as hardline Marxists. But once again, these momentous political events in reality had very little to do with bipolar global politics. These changes undermined the apartheid policies of South Africa, putting Pretoria under simultaneous internal and external military pressure; they stimulated both fear and support among other African states; and they forced Western powers to take seriously the politics of Southern Africa. Before the Portuguese coup, the region could be seen in East-West terms, with the West firmly in control. Afterwards, notwithstanding the victory of radical governments in Angola and Mozambique, Southern African politics was driven by the conflicts inherent in apartheid and underdevelopment rather than by any outside influences.

Superpower co-operation and political diversity

South East Asia, the Middle East, and Southern Africa are only the most dramatic cases of regions where the events of the 1970s triggered the growth of political diversity that weakened the capacity of East and West to structure the most salient international relationships. The growth of political diversity over the last two decades can be seen in subtler ways also. It is noticeable, for instance, that Soviet international policies in the reformist Gorbachev era have done a great deal to stimulate more joint superpower action in conflicts in all of these regions. When they co-operate, the superpowers represent a formidable diplomatic weight and there is no evidence that they are becoming impotent in world politics. But their willingness to co-operate is a good indication of the political diversity they see around them. The fact that they can identify more common interests and that they now *both* have a stake in regional stability around the world, is evidence that they are forced to define events in those regions in quite new ways. Thinking that still derives from the more stark assumptions of the Cold War era explains very little in Asia, Africa and the Middle East, and offers even less promise as a guide to policy responses. Nor does it offer the superpowers a way of thinking about the problems of regions which have not undergone major upheavals in the last 20 years. The Indian subcontinent and Latin America, for instance, have not challenged the core interests of either superpower. Yet both superpowers demonstrated an inability to take a sufficiently sensitive view of some of the mainsprings of political action in both these regions and have been punished with spectacular policy failures: for the Soviet Union in Afghanistan; and for the United States, repeatedly in Central America.

Eastern Europe

Nowhere in the world was political diversity more evident than in

Europe – the continent in which political change had hitherto been so incremental. The communist bloc in Eastern Europe, after 40 years of vigorous suppression by the rigid conservatism of the leaderships in Moscow, Berlin, Prague, and elsewhere, effectively collapsed as, one after the other, those leaderships acknowledged that their countries were in a state of economic and political crisis, requiring nothing less than fundamental reform. Most telling of all, the open acknowledgement of failure and the beginnings of structural reform came from the very centre of the system. After the death of Brezhnev in 1982 the Soviet Union embarked on a process of halting domestic reform, which became an irreversible process after 1985 as the new Gorbachev leadership both deepened and extended it. Domestic reform became part of a more dramatic process of social change that naturally involved a series of fundamental reappraisals of Soviet foreign and defence policies. It took some two to three years before Gorbachev's declarations that the Soviet Union would not physically intervene in Eastern Europe were believed, and it was with some incredulity that the West watched the Soviet leader effectively appeal over the heads of the East European conservatives to the more progressive forces within the bloc to encourage reform. But once it became clear that the shadow of the Soviet tank had been lifted from Eastern Europe, nothing could disguise the crippling lack of political legitimacy from which East European communist governments suffered. Throughout the 1980s the Polish Solidarity movement had waged a protracted campaign against its government, and when it was seen to win through after 1988, other East European governments fell at the first determined push. From Poland to Bulgaria, reformist coalitions and, in many cases, multi-party democracies began to emerge throughout Eastern Europe, making the Soviet Union's original efforts at political and economic reform appear conservative by comparison. When the Berlin Wall was breached on 9 November 1989 it seemed that the very essence of the Cold War was evaporating. The world was witnessing the first spasm of what seemed likely to be a two-stage crisis in the communist bloc: first the breakdown of Soviet control in the satellite states, to be followed by economic and political breakdown within the Soviet Union itself.

Such events, of course, are easier to chronicle than to evaluate, and it is not our purpose here to assess the current nature of relations between the West and the Soviet Union. It is clear, however, that these events are both cause and effect of the emergence of far greater political diversity than has existed in Europe hitherto. Hungary, for example, has more in common with capitalist Austria, both economically and culturally, than it does with either of its other neighbours of the former Eastern bloc. The German Democratic

Republic always had a great deal more in common with the Federal Republic than with its socialist neighbour Poland: and the Poland, Hungary and Czecho-Slovakia emerging from the ruins of the Eastern bloc have every incentive to develop stronger ties with western states than with any of the other members of the former 'socialist commonwealth' with whom they were so closely, and involuntarily, linked. All of these trends become stronger as economic reform requires political reform, and political reform leads to the search for new solutions to different national problems. It has long been observed that the Soviet Union could have 'viable' states or 'cohesive' states in Eastern Europe, but not both. It could have states that were economically and politically viable if it allowed them a measure of freedom that would also reveal the natural diversity between them. Or it could have states that were cohesive to the socialist commonwealth, as long as it was prepared to accept that they would be economically hobbled and lacking in popular legitimacy. By the late 1980s, however, it had become clear that even this choice was no longer available to Moscow: there was simply no alternative to 'viability' and it would be necessary to adjust to the economic and political reform that this would entail. Whether or not 'Gorbachev's' reform was destined to survive through the 1990s, the general direction of the process was manifestly irrevocable by 1987–8.

The Soviet Union

Diversity in Eastern Europe raised questions about the future shape of the Soviet state itself. Nationalism in the Baltic republics, in Transcaucasia and Moldavia and in the large republics of Uzbekistan and Ukraine has posed severe threats to the unity of the Soviet Union. The transformation of the Soviet Union, and possibly its complete break-up, remains on the agenda. Internal change is now unstoppable and it inevitably stimulates political diversity within a superpower that is, in all important respects, one of the last of the great imperial states. There are some 22 major nationalities in the Soviet Union, at least 19 of which use their native tongue as a first language, and all over the country significant minorities – 25 million Russians for example – live outside their own republics. The bitter dispute between Armenia and Azerbaijan over Nagorny Karabakh offered a foretaste of violence and dissent that was to be repeated in many other parts of the Union. The Soviet Union faces the end of the twentieth century having to adjust not only – like the United States – to the external limits on its power in the world, but also to the most powerful type of domestic limitations that can be imposed on the foreign policy of any state.

Western Europe and the Atlantic Alliance

The collapse of Communist governments in Eastern Europe and the transformation of the Soviet Union had major implications for the future of Western Europe. However, it was obvious that no less momentous developments had been occurring since the mid-1970s. Opinions differ about the nature of the growth of political diversity in Western Europe over the past two decades. Certainly, since the height of the Vietnam war the relationship between the United States and Western Europe had been obviously changing, and during the years of the Reagan Administration it had approached a condition of manifest crisis. From the time of the Vietnam War American policy-makers had been repeatedly shocked that the West Europeans no longer interpreted their own interests as synonymous with those of the United States. And the Europeans were generally fearful that the United States, since Vietnam, had become increasingly unilateralist in its approach to common problems. In truth, there is nothing new about these differing perceptions, but in the past they were amenable to quiet diplomacy within a small group of Atlanticist policy-makers. A series of crises, however, arising over the attitude of the Europeans to the Vietnam War, the Middle East War of 1973, the Iranian revolution, the invasion of Afghanistan, the renewed growth of terrorism, and a whole series of specific disputes over defence and economic issues in Europe, made such differences matters of public spectacle and hence of intensive domestic politics in all the major countries of the Alliance. This made such disputes both more visible and more genuinely serious for the political unity of the West. By the mid-1980s some Europeans looked forward to a world in which the political and military influence of the United States in Europe would be considerably diminished; others feared such a prospect, and an increasing proportion of the Washington policy community looked to reduce the level of US commitment to common defence in Europe. Few observers, on either side of the Atlantic, doubted that a structural change in the Atlantic relationship was under way, through many disputed the speed and significance of it.

It was against this background that the dramas in Eastern Europe and the Soviet Union unfolded in the late 1980s, and against which the Gulf War of 1990–1 was fought. Suddenly, an edgy Atlantic relationship was cast into a broader context where the division of Europe had been undermined and the very definition of 'European security' became conceptually unclear. The unification of Germany in 1990 raised in the starkest form the question of what the Atlantic Alliance was now supposed to defend its members from. It also made clear that a Europe containing once more a united Germany could not but be structurally different from anything that had existed since 1939. Whereas many politicians in the West had spoken reluctantly, or fearfully, in the late 1970s about the prospects of new political structures and alignments in European and Atlantic politics, developments in the East after 1985 made such speculation both necessary and acceptable. The Atlantic Alliance now had new roles to perform in a European political constellation that would henceforth be anything but crudely bipolar.

Changes in underlying trends

Changes in broad political alignments, of course, may not be the most significant empirical developments. They are the headline issues which command public attention, and they derive from the Realist perspective which interprets international politics essentially as a great game of statecraft where the actions of states and the diplomacy between them are the key determinants of the nature of international relations at any given moment. On the other hand, perceptive Realists would never assume that even a macro-analysis would be complete if it concentrated exclusively on developments among the key states in the Cold War. Such observers would readily be able to identify underlying trends in the international system which also changed rapidly during these years and which played a crucial part in promoting greater political diversity between the countries that played the great game of statecraft.

The economic transformation

The most notable underlying development of the last two decades is unquestionably the transformation of the post-war economic system. The so-called Bretton Woods economic system established in 1945 was a highly unified financial and trading arrangement, based around the economic dominance of the United States, served by centralised institutions, and operated by specialists who were accorded the luxury of operating in a stable political environment. In reality, Bretton Woods was never a mechanically-operated system. It was rather a 'regime' based on economic and political behaviour that was stimulated by a high degree of consensus among the Western allies, and their dominance over the rest of the non-Communist world.[2] It was a mutually reinforcing process. Bretton Woods was based on political unity, and in turn, Western unity owed more to the efficient and unobtrusive functioning of this system than was ever acknowledged at the time. This regime – the Bretton Woods system itself and the wider behaviour which backed it up – worked spectacularly well for over two decades in both an economic and a political sense. But by the late 1960s it was trying to cope with increasing economic disorder. In 1971 the system effectively disintegrated in the face of the mismanagement of intense problems in the US economy, the growth of world inflation, increasing chaos in monetary relations, and a visible decline in the political consensus by which the regime had been run. And just as world economic management was manifestly entering a period of structural crisis, it was suddenly hit by the dire effects of the first oil crisis, which proved to be the final straw for the Bretton Woods system. Collective economic management had decisively broken down.

The Bretton Woods regime has not been replaced, despite a number of attempts to recreate some of its most salient features. Instead, we are faced with a less coherent and loosely structured set of arrangements – in effect, a non-system that somehow manages to function in a more or less regular way – in which many aspects of economic power have changed hands and the political consensus underlying them has become extremely shaky. A simple characterisation would be that the Bretton Woods regime has been replaced by a global marketplace, though this implies that there is something politically neutral about a 'market' and does not do justice to the myriad interventions and distortions that exist within it. Nevertheless, such a momentous change as the demise of the Bretton Woods arrangements has, as we shall see, had a number of contradictory effects, most of which have given increasing power to market forces. The importance of it for our present discussion, however, is that it clearly added a major dimension to the growth of regional autonomy and the further diffusion of effective political power away from the superpowers and the alliances that had traditionally structured the post-war world.

The growth of regional autonomy   The economy of the United States is still immensely influential, and will continue to be so into the next century. Indeed, some writers contend that the economic power of the United States has not declined in any structural sense: it has merely been grossly misused.[3] But it no longer 'manages' global economic arrangements and it must tussle for economic advantage, not only with other influential states, but also with other types of economic actor. The United States has become the largest debtor nation in the world, while Japan has become the largest creditor: in the second half of the 1980s the United States carried a national debt of over $2 trillion (and rising), while Japan was owed over $500 billion by the rest of the world and is set to have at least $1 trillion in overseas assets by the year 2000.

This has happened so quickly that it is impossible as yet to assess quite what the effects of such a dramatic financial turnaround will be, though as Paul Kennedy has pointed out, it would be historically quite unprecedented for this situation not to have a structural effect on the respective great power status of the countries concerned.[4] There have already been a series of more specific repercussions: Japanese banks and financial institutions have become the most powerful in the world; no fewer than 11 of the world's 12 biggest banks are Japanese;[5] Japanese investment strategies pose challenges to the other states that used to manage the Bretton Woods regime in a way that they can do very little about; and the dynamic of the debtor-creditor nation relationship between the United States and Japan is the single biggest factor that has led to the dislocation of trade and finance, where values of world trade are dwarfed by the scale of financial flows around the world. Not surprisingly, Japan is now proportionately much more important in the economic development of South and East Asia. Its economy underpins the states in the Association of South-East Asian Nations (ASEAN), of which it is not itself a member; and it has mended political fences with China, its most bitter historical enemy, and now holds over 40 per cent of that potentially huge import market.

Saudi Arabia, to take another example, is now a major pillar not only of the world oil market, but also of world financial order, such as it is. Saudi decisions on oil pricing will have a ripple effect throughout the world economy; Saudi money provides essential ballast to key exchange rates; and major Saudi investments can be identified in key sectors of many Western economies. Moreover, the 'newly industrialising economies' (NIEs) – Taiwan, Singapore, Hong Kong, South Korea, Brazil, and others – have made signficant inroads into the markets for sophisticated manufactures that used to be the preserve of the Western economies.[6]

Multinational corporations   Such a diffusion of economic power among states is also paralleled by a diffusion of economic power between states and other international actors. The multinational corporation (MNC) has enjoyed new growth in the last decade, not just because some companies have been particularly aggressive, but because almost all major companies have found it impossible not to become multinational in present economic conditions, and are more than ever the arbiters of international investment. Indeed, the term 'multinational' is no more than a convenient shorthand for business that may be international in a number of different ways. A company may be technically 'multinational' (with foreign subsidiaries as miniatures of the parent company), 'international' (where parent companies based at home simply project themselves all over the world), or – increasingly – 'global' (where the whole company exists for, and is structured around, international comparative advantages). All these types of multinationalism have grown enormously since the 1960s, and the gross trends are remarkable.

By the late 1980s some 20 000 MNCs existed around the world, and over 100 000 firms were controlled from headquarters in another state.[7] Their effect on trade is massive. They are believed to be responsible for over 75 per cent of all world trade: indeed, around 40 per cent of all world trade, excluding the former communist bloc, is accounted for by international transfers of goods within the framework of an MNC. It became clear during the 1980s that many world markets are in effect administered through the coordinated actions of the network of MNCs that are involved in them. By the year 2000 MNCs are likely to be responsible for over half the world's total industrial production. The threat to the autonomy of the state that MNCs pose has stimulated a diffused rather than a united international reaction to them. Some governments welcomed the activities of the MNCs in their territories, others became clearly alarmed about them. Most found it impossible to co-ordinate a satisfactory response to the MNCs with other governments, since their particular interests seemed to differ in each case. Global, or even regional, measures to regulate the activities of multinational companies have not proved to be nearly as effective as national state action, where individual governments deal separately with each individual company.[8] It has been necessary for governments to take each case, and each company, on its merits, so that the relationship between government and MNCs is characterised by an enormous diversity of arrangements and comparative advantages. Since the 1960s the astonishing growth in the scope and number of MNCs has led to the original dominance of US multinational companies being hotly challenged by European and Japanese firms, as well as by those from the NIEs. The 'new multinationalism' of the 1980s did not prove either that the world economy is being taken over by MNCs, or that the state, as an institution, is capable of controlling them; if anything, it supports the thesis that regional variations will become greater as some areas form complex but settled patterns of relations between MNCs and governments, while in others the relationship will continue to constitute a difficult political issue.

Financial institutions   Nor are MNCs now the only major international economic actors. Private banks have taken on some of the roles that central banks used to perform and, increasingly, regulate the international flow of capital: other private financial institutions have mushroomed in the last decade and have added to their powers by performing new domestic and international banking functions. In some countries banks have a more decisive influence on manufacturing industry than governments could ever hope to have. The three big banks in Germany, for instance, hold around 40 per cent of the shares of the 70 largest German companies.[9] Indeed, even constitutionally domestic organisations, such as British local government authorities, and nationalised industries, have become international financial actors by operating on the Eurocurrency markets and borrowing on the international money markets. In 1987, for example, no less than £5 billion in largely foreign loans was raised by at least 24 British local authorities.[10] The reality of the 1980s was that all economic units of any appreciable size were forced to become international actors of some sort because of the essentially global nature of the economic environment in which they operated.

It is clear from this brief description that more countries and more private organisations have come to play a specialised role in the international economic arena. In the post-war years a small group of nations, led by the United States and operating through the Bretton Woods regime, were able to dominate all of the major dimensions of the world economy. In the 1980s, by contrast, even a united triumvirate of the United States, the Federal Republic of Germany and Japan could not effectively dominate world production, world trade or monetary relations, and certainly not all three together. Such a diffusion of economic power is both cause and effect of a similar diffusion of political power throughout the world.

Ideological changes

In other respects, too, the old coherence in world politics has changed. Less visible than diplomatic alignments and their economic substructure, there has also been a significant change in the most prevalent beliefs which lie at the heart of the functioning of the international political system.

Capitalism and communism   The twentieth century world order has been overwhelmingly a Western – indeed a European – conception. The dominant ideologies of the 1950s and 1960s provided a strong political consensus among the prevailing Western and the challenging Eastern groupings of the most powerful states. Liberal capitalism and Soviet communism encapsulated their own views of world order, and the adversarial relationship between them provided a political rationale which would have been understood by any nineteenth-century diplomatist. Now, however, these ideologies are no longer sufficiently convincing for a majority of states and peoples in a world of greatly expanded political consciousness. Yet such disaffection as has occurred has not resulted in clear alternative formulations. As Kenneth Clark expressed it so aptly at the beginning of the 1970s, 'The moral and intellectual failure of Marxism has left us with no alternative to heroic materialism, and that isn't enough'.[11] Indeed so. Marxist governments failed to make inroads into the capitalist world; they have now demonstrably failed to achieve lasting influence in the under-developed world, where they might have been expected to make major gains in the post-imperialist era; and they have singularly failed to offer a more productive model of economic development, still less of political leadership, in their own states. By the end of the 1980s, when the flight from Marxism began in earnest, it had become impossible to point to a single example of an unambiguously successful Marxist government.

The Western capitalist world, however, has meanwhile been in a curious state of uncertainty. The post-war international system, excluding the Marxist states, was established in the economic and political image of the capitalist liberal democracies. The record of liberal democracies throughout the world has always been patchy, but now – half a century after the Second World War – Europe is more widely democratic than at any time in its history, and throughout the world some of the most implacably right-wing governments have found themselves in the throes of irresistible change towards greater democracy – stimulated in many cases by the need to become more integrated into the world economy. World capitalism is certainly more ubiquitous now than ever before, whether or not it is more effective in achieving desirable political objectives. Marxist states cannot avoid being involved in it, and the 1980s witnessed assertive right-wing governments in many Western states which elevated the role of a capitalist market to a political end in itself, so confident were they of the superiority of the model.

Yet it is ironic that the Western world in general is less confident, even less conscious, of its capitalist and liberal values than at any time since 1945. The United States, assertive in itself, has ceased to offer a credible moral lead since the Vietnam War and the demise of the Bretton Woods regime, and European-American relations are in a state of structural and moral change. Conservative governments of the 1980s went out of their way to distance themselves from past conservatism. They tried to establish a distinctively new economic and political model of modern capitalism, a new consensus of liberal values, which broke away from the post-1945 tradition. The capitalist world is hardly in retreat, indeed it may be witnessing its ultimate victory; but capitalism now seems to be more a general condition of existence than a choice, still less a crusade. 'Materialist', in Kenneth Clark's words, it may be, but 'heroic' it is not. The attempts of the Reagan, Thatcher and Kohl governments to inject some heroism into it merely polarised, rather than united, their respective political communities. In the wake of the collapse of communism there has been a vigorous academic debate as to whether the capitalist world has, indeed, won a historic victory, or whether it too is destined to share part of that defeat.[12]

Islam   And yet beyond the increasing influence of the global marketplace there is no clear alternative to the old European ideologies that might provide a focus for a deeper international consensus. Islam accounts for almost 900 million people – more than one in six of the world population – and the forces of militant Islam attempt to provide a political vehicle for the expression of discontent in large portions of the underdeveloped world.[13] But Islam is not united, and parts of it are thoroughly integrated into the structure of world capitalism. The actions of militant Islamic states have been more consensual than their pronouncements, and Islam has shown more political flexibility than is often assumed.[14] Nevertheless, it would be difficult to think of a system of beliefs to buttress international society which offers a greater contrast to post-war liberal globalism than than provided by post-revolutionary militant Islam. Moreover, while there have been repeated cycles of Islamic revival throughout history, the present revival is able for the first time to touch all parts of the Islamic world simultaneously, thanks to the growth of literacy and mass communication. It appeals particularly to the disadvantaged young in the urban concentrations of many countries. The fact that active supporters may display only a shallow appreciation of Islam as a religion does not detract from its appeal as a vehicle of protest against the liberal capitalism that appears to preside over their misery.

The Third World   Similarly, the last two decades have witnessed no lessening in assertions of pan-Africanism as the political map of Africa has changed, even if the policies of many African states have been more equivocal, and regional identities have become notably stronger in the Americas and in parts of East Asia. None of this is 'neutralism' in the sense that it used to be understood in the 1960s, as a delicate position between East and West. Nor is it a rejection of world capitalism, since the non-aligned movement includes more than 120 states whose economies are variously interwoven with Western capitalism. It does, however, reflect the fact that there are different and vehement expressions of political identity and economic discontent throughout the three quarters of the world – 3 500 million people in some 120 states – that is poor. Nationalism, as A.D. Smith has pointed out, not only flourishes in an era of internationalism, but is partly nurtured by it.[15] It is impossible to say how such politicisation of the Third World will continue to evolve. One thing, however, is very clear. The international system which began in seventeenth century Europe and which became truly global in the twentieth century, will not in the future be based so exclusively on the European experience underpinned by European values. In the twenty-first century global politics will be global in the literal sense, not just European relations played out in a global arena.

All of these developments, in balance of power politics, in global economic management and in the decline of prevailing ideologies, point towards a more diffuse international society. It is a society in which there are more states; greater contrast in size and wealth among states; more non-state actors; different modes of characteristic political behaviour; more competing views and a greater diversity of political interests than ever before. In the last two centuries, we have probably never seen a world of such great political diversity and, now, so little state hegemony with which to provide a management structure.

Functional homogeneity in world politics

The empirical, Realist, picture presents powerful evidence of the degree to which diversity has increased in a world dominated by a series of political institutions – states, alliances, organisations – however these may be defined. Nevertheless, there is another side to the picture that indicates other trends, no less true, which create a fascinating paradox in the contemporary global order. From the behaviouralist perspective, the world is undoubtedly becoming more homogeneous – in some respects even integrated.

The last two decades have seen some remarkable functional developments. The most widespread and dramatic has been the extension of the technologies of communication and transport: from this has flowed any number of important secondary effects. The manner and scale of manufacturing processes have changed dramatically since the 1960s. New forms of politicisation have emerged in response to the international effects that such technologies have on political processes, and to the gradual realisation among the peoples of the world that we only have one earth.

To be more specific, it is possible to detect, first, a series of major economic trends in production, trade and finance; second, a series of internal changes in the states of the international community; and, third, a series of political challenges and responses arising out of the increasing interdependence of the global environment.

Major economic trends

Production   Patterns of economic production have changed more quickly than we can easily appreciate. Unit costs of production have fallen dramatically with the application of robotic technologies and it is now generally more economical for firms to produce goods abroad rather than produce in the home country and export. For the same reason, it is also economical for firms to produce particular components of their products in different countries within one region and transport them to another country in that region for assembly. Production itself has come to the customers, and while the real value of manufacture and trade of a good has declined, the value of the knowledge and the software that has gone into it has increased dramatically. The market is global: the capacity of large and small MNCs to operate in it has increased remarkably with the computer revolution; and we can observe a greater international division of labour in certain key sectors of a given manufacturing process – say in the software production – to facilitate a ubiquitous production process for the finished product. Brand-name chocolate bars and soft drinks can be obtained almost anywhere in the world because they are produced everywhere, and the ghetto blaster that is shown off in a village in Sri Lanka is the same make that blasts the ghettos of New York.

Trade   Trade has also shown a similar tendency towards globalisation. It has grown rapidly and unevenly over the past two decades, and there is a general belief that it has increased much faster as an external exchange between states – which is what defines trade for the purposes of measurement – than as an internal exchange within countries – which is conceptually important but never measured.[16] Partly as a reflection of the nature of the modern manufacturing process the composition of world trade has altered a good deal. Primary products are now less vital, even to the trade of under-developed countries, and trade in the service sector has grown, since 1975, by about 10 per cent a year. It now constitutes an average of around 27 per cent of the trade of most countries. This average, of course, hides some very high proportions in the developed world, where around 30 per cent of European and 50 per cent of British trade is in services.[17] All of this represents major economic activity undertaken by non-governmental actors (who may, of course, be subject to national government regulation). But the impact of such changes is that the global marketplace has now become the natural arena for such actors to an unprecedented degree.

Finance   Nowhere is this more true than in the realm of monetary relations and financial exchange. For while in the 'non-system' that has prevailed since the end of Bretton Woods all of the main indicators of national financial activity – interest rates, exchange rates, prices, credit, and so on – have been highly volatile, the scope of financial activity has become genuinely global. This has happened with astonishing rapidity. The deregulation of financial markets during the 1980s, for example, was less a calculated initiative of national governments than a realisation on their part of the inevitable globalisation of national financial transactions. For the financial structure of the world economy has exploited to the full the revolution in world communications to create immediate, sensitive, and vital markets around the globe. The adage that 'money never sleeps' has never been more true. Attempts at national economic self-sufficiency are generally acknowledged as being recipes for disaster, no matter how small or large the economy in question. The massive and ailing socialist economies have been subject to the financial magnetism of the West. Large foreign loans have been required by the Soviet Union and East European states for over a decade and there is every indication that this requirement will increase during the 1990s as their reform programmes go forward. Communist China has joined the World Bank and the IMF, seeing advantages in multilateral western finance over bilateral state to state arrangements: and the Soviet Union, recognising that it must integrate itself into the world trading system, has moved decisively towards the General Agreement on Tariffs and Trade (GATT). The magnetism has affected the small as well. There are a growing number of family businesses – Chinese, Indian and Levantine families who for generations have used their kinship networks as a trading structure – which have used the availability of foreign capital since the mid-1970s to turn themselves into international businesses. They have become family multinationals.[18]

The debt crisis   Typical of the effect of such developments on the world economy was the global debt crisis of the 1980s. The oil crisis of the 1970s created a large surplus of petrodollars that swelled the deposits of western banks and financial institutions. This led major private banks to lend huge amounts of money at high rates of interest to Third World countries. By 1984 some $900 billion had been loaned in this way. Governments did not control the flow, acquiescing in a trade that seemed lucrative, at least on paper. Seeing no official restrictions on such activities, smaller private banks followed big private banks in such business. But by 1982 a number of indebted governments were unable to meet their financial obligations and the world faced an international debt crisis. If the principal debtor countries were declared bankrupt, as technically they were, then some major banks in the West would be ruined and international finance would be thrown into chaos. It was everyone's problem. The socialist bloc was in debt almost as deeply as Latin

America and there was a general recognition that the international banking system had operated recklessly, without sufficient prudence from within or regulation from without. The most pressing debts were deferred for five to eight years, storing up a second crisis for 1987–90. Meanwhile the payment of interest by Third World states to their creditors became greater than their total receipts from aid: by 1985 there was a net annual transfer of some $32 billion from the poor to the rich. By 1989 Third World debt had risen to more than $1.3 trillion and the net transfer of resources from poor to rich was around $44 billion.[19] One can explain this situation, but it is very difficult to defend it. The debt crisis is an international problem: the outcome of global banking and economic incoherence. It provides a dramatic example of the strength of international interdependence in the economic sphere and the tardiness of established political institutions in recognising it.

Social change

The second major facet of greater functional homogeneity in the contemporary world – part cause and part effect of it – is the rate and direction of social change within states. In many respects, domestic politics have changed as much as international politics, though the relationship between the two is seldom studied.

Multiculturalism   One major change within the Western states has been the increase in what is sometimes referred to as 'cultural pressure'.[20] It takes many forms: ethnic and religious transnationalism, the growth of separatism, the internationalisation of pressure group politics, the growth of counter-cultures. Even Reaganite conservatism was accused of having, in effect, finished off the American 'white Anglo-Saxon protestant' – a 'political class that has lost its authority' in a society where the white, black and hispanic mix is rapidly altering.[21]

Meanwhile, nationalism and religious observance has diminished the ability of the Soviet government in Moscow, let alone the Communist Party, to speak convincingly for the peoples of the Soviet Union. Nationalist pressures have grown throughout Eastern and Western Europe, as political boundaries have proved increasingly transparent. There is every prospect that states in Eastern and Southern Europe will come under increasing nationalist and separatist pressures in the 1990s, as different ethnic groups see that political structures are fluid in an integrating Europe. Similarly, separatists in West European countries do not see immediate prospects of statehood but nevertheless look to the European

Community as a forum in which to express their identity and gain more administrative control over their own affairs.

Socio-economic changes   Another important form of internal social change in the last two decades, dwarfing the increasing multi-culturalism of western societies, has been the rapidity of socio-economic evolution induced by the growing integration of the world economy. Every state has its wealthy international elite. Some developed states, however, now have a wealthy international middle class, which is potentially more significant. This is nearly impossible to substantiate empirically, though many have no doubt that it has been happening. As Susan Strange expresses it, 'national capitalist classes are being superseded everywhere by a transnational man-agerial class in which the social and functional distinctions between state and corporate bureaucracies are becoming rather blurred.'[22]

Meanwhile, labour organisations in all countries have faced international management rather than domestic bosses more fre-quently than ever before. Their bargaining position has in any case been weakened, quite apart from the determination of conservative governments to diminish them; and their general aims can now most effectively be pursued through governmental and international action, which is capable of dealing on a more equitable basis with international business. The European Community, for example, makes no bones about the fact that the effects of the 1992 initiative diminish the power of national labour organisations, no less than national social organisations, to deal with problems posed by business and capital operating on an international basis across at least twelve European countries. The century of national trade union power in Europe may well be at an end.

While these developments may be seen as indications of in-creasing political diversity in the world, since they challenge the ability of the nation-state to be the organising device of world politics, they also promote a degree of functional homogeneity. For any socio-economic change within states will reveal new winners and losers. Such changes have encouraged social groups either to operate independently in the international arena, or to demand that governments represent them more forcefully in that arena. No politician should suppose that an appeal to patriotism will succeed in persuading investors to keep their money in their own country, or tourists to stay at home, or separatists to speak through the national parliament, if more advantageous prospects are available abroad. In a multitude of individual cases, social groups have found that they have a capacity, and a motive, to act internationally.

The closed societies of Eastern Europe discovered in the most painful way possible during the 1980s that they could not isolate themselves from comparable socio-economic pressures. Their gradual attempts at economic modernisation could not be carried out without the application of new technologies to production processes and the internationalisation of the management elite. Indeed, they could not escape the information revolution even if they were prepared to give up the attempt at economic modernisation. For information technologies cannot be restricted to government or party workers alone.[23] All the technology of the information revolution – the computers, the software, the satellite broadcasting dishes, the electronics, the teaching methods – can potentially impose the most powerful sort of *glasnost* on any society. Until 1987, the Soviet authorities banned the operations of all but official photocopiers; in Romania all typewriters had to be officially registered; in 1989 the Chinese authorities reimposed their ban on non-official photocopiers. The socio-economic pressures of the 1980s on major communist societies, however, rendered such action as futile as it was ridiculous. In socialist or former communist societies everywhere policy-makers who are mandated to engineer economic, social and political reform have to confront the intractable problems of managing a transition, throughout the whole infrastructure of their societies, that will take them rapidly from carbon paper to computer software.

Global issues

The third major dimension of growing functional homogeneity in the international world can be seen in the increased prominence of issues that are of common concern to all states. Among these are the problems of the global environment; the regulation of air transport and of world over-production of some commodities; the future exploitation of the sea and of inner space, including the distribution of orbits for communications satellites and of the radio frequencies available for them; and the need to co-ordinate actions to combat international narcotics, crime and terrorism.

Such common concerns have arisen both voluntarily and involuntarily. The desire to protect threatened species is an essentially intellectual reaction to an issue of no great political significance. But the need to safeguard against a future Chernobyl disaster or the effects of a hole in the ozone layer is a political imperative. Governments now face the prospect of spending many billions of dollars if the phenomenon of global warming becomes an undisputed fact – either voluntarily, in trying to reverse the warming of the atmosphere, or involuntarily, in huge civil engineering projects to protect major cities from the effects of rising sea levels. If faced with such expenditures, governments of every persuasion will have little choice but to co-operate in some dramatic remedial actions, even though their sense of urgency and enthusiasm may vary.

Or again, all of the forces which compel governments or companies to co-operate more closely, for example, also allow criminals to do the same. The problem of international narcotics is only the most obvious example of globalised crime. Just as family businesses have been able to become international in the last two decades, so have family criminal businesses: computer fraud has reached global proportions, as has the ability to hide and launder money through a single keyboard. Japanese financial frauds have begun to have significant effects throughout the world financial system. Crime, of course, is partly a matter of perception: it increases as we extend the definition of what constitutes crime. In this respect, international crime has arguably come to be perceived by the citizens of Europe and North America as a more immediate and dangerous threat to their own personal security than the possibility of international conflict. As with other common global concerns, the growth of crime is both an empirical and a perceptual development.

A global culture?

In general, the breakdown of the more comprehensible world of the 1960s has focused attention on the untidiness of interdependent arrangements in the 1980s and 1990s, while the demands of a genuinely global economy have created industrial, communications, technical and social processes which have major effects outside national boundaries. This is not to say that the state is going out of business across the globe. Far from it. But it is subject to contradictory trends: political forces are necessarily international, and modern technology gives individuals access to the international environment, enhancing internal diversity. There are many examples in human history of cultures which are international, in the sense that they crossed many boundaries. The twentieth century, however, provides the first opportunity for a truly *global* culture. If any such thing develops it will be through the patterns of individual human behaviour – desires, expectations and the dissemination of knowledge – as much as anything that states may do.

The European context

The paradox of a world of both greater institutional diversity and greater functional homogeneity is seen very acutely in Europe – the most immediate, and the most intensive, arena in which Britain has to operate.

Diversity in Europe

National interests

Western European and 'Atlantic' states exist in a context that is highly structured and institutionalised. The Organisation for Economic Co-operation and Development (OECD), the North Atlantic Treaty Organisation (NATO), and the European Community (EC) form families of institutions which interact and overlap to create powerful organisational webs around the member states. This impressive and unmatched institutional framework makes Europe seem more homogeneous than most of the rest of the world, and has proved so successful that the institutions within it now have to face up to the prospect of structural change, prompted by the new claims of reforming European states to a place within the arrangement. The events of the past 15 years, however, reveal that although this web has strengthened, producing the outward appearance of a highly institutional 'order' in European politics, this cannot disguise the fact that contradictory national trends are at work.

Political diversity can be seen in the extent to which European states – and their leaders – refuse to relinquish willingly any of their sovereign rights in matters which would seem to require an integrated solution. European states have created and joined all manner of new international organisations to handle their mutual problems. Nevertheless, the 1980s offered no convincing evidence that Western Europe is moving towards a form of federalism. The founders of the European Community assumed that the future would pose for all European states a series of problems that could only be dealt with in an integrated way. While they were right about the nature of the problems, however, it is clear that there is nothing inevitable about the nature of the responses: the tendency has been for governments to operate wholeheartedly through European institutions only when it suits them and, in effect, to dash for national and interim solutions to their joint problems rather than put their faith in some grand European compromise. This has been no less true of the United States in its policy towards Europe.

The past two decades have seen continual assertions of national identity and political diversity within Europe, so that progress towards co-ordinated, let alone integrated, policies within the European Community, NATO, or the OECD has been gradual and patchy. Agricultural policy within the EC states provides a long-standing example of a sector that is effectively integrated; external policy has been reasonably well co-ordinated between essentially separate national foreign policies; but industrial, social and transport policies throughout the 1970s and 1980s were little more than a collection of fairly divergent national approaches upon which the institutions of Europe attempted to have some influence. Moreover, though integration or effective coordination has been observed to happen, and in some cases to have increased rapidly, it has not proved able to keep pace with the escalating international problems that have had to be faced.

NATO   The balance sheet, therefore, reveals any number of examples of undiminished political diversity in Europe. OECD and European Council summits have frequently had the greatest difficulty in doing more than ratify the existence of separate national positions – on world interest rates, deflationary policies, or international debt problems. The attempt to rationalise arms production within NATO has proceeded for years at a pace that even NATO officials acknowledge as scandalously slow, and the alliance's military plans have been barely coherent in the face of the separate requirements of its national armies. Contrary to popular belief, NATO always outspent the Warsaw Pact (by between 10 and 25 per cent), yet it got far less for its money because it spent it so inefficiently on national systems which duplicated one another.[24] The nature of the task that NATO faced for forty years could scarcely have been more unambiguously collective, yet the realities of NATO politics over this period reveal a constant struggle to maintain unity. Most of the collective action taken is at the margins of particular policy responses that are merely an amalgamation of more or less co-ordinated national responses.

The European Community   Meanwhile, the European Community has shown itself to be a complex arena in which national politicians play out some traditional, if highly complex, diplomacy. In the 1970s the world economic crisis hit the European Community at exactly the time that it was trying to assimilate its new members, particularly Britain. The immediate response of governments was to adopt a series of unilateral national policies, on energy, employment, exchange rates, and so on. Progress on almost every EC front was stalled indefinitely and the prospects of major reform within the Community, to spend less on agriculture and more on social, regional and industrial policies, became impossible. In 1972 the EC had looked towards a vision of 'political unity' by 1980. Within three years it was clear that the 1970s were to be the most sterile decade in the history of the EC's development, and the optimists were left clutching at straws, pointing to partial successes in what were then peripheral areas of the Community's development. Towards the end of the 1970s the United States, under President Carter, with the support of James Callaghan, Helmut Schmidt, and

Valéry Giscard d'Estaing, initiated new levels of international collaboration to 'manage global interdependence'.

But in 1980 the conservative governments that were to dominate the next decade took power in the key Western states and the nature of such collaboration changed. President Reagan, Mrs Thatcher and Chancellor Kohl all took a more traditional view of European diplomacy than their immediate predecessors. President Mitterrand, though for different reasons, also wanted to demonstrate that the French economy was not driven by the forces of interdependence. All these leaders introspectively concentrated on conservative economic policies, and made domestic political capital by taking avowedly hardline stands on relations with other countries. In 1980 Mrs Thatcher went to her second EC summit in Dublin demanding 'our money back' as a budget readjustment, and set, somewhat over-dramatically, a new tone that was to persist in most EC and OECD summits. Right-wing leaders certainly showed that they can get on with each other, and their summit meetings were not un-productive. But their chief concerns at such summits in the 1980s were to gain international support for their existing national policies, and this generally resulted in agreements to differ rather than package deals, and public assertions rather than flexible negotia-tions.[25] Conservative leaders repeatedly demonstrated in the 1980s that they co-operated in a deliberately old-fashioned way. They played out their diplomatic hands in a complex institutional structure but also in a game that would have been readily understood by a Realist observer of thirty years ago: they assessed their own policies in a confusing environment and defended what they interpreted as their own national interests. Though this may be regarded as anachronistic by a number of the theorists of interdependence, and a surprising number of Whitehall officials, the fact is that the 1980s generation of European leaders clearly felt that they knew how to define and defend their national interests.

Sectional interests

Diverse national policies are also reinforced to an extent by some of the changes in the domestic composition of modern societies. European societies are characterised now by significantly greater vociferousness on the part of sectional interests, which naturally look to their governments to protect them from the effects of European and global forces beyond their own control. This in turn often hardens national responses – or has increased the overtones of 'national security' even where economic logic has seemed to point in the opposite direction.

Aerospace   Thus, European governments have been confronted since the late 1960s by the global competition of US MNCs with a high degree of concentration both in civil and military aerospace and in the development of commercial space programmes. Boeing has sold more than 6500 jet airliners in its history: more than all of the other manufacturers in the Western world put together.[26] This sort of competition was given added point after 1983 by the American Strategic Defense Initiative (SDI). Whatever the SDI may have meant in strategic terms, it constituted a major industrial challenge to the Europeans in both military and civil spheres. For the SDI technologies included almost all of the technologies of modern industrial production – software, new construction materials, modern electronics, chemical engineering – in addition to all the new aerospace technologies. Yet in the face of such challenges the Europeans were riven for over twenty years with sectional interests that hindered a more coherent European response, or even a more collaborative response outside Western Europe. European governments clung tenaciously to their national aerospace industries for reasons involving prestige, their sense of national security and sheer fear of the strength of the competition. Any major aerospace project is necessarily collaborative where the development costs are so high. But neither private companies nor governments have found it easy to agree on multinational projects, since the share of the work to be divided between different countries will have major effects on employment, and even on the survival of some industries that the government may consider to be of 'strategic' interest. Yet the economic logic of the aerospace business has been clear for many years. In 1987 Boeing had 51 per cent of civil airline sales, the European Airbus Industrie 30 per cent, McDonnell Douglas 17 per cent, and the remaining 2 per cent was split equally between Fokker and British Aerospace. In the small aircraft business the American company, Cessna, has about 50 per cent of the market.[27]

In the military market the American domination is even greater, but even Boeing no longer produce aircraft entirely on their own: collaboration is now essential, even for the aerospace giants. As the success of Airbus Industrie has demonstrated, this has not been lost on the Europeans. Nevertheless, only in the 1990s will the Europeans have some real response to the competition. Collaborative products such as the Tornado and perhaps the European Fighter Aircraft (if it comes fully to fruition) and the Airbus A320 would have the ability to compete internationally with the Boeings, and Lockheeds, while the controversial European Space Agency is due to have spent over $30 billion by the end of the 1990s to establish a space shuttle, a spacelab, and the new Ariane 5 satellite-launching rocket.[28] In these respects, the Europeans will be entering a world market more than a generation after its domination by a small number of major firms. In the field of avionics the Europeans have been more competitive for a longer period. But even here it is notable that until recently 'European avionics' has been the sum total of a series of national industries and its competitive edge has depended on essentially national companies.

Other sectional interests   The aerospace industry provides only one example of the problems of timely collaboration that can also be seen in less dramatic ways across a range of areas. This case did not merely demonstrate a failure of 'political will', but was an expression of the growing pressure on politicians from national sectional interests which served to reinforce conservative instincts. Neither politicians nor businessmen can agree easily on common action to prevent environmental pollution, for example, because such action may well increase the costs to hard-pressed domestic manufacturers. Similarly, a radical restructuring of European agriculture within EC countries has proved almost impossible because every set of proposals would disadvantage a major sector of the farming community within at least one of the key member states, and conservative governments felt unable to endure the electoral pressures that would create. The result has been that over the past 30 years the traditional 'national' style of conducting international politics has prevailed, however novel the institutions of Western Europe may be.

Functional homogeneity in Europe

Nevertheless, just as there has been an increase in functional co-operation at the global level, so this has also happened in a very intensive way at the European level.

Informal areas of co-operation

Quite apart from the perceptions and self-images of political leaders and the formal institutions of European co-operation in which they have effective powers of veto, the less formal processes provide rich evidence of evolving co-operation and even embryonic integration in many areas of European politics and economics. We can safely assume that all of the integrative trends identified at the global level exist in a highly concentrated form in the European and Atlantic arenas.

Production   In the manufacturing sector there is a high degree of integrative production in Europe. During the 1980s less than 25 per cent of the components in a Vauxhall car sold in Britain were manufactured in this country, less than 50 per cent of those in a Ford.[29] In early 1987 Ford switched more of its car production to Britain and away from other European countries to take advantage of productivity increases. But in February 1988 Ford UK suffered a national strike which closed its factory in Belgium, and considerably affected production at its plants in West Germany and Spain. Conversely, the 700 British companies supplying components to Ford were not too badly affected, since they had become considerably less dependent on the UK motor industry for their customers and were able to use their sophisticated manufacturing techniques to switch to production for other overseas companies.[30]

This sort of story could be repeated for many of the manufacturing sectors in Europe, though the picture cannot be expressed simply. In domestic electrical production, for example, firms like Philips (Netherlands) and Electrolux (Sweden) both produce and sell all over Europe, whereas most French and many British electrical appliance companies choose to operate on a national basis. Equally, European companies that accept the pressures to operate internationally do not necessarily collaborate with other European firms. In the aerospace, information technology, scientific instrument and pharmaceutical industries, European firms have more frequently sought American and Japanese partners.

Nevertheless, though the picture is not a simple one, the underlying trends became clearer during the 1980s: firms recognise that the market for manufactures is global, and the management strategy of an increasing number of firms is European. The nature of the European market after 1992 is likely to increase this perception and the implications of it are well recognised in the automotive, electrical, chemical and pharmaceutical industries. Daimler Benz, Unilever, Philips, British American Tobacco and Siemens are the biggest employers across Europe, and their management and operations span the whole region. The other side of this coin is that in a country such as Ireland, which has positively welcomed multinational investment, over 30 per cent of all industry is foreign-owned, including over 90 per cent of its electronics and over 60 per cent of its chemical industries.[31]

Trade and finance   In the same way, intra-European trade and financial flows have grown more intensively than in other areas of the world and have promoted even greater flexibility both in Western Europe and in regions that are closely tied to it. The Eurocurrency market is a prime example. In 1960 it was worth some $3 billion. In 1970 it had risen to $75 billion and was growing by over 20 per cent a year. By 1984 the market was worth $1 trillion, and during the 1990s is expected to reach some $3 trillion. Its value is already much greater than the total value of world trade and it constitutes the equivalent of some 30 per cent or more of the total output of the OECD countries. [32] As such, the Eurocurrencies have a major effect on the expansion of credit all over the world, and have so far proved to be beyond the regulation of governments. Eurocurrency markets may be capable of overtaking domestic credit and, 'within a foreseeable period, effectively eliminating state monetary policy'. [33]

Not only has the intensity of financial activity grown but it has also become more integrative over the last decade. After 1973, the pace of economic growth in Europe slowed sharply as the effects of inflation began to bite, particularly in the core countries – the Federal Republic, France, Britain, Italy and Benelux. But though the late 1970s and 1980s witnessed a series of divergent political responses to the problems of the European economy – each individual state's policies to deal with the common problem of inflation were rather different, for instance – the fact remains that the underlying economic reality has been more convergent as a measure of order has returned to the European economy. Inflation rates have fallen, and become more convergent, monetary and fiscal policies have also tended to align themselves and European exchange rates became more closely tied together by 1989 than at any time since the demise of the Bretton Woods regime. Even the poorer states in Southern Europe began to catch up on their richer neighbours during the late 1980s as they were drawn into the new attempts to establish financial order.

Communications Personal and official communication across Europe has expanded by a similar magnitude: broadcasting channels serving all of Western Europe via satellite have become commercially feasible, and international business travel and even travel between divisions and affiliates of the same company account for a growing proportion of total European travel, notwithstanding the boom in the holiday market. In the 1980s world travel and tourism emerged as the largest single industry worldwide, accounting for around 5.5 per cent of world output.[34] By the late 1980s, demand for European air travel had reached unprecedented proportions. Over the decade of the 1980s the number of international airport arrivals grew by almost 30 per cent and was expected by the World Tourism Organisation to continue to grow by at least 4 per cent per annum over the 1990s.[35] In Britain alone, there are no less than 22 main airports operating international flights. This, in itself, provides eloquent testimony to the fact that most of the integrative forces to be found at the global level are also present in dramatic form at the European level.

Formal areas of collaboration

Equally obvious has been the growth in some of the more formal and constitutional expressions of integrative behaviour in Europe. The institutional architecture of European collaboration and integration consists of the families of a number of key institutions: the European Community, NATO, the European Free Trade Association (EFTA), and the Western European Union (WEU).

The European Community   The European Community, with all its limitations, has a dominant impact on certain socio-economic activities of its members (agriculture, intra-EC exchange rates, fisheries, energy, manpower training), and a variable but often significant impact on many other areas (consumer standards, environmental policy, regional development, legal practice, foreign policy, educational and research initiatives, and local government). The EC has had an uneven but growing impact on government below the national level, through its use of funds and regulations which affect local authorities, public utilities, official regional development agencies, and this seems certain to increase.[36] The EC has grown into the most important of all European institutions and its economic magnetism affects the rest of Europe. Turkey has a longstanding application to join the Community and all of the EFTA states have actively reconsidered their relationship with it. In 1989 Austria made a formal application to join, once it was clear that the Soviet Union would no longer use its part in the 1955 Austrian State Treaty to veto such a move. In 1991 Sweden also made a formal application for membership. In October 1990 the Community was effectively enlarged with the reunification of Germany, absorbing another 18 million people. The EC has made it clear that it is not in a position to accommodate further enlargements until the '1992 process' has been digested, but thereafter it is entirely likely that Austria (which is in any case one of the core European economies, straddling one of the trunk routes to Italy), Sweden and possibly Norway will enter the Community. Malta and Cyprus are two feasible Mediterranean members. Other states such as Switzerland, and the reforming states of Eastern Europe – particularly Czecho-Slovakia, Hungary and Poland – may well consider that a closer economic and constitutional relationship with the EC would be advantageous to them. In the early 1990s, the EC needs time to adjust to its Iberian enlargement of 1986 and the conclusion of the Single European Act. As a community of 12, the EC enjoys good commercial and economic relations with the EFTA states through a wide-ranging industrial free trade agreement. The EC and EFTA have been involved in a series of detailed and painstaking technical negotiations since 1984 to redefine the relationship between them. And in 1988, finally bowing to reality, the Soviet Union established formal relations with the EC in Brussels.

NATO Unlike the EC, NATO had almost reached its logical geographical membership limit with the accession of Spain in 1982 though, exactly like the EC, in the 1990s it is having to turn its attention to a series of new issues, and possibly 'associate members', as defence matters inexorably shade into other policy areas. Despite persistent crises on NATO's Southern flank and a major crack in the nuclear consensus among the publics in NATO countries, no one has yet left the alliance. Meanwhile the Western European Union has been revived since 1984 in an attempt both to 'strengthen the European pillar' of the alliance and to fill some of the gaps in European co-operation that NATO does not cover well. Though European-American relations are undoubtedly in a state of more dramatic structural change at the military level than at any time since 1949, intra-European defence relations are more institutionalised now than ever.

Institutional homogeneity

All of this is sufficiently obvious to anyone who has glanced at the recent history of Western Europe. Indeed, it is very easy to look at European politics as if it were nothing but the architecture of regional institutions. Less obvious, but more important, is the development of political, economic and social behaviour that has surrounded the growth of such institutions and which carries on substantially outside them. In other words, apart from the growth of European institutions, the last decade has witnessed an even faster and more dynamic growth of *institutionalism* in Europe. Within the institutions of Europe the presence of sovereign governments always looms large, whether or not they choose to co-operate. But in the confused world that surrounds them, and eventually changes them, there is some evidence of real integrative dynamism.

As William Wallace has pointed out, the European Community is now a far less coherent institution than it was in 1973 because it has acted as the focus for a range of activities that are not formally part of it. The EC is rather the centrepiece of a 'West European system' that is far wider.[37] Thus, the fact that the EC has formal agreements with EFTA is important, but of less significance than the fact that EFTA countries represent such a major force in intra-European trade. The Community's trade with EFTA exceeds in volume its trade with the USA; and Austria, Sweden and Switzerland are each larger export markets for EC members than is Japan. Indeed, if

EFTA represented a single country then it would be the second most important market for EC goods, behind Germany and equal to France.[38] Or again, the European Monetary System (EMS) is a formal institution and has had great significance since its establishment in 1979. But of comparable significance is the fact that Britain, who steadfastly refused to join it until 1990 nevertheless had to behave in most respects as if it were a member: and Scandinavian EFTA countries, Austria and Switzerland, who were not eligible to join it, ensured that their own exchange rates became indirectly linked to it. For in reality, the EMS has constituted a Deutschmark bloc and as such no European states could afford to be too much adrift of it. The European Currency Unit (ECU) therefore represents a medium of exchange that is based upon a more stable monetary regime than exists in any other region, so much so that even Sweden and the Soviet Union, for instance, find it convenient to conduct some of their trade in ECUs.

Business co-operation   Similarly, the institutions of European co-operation do not reveal how much co-operation has developed between private business. When more than 50 per cent of the cost of a new European Fighter Aircraft will be accounted for by the electronics in it (and a modern fighter can have up to 100 000 separate parts), then even major contractors such as GEC-Siemens have no choice but to enter international consortia (though defence consortia often involve US as well as European companies).[39] The trend towards international production on the part of the multinational companies that we identified earlier is not caught at all in the institutional picture of European integration. The international institutions of Europe are mainly concerned with regulation, information, and liaison for the benefit of government agencies. But the economic forces which push defence companies into consortia are far stronger than any encouragement to collaborate from the Independent European Programme Group (IEPG), the Western European Union or the industrial programmes of the EC.

The Single European Act   This is not to argue that institutions are unimportant, or that they have minimal effects on European politics. Rather, we should realise that the institutional architecture constantly interacts with economic dynamism: at some times it might shape developments; at others it may be little more than a reflection of them. Undoubtedly the most significant institutional development in the European Community in the last decade has been the signing, in 1986, of the Single European Act, which amended the constitution of the European Communities and enshrined the aim of achieving a free internal market by 1992. Whatever the effects of this programme, it is clear that it is bound to have wider consequences than were mentioned in the Act both for the members of the EC and, significantly, for non-member European countries.

The most evident consequence of the Single European Act is that it has added greatly to the pressures on governments to act to remove non-tariff barriers to free trade that have been embedded deep in the domestic economy ever since formal tariff barriers were reduced by the establishment of the EC. Another consequence has been that it stimulated intra-Community trade to the extent that the operations of private companies are likely to increase pressure on governments to accept the establishment of a single monetary authority for the Community. For vigorous companies and sensitive financial institutions will punish exchange rate fluctuations by switching their activities to more stable monetary networks. In 1988 David Marquand argued that the practical choice Europe faced was between establishing a Central Bank for the Community with a common currency unit, or else doing nothing and, in effect, letting the Bundesbank determine members' monetary policies and allowing the Deutschmark to become the common currency.[40] This perception proved to be well-founded. Finally, the freer internal market tends to increase the disparities between regions within EC countries, since the intensity of trade between the growth areas – the Rhine valley, South East England, Eastern France, Northern Italy – will increase more than trade between any of them and the regions in which growth is lower. In a relative sense, the rich will get richer and the poor will get poorer after 1992. On the other hand, the less obvious effects of the workings of the Single European Act are on areas outside the European Community. The prospect of a single European market stimulated a good deal of investment in EC countries by the United States and Japan in order to establish production within Europe before 1992; it stimulated the socialist bloc to look for closer relationships within the Community, and it led to a boom in both company mergers and industrial collaboration that straddled the Community boundaries. It is clear that the prospects for the European economy after 1992 have acted as a catalyst whereby the 'central economic regions' of the EC have begun to draw in the bright spots of other European countries that are geographically close – Austria, Switzerland and perhaps also Southern Sweden and Finland.

Official co-operation   A final way in which much greater homogeneity has emerged outside the formal institutions of Western Europe is in what may be termed the 'habits of official co-operation'. Contact between both government and company officials across national boundaries, especially where it is regarded as successful, tends to be habit-forming and spills over into other areas of mutual concern. This has provided an example of neo-functionalism in action: the growing together of elites in different sectors of society. European officials contact each other as a matter of course in much of their routine work; they are carried along by the momentum that builds up behind an issue, and even where their political masters may be standing on their sovereign dignities in a summit, the officials may well be preparing for the eventual compromise they expect. Such behaviour takes place both inside and outside the framework of the institutions. This has probably strengthened institutions within Europe, while it may have weakened some of the more established transatlantic institutions where it is more difficult for officials to operate so freely outside the formal framework. Examination of the specifics of European Community negotiations indicates that 'EC politics' is not merely traditional bargaining at a more intensive level, but has become a different sort of game that crosses most of the conceptual boundaries that exist in other forms of negotiation.[41]

It has become clear, for example, that the real diplomatic relationship between the EC and EFTA states is not the same as that between the two organisations. Matters on the EC's 'political co-operation' agenda will tend to come up on that of the Nordic Council, since Denmark is a member of both. Norway, as a NATO member, has become more visibly, if informally, involved in political co-operation, and Sweden and Norway both became involved in the Eureka programme, which unites both EC and non-EC members since they share the same economic interests in seeing it succeed.[42]

In short, the reality of the growth in European institutions has been that it has not replaced bilateral relations between European states, but rather stimulated them. It has done so in two dimensions: first, it has increased the involvement between societies, as opposed only to governments, and has therefore stimulated greater political interchange among domestic sectors that were formally separate; and second, it has stimulated relations between member states and other states, since the more co-ordinated the core EC states become, the more the interests of the non-members are likely to be affected. The scope and existence of European institutions, therefore, only accounts for the more formal trends in integrative politics, and should be seen not as the totality, but rather as a rough index of the general extent of homogeneous behaviour.

Implications for British foreign policy

Trends as diverse as these, in both the world and the European arenas, raise important conceptual issues for the way in which we think about the general context of British foreign policy. It is important, therefore, to attempt to locate Britain more precisely within this contradictory empirical picture in order to understand the nature of the problems that the 1990s raise for both practitioners and observers of British external relations.

3 Britain in the Contemporary World

The context described in the last chapter, of a world that is both more diverse *and* more homogeneous than ever before, is obviously a gross characterisation of a series of very complex processes. Nevertheless, it expresses an essential truth about Britain's place in the contemporary world. The aim of this chapter is to try to place British external relations in a more detailed context. All of the major dimensions by which British foreign policy has traditionally been understood display diverse trends which are evolving as rapidly as everything else in the world of the 1990s.

Britain's economic status

The economic infrastructure of a country is rightly regarded as one of the key determinants of its place in world politics at any given time. Economic wealth provides direct capability, in that it acts as a source of power in itself, and it underpins the application of other physical and intangible capabilities which are all part of a state's projection of itself in the world. Of course, economic capacity does not automatically create a powerful state in international politics: but lack of economic capacity necessarily translates itself, sooner rather than later, into diplomatic weakness.

The debate about Britain's economic performance has been carried on rather in these terms. Conservative governments throughout the 1980s stressed the extent to which the economic recovery they had engendered had provided Britain with a firmer base for its dealings with the rest of the world. Critics from the Left and Centre disputed both the conclusion and the underlying premise.[1] Such arguments are likely to go back and forth since they raise the most sensitive of party political issues, and there are no definitive answers. There is, however, a more important analytical issue which receives far less attention in the political sphere and yet is crucial to the future of Britain's external relations.

The British economy is more genuinely interdependent with the world economy than most: it is interpenetrated by global economic forces to a remarkable degree, and increasing proportions of its wealth are generated abroad. This is a source of both strength and weakness. In short, Britain has more to gain and more to lose than most other OECD states through its international economic position. This is apparent in all of the four major facets of Britain's economy: production, trade, finance and investment.

Production

The productive capacity of the British economy presents a characteristically mixed picture. Britain's share of world *manufacturing* output has been in both relative and absolute decline for several decades. Productivity growth has slowed steadily since the mid-1950s; Britain's share of manufacturing exports had declined from 19 per cent among the OECD states in 1954 to 8.5 per cent by 1977 and something less than 7.5 per cent by 1986. Moreover, its manufacturing competitiveness has been in long-term decline throughout the century and as Sir Nicholas Henderson observed in 1979, Britain was failing to keep up not only with other world economic powers but with its main European competitors.[2] These trends were arrested somewhat during the 1980s, though it is not yet clear whether this was a structural change or merely a temporary relief. In the late 1980s, the industries that were producing well were in the chemical, electrical and instrument engineering sectors, all of which had tended to move upmarket towards more specialised high-tech products. Those industries where performance had not recovered included metal products, mechanical engineering, automobile production and textiles, where the dramatic decline in absolute, as well as relative, productivity levels mostly occurred.[3] Britain's oil production has served to cushion the blows that would otherwise have befallen the economy in the last twenty years; at its peak it constituted some 20 per cent of visible exports. Some argue that oil production has irrevocably harmed the economy by transforming sterling into an over-priced petrocurrency which has held back export growth. Whether or not this is the case, the productive structure in Britain has irrevocably altered over the last two decades: the health of manufacturing output now depends on oil and on a much smaller sector of high-technology industries.

The growth in the *service* sector is the other element in the transformation of Britain's productive structure. The service industries now constitute almost two-thirds of total British output and over two-thirds of total employment.[4] Invisible exports made up over half of all Britain's export earnings by the end of the 1980s. The financial services sector, for example, more than doubled during the decade. Overall, the export of services grew by more than 12 per cent between 1975 and 1985. Such a trend, of course, is general throughout the OECD countries, though the proportions of service sector output employment in Britain's case are somewhat above the OECD average.[5]

In so far as the British production structure could be described as healthy at the end of the 1980s, therefore, it was thanks to the continuing effects of high technology, oil and the dramatic growth in service industries. There are many possible implications of this for the British economy, but it is significant that all three of these elements are highly dependent upon international developments. The price of oil is something over which no national government has much control: the development of high-tech manufacturing depends heavily on multinational investment within Britain; and the growth of service industries, particularly in the financial sector, is a function of the increased tempo of international monetary relations. Britain is not the world leader in service industries, indeed, its share of world trade in services is declining, but the performance of the rest of the productive economy gives Britain a very strong motive, for example, to press for the liberalisation of services throughout the world, since this is one of the bright spots in a patchy economic performance.

Trade

Most of Britain's trade is with its partners in Europe. By 1985 intra-EC trade accounted for about 52 per cent of all EC trade. Intra-European trade, including non-EC European countries, accounted for over 65 per cent of European OECD trade. Around 46 per cent of Britain's trade is with other EC states and just over 60 per cent with the states of OECD Europe as a whole. Britain is less integrated into the EC trading system than the other major states in Europe. This is not because Britain has held on to its old colonial markets: they were in steep decline before its entry into the European Community and have now diminished to the point where Britain generally has weaker trade relations in the developing world than its Community partners do. Rather, the wider distribution of British trade is due to the strengthening of the trade relationship between Britain and the United States, and Britain and Japan, particularly in the realm of services: only about 25 per cent of Britain's service trade is with its EC partners. The favourable exchange rate of the pound against the dollar stimulated Anglo-American trade in the mid-1980s. Although Anglo-Japanese trade comprises only a small proportion of the total of European trade (perhaps 2 per cent), it makes up over 3 per cent of British trade, with a heavy imbalance towards imports. Britain also has stronger trading relationships with the newly-industrialising countries than most of its EC partners.

Britain is in both a profitable and a vulnerable position. The profits of service trade have not appreciably diminished since 1980, and

Conservative governments throughout the 1980s clearly backed a strategy which hoped and expected to see a boom in service industries throughout the OECD during the 1990s. On the other hand, the general risks of Britain's relatively dispersed trade relations may well increase with the introduction of the free market in the EC after 1992. For Britain's relationship with the United States and success in the US market may be a disadvantage if intra-EC trade becomes even more intense. Added to this, Britain has long held to a belief in free trade which has been strengthened by Thatcherite conservatism. Britain is a uniquely open economy, where international agreements have been honoured and there is comparatively little subsidy to industry to provide hidden protectionism. Britain has nailed its free trade colours to the mast in the past decade, though not everyone else in the system has done so. This is a calculation of national interest, since Britain has much to gain by it, at least in the financial and service sectors. But it is also a gamble, since it could leave the British economy vulnerable to acts of bad faith on the part of other states, especially outside Europe.

Finance

In the financial sector Britain's position is little short of remarkable. Financial services are the backbone of Britain's invisible export earnings, employing 8 per cent of the country's work-force, doubling its output in the decade since 1974, and contributing no less than 14 per cent to gross national product (GNP).[6] The City of London plays host to almost 800 banking institutions, which makes it the largest concentration of international banking in the world. According to the Bank of England, London handled around 24 per cent of all world bank lending in the mid-1980s. Tokyo handled 15 per cent, New York around 12 per cent, Paris and Geneva 6 per cent each, and Frankfurt 4 per cent.[7] London is also the centre of the Eurocurrency markets and handles around 30 per cent of Eurobanking activity.[8] Quite apart from the size of the City, London is also the home of international investment fund management, which makes it the natural centre of investment decisions, wherever securities are actually traded. In short, the position of the City of London, while under pressure from the competition of Tokyo and New York and Frankfurt, has taken full advantage of three interrelated developments of the 1980s: deregulation, which has brought into the stock markets a plethora of foreign firms, as well as established British institutions; innovation, whereby financial conglomerates have become like supermarkets, able to offer a wide range of financial services; and internationalisation, which has aided the powerful growth of international financial liquidity. Like other states, Britain has used this liquidity to reduce its official reserves as a proportion of gross domestic product (GDP). As a result it is now more dependent on the confidence, and hence the ability, of the international financial markets to keep the system going.

Investment

All this is a reflection of the fourth aspect of Britain's economic position in the world, namely the flow of foreign investment. Britain is both Europe's most powerful overseas investor (by a long way) and its most penetrated domestic market for incoming investment. In 1985 its direct investments overseas amounted to £77 billion (around 22 per cent of GNP), while British portfolio investments abroad amounted to around £500 billion. Direct inward investment flows were £41 billion and inward portfolio investment was worth at least £470 billion. (Typically, however, the huge amounts of portfolio investment – greater than the amount of Britain's total GDP – were overwhelmingly made up by banks transacting business among themselves. Direct investments present a more accurate picture.)

The pattern of investment is just as significant as the amount. For it is clear that Britain's position in global investment is the opposite of its trading position. Whereas Europe is the natural, if not exclusive, focus for British manufacturing and trade, the buoyant markets of the United States, Canada and Japan are the natural centres of investment activity in both directions. Thus in the second half of the 1980s 35 per cent of British direct investment abroad was in the United States, compared with just over 20 per cent in the EC, and barely 1 per cent in Japan. Equally, over half the direct private investment in Britain – from multinational companies – came from the United States, as opposed to 30 per cent from the EC and perhaps 2 per cent from Japan. The huge difference here between US and Japanese figures partly reflects the fact that American investments in Britain are very diverse, whereas Japanese investments have, so far, been highly concentrated in a few industries. Nevertheless both figures represent around half of each country's total investments in the EC. Britain, in other words, appears to be the natural home for US and Japanese investment in the European Community.

To combine these four facets of the British economy produces a picture that is patchy and contradictory. The British economy in the world is both strong and weak, poor in manufacturing performance but strong in investment; adventurous and vulnerable, with its degree of outreach and its penetration; European and global, with its different trade and investment biases, and so on. How we balance these characteristics against one another to arrive at either a comforting or an alarming conclusion is a matter of political judgement. For analytical purposes, however, certain conclusions can be drawn:

(i)   It is clear that the long term decline in British economic performance, whether or not it has been arrested, has had an impact on *Britain's role within the world economy*. The absolute size of the British economy measured in the amount of its GDP puts it within the top ten economies of the world. Britain's relative wealth, however, measured in GDP per head, barely keeps it within the top twenty.[9] In this situation, though Britain has global economic interests, it cannot hope to play a really major role in the world economic order of the 1990s.

(ii) Though its significance in the world economy has declined, *Britain's place in the European economy* is still of great significance. Table 3.1 presents a snapshot of Britain's status as one of the core economies of Europe. British-owned companies are significant within Europe and form a natural triumvirate with French and German-owned companies to dominate most markets. Between them, British, West German and French companies constitute over 70 per cent of the biggest European companies in all categories, over 70 per cent of industrial and trading companies, over 60 per cent of insurance companies and over 50 per cent of banks. As Table 3.1 shows, British companies dominate the service sectors, except in banking. For all its manufacturing weakness, and a now widespread self-image as a declining economy, Britain is still a base for some of the core economic activities of Western Europe. In absolute terms, it remains one of the big four economies of Europe along with Germany, France and Italy.

(iii) Although we naturally define international economic structures by reference to the economies of states, *the concept of the 'national economy'*, particularly in the European context is rapidly becoming difficult to invest with clear meaning. A British 'national economy' can be defined easily enough, but even so, that which is defined as the national economy accounts for less and less of the economic activity taking place within its borders. The City of London may be the biggest financial centre in the world, but that is because it is populated by foreign banks – some 370 of them – rather than British ones, which appear low down the international league table in terms of size of turnover. The chemical industry, to take another example, is defined as one of Britain's manufacturing

Table 3.1 National companies among Europe's largest companies (by sales) in 1988

	Companies of all categories			Industrial companies			Trading companies			Banks		
	Top 50	Top 100	Top 200	50	100	200	50	100	200	50	100	200
Britain	15	25	51	11	21	53	18	35	68	5	10	18
Federal Republic of Germany	15	30	55	16	28	52	14	19	41	13	30	63
France	9	20	37	8	22	42	6	18	32	9	14	25
Italy	–	–	–	–	–	–	–	–	–	13	17	29

	Insurance companies			Transport companies			Miscellaneous service companies			Advertising companies*		Hotels/Restaurant companies*	
	Top 50	Top 100	Top 200	50	100	200	50	100	200	50	100	50	100
Britain	18	29	45	11	22	42	18	35	74	24	43	16	26
Federal Republic of Germany	10	26	66	6	9	16	3	9	21	4	9	3	6
France	2	4	11	9	17	32	5	12	21	11	15	6	6
Italy	2	4	9	–	–	–	–	–	–	–	–	–	–
Netherlands	6	9	13	6	7	12	3	6	13	2	10	–	–
Switzerland	6	8	16	–	–	–	–	–	–	–	–	10	15
Sweden	–	–	–	–	–	–	7	11	12	–	–	3	8

Note: Other significant national totals have been included where relevant. * Only 100 companies are listed under these headings.

Source: Extracted from *Europe's 15,000 Largest Companies 1988*, Stockholm, ELC International, 1988 pp 35–8, 98–104, 500–6, 654–717.

bright spots of the 1980s, yet the volume of chemical imports throughout the decade almost doubled.[10] In the world of the ubiquitous multinational, in other words, it is becoming difficult to define a genuinely national company or even a purely national pattern of production. Around 1500 to 2000 British companies operate abroad, the top 100 of which produce more, and employ more people, abroad than at home.[11] Equally, some 3000 companies, covering a wide spectrum of production, operate in Britain as subsidiaries of a foreign multinational. The biggest concentration (26 per cent) of the top 1000 foreign owned companies in Britain are concentrated in electronics, computing, office equipment, oil and chemicals. Otherwise, the other 74 per cent are widely distributed throughout all sectors of the economy.[12] And all major companies, whether foreign-owned or British-owned, have been subject to economic pressures to merge or collaborate in joint ventures. The national economy is constantly compared to a ship on the sea, with politicians at the helm. It is a misleading metaphor. Rather, the British economy, more than most others, should now be compared to a fish or a whale *in* the sea, living precisely because it has water passing through it: an organism in the environment, not an object in relation to it. And like all such creatures, it can be threatened by the predatory behaviour of those who would over-fish the seas or who refuse to give up whaling.

(iv) It is clear that in this situation *the government does have an important role to play*, though it is extremely difficult in the 1990s to establish quite what it should be. The City would not have attracted so many foreign banking institutions had the British government not been noted for its deliberately light regulatory touch on dealings. Yet within two years of the deregulation of the City in 1986 the British government moved to place the Bank of England at the head of the Securities and Investments Board which oversees the regulatory regime of the City. If the touch was to be light, it was nevertheless to be a government touch. The government is able to define its role in relation to other governments and official international bodies: that is part of its job. But the nature of the British economy creates acute difficulties for any government that tries to define its role in relation to increasingly significant private actors. If this is an old conceptual problem to the analyst of British government – there was, after all, the East India Company – the sheer number, diversity, and financial power of private economic actors, both domestic and foreign, with whom the government has to define a relationship in the

1990s makes the problem different in kind from anything previously encountered.

Britain's security status

Britain's physical security has traditionally been based upon three mutually reinforcing premises. First, Britain maintains global security commitments and plays an active role in the maintenance of world order. Second, British security, whether on a global, European, or even a purely national scale, is crucially dependent upon its relationship with the United States. Third, and as an expression of that relationship, Britain maintains an independent nuclear deterrent. Taken together, these premises have underpinned an approach to security that has been noted for its sense of continuity and commitment over 40 years and which focuses on security problems in a specifically military way. It is an approach to security that can be fully understood in Realist terms: Britain responds, through NATO, to direct threats to its own security in Europe; it responds to indirect threats elsewhere by contributing to defence and peacekeeping operations around the world; and it helps to uphold the milieu of the Western world order – in so far as it still exists – through the visible presence of its military establishment alongside those of the other major Western powers.[13]

On the face of it, therefore, Britain still plays a prominent role in the structures of military security. It spends more on defence than most other Western industrialised states both in absolute terms and as a proportion of GNP. Though its armed forces are not the most numerous in Europe, it maintains larger all-volunteer professional forces than most of its European allies and is ranked within the top five military powers in the world.[14] Thus, in 1989 British armed forces not only operated throughout the NATO area, from North Norway to Canada, Gibraltar and Sardinia, but also in at least a dozen other areas of the world, operating in the fourteen remaining dependent territories, in peacekeeping operations and in giving help to friendly powers. In 1989 British forces were deployed from Hong Kong to the Sinai Peninsula, from Namibia to the Falklands. British military personnel had given assistance to some 33 different countries outside the NATO area since 1987 and had made their own training courses available to over 3000 foreign officers from around the world.[15] In 1990–1 Britain deployed a full armoured division as its contribution to the multinational force operating in the Gulf – a physical commitment second only to that of the United States. Certainly, in the afterglow of the successful Falklands War and with the respect accorded to a Prime Minister who pursued a very active relationship with the United States, who was determined to keep Britain in the nuclear club, and who adopted an overtly hawkish attitude to world politics, Britain appeared in the 1980s, both to itself and others, as a military power operating again on a world scale, even though it had not, in reality, been able to deploy a 'global reach' for some 30 years. After decades in which British defence commitments had inexorably contracted, this seemed to come as a pleasant surprise to a public that was becoming accustomed to the language of decline.

By the end of the 1980s, however, the underlying economic situation had shown itself to be depressingly similar to that of the 1970s. The scale of the government's security thinking and the 'global reach' of its defence policy was more apparent than real. Notwithstanding the commitments to the multinational force in the Gulf, British defence policy is concentrated heavily upon its NATO commitments, which the Ministry of Defence regards as absorbing around 95 per cent of the defence budget. Indeed, the Government estimates that rather less than 3 per cent of its annual spending on defence commitments goes on 'out of area' operations.[16] Already, many observers regard any further independent military operation akin to the Falklands as technically impossible. Moreover, the four major roles that Britain performs within NATO – the defence of the Eastern Atlantic, defence of the British home base, the contribution to the defence of Europe and the maintenance of the strategic nuclear deterrent – are under severe cost constraints, quite apart from the pressures to readjust in response to the collapse of the old order in Eastern Europe. Conservative governments insisted from 1983 onwards that no major reviews of defence commitments were necessary and that all of Britain's defence roles could be sustained with an annual budget that in 1990–91 amounted to £21.2 billion.[17] Academic critics tend not to agree, however, and were given sustenance by the fact that the government initiated an internal 'Options for Change' exercise within the Ministry of Defence from 1990 to mid-1991 which reduced British armed forces by around 20 per cent. The critics generally maintain either that at least one of the four roles will have to be jettisoned, or else the performance of the four roles will simply become incredible. Already, for example, the Government's commitment of 1981 to 'sustain' 'about 50' frigates and destroyers has been whittled away and the reality is that the number of *deployable* frigates and destroyers at any one time is now regarded by many critics as being nearer 30, and will be further reduced by the outcomes of the Options for Change process.[18] The armed forces will be lucky to sustain realistic numbers of weapons systems as the price of new generations of tanks, helicopters and aircraft for the 1990s has to be paid. They are all symptoms, says

Coker, recognised even by Conservative defence ministers in the 1980s, 'that present defence policy is bankrupt'.[19]

Though the problems of the defence budget have generally dominated debates about British security policy, they are really an indication of a more ubiquitous trend in the politics of security relations. For it is becoming increasingly difficult to discern sufficient scope for independent British policy in almost all aspects of security policy. In one sense, this is not new since only the superpowers can conceive of a genuinely independent security policy and all other states have to make co-operative arrangements, which are not a diminution of their sovereignty since they are commitments freely entered into. This will remain the case. Britain will be a part of NATO as one of a number of sovereign nations in an alliance to secure collective defence. On the other hand, the context of British security policies is also moving in directions which seriously diminish the autonomy of national governments in ways that cannot be explained by reference to Realist perceptions of defence policy.

Integrationist trends

Multilateral dimensions of security

One major trend is that European security can no longer be satisfactorily defined in predominantly military terms. Already the European political arena is significantly more interdependent than anyone could have imagined at the beginning of the 1980s. Security in the 1990s will revolve around economic relations just as much as, if not more than, around military dispositions and arms control. As such, detente and European security policy involves multilateral economic relations between the states of Eastern Europe and the European Community: it concerns financial arrangements to provide credit and cope with the indebtedness of the East; and the currency of security in the 1990s involves common projects on environment, health and social concerns. Domestic instability in Eastern Europe and the Soviet Union is generally regarded as the greatest threat to European peace: we all, therefore, have a common interest in the peaceful modernisation of the East. Yet the West's military establishment has little power to deal with this threat. The existence of NATO – at least in the form that it has taken to date – is only relevant to deal with the 'worst case' threat that would arise if the economic and political breakdown in the Soviet Union were to lead to a counterrevolution and the installation of a militarily aggressive government. Lesser, and more likely, threats arising from the outbreak of nationalism within the Soviet sphere present a type of challenge that

NATO is presently ill-equipped to meet. It could exacerbate such tensions by overreacting but it has very little direct power to ameliorate them. At best, it might exercise a useful indirect influence in keeping conflicts limited. On the other hand, the European Community and the combined economic power of the Western states may well affect the domestic stability of Eastern Europe, either for good or bad, depending on how the economic magnetism of the West is used. Security relations between East and West, in other words, have become far less bipolar and rather more systemic. In this situation, the characteristic British approach to security, as expressed in the three basic premises underlying it, seems too limited. Military dimensions of British security policies – approaches to arms control for example – are intensely multilateral and have to be hammered out with different groups of partners. It is very unlikely, for example, that Britain will be able to continue to keep the independent nuclear deterrent out of the arms control equation if negotiations continue. And the economic dimensions of security policy – such as decisions on aid or trade access to East European states – are taken within an integrative framework where the outcome is genuinely collective and does not express the policy of any one state. The future of security and detente in Europe requires Western states to integrate their security and economic policies to a far greater extent than hitherto, and to implement them through an institutional framework that is wider than NATO and the Atlantic Alliance.

Collaboration in weapons production

Another major trend in security politics in Europe is the degree to which collaboration has become essential in the production of new weapons systems. European weapons collaboration does not lead to quicker and cheaper production: quite the reverse in fact because of all the problems of co-ordination. Nevertheless, governments are now faced with the choice of having a collaborative new weapon system or no weapon at all since they usually lack the all-round expertise and the investment to produce purely national systems of sufficient quality. Already, the production of a new state-of-the-art aircraft for the European frontline would be beyond the existing resources of the British aerospace industry. Government therefore has traditionally faced the choice of buying American or entering into co-operative projects – usually with its European partners. And yet co-operative projects by their very nature tend to create new forms of defence commitment from which it is difficult for governments to withdraw. Of course, governments can choose which projects to initiate or join, but increasingly, this is becoming less a genuine national choice and more a transnational compromise between countervailing political demands, only some of which are concerned with NATO's military requirements.

This even applies to the British independent nuclear deterrent. For though the decision to replace the Polaris force with a Trident C4 submarine missile system was taken very explicitly and publicly by the Conservative government in July 1980, it soon became clear that the government's options were somewhat limited when the United States decided to develop the more expensive and sophisticated Trident D5 missile instead. Britain had no choice but to announce in 1982 that it too would deploy the D5 since it made little sense to procure a missile that the United States did not intend to operate itself. Britain's Trident D5 would therefore cost over £1 billion more and would constitute a more sophisticated system than Britain required. A Trident submarine can carry five times as many warheads as a Polaris, all of which have considerably greater accuracy. The government does not intend to use the full launching capacity of its Trident submarines, but that simply underscores the point that it is not a weapon which precisely meets the military requirement. Moreover, Trident missiles will be serviced in the United States, and their targeting and communication, like Polaris, will depend on US satellite data for all of its normal operational requirements within the NATO framework. For all practical purposes Trident remains a NATO-based system since it is part of the Single Integrated Operational Plan, controlled from Omaha, which designates all NATO and US nuclear targets. The fact that, *in extremis*, British missiles could be used nationally in accordance with Britain's own target set (traditionally, it was always Moscow)[20], and the fact that it would not depend on US satellites for in-flight guidance in such a situation, is irrelevant to the way it normally operates, and the way in which it *would* operate in any of the scenarios that sensible analysts could possibly devise. Even on this single most expensive, and sensitive, aspect of defence policy, therefore, the government may take a clear political decision to have a nuclear system, but by the time such a system is in service it exhibits a lack of technical autonomy no less important than that which attaches to overtly collaborative European projects.

In sum, Britain's status in the security structure of the world is rather more limited in scope and constrained in practice than a summary of its stated defence policy might indicate. Certainly, Conservative governments of the 1980s made clear political choices over the major defence questions: how much to spend, whether to remain nuclear, what attitude to take to the US commitment to Europe, to NATO's nuclear strategy, how to slim down the forces to meet declining real defence expenditure in the 1990s, and so on. But a clear defence policy does not necessarily produce security, and the 1990s pose a series of quite unprecedented security questions for Britain, only some of which can be answered by reference to defence policy, and all of which require collective political and military responses.

Britain's technological status

If Britain's status in economic and security fields reveals varied pictures that display both strength and weakness, in the high technology sectors the picture is one of almost unrelieved decline: Britain is losing badly in both global and European terms.

There is no easy way of characterising the nature of high technology in the contemporary world. Technical innovation has become central to manufacturing competitiveness, not just in the obviously high-tech industries, such as aerospace or information processing, but increasingly in mass consumer production such as the automobile industry. Technical innovation in the products themselves and robotic innovation in the production processes of them have become crucial determinants of their commercial success. We are moving into an era where the shift towards science-based industries, in all productive areas, creates new patterns of productivity. New production materials (thanks to the potential of biotechnologies) and highly flexible production processes (thanks to computer and robotic technologies) can give capital-intensive industries a decisive competitive edge over low-wage labour economies even in the production of low-tech consumer products.[21] The pace of technical innovation in the production process is little short of astonishing. The three multi-million dollar computers that were fitted into *Voyager 2* in 1977 when it set off on its mission around the solar system, for example, contained only about one-eighth of the memory power of the £500 laptop computers with which journalists wrote about the mission in 1989.[22]

The most significant technological competition is between the United States, Japan and Europe. Two general trends stand out. One is that Europe, under intense pressure from Japanese and American competition, is just about holding its own thanks to the efforts in general of Germany and Europe's strength in certain sectors (especially in chemical, pharmaceutical, plastics, and mechanical engineering, aircraft and civil nuclear technologies).[23] The other trend is that high-tech competition is characterised by the large inputs of big companies, and groups of companies, to research and development (R&D) backed up by strong – sometimes overtly protectionist – government policies to foster development in certain sectors. Thus, in the electronics sphere the United States has operated anti-trust legislation to create an environment in which smaller companies can form a high-tech infrastructure which supports the operations of the giant companies: and the US defence budget and space programme has provided vital markets for US research and development in high-tech electronics. Japan offers its high-tech electronic industries an insular domestic market of 122 million people and its government has played a very active role in the promotion of high-tech electronics exports via the MITI organisation.[24] In Europe, the era of 'flag carrying' national high-tech companies has generally been superseded, for it has become virtually impossible for European states to pursue purely nationalist policies of high-tech promotion, as the French discovered during the 1980s. Instead, Europe is meeting the competition through industrial and intergovernmental collaboration where national governments together try to promote the right conditions for high-tech industrial development.

In all of this Britain is making a poor and ever-diminishing contribution. The total spent by government and private industry on civil and military science in 1988 was estimated officially at £10.3 billion. In 1989 the government spent £4.9 billion on all forms of R&D, around 50 per cent of which was spent in the defence sector (a proportion only paralleled in the United States). British industrial funding for R&D is relatively the lowest among all its major competitors. Industrial R&D spending in the Federal Republic, France, Italy, Sweden, Belgium, Denmark and Ireland all grew between five and seven times more than spending by British industry between 1967 and 1983. At the end of the 1980s Britain was patenting fewer inventions than in the 1960s, while Japanese patent applications had increased more than elevenfold; and France and Germany had virtually doubled their levels.[25] The pattern of industrial R&D in Britain, in fact, owes much to the decisions of a small number of large companies. Thus, while the pharmaceutical companies have witnessed the fastest growth in industry-funded R&D in the last twenty years and while chemical industries account for almost the whole increase in industrial R&D since the mid-1980s, major British companies in the electronics and automobile industries have signally failed to maintain competitive levels of funding.[26]

The results have been all too predictable. Between 1964 and 1980 Britain's share of world exports in technology-intensive products declined by 10 per cent: between 1980 and 1984 it declined by a further 21 per cent, while during the same periods Japan's share increased by 96 per cent and then 41 per cent.[27] Britain's longstanding advantages in new biotechnologies, for example, have been whittled away as its research base has dwindled in the face of public expenditure cuts and the unwillingness of important companies to invest in high-risk projects.[28] As we have seen, Britain has no difficulties in attracting inward investment and many high-tech foreign companies operate in Britain. They do not, however, normally bring the core of their high-tech processes with them. Britain increasingly faces the prospect of being a 'branch economy' with assembly plants and service industries serving other core economic areas. Where British high-tech companies themselves are successful, this tends to be in niche markets. Although some of the niches are fairly large, particularly in the United States, such markets do not provide a basis for sustained economic growth in a major economy. High-tech skills in certain key sectors are not merely a facet of industrial success: for a Western economy of the 1990s wishing to retain its high-wage workforce, they are the essential prerequisite to competitive production in a fierce global market. The response of successive British governments to these trends has been continually uncertain. The policy of supporting 'national champion' companies during the 1970s gave way in the 1980s to a faith in the dynamics of the free market. In this respect, governments look forward to the European free market of the 1990s as an environment that will encourage high-tech research and development. British governments have also been continually sceptical about very public high-tech collaborative projects where their short-term profitability has been in question. They insisted, for example, that Europe's Eureka initiative should involve no extra public expenditure and effectively pulled out of the further development of the European Space Agency on the grounds that it was not an appropriate use of public money when private industry should fund such research.[29] Moreover, the government's commitment to privatisation has put more high-tech industries into the free market. But though the Conservative governments of the 1980s took a minimalist position in relation to technological development, the fact remains that the international high-tech market is far from free. It is one of the sectors where certain governments have chosen to be actively involved in industrial policy, where they have provided extensive infrastructural support for high-tech R&D, and where they have worked in close partnership with selected commercial interests. As Tugendhat and Wallace wryly remark, high technology is 'A world in which the Japanese example is accepted as the model, rather than the British'.[30]

Britain and international institutions

Formal institutions

British external relations exist in an ever-deepening network of international institutions, particularly within the European arena. This is not to be wondered at, given the nature of contemporary international relations and the fact that Britain has traditionally tried to play a significant role in the promotion of world order. Britain is a member of a great variety of international institutions: 18 major institutions under the United Nations rubric; 7 major institutions in Western Europe; and since 1944 it has been party to 62 international agreements that create some form of political or financial commitment, from Yalta in 1945 to the INTELSAT or Lomé Agreements, to the settlement over Hong Kong in 1984; not to mention over 100 various constitutional agreements since 1944 in respect of the Commonwealth.[31] Again, the contradictory nature of the present international context is very apparent here. For in some respects Britain's membership of so many international institutions is evidence of a rather traditional world. To be sure, there are more international institutions now than in any previous period and they cover an enormous variety of subjects that were not previously matters for external policy-makers. But 'Britain', as a former Head of the Diplomatic Service observed, 'is a member of every international organisation of universal scope for which we are eligible'.[32] It chooses to belong to more than 120 international organisations around the world and pays subscriptions of around £90 million annually to them. Equally, it can withdraw from them, as it did in the case of the United Nations Educational, Scientific and Cultural Organisation (UNESCO) in 1985, if it disagrees with the direction the organisation is taking.

According to this traditional perspective, therefore, it is possible to pinpoint Britain's status within the network of international institutions with some precision. Britain was a founder member of the United Nations Organisation and as such holds one of the five permanent seats on the Security Council, which gives it the power of veto over its resolutions. Almost 40 of the 161 members of the UN General Assembly are ex-British colonies or dependencies. Britain is also a prominent member of the other organisations in the family of United Nations institutions, particularly the International Monetary Fund (IMF), the World Bank, the General Agreement on Tariffs and Trade (GATT) and the United Nations Conference on Trade and

Development (UNCTAD). In the same way, having been the backbone of the forerunner of the OECD in the 1940s, Britain is a notable member of the modern organisation, and the OECD's structure owes much to the work of British officials in earlier days. Britain was the principal architect of NATO, and its commitment to that body has never been in doubt. As such, it is a part of all the organisations that flow from it, the Western European Union (WEU), the North Atlantic Assembly, the Eurogroup, the Independent European Programme Group (IEPG), and so on. Finally, and most significant of all, Britain has been a member of the European Community since 1973 with all the attendant institutional commitments implied by that. Table 3.2 gives some idea of the scope of Britain's formal institutional commitments. It lists what may be regarded as the most important institutions, together with some of the most significant members of their institutional 'families' and other organisations associated with them, if not formally a part of them. Figure 3.1 shows how the most salient of these institutional commitments overlap, if seen from a purely functional perspective. The previously stable distinction between security and economic/social matters is becoming blurred: if the 'family' and 'associated' organisations listed in Table 3.2 were also included, they would be comfortably separated by the dividing line on the first diagram and would clutter up the overlapping centre ground between security and economic/social issues on the second.

From a traditional perspective, Britain generally plays a well-understood and respected role in most of these organisations. Having been one of the architects of the post-war world, Britain's attitude to the workings of these institutions tends to be very correct, almost legalistic. British officials are trained to put the accent on practical improvements rather than flights of rhetoric in any negotiations, and they are adept at working subtly behind the scenes to arrive at compromise documents that frequently owe a great deal to their own drafting. They are not usually noted for attempts to bend the rules, and they can take a justifiable pride in the degree to which they are trusted and believed within the formal institutions of the international community. In Ralf Dahrendorf's phrase, 'Britain does not need to seek a place in international politics, for it already has one'.[33] In many respects, therefore, Britain's intensive membership of international institutions is fully explainable by reference to Realist thinking and it does not raise any fundamental questions about the definition of external relations or the sovereignty of the state.

Table 3.2   Britain's major international institutional
commitments

Organisation	Family	Associated
NATO	Eurogroup	Independent European Programme Group (IEPG)
		Co-ordinating Committee (COCOM)
Western European Union (WEU)		
Council of Europe		
European Community (EC)	European Political Co-operation (EPC)	
	European Monetary System (EMS)	
	Lomé Agreements	
		Eureka Programme
Organisation for Economic Co-operation and Development (OECD)		
Commonwealth		
United Nations (UN)		
	International Monetary Fund (IMF) World Bank International Atomic Energy Agency (IAEA) General Agreement on Tariffs and Trade (GATT) International Labour Organisation (ILO)	
Bank for International Settlements (BIS)		

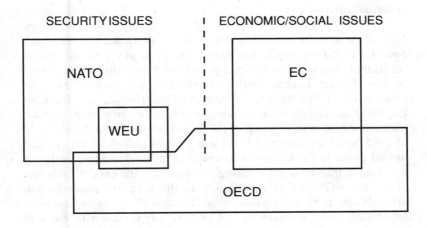

Figure 3.1(a) European institutions prior to 1988

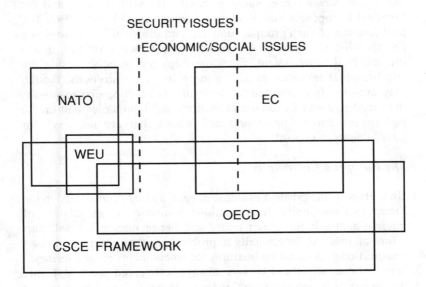

Figure 3.1(b) European institutions in the 1990s

Informal institutions

Nevertheless, there is another side to the institutional picture which does raise more complicated questions. In a world of increasing functional homogeneity it is necessary for Britain to join networks of less formal international and transnational institutions. The Chancellor of the Exchequer and the Governor of the Bank of England became part of the informal financial co-ordination mechanisms embodied in the 'Group of 10' formed in 1983, the 'Group of 5' of 1985, and the 'Group of 7' formed in 1986 (which rapidly tended to boil down to the Group of 5) and their officials are permanently involved in transnational working groups to implement the decisions of the main G5 or G10 meetings.[34] In the security sphere British officials take part in the confidential 'London Club' on nuclear non-proliferation, for instance, the 'COCOM' organisation in Paris to oversee restrictions on exports to adversary states, or the IEPG to try to develop common weapons procurement policies. The Home Secretary is part of the 'Trevi Group' or the Council of Europe's 'Pompidou Group' to coordinate policies on terrorism and policing. Not least among these arrangements, the Prime Minister is part of the regular seven-power summits among the OECD states and the biannual European Council summits among the 12 of the EC. The proliferation of such groups, summits, and informal institutions is a functionalist response to the growth of common problems in the international environment. Such meetings are usually outside the constitutional frameworks of the more formal institutions, though they are closely connected to them and as functionalist responses they tend to cross national and institutional boundaries and create patterns of commitments and obligations that are not easy for governments to control.

The European Community

Undoubtedly, the greatest example of such a trend is embodied in the European Community. It is a unique institution in the history of international relations: part treaty and hence intensely legal; part informal, reacting functionally to problems as they emerge; and part constitutional, demanding institutional amendments among its members. Above all, the EC was always conceived as a dynamic institution. It is 'integrationist' in that it intends to go somewhere: it is a vehicle of transition to something else. There are endless arguments, of course, about what it should become, but the fact remains that unlike the vast majority of treaty-based international institutions, the EC is not an attempt to bolster a status quo. It is, in a genuine sense, politically subversive.

It is impossible to divorce Britain's membership of the European Community from any consideration of the context in which its external policy exists. Given Britain's history, its relationship with such a hybrid organisation as the EC could never be less than complicated. Britain encouraged European union in the 1940s, but in the event refused to join with it in the 1950s and tried to sabotage the foundation of the EEC by establishing EFTA. It then changed its mind in the 1960s and applied for membership, only to be excluded by two French vetoes. After finally managing to get into the EC in 1973, Britain conducted a referendum within two years over whether it should stay in. Having decided that it was irrevocably 'part of Europe', Britain spent the first half of the 1980s arguing about the budgetary terms of its membership, and when that was settled, the second part of the decade trying to limit the effects of any further progress towards European union. Clearly, therefore, there is some ambiguity between Britain's perceived interests in the European Community and its general political attitude to it.[35] For in a sense, though it has never been expressed in such terms by political leaders, Britain has an intuitive grasp of the subversive implications of the European Community.

In the 1990s Britain finds itself amid a network of European Community commitments which span the full spectrum of institutional restraints. At one end of the spectrum it has been able to rely on the precision of the Treaty of Rome to which it acceded in 1972. The British attitude to this has always been one of dogged practicality and for almost two decades British officials have claimed that their main efforts are directed at attempts to make the precise details of the Treaty work better.[36] Nevertheless, even this was modified by the Single European Act of 1986 which threw some of the old legalistic certainties into confusion. The British government was unenthusiastic about the calls for institutional reform of the EC that lay behind the negotiations for the Single European Act. It feared that such reform would try to elevate the EC to be a genuinely supranational institution and it worked to head off such a move by pushing for an Act that would further free the internal market and develop even greater foreign policy cooperation. By the end of the negotiations in 1985 it was clear that Britain was not against the notion of reform: indeed was pressing vigorously for it in certain particular spheres. But Britain was implacably opposed to major structural reforms that would transform the EC into something else. In the event, the Single European Act was a classic Euro-compromise in which the British position appeared to be well protected.[37] The Rome Treaty had been modified but in a way that was less than fundamental. Nevertheless, within two years, the nature of the Single European Act and its implications for the member states had become the focus for a debate within the EC over exactly the sort of fundamentals the British had thought were excluded. For like all Euro-compromises, this one was based on a series of divergent national views of the nature of the EC itself, from which all drew their own implications. From 1988 to 1990 the British government insisted that '1992' was only about the implementation of a free market within Europe. Other states, along with the European Commission, however, interpreted it variously as a catalyst for the development of a considerable 'social dimension' to the Community, of a common currency and central banking system, and a further expansion of intra-European free movement, in all of which the institutions of the EC would have a significantly increased role. Far from settling the question of structural reform in the EC and channelling it into a legal framework, Britain discovered that the Single European Act only focused the discussion.

The Single European Act is the most obvious example of the way in which international legal commitments have become dynamic, perhaps even subversive. There are many other less publicised instances that point in the same direction. The European Court of Human Rights, in existence since 1959, is now arguably a higher court than Parliament in relation to personal cases. Between 1975 and 1985 the British government was taken to this court by individuals and other governments on 13 occasions, over the rights of prisoners, closed shop arrangements, telephone tapping, corporal punishment in the Isle of Man and in Scottish schools, and so on. In all but one case the judgements went partly or wholly against the British government, and while they cannot be coercively enforced as in domestic law, British practice has nevertheless changed as a result of them.[38] In the same way the Court of Justice of the European Community adjudicates on the Treaties of Rome and the actions of EC institutions and on complaints 'by or against Community institutions, member states or individuals'. European rulings have normally been incorporated into British law or political practice. Britain's Equal Pay Act, for instance, was amended in 1984 to incorporate the European Community definition of 'equal value' which became a lever for women workers in several individual court cases and which, according to the Confederation of British Industry, threatened to add 10 per cent to company pay bills.

Less formally, Britain was pressured by its EC partners into accepting the UN Code of Conduct on shipping rules. Having declared itself not bound in international law to observe the Code, Britain nevertheless found itself having to agree to the so-called 'Brussels Package' compromise deal, wherein the Code would be substantially observed and the EC was treated as a single state for the purposes of assessing shipping within it.[39]

Or again, European conventions on the problem of insider dealing on stock markets, from both the Council of Europe and the European Community, have major implications for British company law. The British Company Securities (Insider Dealing) Act of 1985 is generally recognised as inadequate to deal with the problem, but effective amendment of it depended on the harmonisation of other regulations, not just in European Community states but also in Switzerland and Liechtenstein, through which many illegal funds are known to pass. National company law is becoming increasingly inadequate to the task of regulating international company practice.

At the other end of the spectrum from legal requirements Britain finds itself enmeshed in a web of deep functional commitments throughout the European Community which have become no less binding. The Eureka programme emerged, among other reasons, as a direct response to American high-tech competition. Britain became enthusiastic about it, if not about its funding, apparently because it served to forestall the European Commission from taking a more active and *dirigiste* role in the promotion of advanced technology. Backing Eureka would keep the issue in the hands of individual governments. And so it has proved. Though in constitutional terms Eureka is both inside and outside the formal framework of the EC, there is, nevertheless, a Eureka Charter which gives the programme a legal basis, and a secretariat which operates in Brussels. By 1986 the programme was backing well over 100 transnational projects, in more than 70 of which British companies were involved.[40]

Or again, the British attitude to foreign policy co-ordination through the machinery of European Political Cooperation (EPC) similarly reveals the evolving nature of European commitments.[41] Britain has always been enthusiastic about EPC and has done a good deal to develop it: through the 1970s where it was essentially procedural, and through the 1980s when it became rather more substantive. As ever, the British attitude was essentially practical, since officials were acutely aware of the common gains that could be made at the price of relatively small improvements in the co-ordination process. Equally characteristically, the British attitude showed great respect for existing institutional structures. Like their French counterparts, British officials were keen to preserve the distinction between business that fell within the terms of the Rome Treaties and that which should be dealt with through the non-Treaty channels of EPC. British officials also began to argue during the 1980s that EPC should begin to tackle some defence and security questions, though there was absolutely no desire in this to attack or modify the institutional divisions between NATO and the EC. British officials, still less British politicians, simply did not think in such terms. For them, the institutions were already there: the challenge was to make them more effective.[42]

Despite such an approach, however, EPC now constitutes a powerful set of commitments in the foreign policies of its members. The distinction between EC and EPC business could not be sustained in the face of substantive issues and has been greatly relaxed, with the result that in the field of foreign policy the European Community now has a wide remit in the co-ordination of national activities. The desire to include security issues in EPC helped stimulate an interest in the problem during the late 1980s which raised the very institutional issues that British officials regarded as beyond question. Politicians in France, Spain, Italy and the Netherlands (and even some in Germany) have raised the question of the appropriate security relationship between NATO and the EC in response to the WEU revival and the emergence of common European economic interests in defence and detente policies, the declining US defence commitment to Europe, the collapse of the communist threat and finally the European reaction to the Gulf War. Perhaps most significantly, the Single European Act codified most of the existing EPC arrangements, established a secretariat in Brussels, and made explicit a series of commitments to co-ordinate 'foreign and security policy' so as to recognise the EC as a 'cohesive force in international relations or within international organisations'.[43] British officials were greatly in favour of this arrangement, which is testimony to their practical enthusiasm for EPC. It illustrates the distance that the EC has travelled in certain sectors over the last decade. National foreign policy still remains under national control, but EPC is both cause and effect of an intensifying web of European foreign policy commitments.

Britain's diplomatic status

As a diplomatic actor in world politics Britain is, yet again, in an ambiguous position: both strong and weak, having a diplomatic status beyond its tangible power and natural diplomatic advantages, but an official unwillingness to capitalise upon them; and displaying a somewhat different diplomatic personna inside and outside Europe.

The statistics of British external diplomacy reveal a state that is well represented around the world. In 1987 Britain maintained 220 overseas posts in 165 different countries. This included 10 permanent delegations to international conferences, 8 miscellaneous posts, such as the British Military Government in Berlin, and 60 subordinate posts, such as deputy high commissions or consulates. In addition to 207 official posts – staffed by at least one officer of the Foreign and Commonwealth Office (FCO) – there were 13 subordinate posts staffed entirely by locally-engaged staff.[44] There are very few states or territories in which Britain does not maintain a diplomatic presence. And where it did not, as in the cases of Kampuchea and Libya, there were clear political reasons for the lack of diplomatic relations. Apart from the formal diplomatic posts run by the FCO, the British Council operated (in 1987) in 81 different countries, promoting British values and arranging for educational and cultural exchanges.[45] In addition, the BBC External Services, which is funded by the FCO to the tune of £116 million annually, broadcasts for 734 hours a week in 37 different languages, to a regular audience of at least 120 million people.[46] Finally, the British foreign aid programme committed £1.3 billion in aid for 1989, of which some 53 per cent was allocated as bilateral aid across 72 countries and more than a dozen regional organisations of the developing world.[47]

Just as significant, British diplomacy is backed up by a number of less tangible advantages rooted in its history. Whatever the so-called 'special' Anglo-American relationship has come to mean in reality between the two countries, it is still the case that in many parts of the world 'Anglo' still derives some psychological benefit – and in some cases detriment – from its connection with 'American'. Certainly, the Soviet Union paid Britain the compliment of believing that it had some useful diplomatic leverage with the United States in the 1980s just as it did in the 1950s. Such leverage appears to be taken most seriously by Soviet leaders at times when US-Soviet relations are more tentative, but the persistence of the belief was surprising during the 1980s. Britain's wartime role still carries some diplomatic weight, in Eastern Europe and in the wider world, as witnessed by the still largely unchallenged position of Britain as a permanent member of the United Nations Security Council. So too with its Commonwealth links throughout the former dominions and empire. There is much debate about the vitality of the Commonwealth, witnessed by the fact that it could not settle even the sport and politics issue in relation to South Africa. Nevertheless, the organisation continues to exist. In 1989 it spanned 49 states and around 1200 million people, and must be counted as a diplomatic forum for Britain, however slightingly it has been used in recent years. In this respect, the Queen constitutes a valuable and unique diplomatic asset. Having presided personally over the independence of the majority of the states in the Commonwealth, Queen Elizabeth II remains Head of State in 17 Commonwealth countries and commands a diplomatic esteem around the Commonwealth that may be as much personal as constitutional. Certainly, though there is no indication that the fascination of the world's media with the British royal family is wearing off, it may be that the Queen's successor will not command the same affection or carry as much authority in the

Commonwealth. As we enter what is almost certain to go down as a decade of great change in South Africa, it may be that the present monarch has become the most potent focus for unity in the Commonwealth. Perhaps most intangible, and most important to diplomacy, Britain has the advantage of English as an increasingly global language. It is impossible to do more than guess what this might imply, but in 1985 the FCO defined the English language as Britain's 'cheapest diplomatic asset': one reason why the BBC External Services, in the words of Simon Jenkins, 'transcends every other aspect of Britain's overseas projection'.[48]

The anomaly in this generally advantageous picture is that successive governments have done little explicitly to capitalise upon these assets. There appears to be some real confusion at the centre of British government over what constitutes 'diplomacy' and how the political and financial resources devoted to it should be assessed.[49] In 1977 the Central Policy Review Staff (CPRS) conducted a celebrated survey into Britain's external relations. It began by trying to define the nature of foreign policy and government's responsibilities to it. Its recommendations, many of which were very good, generally took an accountant's tone over the matter of resources for diplomacy. The report was sceptical about those alleged diplomatic advantages that were merely atmospheric, unquantifiable, or extremely long-term. And in its most celebrated and ill-judged phrase the report criticised the FCO and the British Council for doing their jobs 'to an unjustifiably high standard'.[50] The FCO, of course, pleaded guilty and sat back while everyone else demolished the report. Very little of it emerged from the barrage of criticism and those reforms that were implemented in the late-1970s were generally what Whitehall had in mind in any case.

The irony of the history of the CPRS report was that no one in positions of power at the time accepted its downbeat, cost-conscious approach to the business of foreign policy, and on the whole the report was ignored. Yet ten years afterwards it had become clear that, by default – indeed almost by accident – such an approach had been embodied in the thinking of the Conservative government. There had been no fundamental reform and no political rethinking about the best use of Britain's diplomatic assets. Instead, the resources had dwindled in the face of public expenditure stringency. Between 1981 and 1987 FCO expenditure fell by 4 per cent: manpower by about 9 per cent.[51] Its present number of overseas posts (220), while extensive, represents a significant reduction in the 273 that were operational in 1970.[52] Equally, funding for the BBC External Services was static in real terms and the government would not agree to finance a new Korean service, or contribute £1 million to a BBC initiative for a satellite-based World Television News

Service. The Commonwealth Institute's budget suffered a cut, and while the foreign aid programme was increased slightly in 1987 it still represented a smaller percentage of GNP than previous years, falling to 0.28 per cent – well below the average for the OECD countries. In 1990 the government made it clear that recipients of foreign aid would, in future, have to meet more clearly certain criteria of 'good government' to benefit fully. Nor was anything done to capitalise on the English language as an asset. Subsidised fees for overseas students were abolished in 1980, prompting a drop in overseas student enrolments by 1984 of 35 per cent, the bulk of the loss among Commonwealth students and those from the poorest 50 countries of the world.[53] Meanwhile, rows over South Africa that set Britain against most of the rest of the Commonwealth, the failure of the government to apply the Gleneagles Agreement on sporting links more vigorously, and its attitude to refugee problems in Asia, all created a mutual sense of disillusionment within the Commonwealth. In addition, the government's free market approach to the future of broadcasting, higher education, the arts and the work of charitable institutions, all conspired against the articulation of a more coherent policy that would have sought to capitalise on Britain's intangible diplomatic assets and hold them in some sort of constructive balance.

The result of all this has been a curious mixture of the complacent and the quietly effective. It is clear that Britain does still have some natural diplomatic advantages: perhaps quite considerable ones in an English-speaking 'American century'. But it does far less than any of its closest diplomatic rivals to capitalise upon them, and it would be very surprising if such advantages continued automatically to apply when diplomatic competition has become noticeably more fierce throughout the OECD world. It is clear that the British foreign policy establishment generally does an effective job within a narrow definition of overseas representation. In a broader sense, however, Britain's diplomatic status exists somewhat uncertainly between a European diplomacy that has the reputation – for both good and bad reasons – of being half-hearted and comparatively ineffective: and a more independent, global diplomacy that Britain seems to have done little to maintain or foster. As Tugendhat and Wallace say, there is no clear definition of political priorities in all of this.[54] In a narrow sense it is directed too exclusively at the wrong target, cost efficiency: in the broadest sense, and in a world of unique political challenges, it is not directed at anything in particular.

4 Policy Processes in a Changing World

The formulation of British policy in relation to the outside world is subject to all the contradictory and conflicting trends we have identified in the previous chapters. The policy process is a mixture of unchanging realities and new developments. The unchanging realities are important, for they express some of the simplicities of impressive political power: the nature of foreign policy in the British constitution, or the role of the civil service in the workings of cabinet government. In this respect a general understanding of the nature of British government constitutes at least a partial understanding of how the foreign policy process works. In this sense, none of the major books that have been written on the policy process over the last 25 years are actually out of date. What Vital, Frankel, Barber and Wallace – indeed what even Strang and Morrison – said about British foreign policy-making is still essentially true.[1]

Nevertheless, there are powerful forces of change at work and the conceptual problems that were identified in Chapter 1 are no less acute when we consider the specifics of the modern policy process. The essence of the problem is that 'foreign policy' and 'external relations' are not interchangeable terms. Foreign policy refers to the relations between one government and other governments and international institutions. External relations has broader implications and refers to the totality of relations between different societies. In Britain's case, there is now an acute tension between these two definitions of the subject matter, and an uncertainty over how far the government's responsibility for foreign policy can, and should, extend into external relations. For this reason it is comparatively easy to describe the foreign policy-making process in Britain, but much harder to grasp the processes of policy-making for external relations. The best way to capture this tension and consider some of its implications is to analyse the policy process from constitutional, administrative, and reformist perspectives.

Constitutional perspectives

A constitutional view of the nature of British foreign policy is not

72

often articulated, but it is always important. In essence, foreign policy-making has always been bound up with the executive. When the executive was expressed through the power of the Monarch, foreign policy was very much a Royal Prerogative. For this reason it was centralised, personalised and necessarily mysterious. As executive authority in the British constitution was wrested from the Crown to be exercised by Parliament, the strength of the Monarch's role in relation to foreign policy became even more pronounced. For foreign policy became the final function of government over which the Monarch retained control: and when control irrevocably slipped in the nineteenth century, it was the area in which the Monarch – then and now – proved to have the greatest residual influence. When control was effectively lost to the Monarch, it automatically switched to the political executive and resided firmly in the hands of senior ministers. Foreign policy has never been controlled by Parliament, even though, at particular times, it could be much influenced by it. It has always been directed from the centre; whether that centre has been expressed through royalty or through a powerful political executive.

The symbolism of the state

The implications of this domination of foreign policy by the executive are not often spelt out. The most obvious implication is that foreign policy embodies a powerful symbolism about the nature of the state. No matter how much the modern state is subjected to interdependent pressures, or how mixed up with domestic politics foreign relations have become, the fact remains that the symbolism of sovereign, independent action is still extremely powerful in the minds of both politicians and public. The personality of the executive, whether expressed through the Monarch or the Prime Minister is, in itself, a major source of symbolism: the deference paid to the Queen when abroad, or the way in which the Prime Minister deals with foreign heads of state and government, provides a focus for public images of the British state. In the popular mind, and not least in the minds of journalists, foreign affairs are qualitatively different from domestic matters, so that the dominance of the executive is not only taken for granted but is almost expected. Thus the popularity of the Monarch at any particular time, or the personality of a given Prime Minister, has more than a passing relevance to the British public's self-image, and to its view, therefore, of the rest of the world.

The power of the Monarchy

Second, executive dominance is important because the Monarch plays a tangible role in foreign policy. It is no accident that ambassadors are sent abroad as direct representatives of the Queen.[2] They enjoy many Crown privileges when abroad and they have some direct contact with the Queen when at home. This is only one expression of the fact that the Monarch, as a symbol of independent foreign policy, is also an agent of it. In constitutional terms, the Monarch has a right to be informed, to advise, and to warn on all aspects of policy. In foreign affairs, the Monarch is kept well-informed, and builds up a large enough fund of experience to be listened to attentively when advice or warnings are offered. Indeed, until 1936, it was an established rule that all important Foreign Office despatches had to be submitted to the Palace in draft form before they could be sent, and while this rule can no longer be enforced in the world of instant telecommunications, the present Queen is noted for her assiduous reading of all the important papers concerning foreign relations.[3] As Harold Wilson observed in 1976 when he retired as Prime Minister, 'I shall certainly advise my successor to do his homework before an audience [with the Queen], or he will feel like an unprepared schoolboy'.[4]

There is always debate among students of Politics about the practical power of the Monarch in the late twentieth century. In arguing about the reality of powers which are notionally constitutional, both detractors and defenders rather miss the point, for as James Cable puts it, the Monarchy does have an important constitutional role to play, and the powers of any particular Monarch are not inexorably declining: 'A very little substance is enough to sustain the symbolism of tradition and ceremony, but there must be some if the Sovereign's discharge of the dignified duties of Head of State is to have any meaning'.[5] In day to day matters, as opposed to constitutional crises, external relations provide most of the 'little substance' that is required. As Head of State the Monarch provides a continuity which spans many different governments, and the Royal Family constitutes an effective instrument of formal diplomacy through its connections, official visits and personal interests. Certainly, George VI made notable contributions to British diplomacy in both war and peace.[6] The present Queen's reign now spans some nine different prime ministers and twelve separate administrations. She has witnessed most of the process of decolonisation and has presided over the establishment of a multi-racial Commonwealth to which she is known to feel a strong and personal commitment. Indeed, in so far as one can gather evidence about such matters, it appears that the Queen and Mrs Thatcher, as Prime Minister, did not see eye to eye in their attitudes to the Commonwealth, and took different views about the weight to be accorded to black African voices raised against the South African government. The Queen is thought to have had some misgivings about the Government's decision to allow the United States to use its British bases from which to bomb Libya in 1986. And she is widely known to have been furious over the US invasion of the Commonwealth island of Grenada in 1983 wherein the British government was not only ignored but, in effect, lied to by the US Administration.

It is difficult to assess how much difference royal attitudes can make on such specific issues. On matters concerning general 'friendship between states', however, it is possible to discern some explicit royal influence. Anglo-Spanish relations, for example, have been notably improved by the friendships between the Spanish and British royal families: a not inconsiderable advantage when the problem of Gibraltar has loomed so large in their past relations. Equally, relations between Britain and a Monarchy such as Brunei, or the Monarchical states of the Gulf – particularly Saudi Arabia where the royal family is synonymous with the government – are naturally affected by friendships between royalty, no less than by friendships between political leaders in the rest of the world. In so far as the Monarch plays a genuine role in the work of the executive, in other words, it is played in foreign policy both as a counsel and as an instrument, and it is played rather well. As Peregrine Worsthorne pointed out in evident frustration in 1984, Bagehot called the Monarchy the 'dignified' and the cabinet the 'efficient' part of the constitution, but 'these days the only efficient part of the British constitution *is* the Monarchy'.[7]

Constitutional evolution

Thirdly, the fact that foreign policy is essentially the business of the executive creates something of a paradox. On the one hand this appears to make it constitutionally simple: it was the responsibility of the Monarch, then it became the responsibility of the most senior members of the executive. On the other hand, it is in the nature of the British constitution that the role of the executive is not clearly defined, for all its power. It is in a constant state of evolution in response to changes in the nature of the British state and in the international environment. Thus, as the British constitution evolves, foreign policy finds itself at the frontier of the evolution. The power of the executive has been deeply affected by Britain's European commitments and not least by entry into the European Community. It is affected by the penetration of the British state by outside influences: by the development of European Community law, or the application of US law to British subsidiary companies; by the physical inability to control trans-border data flows, or by the near impossibility of protecting what is widely defined as security information. Everything, in fact, that has been identified in the first three chapters raises questions about the nature of the British state and of what we mean – or used to mean – by the term foreign policy. This is reflected immediately and most starkly in the administration of external relations. When British foreign policy-making has been reviewed, either in the Duncan Report of 1969 or the Central Policy Review Staff Report of 1977, one of the most important questions, spoken or unspoken, was the role that the executive should play across the spectrum of Britain's external relations.[8] For all the traditionalism which surrounds it, foreign policy-making is remarkably innovative in constitutional terms. Foreign policy-makers must adapt to changes in both the international and the domestic environment. There are few settled institutions on which they can rely, though there are many institutions in which they are deeply involved. As a manifestation of the political executive, the adaptations which policy-makers go through – whether wisely or not – are inevitably expressions of changes in the nature of political authority and in the expressions of British statehood. The fact that the British foreign policy establishment, rather than, say, the Treasury or the Department of Trade and Industry, is at the forefront of Britain's relations within the European Community, is not simply an expression of the enthusiasm and seniority of the FCO. For something which is as important to the political executive as membership of the EC, it could hardly have been otherwise.

Administrative perspectives

If foreign policy exists at the frontier of constitutional evolution then it is not surprising if the uncertainties associated with this are reflected in the policy machinery. In Britain's case, the formal structure of the process for dealing with foreign policy, as traditionally understood, has not fundamentally changed over the years, though there have been many major adjustments as Britain's status in the world has altered. The shape of the formal machinery remains essentially traditional. The dynamics by which the machinery works, however, are in a state of flux which appears to be ever-increasing. This creates a tension between the demands, on the one hand, of a world in which events mesh into a complex of issues that can only be described loosely as 'external relations', and on the other, of an official response which is still predicated on the narrower definition of 'foreign policy'.

The formal machinery

From the vantage point of Whitehall, the structure of the foreign policy process can be described in a straightforward way. Even within a simple statement of the bureaucratic map of Whitehall there is a ubiquity about foreign policy and external affairs which easily rivals even 'economic management' in its extent, if not quite in the political prominence which it is accorded. The Foreign and Commonwealth Office (FCO), which now encompasses the Overseas Development Administration (ODA) constitutes the centrepiece of the constellation of relevant ministries. The Ministry of Defence (MoD), the Treasury, the Department of Trade and Industry (DTI) and the Ministry of Agriculture, Fisheries and Food (MAFF) are the other ministries which most often have a common interest in the business of the FCO, and vice versa. In addition, the Bank of England must be counted as part of this general structure. All ministries will have an involvement in foreign policy at some time, however, according to the issue, and circumstances are such that an increasing proportion of the routine of most ministries now falls somewhere within the sphere of external relations. Whatever constellation of relevant ministries or departments is brought together by particular circumstances, the whole is given central co-ordination through the extensive machinery of cabinet liaison and, in some cases, cabinet direction.

The Foreign and Commonwealth Office

As an independent ministry, the FCO has a long and interesting history. The Diplomatic Service can be traced back to 1479 with the establishment of a permanent British Ambassador. The Foreign Office itself dates from 1782. It always co-existed with a structure for colonial administration; originally a Council of Trade and Plantations (1672), then an India Board of Control (1786), and then a separate India Office (1857) and Colonial Office (1854). Until the mid-1960s, in fact, there were three separate strands to the administration of foreign relations: the Foreign Service, the Commonwealth Service and the Trade Commission Service.* Following the Plowden

---

* The Foreign Service was formed in 1943 from the Foreign Office and Diplomatic, Consular and Commercial Diplomatic Services. The Commonwealth Service originated in 1947, under the title of the Commonwealth Relations Office (CRO), when the Dominions Office and the India Office were merged. The Trade Commission Service was formed in 1946 when the Board of Trade took over from the defunct Department of Overseas Trade the responsibility for staffing Trade Commission posts in Commonwealth countries.

Committee Report of 1964, these three services were amalgamated in 1965 to form the new Diplomatic Service. The Foreign and Colonial Offices and the Commonwealth Relations Office (CRO) remained separate Departments of State in London, but the responsibilities of the Colonial Office were gradually transferred to the CRO and the Ministry of Overseas Development. In 1966 the Colonial Office and the CRO merged to form the Commonwealth Office, which was itself merged into the new Foreign and Commonwealth Office in 1968. In 1979 the ODA was, for the second time in its brief history, brought into the FCO organisation, to create the present structure. With this sort of pedigree, therefore, it is hardly surprising that the FCO is both highly prestigious and politically senior within the official bureaucracy.

The number of people involved directly in FCO work is remarkably small. In 1987 the FCO staff in London numbered just over 6500 people; the Diplomatic Service numbered some 4600 people, of whom around 1600 carried official diplomatic status. Around the world, about 7000 locally-engaged people worked for the Diplomatic Service.[9] As one senior official pointed out with some pride, the FCO employs fewer people than Harrods and has no problems in recruiting high quality entrants. The direct expenditure on the FCO and on foreign representation is also noticeable for its economy. In 1988–9 the financial provision for the FCO was £725 million, which amounts to less than 0.7 per cent of central government expenditure.[10] This should not, however, be confused with the expenditure devoted to external relations, which is a wholly different matter. It is clear, nevertheless, that the central administration of British foreign relations is a very cost-effective business. Indeed, the cost of running the FCO at home and overseas in 1988–9, including pay, accommodation, travel, allowances, and capital expenditure, was only £435 million.[11] The FCO, therefore, is not one of the big battalions in terms of numbers; nor is it one of the big spenders in Whitehall. Its political strength in the bureaucracy flows from its tradition, its identification with the nature of the executive and its constitutional importance as the ministry which deals with the external manifestations of statehood.

The British Council

The FCO also deals with a number of subordinate agencies which make up the institutional base of the foreign policy bureaucracy. Appendix 1 indicates the major organisations which contribute to the FCO's organisational structure, and those public bodies for which it has some responsibility. The most important is the British Council whose purposes under its Charter are to convey British culture abroad and promote cultural, technical and educational co-operation between Britain and other states. It is financed through both the FCO and the ODA financial provisions, since its role covers both cultural and foreign aid work. In 1988–9 it received around £58 million from the FCO, £44 million from the ODA and earned some £44 million from its own activities in the previous financial year.[12] Thus with a total budget of some £146 million and a staff of home-based and overseas-based officers, the British Council is responsible for much of the cultural, educational, scientific and technological aspects of normal diplomatic relations, and for many educational and technical training tasks required under the aid programme. Staff at the British Council are neither FCO nor Home Civil Service employees, though some of them may enjoy diplomatic status in certain posts: in essence they work independently for the Council, while the Council operates very much as an associated agent of the FCO.[13]

The Central Office of Information

Closely related to the work of the British Council is the overseas work of the Central Office of Information (COI). The FCO pays for some £20 million worth of COI services annually, which constitutes over one quarter of the COI's turnover. Half of the COI's staff work to promote the FCO's 'policy objectives overseas'.[14] The COI is a separate governmental agency but there is little doubt that the FCO has a major voice in a large proportion of its work and entirely determines the nature and shape of its overseas information policy. Indeed, a senior official at the COI has described its role in foreign policy work as 'an extension of the arm of the FCO's own information department'.[15]

The BBC External Services

Almost 16 per cent of the FCO vote is spent on the External Services of the BBC, which constitute a major agent of British diplomacy. They began operations in 1938, and are financed entirely from the FCO – in 1988–9 to the tune of £114 million. The External Services enjoy complete editorial independence in their own day to day administration and guard it jealously. The FCO, nevertheless, has a large measure of overall control. The FCO is responsible, in its own words,

> for prescribing, in consultation with the BBC, in what languages, at what times, and to what countries the External Services shall send programmes... The Corporation is obliged to consult the FCO

and to obtain and accept from them such information ... as will enable the Corporation to plan and prepare its programmes in the External Services in the national interest.[16]

The reality, of course, is less dictatorial than it sounds since the FCO is involved in constant liaison with the BBC, but as paymaster and political director of the service, the role of the FCO is clearly the single most important determinant of the way the external services operate.

The Crown Agents and the Commonwealth Development Corporation

Under the remit mainly of the ODA, two other organisations are important agents of foreign policy, the Crown Agents and the Commonwealth Development Corporation (CDC). The Crown Agents provide goods and services of all kinds to foreign governments, either on behalf of the British Government or other public bodies, or more commonly to assist in the practical work of the ODA. They administer aid loans and grants, supervise projects and are expected to operate in a financially independent and profitable way. They run their own overseas offices and independently administer the procurement and flow of materials for which they are responsible.[17] The Crown Agents themselves – normally 6–10 people to act as a board of management for the organisation – are appointed by the FCO Minister of State responsible for Overseas Development. Thus, though the Crown Agents operate independently and are subject to general ministerial guidance under the terms of the Crown Agents Act of 1979, they are effectively under the wing of the ODA within the general FCO structure. The Commonwealth Development Corporation is financed through the ODA and has a consultative role in policy-making on particular issues. Other bodies for which the FCO and the ODA have some responsibility are rather less important than any of these and have the status of consultative organisations rather than of parts of the policy-making or implementation process.

FCO structure

The administrative structure of the FCO has not noticeably altered for about 20 years. The basics of it are set out in Appendix 2, which for comparison offers two snapshots of the structure in 1974 and 1990. Essentially the departments break down into well-understood and traditional categories: the geographical departments – the 'desks' for various parts of the world; the functional departments which specialise in particular sectoral subjects; the specialist advisers and departments to provide news, research, legal and historical advice, economic analysis, library services and so on; administrative departments which manage the FCO organisation; and finally, the extensive Communications (now Information Systems) Division, which is responsible for a mixture of radio, telex and leased teleprinter communications between Britain and all its overseas posts, with the distribution of telegram copies to other Whitehall departments and with the operation of the diplomatic bag service. Appendix 3 offers a breakdown of the staffing of the FCO. The structure of FCO departments shows relatively minor but understandable changes over the years: some of the 'colonial' desks have been wound up or consolidated into other regional desks, the Soviet Department has become separate, the Passport Office has been taken out of the FCO altogether; there is an Environment, Science and Energy Department, 'space' is now a part of the bureaucracy, and the Consular Department now fields, alas, a Football Liaison Officer. These are the sort of evolutionary changes which are taking place all the time and generally represent a series of sensible rationalisations. It is a testimony to the general flexibility and sensitivity of the basic structure. It is also a telling symptom of the ethos and expertise of the FCO.

The organisational ethos of the FCO is less resistant than most of Whitehall to internal change. This is partly because the present structure of the FCO represents a fusion of older Whitehall ministries which each brought to the new structure their own particular ethos. The old Commonwealth Office, for example, had a different official style to that of the Foreign Office, and the ODA still does its job in a rather different atmosphere to the rest of the FCO. In a sense, the FCO is still an official melting pot. Moreover, this has happened at a time when the political orientation of the country has moved decisively towards European commitments, and this has affected the style and procedure of a great deal of FCO work. The organisational structure of the FCO does not give a complete indication of the degree to which the ministry has really changed over the last decade. As one Assistant Under Secretary has pointed out, for example, the EPC process fitted in with some European foreign ministries more than others and the FCO 'has had to adapt more than most': though from the organisational map of the FCO this would not be obvious.[18]

One aspect of the ethos that has always prevailed in official foreign policy circles is that of expertise and high administrative ability. This too has stimulated bureaucratic flexibility, for there is a high rotation of staff between different departments and between home and overseas postings. Career-minded officials know that advancement does not reside in defending entrenched interests, so much as in building up a core of varied FCO experience. FCO officials are noted, both inside and outside government, for their ability to master complex material quickly and in some detail. They read an enormous amount of documentation and the FCO circulates a great deal of material to all relevant departments so that officials are well-informed on a range of issues. Desks have to be cleared of work at the end of the day; only two years' worth of documentation on a given subject is kept in offices. The rest goes to the archives. So the positive aspects of this sort of ethos are a high level of flexibility, efficiency and an impressive command of immediate detail. The disadvantages are that officials do not have time to read more widely and generally about their subjects, and since they do not usually spend more than three years in any one department, the FCO's institutional memory on a given issue tends to be rather short. The acknowledged expertise of the Research and Analysis Department partly offsets such short-termism. Nevertheless, there are many more clever officials than reflective ones in the FCO, and while there is no shortage of radical perspectives in the conversations that take place in the Travellers' Club, or in round table meetings with outside bodies, the pressure of events and the high expectations of immediate performance on the part of officials tend to militate against any collective radical thinking. It is impossible to assess whether the predominance of Oxbridge graduates in the highest echelons of the FCO has a liberating or a convergent intellectual effect on the ethos. Certainly more than 70 per cent of the current Administrative Grade staff at the top of the organisation have an Oxbridge background, less than 10 per cent are women and less than 0.2 per cent are from black or coloured ethnic groups.[19] The FCO claims, rightly, that its duty is to take the most appropriate candidates coming forward, and that it is trying to encourage a wider range of graduates to apply for the Administrative Grade. Nevertheless, it is possible to argue that with a senior staff whose intellectual background is heavily biased towards History, French and Classics (in that order); where Economics, Politics or Law are not well represented; and where the *esprit de corps* is in any case powerful because of the unique demands of the job, official thinking inside the FCO is more likely to be convergent than divergent and to operate within its own frame of reference.

Overseas Development Administration structure

Apart from the FCO proper, the Whitehall foreign policy machinery is also made up of other ministries' external divisions. The ODA began life in 1964 as an independent Overseas Development Ministry with its own cabinet minister. It was absorbed into the FCO in 1970 when the Conservative Government came to power under Edward Heath; in 1974 the Labour Government restored its independence as a separate ministry, before it was reabsorbed into the FCO in 1979 when the Conservatives returned to power. The ODA is part of the Home Civil Service and it is described by the FCO as 'an administratively autonomous unit' within it.[20] Appendix 4 shows the organisational layout of the ODA. In both its authority structure and its distribution of departments it mirrors that of the FCO 'diplomatic wing' (as it is termed, to distinguish it from the 'ODA wing'). Since ODA geographical desks are responsible for all stages of the aid programmes they administer, contact with the appropriate desks in the diplomatic wing is close and continuous. Indeed, from an organisational point of view, the incorporation of the ODA into the FCO structure is entirely logical, and senior officials in both organisations professed themselves to be happy with the arrangement.[21] Problems arise in staffing arrangements, since ODA officials operate under Home Civil Service terms of service and are less willing to serve abroad without the allowances, and career expectations, of their diplomatic counterparts. Nevertheless, the administrative arrangement works well, and in 1987 there were six joint FCO/ODA departments dealing with aid policy. The case for a separate Overseas Development ministry is, in truth, a political one: that a separate ministry with its own cabinet minister would give aid a higher political profile and attract more resources for aid programmes. It would also institutionalise the notion that aid is primarily for the benefit of the recipient country. The present integration between the FCO and the ODA, of course, makes perfect sense in Whitehall terms and could be regarded as administratively unavoidable. Nevertheless, the present arrangement institutionalises a contrary notion: that foreign aid is an explicit instrument of foreign policy. As such, while the FCO and ODA structures operate as mirror images, it is still the case that their respective approaches to their work and their status within the Whitehall pecking order are rather different.

The whole FCO network is presided over by a political team consisting of the Foreign Secretary and normally three Ministers of State, one of whom is designated as Minister for Overseas Development, and one of whom is likely to be in the House of Lords. There is also a Parliamentary Under-Secretary. Needless to say, the personal relationships that exist within this team, and in the broader political configuration between Foreign Secretary, Minister of Defence and the Prime Minister, are a vital determinant of how well this core of the external policy-making machinery will function. In particular, the relationship between the Prime Minister, Foreign

Secretary and Minister of Defence is more important than ever before. Since a Prime Minister must now be more involved in the substance of external relations, there is a necessary closeness – almost an intimacy – between the three of them.

The Ministry of Defence

The Ministry of Defence is probably the closest cousin in Whitehall of the FCO itself. But like many cousins, they could hardly be more unlike. The MoD is a major employer since more than half a million people are on its payroll. It alone employs almost one-third of all civil servants. And it is undoubtedly one of the biggest of big spenders in Whitehall, responsible for a budget of £21.2 billion in 1991. Whereas there is a distinct homogeneity about the FCO, the MoD is a sprawling, heterogeneous organisation. Like the FCO, however, the present ministry is the result of a series of major post-war rationalisations made in response to changes both in global politics and in Britain's role within them.[22] It has been the subject of a major review no less than eight times since 1949.

The most dramatic post-war reorganisation was that of 1963 which merged the separate ministries for the three armed services to create the present structure of the MoD. Scarcely less important, however, were the Heseltine reforms of 1984, which did not alter the essential structure of the ministry but radically altered the lines of communication and authority within it.[23] Appendix 5 sets out the higher organisation of the ministry as it currently exists. From this it is apparent that the MoD is divided between three chief functions: the administration of the three services, for which there is an Admiralty, Army and Air Force board; the Defence Staff responsible for co-ordinating defence planning under the Chief of the Defence Staff; and the civilian sector dealing with management, budget, equipment procurement, collaboration, scientific research and so on. The effect of the reforms carried through by John Nott and then Michael Heseltine on this structure was effectively to deprive the separate service chiefs of a role in general policy-making. The effort to tighten up the management structure of the sprawling ministry had involved a much greater degree of cost consciousness in every area of its work, and a political determination to prevent inter-service competition from driving policy, especially its spending priorities. Accordingly, the Chief of the Defence Staff and the Permanent Under-Secretary now play significantly more important co-ordinating roles throughout the organisation and, with the Minister, form a centralised trio of policy-makers at the top. It is fair to say that the organisation of defence in Britain is now more coherent than at any other time. Given the history of British defence policy-making, of course, this may not be saying a great deal, and we are only concerned with reorganisations at the top level in Whitehall. The management of some other defence organisations, such as the Atomic Weapons Research Establishment at Aldermaston, attracted repeated criticisms during the 1980s. At least, however, it is clear that the effect of the Heseltine reforms was to complete a process which distinguished between the management of the defence sector and policy-making for it.[24]

Management reform in the Ministry of Defence, however, has to be judged against a burden that does not afflict other ministries in Whitehall: the MoD has to plan for both peace and war. Its management reforms are undertaken in time of peace when cost-efficiency is an obvious criterion of success. Yet in its role as a commander and administrator in time of conflict, the key criterion of success has to be the performance of people and equipment in operational conditions. And if the history of the last half century indicates anything to the planners it is surely that the incidence of conflict is no more easy to foresee than it ever was. Not only is the task of MoD management based on such an acute ambiguity, but the public expectations of which role the MoD should more completely fill swings one way and then the other according to political mood. A degree of schizophrenia is understandable.

Given that defence covers such a wide area, it is no surprise that liaison with the FCO is very close, especially on policy issues. Indeed, the two ministries, however unalike as cousins, tend to be natural allies within Whitehall. The Foreign Secretary and the Minister of Defence are the only two ministers whose brief is explicitly external. In the days of the Commonwealth Office, the Dominions Office and the separate service ministries there were more senior political voices who were formally concerned with external relations. Now, however, external affairs affect virtually every minister's brief and the FCO and the MoD frequently find themselves defending a broad foreign policy picture against the special pleading of ministries in whose world external affairs are only one dimension. The annual statement on the defence estimates, now that it has come to include a series of essays and more general discussions, is the closest the British government ever comes to producing an annual statement on foreign policy, and there is a good measure of FCO input to it as the writing of the annual statement goes through its second draft. Similarly, both ministries have some overlapping departments.

The FCO's Security Policy Department has extremely close relations with a number of MoD departments to co-ordinate on NATO, Western Security and disarmament issues, for example. Equally, both handle a good deal of intelligence information: in the

FCO through the appropriate regional or functional departments, in the MoD through the very extensive Defence Intelligence Staff. But aside from the obvious overlap between departments, there is an immense commonality of interests in most matters relating to arms procurement, overseas arms sales, military aid, scientific research, international technical collaboration, and so on, often recognised in mutual opposition to the Treasury or to antagonism from the Department of Trade and Industry. In 1980 the FCO defined four general areas in which the two ministries work closely together; defence within the NATO area; defence outside NATO; arms control and disarmament issues; and arms sales policy. They would now have to add to that list the whole area of West European technical and military collaboration as it has developed since 1984. Thus, the FCO 'takes the lead' on issues such as arms control and disarmament or Western European Union matters, the MoD on issues such as arms sales, or any essentially operational matters.[25]

The Department of Trade and Industry, Ministry of Agriculture, Fisheries and Food, and Department of Energy

Of the other Whitehall ministries which most commonly share issues with the FCO, the most prominent are the Department of Trade and Industry (DTI), the Ministry of Agriculture, Fisheries and Food (MAFF), the Department of Energy (DEn) and the Treasury. The DTI oversees the Export Credit Guarantee Department and runs the British Overseas Trade Board, both of which have close links with the FCO. In addition the DTI runs four major Overseas Trade Divisions which, roughly speaking, divide up the geographical areas of world business and pursue some key sectoral interests. There are also divisions for European Commercial and Industrial Policy, and International Trade and Policy. Clearly, the involvement between the DTI and the FCO has increased exponentially with Britain's entry into the European Community, but quite apart from that they now share more common problems than ever before as a result of the greater importance in the scale of political priorities accorded to commercial relations during the 1980s. The FCO went to some lengths, in the climate of the decade, to prove that it devoted a high proportion of its resources to commercial work and trade promotion, and the degree of personnel interchange between the two ministries is now fairly high. Over a quarter of the 40–50 members of the Diplomatic Service on loan to Home departments go to the DTI and at any one time over 20 DTI staff are normally serving overseas with the Diplomatic Service.[26]

The MAFF operates a large European and External Relations sector – the largest external sector in Whitehall outside the FCO itself – with two major European Community divisions, in addition to the international 'desks' it operates to deal with particular sectors such as fisheries, environmental protection, or food and drink marketing. Its major involvement in external relations is through the European Community where it has now amassed some considerable expertise.

The Department of Energy, roughly speaking, allocates its major divisions to the type and application of the various energy sources for which it has responsibility: petroleum, oils, gas, atomic, offshore technology, and so on. In each division there is at least one branch which is responsible for the international implications of the relevant work, and with relations with international organisations.

The Treasury

Finally, but perhaps most significant of all, are the Treasury and the Bank of England. Clearly, the Treasury has a potentially deep involvement with any ministry to monitor its finances and suggest ways in which it might better manage itself, and Whitehall has always been noted for the particular rivalry – among many – between the FCO and the Treasury as two of the three most senior offices within the government. More importantly, however, given the nature of their respective portfolios, it is not surprising that the Treasury runs a major Overseas Finance sector which deals with aid and export finance, international finance and the European Community. The FCO has constant and close dealings with the Aid and Overseas Services Division of the Aid and Export Finance Group. Treasury officials are also involved in some of the most important FCO posts overseas in order to deal with exchange rate policy and to take their part in international economic organisations. The British mission to the Organisation for Economic Co-operation and Development (OECD) in Paris, for example, has been led by a Treasury official rather than one from the FCO (though this is not invariably the case). Moreover, the Treasury is inevitably involved in its own network of international contacts with bankers, finance and industry ministers and international secretariats of all shapes and sizes. Though the personnel involved in such networks are far less numerous than those of the normal 'diplomatic' or 'defence' circles, they are extremely influential and of great relevance both to the business of external relations and domestic policy-making. Treasury officials know the City very well and are dealing in a centralised and sophisticated environment. They can transact major business with a telephone call which, in truth, leaves the FCO struggling to keep up with the flow of events. The Treasury always has the natural advantage of expertise in an international sector where knowledge is everything. Quite apart from such natural connections, however, the FCO and the Treasury have found their political territories over-lapping more completely in the last two decades than at any time this century. For as described in the last chapter, domestic economic management has become intensely politicised since the breakdown of the Bretton Woods regime, and economic issues, if they are not in themselves international, normally have significant transnational dimensions. The influence of Thatcherite conservatism throughout the 1980s gave the Treasury increased influence at the centre of the Whitehall structure, so that not only has 'Treasury thinking' become thinking about economic policy or careful accounting – though it is certainly that as well – but it represents, rather, a prevailing approach to some of the widest aspects of governmental policy, many of which are inherently external.[27]

Customs and Excise

Also within the Treasury's immediate remit is the Customs and Excise Service, presided over by a Treasury Minister of State. HM Customs and Excise is a big organisation, employing over 25 000 people: not much smaller than the total size of the Home Office and twice as big as the DTI. Its involvement in external affairs goes well beyond the collection of indirect taxes, for it is concerned with all matters relating to Value Added Tax, which is intimately connected with Britain's membership of the European Community: it is on the front line in international efforts to co-ordinate policies against terrorism, international narcotics and organised crime, or any imports and exports subject to official sanctions, and it is responsible for the compilation of various sorts of information, not the least of which are British trade statistics. Since external relations have become more integrated with commercial relations, and since Britain's economic future lies predominantly with the European Community, departments such as HM Customs and Excise have become essential elements in British external relations. As such, they strengthen the role of the Treasury in the process, though they do not always reflect Treasury thinking about the nature of the external world.

The Bank of England

Another department connected to, but not of, the Treasury is the Bank of England. In theory, the Bank is an agent of the Treasury, though as William Wallace has put it, 'the relationship between the Treasury and the Bank of England is one of the cardinal mysteries of British government'.[28] The same could be said of its role in external relations. Very few of the old textbooks on British foreign policy even mention the Bank of England as a significant actor, yet it has always played an important role in Britain's relations with the rest of the world. It is responsible for funding the government, for managing the currency and, through the Banking Acts of 1979 and 1987, for regulating the banking system. The Governor of the Bank of England is separated from the political hurly burly of Whitehall and yet has regular and direct access to the Chancellor of the Exchequer and the Prime Minister. The Bank of England is an agency of the government, and yet is a representative of the domestic and international banking interests of the City. Harold Wilson records how he established a series of 'City dinners' alternately at No 10 and in the Governor's flat at the Bank of England, whereby the Governor invited financial leaders to a series of 'extremely valuable' discussions.[29]

Thus the Bank of England acts for the government in the domestic context by managing exchange rate policy and in regulating the terms under which the City of London will operate. In typical Bank of England style, the most important rules are the informal ones, where the Governor has traditionally operated 'more like a headmaster than a judge, with a system of frowns, nods and occasional deadly disapproval'.[30] Yet in the global context the Bank of England also upholds certain principles of international finance and operates within its own highly specialised network wherein bankers interpret their task as an exercise in public goods: to uphold an international finance system based on good banking practice. As the world confronts the international debt crisis in the 1990s, to take the most dramatic example, the prevailing consensus among central bankers within this specialist network probably does more to establish the boundaries and terms of the international response than any initiatives of political leaders. The tradition of secrecy, upheld by all central banks, is an article of faith for the Bank of England. Thus it is able to participate in the Basle Group of the Bank for International Settlements, which informally regulates levels of international lending, just as easily as it played a mediating role in the financial deal that lay behind the Iranian release of American hostages in 1981, since even the Iranian revolutionary government was prepared to trust it.[31]

Other departments

This, however, is only a brief sketch of some of the most relevant departments within the constellation of ministries which most regularly and closely liaise with one another. Even a formal sketch, however, creates a picture where the degree of overlap is very obvious. And when particular policies and cases are considered, it is necessary to include in the picture many other departments of these ministries which will have an interest in a given case, and large areas of other ministries which are not normally thought of as part of the core constellation defined here. The Department of the Environment and the Home Office, for example, have found that increasing amounts of their work have a significant external dimension. Even the Home Office has found it necessary to join various international networks in order to cope with modern policing problems or the internationalisation of broadcasting, some of which touch upon the most sensitive issues of sovereignty and government autonomy. Thus, in 1988 the Home Office made a determined attempt to water down the proposed regulations for the future of television advertising that had emanated from the European Community and the Council of Europe. In an attempt to champion both the British broadcasting industry and the advertising sector, Timothy Renton, as a Minister of State, and Douglas Hurd, as Home Secretary, engaged in a round of international and conference diplomacy in all of the major European states, including Switzerland.[32] There is, in fact, almost no area of government which does not, in some way, relate to external affairs at fairly regular intervals. Co-ordination, therefore, is necessarily a constant and major problem. Co-ordination has to flow from the centre, and it is here that the cabinet system of government is seen at its most impressive and yet its most elusive.

The cabinet system

In formal terms the cabinet system is very easy to define. It is the system whereby the political executive co-ordinates governmental activity and takes important decisions collectively, from the centre of government. The cabinet system is extremely powerful: it shapes and adapts itself to the preferences of a given prime minister; it is dominated by the personality of the holder of that office, and yet it constantly proves itself to be more powerful and durable than any one prime minister. The impressive combination of personal leadership and the weight of collective decision-making – or at least of the responsibility for whatever decisions are made – provides a flexible and strong centre of political power in British government.

While such principles of cabinet government can be stated fairly simply, however, the reality always proves somewhat elusive. To begin with, the secrecy which surrounds the cabinet system, and which is a prerequisite for collective responsibility, means that even senior politicians will not know the full extent of the decision-making structure which is being operated in their name. All cabinet committees and sub-committees are formally secret and many decisions are taken in informal groupings on a 'need to know' basis. There are very few people indeed – and most of them officials – who could draw an accurate and complete picture at any one moment of the 'cabinet government' network of which they are a part. For this reason, all assessments of the cabinet machinery must be provisional and are unlikely to be totally inclusive, though clearly some researchers have achieved an impressive degree of accuracy and coverage in their assessment.[33]

Second, since the cabinet system depends so much on the personality of the Prime Minister, it is evident that it is very difficult to say anything useful about the cabinet unless we establish whose cabinet is under discussion. And even within one premiership, it is unlikely that the approach will be consistent over a period of time. Mrs Thatcher's approach, for example, always embodied both consistent and inconsistent elements, and the Thatcher cabinet system of 1979 worked somewhat differently from the Thatcher cabinet of 1987. As a working manifestation of the political executive, the machinery inevitably responds to changes in the political climate.

Third, like all really powerful arrangements, the cabinet system is remarkably informal. As Wallace observed in 1977, the system 'is less a machine than a network of well understood procedures', or in the words of a Senior Treasury official, 'the Cabinet is a personal business'.[34] What are commonly known as 'Cabinet procedures' span a plethora of formal and informal committees and meetings, of both ministers and officials, in regular and *ad hoc* groups. Arguably the least significant part is the meeting of 24 or so ministers, 'in Cabinet' normally for two hours every Thursday, at which a regular foreign policy report is delivered by the Foreign Secretary. Key political choices may be made in this forum, of course, though it is just as likely that they will not, and in the later Thatcher years it became extremely likely that they were not. Instead, the real locus of cabinet government is in the everyday work of this network of procedures. In 1985 Hennessy pinpointed some 43 standing cabinet committees or sub-committees and 29 ad hoc ones.[35] Some are ministerial, others are 'shadow' committees of civil servants to support the ministerial committees; a few are mixed between ministers and civil servants. On top of these a further 80 odd groups are believed to exist in a less official but extremely powerful limbo: liaison groups, interdepartmental groups and whatever bilateral and private arrangements the Prime Minister chooses to make. At any given moment there will be up to 200 odd committees or meetings forming the network of what is glibly termed 'Cabinet government'.

The Cabinet Office

At the centre of all this is the Cabinet Office and Number 10 itself. The history of the Cabinet Office has reflected the vicissitudes and fashions of cabinet government, being expanded and contracted, having its responsibilities and authority adjusted according to the taste of different Prime Ministers. At base, however, its role is to act as secretariat to the cabinet. Given the nature of the system, it therefore has a key part to play in organising and liaising between the various networks of Whitehall committees. In general, the role of the Cabinet Office has become more settled over the last decade, partly because more detailed policy-making has taken place within Number 10. Nevertheless, in its more settled existence the Cabinet Office is extremely powerful. It is staffed by fairly young civil service high-flyers, usually seconded from their own departments for two or three years, who are there as co-ordinators rather than explicitly as policy-makers – though as co-ordinators they can shape the nature of the negotiating arena between different ministries and can structure the way in which the networks of overlapping committees will operate. The Cabinet Office keeps the 'List of the Great and the Good' from which are drawn the names of those civil servants who will play important roles in any of the myriad Whitehall committees, and it will sit in on, or host, all of the most important ones. Where power over the agenda constitutes power over the outcome, the Cabinet Office has an important bearing on the detail of cabinet business. It works closely with the Prime Minister, but it is not an office of the premier's: it is a co-ordination mechanism under the leadership of the Chief Secretary to the Cabinet which 'belongs' to the Civil Service.

Number 10

The most significant office of central co-ordination, of course, is Number 10: 'a small village', as Harold Wilson described it.[36] All prime ministers have access to whichever personal advisers they choose and there is a long tradition of Number 10 staffs who have informal but extraordinary powers in relation to the rest of Whitehall. In the last twenty years, however, the staffing of Number 10 has become more formalised, though in numerical terms it is not particularly extensive. In 1986 Mrs Thatcher employed 27 people on the Number 10 staff, divided between the Private Office, which is entirely staffed by senior civil servants, the Press Office, which is normally staffed by officials on secondment from their own minis- tries, and the Political Office which usually consists predominantly of party supporters to manage the Prime Minister as a party leader, rather than as head of the government.[37] The Political Office, however, also houses what became in the Thatcher years a very influential Policy Unit, where the Prime Minister can second officials or private individuals as personal advisers to offer strategic counsel on any issue. In 1986, Mrs Thatcher's Policy Unit had reached the most formal expression it has ever known: it was headed by Professor Brian Griffiths, formerly of the City University Business School, and consisted of eight separate advisers, two of whom were seconded from Whitehall ministries, six from the private sector. And just to emphasise the personal preferences in such an elusive power centre, Mrs Thatcher also appointed to Number 10 in 1982 some senior personal advisers for foreign affairs and defence to complement her (sometime) adviser on economic affairs. Such personal advisers are complementary to the Policy Unit, though not actually part of it. They can be employed and dismissed as and when the Prime Minister deems it necessary.

The role of the Prime Minister

Within this nexus of political and administrative power at the centre of cabinet government, external relations figure more prominently than most observers normally assume. All Prime Ministers choose the degree to which they will be personally involved in foreign policy and most of them grow into a 'world leader' role which they positively enjoy. It is no surprise, therefore, that major foreign policy questions will normally be dealt with at the political centre of government. What is less often appreciated is the fact that while the Prime Minister's involvement in foreign affairs has grown, the premier now has far less choice over whether or not to play a prominent role and over which issues will have to be handled at prime ministerial level. For any Prime Minster is now timetabled into several structures of international negotiations by the institutionalisation of international politics within the OECD world. Thus, quite apart from summit meetings arising out of the normal round of official visits, tours and funerals (which are well-noted for their brisk summitry), the Prime Minister is timetabled not only into regular Commonwealth summits in alternate years, but more significantly, into annual OECD seven-power summits, biannual European Council summits, (normally) annual North Atlantic Council summits, and several other regular meetings at Head of State level arising out of long-standing commitments. These range from the Intergovernmental Conference of 1985, hammering out the final terms of the Single European Act, to the fortieth anniversary celebrations of the NATO alliance, or the two hundredth anniversary celebrations of the French Revolution in 1989. In this sense, therefore, prime ministerial interest in external affairs, and the need to co-ordinate the Whitehall structure to service it, is now built into the domestic political system by the nature of Britain's international context.

Cabinet co-ordination

The international context also requires more cabinet-level co-ordination, regardless of the Prime Minister's own role in it. Within the Cabinet Office there are six major secretariats to co-ordinate ministerial interests and serve the relevant cabinet committees. Of these six, three of them directly cover external affairs: the Oversea and Defence Secretariat; the European Secretariat; and the Security and Intelligence Secretariat. Of the various cabinet committees and sub-committees, Hennessy is able to name and locate 72 as of December 1985. Of this number, 28 had some direct external or defence policy relevance. Even more significantly, no less than 20 of the 43 standing committees, as opposed to the *ad hoc* groups, fell into this category.[38] It is no surprise, therefore, that foreign affairs looms large in the routine work of those ministers and officials charged with making the cabinet system work efficiently. Within the Number 10 staff, the Private Office (of officials) offers specialist advice on foreign affairs. One, and sometimes two, of Mrs Thatcher's personal, special advisers were concerned with foreign and defence matters. In 1986, within the Policy Unit, not only the head of the Unit but no less than five of the eight regular advisers were charged with responsibilities that covered matters which touched directly on external affairs. Such a concentration of central advisers with responsibility for various aspects of external affairs reflects not only the importance of the Prime Minister in this area, but also the pressing need to co-ordinate so many relevant external aspects of other areas of policy. It is eloquent testimony to the ubiquity of external affairs in contemporary British Government. Nor is it surprising to discover senior officials seconded from the FCO to run key cabinet shadow committees or parts of the Cabinet Office before returning to senior positions in the FCO or to major embassies. While it would not be true to say that the FCO dominates either the bureaucratic structure of external affairs or the issues involved in them, it is certainly the case that FCO personnel now play a more central role in Whitehall's co-ordination mechanisms as the ubiquity of external relations has manifested itself.

The dynamics of the process

All organisations have characteristic patterns of operation which are to some degree at variance with the map of their structure. In the case of external relations it is clear that power tends towards the centre of government. As Sir Kenneth Berrill put it, there is a troika at the heart of the power map of British government, consisting of Number 10, the Treasury and the FCO.[39] But if this expresses in stark form the most obvious feature of the unchanging reality of British foreign policy, it does not satisfactorily express how the process *characteristically* works.

Overload and co-ordination

Probably the most consistent and tantalising problems throughout the governments of the developed world are policy co-ordination and the dangers of political overload. British external relations, on the frontiers of constitutional evolution, suffer from both these problems in full measure, and some characteristically British ways of coping with them exist.[40] Co-ordination is an obvious problem since issues simultaneously cross so many ministerial and national boundaries. FCO personnel have to deal with the implications of issues which are matters of specialist knowledge, say, to the MAFF or the DTI, and they have to work with Home Civil Service officers who have learned to react to domestic political and administrative pressures which are normally more immediate and tangible than those under which the FCO works. Equally, domestic departments are increasingly having to operate in the international environment in order to fulfil their responsibilities. Every month some two hundred officials from the MAFF alone are required to travel to Brussels, for example, and they can only do this with the support of, and within the structures provided by, the FCO.[41]

The second all-pervading problem is that of political overload. In the analysis of domestic politics this normally applies to both the work that governments have to do and the expectations that they are required to meet. This is no less true in the realm of external policy, though few of the analysts of the 'overload problem' have considered it in relation to the international environment.[42] Indeed, it is arguably more pervasive in the international context since a government cannot so easily affect the environment in order to fulfil minimalist notions of the governmental role.

A good symptom of the problems of political overload is the amount of attention that political leaders are able to devote to any one issue. Human comprehension can only be stretched so far and is constantly under threat from the punishing schedules that ministers have to follow. It was widely believed that the physical strain of the Foreign Secretaryship, wherein less than half the working hours were spent within the FCO, was mainly responsible for the death of Anthony Crosland whilst in office. Geoffrey Howe, whilst he was Foreign Secretary, visited no less than 75 countries and clocked up over 700 000 miles in official travel as part of his job. Forty years ago, Ernest Bevin, who served as long as Howe in a single stretch in the post, was never subject to physical pressures on such a scale. In July 1989 John Major replaced Howe as Foreign Secretary. Within three hours of assuming the post on 25 July he was involved in discussions with the President of the United Arab Emirates: during the afternoon he was faced with demands to arrange an early visit to Hong Kong to stem the crisis of confidence following the Tiananmen Square massacre. In the evening of his first day he hosted a dinner for the Prime Minister of St Vincent and the Grenadines. The following day he had to meet the Soviet Defence minister. Within four days he had to attend the 20-nation peace conference in Paris to speak about South-East Asian affairs at which he also had to deal with the US Secretary of State and the Soviet Foreign Minister. And within seven weeks he had to visit the US President in Washington and speak at the United Nations General Assembly in New York, where he would meet most of his international counterparts. Within twelve weeks he had to attend the Commonwealth Conference in Kuala Lumpur. His immediate agenda during his first three months in office was not difficult to discern. He was deeply involved in East-West relations over aid to Poland and reactions to the refugee crisis in East Germany: there was another round of hostage diplomacy with Iran and Syria; East-West conventional and chemical arms control talks were at a critical stage and British defence interests were directly at stake; the issue of sanctions against South Africa dominated all diplomacy surrounding the Commonwealth Conference; the implications of the Single European Act on foreign policy co-ordination within the European Community was a continuing issue, while the refugee problem in South East Asia and the crisis over Hong Kong absorbed a great deal of his immediate attention.[43] Fourteen weeks after becoming Foreign Secretary, John Major found himself switched to Chancellor of the Exchequer in a crisis reshuffle prompted by the resignation of Nigel Lawson as Chancellor, and the learning process for his successor, Douglas Hurd, had to begin again. As John Major himself was subsequently to discover, the Prime Minister's load in relation to external affairs is no less than that of the Foreign Secretary. Mrs Thatcher averaged more than eleven official overseas visits each year: between 1979 and 1987 she had made some 95 visits, to more than 50 countries, at a total cost of around £3 million.[44]

The problems of overload and of co-ordination are not that the system will fail to work, or will be paralysed, for this clearly does not happen: the problem is rather that it will work badly, lacking consistency and sufficient thought and analysis. The British response to the problem remains contained within the essential structures outlined in the previous section. There have been very few institutional innovations, but the system has shown a capacity to learn and adapt. Relations between the FCO and the Treasury, and the MoD and the Treasury, have always been delicate: in the FCO's case because it is a senior ministry, in the MoD's case because it is a big spender. The Treasury is naturally discrete and tends to operate individually with different Whitehall ministries. It generally does not criticise the detail of particular programmes (though it can), but tries to apply certain economic principles at cabinet level with a delphic but iron touch which other ministries find difficult to handle.

Nevertheless, over the 1980s when the Treasury was clearly ascendant in Whitehall, the FCO and the MoD, like other ministries, learned to adapt to a new mood. Similarly, the FCO acknowledged twenty years ago that it needed to do a good deal more in the way of export promotion. By the late 1980s, at least in formal terms, the FCO and the MoD had learned from experience the problems of co-ordinating policy on specific commercial deals. Many would argue that the government lacks the political will to contribute more directly to British trade and industry abroad, and some consider the structure of policy-making as being inadequate to the task. But there is little doubt that officials in overseas posts, particularly in Western Europe, East Asia and the Middle East, have explicitly undertaken a lot more export promotion in the last decade. The British deal with Saudi Arabia to sell Tornado aircraft was regarded as a model of effective co-ordination: equally, the machinery for export credit arrangements in Whitehall involves an efficient interdepartmental machinery which brings together the Export Credit Guarantee Department, the Treasury, the DTI and the FCO.[45] Many regard these as the exception rather than the rule, but officials can point out, fairly, that their co-ordination is improving all the time and that their role is not directly to win exports as such, but to give effect to the prevailing view of the government about the appropriate place of the state in the performance of British industry. British officials have proved themselves to be very capable of adjusting and learning: there is an ethos of flexibility among those dealing with external affairs, though it is all within the prevailing structure and the political mores, and it normally shows its worth mainly as a response to tangible problems. They can certainly be caught out by individual problems which cross established boundaries. The handling of the 'Libyan People's Bureau' which led to the crisis over the shooting of a British policewoman in St James's Square in April 1984, revealed a clear lack of co-ordination between the FCO and the Home Office, as did some of the policing arrangements for South Africa House.[46] Officials have made bland statements that all necessary co-ordination takes place on such matters, but it is apparent that co-ordination over diplomatic and espionage incidents in Britain has been slow to develop in light of the growth of such problems.

Adaptation and learning within the general framework has taken place across the board in British external policy, though to differing extents depending on the arenas involved. There are different patterns of issues and relevance in external relations which lead to the development of packages of issues and areas of geographical concentration that sometimes overlap: economic relations predominate in Britain's relations with East Asian states; international financial issues have a major relevance to Britain, wherever they arise; economic, security and diplomatic relations overlap and interact in Britain's European and Atlantic relations; while there is much less intensity in most of its relations with Latin America. To make a crude distinction, however, it is possible to divide the degree of adaptation exhibited in the policy-making machinery according to a distinction between the non-OECD and the OECD world.

Diplomacy in the non-OECD world

In the non-OECD world essentially traditional patterns of policy-making still apply. The FCO sets the framework and is primarily responsible for the co-ordination mechanisms, at home and abroad. The policy machinery has certainly taken on new issues and problems, such as the co-ordination of EPC in regions outside Europe, the greater emphasis on commercial work, or the vastly increased number of British official and business visitors to an area. There are any number of new demands. But in essence, bilateral relations between Britain and Third World states; or relations with an international organisation such as the Commonwealth, or even the United Nations; issues concerning military aid outside the European context; or within the new FCO department for the Falklands Islands, all reveal that the bureaucratic map indicates most of the relevant processes. Policy is made through liaison between relevant FCO or MoD departments and domestic ministry departments, with the FCO normally taking the lead. Political direction is applied in the form of a monitoring and supervisory role from above by ministers of state. Co-ordination is performed through the cabinet machinery, and any key decisions, where they apply, will normally be taken in the Oversea and Defence Policy Committee of the Cabinet.

Political decisions will be made, or failing that, the flow of standard practice will be conveyed to the agencies charged primarily with the detailed implementation of policy; the British Council, the ODA, the British delegation to the international conference, or the network of 207 overseas posts. Overseas posts come in all shapes and sizes – major embassies, consulates, delegations, mini-missions, information services offices, and so on. This network is one of the major instruments through which British foreign and external policies are enacted, in those policy areas that may be broadly defined as being outside mainstream OECD concerns. Within the OECD compass overseas posts can be seen to perform a different combination of functions: they are not central to the implementation of policy. But in Lagos, for example, the British Embassy continues to perform the role to which it has been accustomed for many years, and which would broadly be repeated in embassies and missions throughout Africa, Latin America, East and West Asia and, to a lesser extent, within the former socialist bloc. The embassy serves as a base for military attachés, who are responsible to the Ambassador, not the MoD, while they are in post. It often provides the home base for British Council operations, and will normally run a commercial section for the benefit of British business interests in that country. It will probably also house the consular and immigration services and is bound to have an information section and other supporting services as required. Thus the tasks of contemporary diplomacy between, say Britain and Nigeria, and the way in which they are handled, are all comprehensible within the traditional framework by which British foreign policy is understood. Issues change, of course, and the emphasis has shifted to deal with almost every issue on a more multilateral basis. For this reason a great deal more political decision-making takes place in London, or in Brussels or Washington, rather than in post. But this merely bears witness to the contradictory nature of modern world politics. For while the growth of interdependence affects the whole world, and in particular the relations between OECD states' missions *within* Third World countries, it does not therefore follow that such interdependence will be the most dominant factor in relations between any one OECD state and, say, any one developing state.

Diplomacy in the OECD world

Within the OECD-dominated diplomatic world, however, and particularly in relation to Europe and European Community issues, the pattern is rather different. The very nature of the flow of issues within the OECD context challenges any categorisation of departments and ministries that exists in Whitehall. The need for officials from both 'domestic' and 'external' ministries to liaise constantly with their opposite numbers in other Western countries, and the sheer interdependence and complexity of the issues with which they must deal, creates new patterns of policy-making and implementation which are barely comprehensible within the usual assumptions we make about the nature of British government. In this case, processes of learning and adaptation have evolved to a point where, though they take place officially within the formal structure of external policy-making, they are nevertheless not easily understood by reference to it. A number of trends can be discerned.

Firstly, the nature of liaison within external affairs policy has become significantly cross-national. Officials deal directly with their foreign counterparts under a general political and bureaucratic framework laid down by their superiors. And very often such a framework is not consciously laid down, but is merely continued over a period through benign neglect. As a British official in the Paris embassy expressed it, the 'framework' is rather less important than the network of individual contacts. Their informality is the source of their effectiveness and their scope is deepening all the time as such contacts go down to the lowest working levels. The working networks that are established are quite different to the 'social' and 'general' networks that are traditionally fostered by an ambassador and senior embassy staff.[47] So in some policy areas, the scope for the exercise of discretion can be very wide. More importantly, the nature of the liaison process – difficult enough in any complex bureaucracy – has a significantly new dimension. Liaison is not only a cross-departmental matter but is now essentially a cross-national-cross-departmental task.

Second, and for this reason, the centre of the process – the cabinet machinery – is both more and less important. It is important because the need to achieve co-ordination is even greater, and generally speaking, the co-ordination of external affairs is very impressive. It may be less important, however, because co-ordination should not automatically be seen as synonymous with control. The cross-national nature of so much day to day liaison is evidence of the constraints and limitations that are inherent in an interdependent environment. The intensity of contact and co-ordinating arrangements may indicate sheer confusion, as officials fight a losing battle to retain some shape to their policy objectives. More likely, however, what we may be witnessing is the creation of several different, functioning, policy processes. The machinery becomes progressively disaggregated as certain cross-national arrangements establish their own *modus operandi* according to the range, seniority and nationality of the officials responsible for them, and the length of political leash allowed them by their over-burdened ministers.

Third, the issues generated by the politics of the OECD world demand – and are beginning to be accorded – perceptual changes in the ways in which British interests are articulated. An example of how wide are British external interests, and of how much they interact with predominantly domestic perceptions of interest, is provided by the case of Britain's international expenditure. A study by Wallace conservatively estimated the internationally determined proportion of central government public expenditure as 24 per cent, divided between at least ten different spending ministries and numerous subordinate agencies.[48] Within this total, the major share is provided by the defence budget, which accounts for almost three-quarters of 'international expenditure'. The defence budget, however, is also the single biggest category of expenditure within the hands of central government, so it is not surprising that government tends to use it as a lever on the domestic economy. The MoD Procurement Executive, for example, in line with the thrust of government economic policies, operates a small business office, and there is a constant tension inherent in major weapons procurement decisions between the need to obtain the weapons and the regional and employment effects on the economy of obtaining them in any particular way. Dealing with issues of such complexity, efficient liaison may not be enough. The fact that the disastrous decision to try to build a British airborne warning and control system (AWACS) had to be dealt with under so many different headings – foreign, defence, economic, technology support, allied relations, and so on – made it difficult to conceptualise the issue for the purpose of articulating British interests. Of course, it is not difficult to imagine ways in which the policy process could have worked better in the AWACS case to produce a clearer choice early enough to have made cancellation less expensive and damaging. But given the way in which the security environment is changing, as indicated in Chapter 3, even good co-ordination does not guarantee a full appreciation of the nature of the AWACS issue still less an appropriate political choice.

Fourth, the concentration on OECD matters in British external relations inevitably affects the pattern of staffing. Around 43 per cent of all the FCO's overseas staff are occupied with work within the West European and OECD world. This concentration is accentuated when the number of MoD and home ministries' staff working abroad in the OECD context is added. More important than numbers, however, may be the pattern of career experience that brings seniority. The calibre of officials dealing with Europe and with economic management is generally very high and experience in these fields is regarded as essential to the high-flyers in key ministries. Functional departments within the FCO loom even larger in OECD politics and there is a general trend for senior FCO staff to spend more time in London rather than at foreign posts, and to travel to and from working groups, meetings and conferences. A first secretary grade official can expect now to do two only one overseas and two home tours in a decade. Delegations, and a great deal of delegated authority, has replaced much of the work that would otherwise be done by embassies in the rest of the world. British embassies in Western Europe share the stage with the major permanent delegations, particularly with the United Kingdom Representation to the European Community (UKREP) and the delegation to NATO (UKDEL). They spend a great deal of time working on behalf of such delegations, preparing for summits, or acting (as one official in the Hague put it) 'as a messenger boy for London'. Much of their time is spent in receiving and briefing visitors and visiting groups, and they normally operate a fairly high-powered commercial section as a service to the business community. A former ambassador estimated that in an embassy such as Damascus some 80 per cent of the work would be bilateral, whereas in one such as Rome or Bonn, only 25–30 per cent of the work would fall into this category. Another 30 per cent would be to 'run around for UKREP' and perhaps 40 per cent would be impossible to classify in this way, being a mixture of a wide range of functions, bilateral, multilateral and international.[49] In short, trends in the deployment of personnel and the nature of senior foreign policy work, both in the FCO and home departments, tell a story of consultation between Britain and its close partners which has grown exponentially in both scale and scope over the last 15 years.

Relations with the European Community

The most important manifestation of all of these trends is in Britain's handling of its European Community relations. The FCO operates an 'internal' and an 'external' European Community Department (ECD) under the supervision of an Assistant Under-Secretary. These departments play a key role in co-ordinating policy within the FCO, within Whitehall, and in relation to UKREP and to British embassies in Community capitals. None of this is out of the ordinary, except that both ECDs are prestigious and dynamic departments within the FCO. The importance of the Community to the FCO, however, is very clearly highlighted by the appointment of the Political Director in London: a very senior official whose responsibilities for European political co-operation cut across the territories of the deputy under-secretaries. On occasion, this official is deputy to the Permanent Under-Secretary – the head of the FCO. The appointment of the Political Director and the job description represents a significant new development in the evolution of the bureaucracy, though it does not imply any explicit structural change.

The European Secretariat One of the keys to policy co-ordination in EC matters lies in the European Secretariat of the Cabinet Office. The Secretariat is small. In 1988 it was headed by a Deputy Under-Secretary with an Assistant Under-Secretary (equivalent) below that, an Assistant Secretary, four principals, and a support staff of about 12. Its function is not to make policy itself, but to co-ordinate and give coherence to the essentially disaggregated evolution of policy among the responsible ministries. In this respect the ECD is a more important policy-maker than the European Secretariat. But the Secretariat's job is to investigate sins both of omission and of commission. It can initiate a meeting at any level from a ministerial meeting downwards if it feels that one is necessary: it performs a managerial function for those parts of the bureaucracy that are involved in the Community, and an educative function for those that are not. Over the years, its educative function has declined as those ministries which habitually deal with Europe have learned the routines. In reality, there are only six major players on most EC issues: the FCO, UKREP, the DTI, the MAFF, the Treasury and the Cabinet Office itself. This has become a very close network in which all the important material is handled – to some a veritable 'Euro-mafia'. The full Cabinet receives a separate weekly briefing on Community matters, in the same way that it is briefed on foreign affairs, but this is only for general information purposes. The Cabinet's ministerial committee dealing with EC matters, the OD(E) Committee, meets only five to eight times a year. In these meetings it will look in more depth at one, or perhaps two issues. But even then it will scarcely spend more than 45 minutes on any item. So policy-making has to take place inside the network of departments. And within the network, relations between UKREP, the ECD, and the European Secretariat are a driving force. For more than a decade the success of the arrangement has rested as much as anything else on the strength of the key personalities involved. They have galvanised Whitehall, and created a high morale in Euro policy-making circles. Every Friday, the head of UKREP is in London to join the ECD (and other relevant officials as necessary) for a detailed two-hour planning meeting chaired by the European Secretariat. This is the trinity of officials who push the process along.

Diversity in EC policy-making The nature of EC issues is also a major factor. For the EC, like the Kaiser's war plans, runs on timetables. There is a constant pressure to meet deadlines. The British Government has little ability to affect the rhythm of EC policy-making, and there are many other players in Brussels who will initiate, or hinder, policy. As one senior official expressed it, the nature of EC affairs is such that officials 'will keep running with the ball unless their minister stops them'. This is not true of Whitehall in general. Britain's approach to the EC is a good example of a policy area in which most of the immediate substance falls under the rubric of MAFF or the DTI, but it is the foreign policy establishment, through the FCO, and FCO personnel who run the European Secretariat and UKREP, which dominates the style and presentation of the business. And it is the FCO which runs and organises the key embassies and delegations, even though their work is to facilitate the detailed day to day operations of home departments. In the wider context, the mission to the OECD, for instance, is run chiefly by FCO personnel but the majority of those who use and visit it are from the DTI, the Treasury, the Bank of England, or the Department of Transport or Environment. The same applies in UKREP, where an FCO organisation acts as home for officials from all the major ministries dealing in the EC, in particular those from the Treasury, MAFF and the DTI. Even in UKDEL, where the staff are pre-dominantly from the MoD, dealing with NATO issues, the Head of Delegation and immediate staff are from the FCO. This is the essence of modern cabinet government in a contemporary setting. The policy issues are dynamic and interdependent. Policy cannot be formulated only at the centre, because the issues defy easy definition that would allow the centre to handle them. Policy *has* to be made throughout Whitehall, but equally, it must be carefully co-ordinated. For all the concern by outside observers about the power of the Cabinet machine and its committees, the reality on EC matters is not that the cabinet system has spawned a huge, presidential bureau-cracy, but rather that it tries to give coherence and rationale to different levels of policy-making throughout a bureaucracy which is becoming internationalized. Britain's European policies, in a sense, have become well co-ordinated in their diversity.

The effects of the Thatcher decade

A final major dynamic of the foreign policy process was provided by the style of Margaret Thatcher as a three-term Prime Minister over more than a decade. Mrs Thatcher's contribution to foreign policy substance will be discussed in other chapters, but the contribution of her government to the policy process was not to reform the structure or alter the role of the FCO within it. There is every indication that she would have liked to do both of these things since her instinctive distrust of governmental institutions was matched only by her distrust of the FCO itself. Nevertheless, though she failed to break down and change the basic shape of the external relations policy-making structure, her reduction of civil service numbers – by about 130 000 to 600 000 – and her devolution of the functions of 70 000 of the remainder to separate agencies, indicates at the very least a determined attempt to affect the civil service ethos.[50]

Mrs Thatcher committed herself to introduce a 'management style' into the system and after a decade of attempts and the emergence of a 'Thatcherite generation' of civil servants and ministers taking up key posts, the external relations bureaucracy showed many signs of adaptation. Mrs Thatcher's cabinet style favoured less multilateralism in almost every respect. There were fewer full Cabinet meetings, many fewer cabinet committees, and dramatically fewer cabinet papers in circulation. She preferred to deal bilaterally with ministers. In addition, attempts at stringent financial management were introduced into all Whitehall ministries. In the case of the MoD this involved major management restructuring under John Nott and Michael Heseltine; in the case of the FCO, more of a change of attitude and accounting methods in response to expenditure cutbacks. The emphasis was put on greater management autonomy, whether in Whitehall departments or overseas posts. As a result, missions and embassies are now responsible for 80 per cent of their own expenditure. Within the FCO financial limits are set and officials must be responsible for the spending of their own departments. Posts in the financial and management departments of the FCO and MoD are no longer regarded as career sidesteps: they are now routes to promotion for high-flyers. In fact the FCO has performed better than most of the rest of Whitehall in meeting tight expenditure targets and the MoD has been able to save an estimated 10 per cent in its £8 billion procurement budget, thanks to the introduction of competitive tendering, and has hopes of finding further efficiency savings to get the best out of its declining 'real' defence budget. Ministers, it has been observed, came so to dread their 'annual bilateral' with Mrs Thatcher, in which their ministerial housekeeping was scrutinised, that they would move bureaucratic mountains to get a sympathetic hearing.

Mrs Thatcher's management style as Prime Minister increased the paradox of contemporary external policy. It centralized the co-ordination of policy and made some of it susceptible to very high level political direction; the Prime Minister was clearly in control of those areas in which she chose to be involved. She was prepared to bypass the FCO by appointing personal foreign policy and defence advisers after the Falklands War, though in reality, she did not use them in that way. On the other hand, she increased the trend towards more disaggregated policy-making by giving officials, if not ministers, more discretion. Her cabinet machine was not a massive

structure and Whitehall has reacted more to the pressure of international events in the last decade than ever before. Her style
strengthened the argument that it is more accurate to see the British
external policy process as a series of *ad hoc*, cross-national processes which work in their own characteristic ways.

Reformist perspectives

From what has been said above it is clear that the machinery for
external policy-making has shown itself capable of adaptation and
learning. It would be difficult to substantiate an argument that the
process is not well managed. But clearly all this is not enough.
Britain's foreign policy process is, in a deeper sense, unsatisfactory
as it tries to cope with the nature of contemporary external relations.
In the case of Britain's EC policy-making process, for instance,
where we have described the success of co-ordination, it is also clear
that an awareness of the wider implications of the European context
is not universal within Whitehall. Co-ordination is clearly very good
on particular issues. Indeed, it is recognised as being probably the
best throughout the member states of the Community,[51] for the
requirements of British membership of the EC have given the FCO a
framework within which to work: a distinctive role within Whitehall
which it performs with enthusiasm and some panache. This, however, has not in itself given the British government as a whole a head
start in dealing with broader European issues, or in anticipating the
effects that the EC will have on British society and politics. The
determined pragmatism of the British approach is very efficient but
essentially reactive. And as has been pointed out in earlier chapters,
an overly reactive approach to the divergent and confusing trends in
modern world politics – even more in modern European politics –
will fail to establish meaningful influence over the international
environment.

   All ministries are increasingly affected by 'Euro-politics' though
some are much better at dealing with them than others. The Treasury
and the Home Office are not noted for their Euro-mindedness and
certainly tend to be reactive in their collective approach to Community business. HM Customs and Excise, on the other hand, have
shown themselves very sensitive to the implications of the Single
European Act and used their knowledge of the European scene to
develop schemes that would speed up border traffic in anticipation of
the more integrated market. The Department of Health and Social
Security, or the Department of Employment, are no less affected by
the implications of the single European market, but as long as the
prevailing political wisdom is that such a development is almost

exclusively economic, their approach also has been essentially reactive. Too much depends on key personalities, and prevailing attitudes will vary with changes in their political fortunes. Norman Fowler, as Minister for Employment, envisaged the work of his department in a peculiarly national way and was not noted for a willingness to approach interdependent issues in a broader context. Lord Young, in contrast, as Minister for Trade and Industry, lifted the profile of the DTI on all European issues as a matter of personal commitment and established it as the leader on all 1992 developments. Michael Heseltine explicitly tried to take an active European view at the MoD, though George Younger, his successor, was a notably less-committed 'European'. Or again, Nicholas Ridley, when Minister for the Environment, never attended Brussels meetings, but was compelled to spend a good deal of energy fighting rearguard actions against EC transport and water regulations which became increasingly confused with the government's privatisation programmes.

Throughout the 1980s, in fact, Britain's European policies were the subject of embarrassing rows within Whitehall, where it was evident that there existed rather different definitions of what constituted British interests in the European context. It all added fuel to the wide-ranging criticism of the foreign policy establishment that ran throughout the decade: from the attitudes to Britain's budgetary problems with the EC in the early 1980s, to the notorious Falklands hiatus in 1982, to niggling rows ranging from recognition for the PLO, or sanctions against South Africa, to disagreements over whether Mrs Thatcher should visit Commonwealth war graves during a visit to Japan in 1989.[52] Criticisms from outside Whitehall also simmered throughout the decade. Three successive 'Conservative' Parliaments became wary and suspicious of the civil service in general and the FCO in particular. There was a ready indignation in Parliament at the FCO or the MoD when British institutions or firms appeared to be compromised by external developments. Whitehall seemed to be confused in its attitudes to key companies, particularly defence companies, when they were subject to foreign takeovers: the Royal Navy mounted a series of partisan defences of its status, putting its case strongly – and indiscreetly – to Parliament and the public; and the FCO, particularly under the stewardship of Sir Geoffrey Howe, attracted constant criticism for its 'Europeanness' when important British interests were at stake. As Norman Tebbit put it 'The Ministry of Agriculture looks after farmers. The Foreign Office looks after foreigners.'[53]

Talk of reforming the machinery has not subsided since the debate over the Central Policy Review Staff's report in 1977. In 1988 and

1989 there were renewed calls from across the political spectrum for an independent foreign policy unit to offer the government clear thinking on major international issues. 'The question that should now be asked', said the International Freedom Foundation, 'is whether the will of the Executive is being frustrated by the FCO'. 'The Foreign Office has transferred its allegiance from Britain to Brussels' declared Tony Benn; 'the Foreign Office finds it difficult to believe that it *can* be wrong', said Roy Hattersley.[54] In November 1988 *The Times* called for a separate foreign policy unit somewhat akin to the National Security Council in the United States, and thus entered into an acrimonious press debate. But most of these calls for a separate foreign policy unit were for rather different reasons: some because no policy was being made in Number 10 for lack of proper advice; some because very clear policy was being made in Number 10, but frustrated once it travelled the 20 yards across Downing Street to the FCO; some because policies were being faithfully enacted but were simply the wrong policies; others because they felt that what Herbert Morrison had once called 'the Chinese wall round the Foreign Office' was still very much in place.[55] In general, the 1980s left an impression that the proper handling of external affairs was not merely a political argument between the zealots and the recalcitrants in the Thatcherite revolution. In short, there was abundant evidence of a deeper malaise – and hence a louder argument – about the very comprehension of external affairs: a malaise that was disguised and partly ameliorated by the essential competence and unity with which the machinery handled the details of policy.

The malaise concerns the way in which the machinery articulates choices and objectives for British external relations. A typical civil service response to this criticism is to plead that the machinery can only respond to whatever political direction it is given on key choices and objectives. But the reality is that there is a dialectical relationship between civil servant and politician in the expression of objectives. Administrators cannot wash their hands of responsibility for political choices, any more than politicians can for the way in which they are administered. The danger for Britain is that it may have slipped into a syndrome where its policies are, in a tactical sense, beautifully co-ordinated but, in a strategic sense, incoherent. It is an aspect of the problem that Sir John Hoskyns, who worked in the policy unit in Number 10, characterised as government being 'a creature without a brain' where there is 'no policy on policy-making': what Lord Hunt, an ex-cabinet secretary, called 'a hole at the centre'.[56]

Research and planning

None of the major ministries involved in external relations are short of research or planning facilities. The FCO's Research and Analysis Department is intended to provide it with expert background material from specialists drawn from outside the civil service, and its Policy Planning Staff have been accorded more influence and prestige within the organisation during the 1980s than at any other time in the troubled history of foreign office planning and research.[57] Likewise the Heseltine reforms of 1984 established in the MoD a Secretariat for Policy Studies, whose remit was to act as a 'think tank' within the ministry, though it coexists with three other such units, in the Procurement Executive, and within the Defence Staff. The FCO also runs an Arms Control and Disarmament Research Unit which has been in existence since 1965. Its first director was Hedley Bull and over the years it has drawn personnel from the academic world and acted as a think tank on a number of arms control and related issues. It had a significant effect on British arms control policies in the 1960s, though its present influence is rather less than it was. In addition to such in-house units, ministers are normally allowed up to two Special Advisers each: people brought in from outside the civil service to offer their minister independent advice on a complete range of ministerial work. Last, but not least, Prime Ministers can take advice from anyone of their choosing and during the 1980s, Sir Anthony Parsons, Sir Percy Craddock, Charles Powell, not to mention Bernard Ingham as press secretary, were all in a prominent position to give the Prime Minister strategic advice on foreign affairs.

Controlling expenditure

The problem, therefore, is not so much that the external policy machinery is overwhelmed by pressures to the point where it cannot think straight. It is rather that both internal and external pressures on the policy process have encouraged the growth of particular *types* of goals and objectives that have tended to mortgage future thinking. Foremost among such pressures has been that of cost-cutting. The need to manage its own administration more efficiently has provided a very clear performance objective for the FCO. Since 1984 FCO departments have been made to set their own particular objectives and evaluate them: the office has coped with a 20 per cent cut in manpower over the last twenty years and a 3–4 per cent cut in financial provision in real terms over the last seven. It has cut back in those areas where it has been easiest to cut – in information work, for example, or in the staffing of overseas posts, where it has some independent control over the expenditure. As a department which is not a big spender, economies mean cuts in manpower and the FCO has had to organise a reduced staff to cope with greatly increased demands. A good proportion of FCO expenditure is demand-driven, so as expenditures have increased on work such as that relating to narcotics, AIDS, terrorism, or in providing consular cover (for the doubling of British travellers abroad in less than a decade), relative expenditures on other items have tended to be driven down. Similarly, the MoD has been subject to intense pressures to achieve economies through greater efficiencies. This it has tried to do, but the switch to a greater emphasis on equipment rather than manpower between 1978 and 1985, and then the determination to further restrain equipment costs after 1985, put the defence budget into an ever-tightening strait-jacket which satisfies the short-term thirst for economy but clearly begins to constrain medium- or longer-term choices. In response to academic seminars and political enquiries many formal papers are produced which attempt to specify foreign policy objectives, but officials admit, like Lord Carrington when he was Foreign Secretary, to being 'rather nervous' about them: there is a general acknowledgment that policy is reactive.[58] In the words of a deputy under-secretary, 'Our skill is in *not* having a grand strategic concept'.[59] Expenditure targets and departmental performance targets, on the other hand, are both expressible and achievable and have the added blessing that they can head off external criticism.

The pressure on expenditure also creates working practices which militate against the articulation of longer or broader objectives. When expenditure is tight, departmental and institutional boundaries become more rigid. If one ministry tries to set broad objectives it will inevitably involve several other ministries, and immediately it becomes a scheme to spend their money for them. The DTI repeatedly pressured the FCO to allocate more of its budget to the promotion of commercial relations abroad. This the FCO could not afford to do. On the other hand, it would be loath to give responsibility to the DTI for commercial promotion overseas, since that would carry the grave risk of a major – and perhaps more than proportionate – shift in budget to the DTI to do it. Even where ministries, or even departments within a ministry, may agree on an adjustment of responsibilities, officials are well aware that the money withdrawn from one may not be made fully available to the other. The only gainer is the Treasury. As John Nott wrote in evident frustration after his term as Minister of Defence; the system of annual Treasury control

is so organised as to prevent any serious long-term financial planning. If a prudent degree of flexibility is built into a programme ... it is seen by the Treasury as a money box to plunder for the fashionable political orgasm of the day, be it lower public expenditure, lower taxes or whatever.[60]

Indeed, the general year on year stability of the budgets of the FCO, the MoD and the DTI over the last decade, at a time of great change in their international context, may be regarded as strange. Many observers have argued that a broad, and rational, approach to British external relations would long ago have cut the defence budget and reallocated resources to some of the less tangible aspects of diplomatic relations, on the assumption that the loose change of the defence budget could double or triple the size of educational programmes, commercial promotion, and so on. But while cutting the defence budget has become conventional wisdom, the idea of such a fundamental redistribution of resources from one programme to another is simply beyond the range of the possible in the present Whitehall climate. Treasury thinking reinforces all the tendencies, already strong in any bureaucracy, to defend departmental boundaries.

Conceptualising choices

Another type of pressure which reinforces a sense of malaise in the definition of clearer policy objectives is the continuing tendency in British politics and British business circles to cling to a narrow conception of the 'national economy'. As we have seen, Britain's economic context makes this a controversial notion, but it remains the conviction of present governments. The defence of the national economy in a highly interdependent context becomes conceptually ever more difficult. All Whitehall ministries have suffered from the problem of trying to reconcile external economic pressures with internal political ones. Proposals that make good sense in a European context invite derision in the domestic one. And the implications of the European context – in particular of 1992 – have only seriously been taken up by the companies that are already major exporters, or social groups who see themselves as explicitly transnational: there is not a wide domestic constituency for European proposals that are not framed in terms of the direct benefits to the national economy. Public expenditure is examined without serious reference to the international conditions in which it will take effect and becomes a matter, in the words of Sir Burke Trend of, 'mere austerity' and 'indiscriminate horse-trading between Ministers'.[61] In these circumstances there is no clear conception within the external policy machinery of how the growing institutionalisation of the European economy should be approached. Certainly, there is a widespread conviction in Whitehall that there are more than enough institutions in Europe and there is no case for any more. But the increasing institutionalisation of behaviour between European societies creates a tension over how Britain's interests can best be furthered in such an environment. In a political climate which takes a minimalist view of government's role in the British economy and society, it is natural that individual ministries will tend to have ministerial objectives rather than national objectives, as such. There is no political pressure from above to become more involved in British society's dealings with the external world (quite the reverse, in fact), and insufficient recognition from economic groups below that the national economy is probably no longer a sustainable framework for their existence.

British external policy-making remains uncertain about all of the major issues it confronts: a European, as opposed to an Atlantic and world orientation; its relationship with European integrationism; its relationship to the British economy and to the European economy; its conception of appropriate defence and security; the role of external policy in the increasing internationalisation of British society.[62] These are daunting questions in any case, and are certainly being faced by other European states, but the policy system hardly recognises them as genuine political choices at all. Intellectually it falls back on the somewhat comforting constraint that it must maintain its formal international commitments: and for practical purposes it concentrates on efficiency and financial austerity. Such a malaise is not merely a political problem, though it contains political elements since the final Thatcher government was convulsed by political uncertainties over the appropriate role for Britain in the more integrated context of the 1990s. Nor is it just a management problem, though administrative reform could be one of the keys to unlock some of the puzzles. At root, it is a conceptual problem, where a system organised according to domestic functions – employment, social provision, transport, and so on – is confronted by issues that are less and less comprehensible by reference to domestic categorisations. The policy system can react to the immediate manifestations of such issues but it cannot establish meaningful priorities within a context that it barely comprehends.

In the next two chapters we will examine some of the ways in which these barely comprehensible pressures feed into the policy process.

5 Institutional Influences on External Policy-making

Earlier chapters have concentrated on the new context in which British external policy is now made. Clearly, the context of policy will have an intimate effect on the content and the making of it. But we must be careful to distinguish the context of policy from influences upon it. For the 'context' is something within which Britain exists according to the view of the beholder. Governments may or may not agree with the observer's particular characterisation of the context, and to a large extent, the context of policy is whatever governments perceive it to be. They may, of course, be wildly inaccurate and will pay the price of misperception, but they have nothing but their honest opinions on which to rely.

Influences on policy, on the other hand, derive from the international and domestic contexts and will obviously reflect them, but they are of an altogether more tangible character. Influences on external policy can be perceived more objectively since they have a discernible impact on the policy process. There is plenty of room for argument over what any particular influence tells us about the general context, or over how powerful an influence it may be, but analysts can normally agree on a rough list of prevalent influences that have some sort of impact on policy.

On the other hand, the context that we have identified is a very complex arena in which foreign and domestic influences have become inextricably mixed in the developed world, and where diverse and homogeneous trends develop side by side. It would not be consistent with our approach in this book to analyse influences on the external policy process as if they were simply 'domestic' and 'international': nor would it be wise, since such distinctions soon break down once serious analysis begins. Instead, it is more useful to analyse those influences that are generally institutionalised as opposed to those which generally are not. For in a context of rapid change institutional distinctions are important. As some institutions lose power and others gain it; as some institutions continue to exist while others establish themselves in response to a need; above all, as some forms of behaviour remain essentially ad hoc and others become institutional*ised*, we can begin to perceive some of the directions of political change to which the policy process is responding. This approach allows us to view the external policy

113

process within its overall political structure, both domestic and international, and to take account of the contradictory trends that we have identified.

In the 1990s it is simply not the case that the domestic environment encompasses essentially institutionalised influences on foreign policy while the international environment includes less potent institutional influences. This traditional distinction between domestic 'society' and international 'anarchy' that has so influenced the literature of Political Science was always overdrawn and certainly lacks credibility in the European and the OECD context.[1] The fact is that external policy is made within a web of institutions that derive from British domestic society, from other domestic societies, and not least from the international polity itself. The pattern of the most influential institutions changes over time and, at the risk of making too crass a generalisation, it appears that in the 1990s the established institutional influences on British external policy are less important now than the growth of new institutions and the rapid development of institutionalised behaviour in sectors that were not previously central to the perception of the context of British policy.

This chapter, therefore, attempts to analyse the most obvious and well-understood institutional influences on British external relations, while the next looks at the essentially non-institutionalised influences.

Parliament and external policy

The influence of Parliament on policy-making for external relations has always been a mixture of the formal and the informal. The formal powers of Parliament in the realm of foreign policy are, by the nature of the British constitution, extremely limited. What influence Parliament does exert over foreign policy is through its informal powers, which on occasion can be significant, especially if the political parties are closely balanced within the House of Commons. There is little dispute, however, that in the normal run of British politics Parliament is a relatively weak influence in the foreign policy process. The perspective of the 1990s suggests two particular variations on this truth. First, it is clear that the contextual changes we have already outlined have affected Parliament no less than any other institution in the last 20 years, and have had an impact on the way in which it exercises its essentially informal powers. Second, for the same reasons, Parliament finds itself involved less in foreign policy-making and more in external relations policy, broadly defined. And this creates a paradox, for while Parliament in the

1990s cannot help but be more engaged in matters relevant to external affairs, it is nevertheless confronted by a succession of issues over which it can exert less influence than ever before.

Parliament's formal powers

The formal powers of Parliament, such as they are, derive from the notion that British sovereignty is essentially parliamentary sovereignty.[2] For sovereignty was assumed to be exercised in relation to the rest of the world on behalf of Parliament, not directly on behalf of the nation. The prospect that Parliament would not support the foreign policy that it undertook did not arise, and in an unwritten constitution, the powers of Parliament in this respect did not have to be specified. Thus, foreign policy was both a Crown prerogative – being the last area of policy that was effectively given up by the monarch – and yet was assumed to be exercised by the grace of Parliament, to whom the King's or Queens's ministers were responsible.[3] It was therefore axiomatic that Parliament would support foreign policy but take no active part in it. Indeed, in Bagehot's classic 1867 analysis *The English Constitution*, wherein the powers of Parliament were judged to be considerable in relation to the executive, foreign affairs were not even mentioned: nor, by nineteenth century standards, should they have been.

Thus, the formal powers of Parliament over foreign policy can be stated briefly. In foreign affairs Parliament has the same delegatory power in relation to the executive that it has in any other matter: that is, in theory Parliament could bring down a government on a foreign issue, just as it could on a domestic one. The replacement in 1940 of the Chamberlain government by Churchill's is the most recent example of the exercise of such power, though even here the Chamberlain government was not actually defeated in the Commons: it simply lost support to a humiliating degree.

Apart from the ultimate power over the survival of governments, Parliament is also constitutionally in control of the armed forces, and has been since the 1688 Bill of Rights. It votes every five years for the continued existence of armed forces in peacetime and every year, under the Armed Forces Act, for the continuation of the existing three armed services.[4]

Of more practical concern, Parliament's formal influence over the legal substance of foreign affairs lies essentially in the strength of convention. Parliamentary ratification is not required for treaties to enter into force, unless such treaties require some alteration in existing legislative arrangements, or the creation of new legislation; unless they would increase the rights of the Crown, or their wording explicitly demands parliamentary consent; or unless they involve the cession of territory which would affect the rights and nationalities of British subjects.[5] By convention, according to the 'Ponsonby rule' of 1924, any international treaty entered into by the government is laid before both Houses of Parliament for 21 days prior to its ratification. There is some debate as to how binding this convention may be, and in any case there are exceptions, as the Government specified in 1961.[6] Where aspects of foreign policy require a formal enactment of some kind, it takes place through Agreements, Conventions, or Exchanges of Notes, which are normally presented to Parliament as a matter of information rather than for discussion. The exchange of notes between Britain and France regarding the future of the New Hebrides, as one example, came into effect on 19 April 1972, but was not presented to Parliament until some two months later.[7] Parliament therefore has no constitutional rights to be consulted about foreign affairs and no constitutional role at all in foreign policy-making. On the other hand, governments would be very foolhardy simply to ignore Parliament in foreign affairs, since Parliament clearly has a political significance in the same way that it has in all aspects of government.

Parliament's informal powers

If we turn to Parliament's informal powers, the focus of our interest is on the way in which Parliament represents an institutionalised political dialogue between legislators and rulers. For analytical purposes, it is sensible to see this dialogue as consisting of three distinct but related political arenas: Parliament as the chambers of the Commons and Lords; as the focus for party organisations, and as the framework for the detailed work of the select committees. In all of these three arenas it is possible to see at work the general trends we have outlined above: a shift in the way informal powers are exercised towards more specialised Parliamentary functions in an attempt to keep up with the pressures of a complex political environment; and yet a continuing failure to come to grips with the real substance of external relations.

The two Houses

Foreign affairs debates on the floor of the Commons or Lords are dominated by the simple reality that Parliament is not concerned with what is important but with what is controversial. For this reason, certain issues will tend to dominate the parliamentary agenda and others will only ever be mentioned in passing. The debate on the Queen's Speech devotes a day to matters of foreign affairs – traditonally defined – and there is normally one general two-day debate on foreign affairs in each parliamentary session. Other debates affecting foreign affairs and external relations more generally will arise in an *ad hoc* way according to the emergence of particular controversies or in relation to questions asked of individual ministers. The Opposition will normally allocate half, or perhaps a whole day, per session to a foreign or defence issue, to deal, say, with developments in South Africa, or as has happened, on elections in El Salvador. The Opposition normally allocates such time and such topics according to what it thinks will most embarrass the government, rather than what is intrinsically most important. Adjournment debates may also cover foreign affairs, though since opportunities to take part in them come round infrequently to individual MPs they much prefer to put local or constituency matters forward. By their nature they are a good general indicator of the salience of various issues to back-bench MPs, and in most sessions somewhere between 5 per cent and a maximum of 10 per cent of adjournment debates cover either foreign affairs or defence matters.

The standard of debate on all of these various occasions is not high. Foreign Secretaries are used to providing Parliament with general overviews of the 'foreign' situation, and Ministers of State with more detailed information on their own areas of responsibility. Members of Parliament (and their Lordships) are noted for their ability to ride personal hobbyhorses on the occasion of any parliamentary debate or to score their own party-political points, and in general it could hardly be said that these particular forms of political dialogue merits the title of a 'debate' at all.

Equally, the tabling of early-day motions (EDMs) or Parliamentary Questions (PQs) is nothing if not ritualistic, and apparently becoming ever more so. EDMs are written resolutions placed by MPs on the Order Paper, unlikely to be discussed but intended to attract signatures from sympathetic colleagues as an expression of back-bench opinion.[8] In the last two decades EDMs have become effectively devalued and now fail to convey any meaningful trends of opinion. MPs have come to use EDMs to make special mention of particular things in their own constituencies, even to congratulate their local football teams on winning trophies: so that whereas in the 1950s there were perhaps 60 or 70 EDMs in a session, the number ran at more than 1400 in 1989. The noteworthy ones contain a high number of cross-party names or else EDMs of the governing party with (in present conditions) more than about 150 names on them. During the years of a dominant Conservative government, Labour or Liberal Democrat EDMs indicate nothing much about anything.

PQs have always been a useful device for MPs to extract information or policy statements from a government, especially when they are written PQs seeking information on a matter of detail. The number of PQs put down presently runs at almost 50 000 a year, of which the Ministry of Defence alone has to deal with over 2000.[9] The vast majority of PQs are written, which is where the growth in PQs has mainly occurred; but the sheer number of PQs diminishes their individual impact and where oral PQs are put down as a device for debate on external relations they have been increasingly dominated by syndicates of six or a dozen MPs who all prepare similar questions so as to get their cherished topic debated. Cherished topics are seldom mainstream external affairs issues. PQs are potentially a useful way for Parliament, and in particular Opposition MPs, to tackle governments about difficult issues; but because they are such a useful weapon, they are subject to the sort of parliamentary tactics which emphasise the eccentric and the singular over the general run of external relations in the dialogue between Government and Parliament. Taken together, debates on foreign or defence matters, oral PQs and government statements on some aspect of external affairs normally take up around 100–150 hours a year on the floor of the House of Commons – equivalent to three or four weeks of parliamentary time annually.

Modern Members of Parliament display increasing degrees of specialisation in order to cope with the more and more complex demands made upon them. Such specialisation tends to create relatively small groups of foreign or defence policy experts. Out of 650 MPs there are perhaps 20 to 30 who regard themselves as specifically interested in foreign affairs, apart from the 11 members of the Select Committee on Foreign Affairs. In defence matters the core of interested MPs is rather smaller: 11 Select Committee members and perhaps another dozen or 15 MPs who take an active interest.[10] Above all, MPs are creatures of their party machines. In 1988 the Gallup organisation conducted a survey of MP's knowledge and views about defence and foreign issues. Their views ran true to party type on most issues, and defence and foreign affairs were both put within the top three 'areas of interest' of MPs – more so by Conservatives and more so by those who had been longest in the House – probably reflecting a degree of party politicisation in recent years on foreign and defence matters. Their knowledge, however, provides a more accurate reflection of their true specialisation. More than 80 per cent did not know who the NATO Secretary General was: more than 75 per cent did not know what proportion of GNP is spent on defence, and more than 50 per cent significantly overestimated aspects of British defence expenditure. Gerald Frost suspected 'that an A-Level Politics and General Studies student would have performed better'.[11] Clearly, the relationship between MPs and external relations is somewhat curious. Most of the foreign policy specialists are, by background, more interested in the essentially traditional areas of British policy: the Commonwealth, British policy in relation to the world outside Europe, or the well-being of particular countries and causes, such as Southern Africa. Defence policy specialists are very much concerned with the Atlantic Alliance, the Anglo-American relationship or the British armed services: there is always a powerful Commons lobby for any of the armed services, particularly the Royal Navy. Those MPs with a high level of experience in a whole range of foreign and defence issues sufficient to enable them to comment effectively on the complexities of contemporary government policies constitute a small core of MPs. The fact that this core is so small is probably because rather fewer MPs these days are old enough to have done national service, which frequently had the effect of interesting them in particular foreign countries or defence issues in general. Another reason is that MPs tend to have only one 'foreign' area or issue in which they take any personal interest, usually because they have been there on a sponsored visit or are part of a particular lobby to promote some external cause.

This touches upon the crux of one of the changes in Parliament's relationship to external affairs. For the House of Commons, in particular, is subject now to more effective lobbying on behalf of both domestic and foreign interests. Individual MPs normally receive well over 100 letters each week, many of which are elements of carefully orchestrated postal campaigns through which they discover they have been targeted. And within the immediate orbit of Westminster, professional parliamentary lobbying has become part of the political scene, rather in the style in which it is known on Capitol Hill. More than ever before, foreign interests have set up offices in London to run campaigns, produce glossy brochures and establish personal relations with MPs. Above all, they are there to arrange personal visits by MPs to whichever parts of the world are relevant to their issue. Indeed, however they are arranged, MPs' fact-finding trips to foreign parts often provide the only ready means by which members can travel abroad. Flushed with local knowledge they then, in the words of one Labour MP, 'fall off the plane and stumble into the Commons to show off their great authority on the subject'.[12] And when they have had some sleep they take their 'travellers' tales' into their party committees and their informal meetings and conversations so that the salience of particular foreign issues is consequently seen to rise in parliamentary circles. For many years the pro-Israeli lobby has been successful in facilitating MP's visits to Israel, and the Communist Parties of the Soviet Union and Eastern Europe paid for a number of parliamentary visits over the years. More recently the Conservative MP Nicholas Winterton seemed to have discovered the Namibian issue in the late 1980s, following sponsored visits there, and as an energetic politician managed to get it put on several different party agendas. Five Labour MPs visited Central America during the same period and elevated the problems of that region to a prominent position on the Parliamentary Labour Party's foreign affairs agenda. MPs are prepared to admit that the conditions in which they work and their financial arrangements make them vulnerable to the pressures of sophisticated lobbying. By the end of the 1980s there were over 30 recognised professional lobbying companies operating around Westminster, serving a wide range of domestic and international causes (of which over 100 formally existed). There is, inevitably, a thin line between the legitimate representation of outside interests and the creation of overly-funded special interest campaigns for which MPs are a prime target. The problem for MPs is not that they are more inclined towards corruption than anyone else, but rather that corruption comes looking for them in several subtle disguises. Groups generally regarded as legitimate that have been notable for promoting foreign causes to some effect have in the past included the Israeli and South African lobbies, and groups to promote particular points of view over Cyprus, Gibraltar, Hong Kong and the Falklands. In 1989 a semi-formal 'Bruges Group' was formed to propagandise Mrs Thatcher's approach to the European Community, in the face of a Parliamentary consensus that was not so strident, and achieved some notable success among MPs in its early months. More recently, the Turkish government employed Saatchi and Saatchi to press its case for membership of the European Community. The operations of such sophisticated lobbies have reinforced the trend whereby all MPs have one 'foreign issue' on which they take a position, but could not otherwise be regarded as interested in external relations.

Another development which increases the specialisation of MPs is that which leads them to have to spend more time doing a professional job on issues of some technical complexity. As one senior Conservative member observed, 'MPs are more businesslike now... less like the older members: the new boys are more for talking and less for listening'.[13] More particularly, there are only so many interests that any MP can actively sustain at one time. This is particularly so for opposition parties who, by definition, have fewer available members than the governing party. Of the Conservative Party's 374 members in 1989, 85 of them were in the government (along with 24 peers), more than 120 of them were involved in select committees, which tend to dominate the personal interests of their members for as long as they are on them, and at least another 50, not also on select committees, served as chairmen or vice-chairmen on the most central of the back-bench committees. Within the Labour Opposition the pressure on individual specialisms was rather greater.

Of the 227 Labour MPs, more than 80 were on the front bench with specialisms designated to them, over 60 were involved in select committees, and around 20 others not on select committees helped organise Labour's back-bench committees. None of this gives many MPs of any party the luxury of being useful generalists, particularly when 60–100 of them know that they are taking part in their final Parliament and are regarded as 'extinct' by their party managers. It has also been said that such pressures have taken the importance out of debates on the floor of the House and reduced its effectiveness as a political arena in a way that has reinforced the need of career-minded young MPs to develop a particular area of expertise. The net result is that most MPs have their 'designated' specialism, given to them by their party managers, plus one area of greater or lesser interest in external affairs, nurtured by outside interest groups.

Political parties

The second parliamentary arena in which external affairs figure is that which exists within the political parties. The major parties at Westminster run a series of back-bench committees. In 1989 the Conservative Party ran no fewer than 26 main back-bench committees, 7 subcommittees and 6 committees representing regional interests throughout Britain. Technically, all of these bodies were subcommittees of the party's 1922 Committee which assumes a co-ordinating role between them. Of these, there were committees on defence, foreign affairs, aviation, European affairs, trade and industry, tourism, environment and transport, all of which had some bearing on external relations. The Parliamentary Labour Party operated only 14 back-bench committees, plus 8 regional committees, which generally corresponded to the structure of ministries in Whitehall. The work of this network of party committees varies a good deal according to circumstance, in particular, whether or not the party is in government. Where it is, back-bench committees play an important political role in building support for government policies and acting as a two-way channel of communication. As one ex-Foreign and Commonwealth Office minister expressed it, the Conservative back-bench committee was more important in his life than the Commons Select Committee on foreign affairs, since in the world of practical politics he had ultimately to answer to his colleagues in Parliament, and the back-bench committee had the power to make his life extremely difficult on the floor of the House if he did not carry it with him. It was, after all, the attitude of, 'a fairly disagreeable meeting of the 1922 Committee' which convinced Lord Carrington that he should resign from the Foreign Secretaryship in 1982, just as it had been a group of back-bench Tory 'Falklanders' who had savaged Nicholas Ridley over the issue in 1981 both in the House and in the committee.[14] During the 1980s the Foreign Secretary would see the chairman of the Conservative back-bench Foreign and Commonwealth Affairs Committee if the latter requested it, if necessary, at an hour's notice. An important trust builds up between such committees and government ministers. Lynda Chalker, for instance, was regarded with deep suspicion by right wingers on the Conservative backbench committee when she became a Minister of State in the FCO, though she was able to win a grudging respect from the whole committee after about two years. In the case of the Labour Party's committees there was an attempt to reintegrate them with the work of the front benches after 1980, which proved to be critical as the Labour Party underwent a series of major policy reviews in 1988 and 1989. When a party is in opposition its back-bench committees do not have the same bite as in government, though in the case of the Labour Party of the 1980s, the problems of internal unity, particularly over defence issues, kept the Foreign Affairs and Defence committees extremely busy.

There is no shortage of all-party groups and committees, very many of which relate to external affairs. Since 1988 groups have been classified as 'All Party Groups' where they involve at least ten members from both sides of either House, and 'Parliamentary Groups' where they may involve non-members, may indeed, be administered by outside bodies. In 1989 there were 100 All-Party or Parliamentary subject groups, including at least 24 which covered aspects of external affairs, from the Fisheries Committee to the Refugees Parliamentary Group or the Parliamentary Committee for the Release of Soviet Jewry. In addition to subject groups there are even more All-Party or Parliamentary country groups, generally affiliated to one of the two umbrella organisations.The Commonwealth Parliamentary Association, founded in 1911, included 955 British parliamentarians in 1988, while the Inter-Parliamentary Union (IPU), dating back to 1889, included 770 British parliamentarians among its number. Within the framework, mainly of these two organisations, there were no less than 113 All-Party or Parliamentary country groups in existence in 1989, from the UK-Manx Parliamentary Group to the British-Mongolian Parliamentary Group. In an average year the IPU will receive representatives from up to 60 foreign parliaments for informal conversations. These groups and their activities meet some of the travel needs of MPs and peers: they (usually) add to the stock of international goodwill, and they ensure a flow of more or less accurate foreign information into Parliament. Some of them, of course, are the long-term efforts of the more sophisticated lobbying organisations and the extensive number and coverage of such groups should not be taken as an indication of political significance. As one Labour Party manager pointed out, he had never handled any papers for the shadow cabinet that had come from or through an All-Party or Parliamentary Group.[15]

In the arena of party political debate the most prevalent external policy concerns are not difficult to guess. All parties share a current concern with the new intricacies of European relations, though for the Labour Party and the Liberal Democrats the accent is on appropriate Western defence policies and detente in Europe. For the Conservative Party it is rather upon NATO and Atlantic unity and the relationship between the two superpowers. Middle East issues similarly figure prominently on both parties' foreign agendas, though the focus has shifted somewhat from a traditional concern with Israel and its neighbours to a degree of unity in the face of the Islamic revolution and its effects on the region. Beyond these subjects the parties take significantly different positions – though not always antagonistic ones – over South Africa, Central America, refugee and human rights issues (depending normally on the origins of the refugees or the imprisoned) and on development problems in the Third World. The external policy agendas of all parties are driven partly by special interests, where a small number of MPs keep an issue in the public eye, but mainly by Whitehall, since Parliament has little choice but to shadow government concerns. For this reason the observer will not find any new conceptual thinking about external affairs in the Parliamentary or party arena. They will find more reflective thinking on the floor of the House of Lords, and a better background of specialist research on certain topics: the Lords' select committees on the European Communities, on Overseas Trade, and on Science and Technology, are well-run and have both the inclination and the opportunity to look in a more leisurely way at some of the broader and more sensitive aspects of external relations under these headings. Nevertheless, their Lordships' agenda is also a prisoner of the government's timetable, and the quality of Lords select committee reports is more well-recognised by academics than by journalists. Meanwhile the Commons drives forward at a frenetic pace, voting the government some £200 billion of public money every year, and then pursuing both it and the government in a constantly unequal race. It is not surprising, therefore, that parliamentarians are essentially reactive in the way they approach external affairs: and since very little legislation attaches to foreign issues, external issues do not demand parliamentary attention in the way that traditional domestic issues do. It takes a certain amount of experience before MPs develop a sophisticated grasp of external relations and a sense of the most important role that they can play in them.

Commons Select Committees

Such a role for MPs interested in external relations is best played in the third parliamentary arena: the realm of the House of Commons Select Committees. Parliamentary select committees have a long but very *ad hoc* history. Contrary to popular belief, defence matters, at least, have been scrutinised more than any other single sector of British government, precisely because in the nineteenth century so much public expenditure went on the armed forces and Parliament was traditionally interested in military affairs. There were many reports on the state of the army, and a good deal of the work of the Public Accounts Committee and then later the Estimates Committee was concerned with defence issues. This, however, did not extend to foreign affairs because foreign policy did not require the monitoring of extensive expenditure or of complex legislation; as such, detailed parliamentary scrutiny was, at best, incidental. By the 1970s external affairs were covered across an untidy range of committees: chiefly the Defence and External Affairs sub-committee of the Expenditure Committee (which had superseded the Estimates Committee in 1971); and, as and when relevant, its Trade and Industries or Environment subcommittees, and other particular committees such as the *ad hoc* Select Committee on Cyprus and the Select Committee on Overseas Development.[16] But the structure of these committees was purely incremental and their terms of reference did not encourage them to be assertive or permit MPs to become involved too closely in important policy issues. Between 1949 and 1965 the Estimates Committee had published no fewer than 34 reports on some aspect of defence policy, almost all of which were completely ignored both in Parliament and the press.[17] In 1979, however, partly as a reflection of a period of unusual parliamentary power during the 1970s when clear majorities had been hard to come by, the old system was replaced by a series of 14 select committees to shadow all of the major government ministries. Henceforth, Parliament was to scrutinise the whole range of central government's responsibilities, and external affairs were to be covered principally within a Foreign Affairs committee and a Defence committee.

   Established in the wake of a change of government that had been engineered by a parliamentary defeat, and inviting parallels with the powerful committees of the US Congress, the new select committees were created in a wave of excitement and optimism. Norman St John-Stevas who, as Leader of the House, launched the new system, claimed that the reforms would 'redress the balance of power' between Parliament and the Executive and that they 'could constitute the most important political reforms of the century'.[18] The reality, however, has been somewhat different and many of the early claims made for the select committees proved to be unfounded. There is no useful parallel with US Congressional committees mainly because Parliament does not occupy an analogous place in the British constitution to that of the US Congress in America. They got off to a difficult start and had not visibly redressed any imbalance of powers within British government by the end of their first Parliament in 1983. After more than a full decade of existence, however, it is fair to say that the select committees have proved to be both less and more significant than many observers expected, particularly in relation to external affairs.[19]

Select Committees have proved to be less effective than might have been hoped, partly because the reform was rather less radical than it was made to seem at the time. The existing, rather messy, system was rationalised and extended, minimum staffing was laid down for each committee, and permanent outside advisers were instituted in the service of the new committees. The new committees were a reorganisation rather than an innovation and it is not surprising that they have manifestly failed to shake governments deeply or to become grand inquisitors of policy. Whenever a confrontation has loomed within a select committee between Parliament and government – as when the Defence committee tried to get key testimony over aspects of the Falklands campaign, the Westland affair, or when the Agriculture committee effectively compelled Edwina Currie to give evidence before it – the result has normally been an anticlimax. The new committees, no less than the old, depend upon the quality of the personalities involved in them and the personal chemistry within the committee. There is no difficulty in recruiting MPs to serve on them: their popularity as a useful career move is one of their successes. But each committee has to establish its own working ethos according to who is on it, how it is chaired by a senior governmental MP, and how it is supported by the influential Clerk to the committee and the staff of half a dozen or so who back it up. MPs 'emerge' to serve on select committees in a process of discreet inter-party negotiation. In the case of the Foreign and Defence committees, where it is important that they win the confidence of Whitehall that they can be trusted with sensitive – even classified – information, it is vital, in the words of one senior ex-member, 'to exclude drunks, big-mouths and extremists'.[20] Given, in any case, the limited number of foreign and defence policy specialists among MPs, this does tend to limit the field somewhat. The members of either committee must be 'clubbable' and to do their job effectively they must win the confidence of the ministry with which they deal.

A more obvious limitation on the work of the select committees is that the government established very clearly during the 1980s what the limits of Whitehall co-operation would be. Not surprisingly, it was in the realm of external affairs that the most acute problems of information and authority arose. After a series of controversies involving, in particular, the enquiries into the *Belgrano*, and the Westland issue, the Thatcher government established its response to a number of expressions of parliamentary concern over the access that select committees could have to ministers and officials.[21] It maintained steadfastly that ministers could not be compelled to attend a select committee without the specific authority of the House as a whole: that civil servants giving evidence to the committees do so 'subject to their duty and accountability to their minister';[22] and that it is important to observe a distinction between the 'actions' of a civil servant, which a committee is quite free to question, and the 'conduct' of a civil servant, which it is not, since that would be a matter for the minister.[23] In short, the government asserted that it had no intention of allowing the select committees any separate powers that did not derive directly from the floor of the House of Commons, over which it normally exerted an assured control.

A third limitation is that the particular situation in the House of Commons itself is the most important determinant of the outcome of select committee reports. The committees have only the power of publicity at their disposal, and they are composed so that the government holds an automatic majority on them. Critical reports are therefore a compromise of different ideological views, and governments have to be exceptionally high-handed to unite a whole committee against them (though they did manage it during the 1980s). Just prior to the 1983 election the Foreign Affairs committee was about to produce a report on the Falklands issue which gave some limited credence to Argentine legal claims. The appearance of the report, during the last hectic days before a parliamentary dissolution, would have been delicate at the best of times, nevertheless many on the committee were confident that an agreed version would surface before the session was concluded. In the final days, however, Conservative members suddenly tabled several dozen amendments to the draft and effectively killed it, on the instructions, apparently, of the government. In the words of one observer, 'the Tories had been knobbled by Number 10'. In the following session the committee and its Conservative chairman were all the more determined to produce a report on the Falklands, though its conclusions carried far less weight by the time of its eventual appearance in December 1984. For the most part, however, political compromises are made among select committee members and both the Foreign Affairs and Defence committees have produced reports critical of the government, though the tone of their criticism is normally muted and centred on technicalities rather than basic approaches. The Governments are required to reply to committee reports, normally within two months, though the substance of government's polite observations seldom admits to error. Quite apart from the political compromises, only a very small proportion of select committee reports are debated on the floor of the House and reports have a very brief shelf-life. The power of publicity that the select committees possess is heavily conditioned by luck, their sense of timing, and the willingness of the House of Commons and the press, to express an interest. In this respect, the televising of Parliament, and the presence of TV cameras in the Select Committees, may turn out to be very significant.

On the other hand, the select committees have in some ways achieved more than might have been expected as they have evolved over the whole decade. The first four years of their existence witnessed a series of particular difficulties. In the case of the Foreign Affairs committee, there was an unhelpful division of interest between the committee proper and the sub-committee it appointed on Overseas Development. The Foreign Affairs committee is one of only 3 of the 14 committees that is empowered to appoint sub-committees, and this one was a direct descendant of the pre-1979 Overseas Development Committee. It was maintained after 1979 to satisfy Labour Party MPs and hence was composed of Labour members who showed less interest in the work of the full committee, whilst Conservative members were only genuinely concerned with the full committee's work. The result was some tension between them and a degree of inefficiency. The sub-committee was not continued in the new Parliament beginning in 1983. Both Foreign and Defence committees also found in the early years that their special advisers were tending to take over their agendas, even argue among themselves, leaving MPs uncertain as to their own role on the committees. Then too, the committees had to fight every inch of the way to be taken seriously by ministers and senior civil servants. Nevertheless, by the mid-1980s the Foreign, Defence, Treasury and Civil Service and the Environmental select committees, in particular, had won good reputations for themselves within Whitehall, by working with the grain of government, though in a highly organised and professional way. In this respect, the *Belgrano* and the Westland issues were a turning point for all the committees. The Foreign Affairs committee won a major procedural battle in getting access to the 'crown jewels' over the Belgrano enquiry, and the Defence committee witnessed its finest hour to date in, '*the* classic confrontation ... of the reformed select committee system' when Labour's John Gilbert challenged Sir Robert Armstrong, the Secretary of the Cabinet, and then Sir Leon Brittan, ex-Industry minister, over the irregularities of the government's behaviour in the Westland affair.[24] Meanwhile the Treasury and Civil Service Committee had established its right to question the Treasury and the Bank of England on their annual financial strategy, so that their reports have become part of the continuing debate about the management of the British economy in an international context. The Treasury Committee has also investigated questions such as budgetary discipline within the European Community, the financial and economic consequences of EC membership on Britain, arrangements for international monetary control, and the question of whether Britain should join the European Monetary System.[25]

After the Westland affair and the experiences of the first Parliament, in fact, the general atmosphere changed in the select committees. The quality press began to take more notice of the work of the committees and, since Westland, have allocated correspondents to monitor their work permanently. Given that the only weapon of the committees is publicity, this represents a great step forward. Members serving on committees have become more assured about their role and power and have responded to the psychological boost by being more ambitious in their programme of scrutiny. A full list of Defence and Foreign Affairs committee reports to date is provided in Appendix 6. Whitehall sometimes tries to discourage the committees from certain topics. The FCO consistently tried to keep the Foreign Affairs committee off Cyprus and Hong Kong, since they were concerned that any report would interfere with diplomacy that was then in a sensitive state. But eventually the FCO agreed to co-operate since the committee was both patient and persistent and reports subsequently appeared on both topics.

Another victory for the committees is that Whitehall has recognised that their work can be directly useful to the government. It was happy to suggest that there should be a report on the question of diplomatic immunities following the shooting of PC Yvonne Fletcher from the Libyan People's Bureau in 1984, and both the MoD and the FCO have found it convenient to have parliamentarians investigate the effects on their work of successive expenditure cuts and staffing difficulties. Contact with the committees has also provided a regular channel of communication between officials and parliamentarians that did not previously exist except in infrequent and unstructured ways. In short, during the second Parliament in which the committees existed it became clear that both officials and MPs had learned from their earlier experiences and discovered, certainly in the committees relevant to external affairs, a constructive tension built upon a greater respect than hitherto.

The Foreign and Defence committees also offer Whitehall the mutual advantage of a number of foreign visitors and foreign visits of their own. Their ability to offer a semi-official audience to distinguished foreign visitors is, in itself, a diplomatic asset. More interestingly, their own fact-finding visits abroad sometimes take on a semi-governmental status. There are few reliable generalisations about select committee visits overseas. On some, the FCO is thought to be extremely helpful, both in offering preliminary briefings in London and at overseas posts *en route*. In other cases, the FCO is accused of going through an elaborate charade whereby MPs are taken ostentatiously into embassy 'safe rooms' to be given a 'confidential briefing' that any of them could have read in the press. For their part, MPs are observed to work very hard on these trips, just as they are also observed to be more than half asleep more than half of the time. And again, select committees are treated as VIPs by their hosts in some countries and given short shrift in others. In Hungary in 1988 the Foreign Affairs committee was fêted as if it was a direct representative of the British government. In the Soviet Union it was little more than another group of official visitors: indeed in addition to its own hotel bills (which the committee insisted on paying itself) it was charged for the accommodation of the KGB officer who spied on it. The work and visits of select committees, however, can have a discernible diplomatic effect in their own right on some countries and certain issues. The report of the Defence committee on the future of the Brigade of Gurkhas, or on British forces in Belize, for example, received little attention in Britain but were of some importance in Nepal and Belize. Equally, the Foreign Affairs committee's report on Cyprus made a big impact in that country though, for that very reason, it alarmed the FCO, which was privately hostile to it. Its Falklands report was too late to affect debate on the issue in Britain after 1982 but the taking of evidence for it in the Falkland Islands was a major political event in itself – it was broadcast throughout the islands in its entirety – and when the report eventually appeared it had a discernible impact in Argentina. Similarly, its report on South East Asia won no coverage whatsoever in Britain but was much quoted within diplomatic circles in certain South East Asian countries, since its tone was rather less pro-American than the government's own position. Its overseas aid reports can also have a major impact within aid-recipient countries, since they normally take a more generous tone than the government. Select committees undoubtedly constitute the most specific parliamentary influences that bear on the government's handling of external relations. Given the context in which external relations exist, however, even the evolution of select committee work cannot compensate for some of the problems that parliament faces in relation to external affairs.

External pressures on Parliament

As was pointed out at the beginning of this chapter, Parliament is subject to the same external pressures that affect the government itself. In particular, Parliament has found that matters which are politically important, and hence a subject of legitimate concern, now cover a very wide range of interrelated issues indeed. When Parliament becomes concerned at job losses in Scotland, it usually finds itself fulminating at the withdrawal of a multinational company and at a government that, in truth, can do very little about it by itself. When it discussed the details of various Conservative privatisation plans, it had to do so in relation to European standards on environmental protection or industrial policies, and when it discusses defence commitments or NATO's high technology future, it has to do so in the domestic context of the effects on British industry, and so on. Like the government, MPs have the same problems trying to conceptualise the true nature of such wide-ranging issues. And like the government, it constantly finds itself trying to square an impossible circle between the protection of formal sovereignty, as when the free movement of European peoples compromises Britain's ability to police itself independently, against a calculation of what is in the interests of the British community, as when the European free market of the 1990s requires there to be free movement of peoples. Unlike the government, however, Parliament does not face these difficulties in full possession of the relevant facts, or at a stage in the decision process where realistic options are still open. Like the coaches behind a locomotive, Parliament is pulled along by the Government, with a communication cord at its disposal but no brake. Parliament has never been in a position directly to affect external policy-making; it is not in a good position to think more widely or reflectively about the problems of external relations; and now it is finding that it cannot easily scrutinise even *post hoc* the work of an executive that does the policy-making and thinking for it. Select committees notwithstanding, Parliament is in danger of losing what genuine influence over external affairs it currently has, let alone that which it could hope to have in the circumstances of the 1990s.

Parliament's problems in this respect are both general and specific. For one thing, Parliament cannot help but be dominated by the executive's agenda: that is in the nature of the British constitution. Since that agenda in turn is dominated by commitments and restraints that flow from the complex nature of modern European international relations, there is less perception of choice among decision-makers over the more fundamental issues. Parliament therefore finds itself participating in choices over very major issues, where the executive determines that it should do as a matter of constitutional propriety. And at the other extreme, it participates in the role of a commentator on the administrative details and the fine-tuning of policies. The problem is that the government's agenda on a day-to-day or medium-term basis is not susceptible to parliamentary participation and is effectively beyond Parliament's immediate competence. There may seem to be more for Parliament to monitor but less to argue about in external affairs.

Second, Parliament is also dominated by the structure of the executive, in particular by Whitehall's ministries. At a time when external affairs are seen to cross so many functional boundaries within government, it is extraordinarily difficult for parliamentarians to operate with authority across existing ministerial boundaries. The select committees shadow their 'own' departments and do not generally undertake joint operations between themselves. Thus, external affairs issues on which neither the FCO or the MoD take the lead in Whitehall come up in other select committees. The Trade and Industry committee has examined Britain's trade relations with its EC members: it has examined the crisis in the international regime for the regulation of tin production; and Britain's trade with China. The House of Lords Select Committee on the European Communities, as well as the Commons Treasury and Civil Service Committee, have both investigated the EMS (though they came to different conclusions over Britain's role in it). The Transport Committee has examined some of the broader aspects of the Channel Tunnel, and so on. Though all of the relevant ministries in Whitehall are normally consulted on any of these investigations, the relevance of the conclusions is usually perceived to remain peculiarly within the subject pigeon-hole in which it began. The only parliamentary committee that explicitly crosses policy boundaries is the Public Accounts Committee (PAC) which since 1983 has had the National Audit Office (NAO) to back it up. With the 650 people in the NAO to work for it, the Public Accounts Committee remains one of the more impressive of Parliament's committees and can range across the accounting of any department in relation to all patterns of expenditure. Even then, however, it can be evaded on occasion. In 1988 the MoD attempted to spend money on a new nuclear war command bunker for the Prime Minister in such disaggregated amounts that it would not have to notify Parliament, and thus would not be subject to PAC scrutiny.[26] Over the vast majority of expenditure, however, it is clear that the PAC has a powerful brief. But the brief remains financial rather than directly political, and there is some friction between the PAC and some of the select committees since in reviewing financial provisions it takes up highly political issues, such as the cost of foreign diplomatic residences or the efficiency of the British Army of the Rhine, without also setting them in their wider international or political context. The PAC, in short, has all the equipment to review external affairs effectively except for the appropriate terms of reference. The same is broadly true of party back-bench committees. If they are to perform their roles as sounding board for party leaders and centre of party debate on the policies of the day, then it is inevitable that, like the select committees, they should also shadow Whitehall in their structure. It is no less inevitable that Parliament is regarded as performing its scrutiny functions more effectively when relations between it and the executive are generally good. For then there is a sense of mutual understanding and undoubtedly greater access both to formal and informal information. It is no coincidence, for instance, that both the MoD and the FCO reassessed their relations with Parliament after the Falklands War. They both formed Parliamentary Units within their ministries to co-ordinate more carefully their relations with the legislature, and have been pleased to see that their various efforts at better liaison have borne fruit in a greater understanding on behalf of specialist MPs of the nature of foreign and defence problems. But in creating better relations with MPs, officials have also, in effect, locked them more completely into Whitehall's problems and the categories in which they are expressed.

Third, in order to perform even *post hoc* scrutiny of external relations effectively, Parliament needs to be conceptually a little way ahead of the executive in order to be able to think of realistic alternatives to the policies it is examining. Anything less is more accountancy than scrutiny. But this too is extremely difficult. Whether or not MPs or active members of the Lords are foreign or defence policy specialists, they constantly become engaged with external issues in a high proportion of the other work they do. The conditions in which they work and the immediacy with which governmental business has to be tackled make it virtually impossible for them to offer intelligent comment – and be listened to – on matters not directly related to contemporary government policies. One might argue that this is as it should be within a cabinet system of government. On the other hand, what is conventionally regarded as 'policy' on home affairs, environmental issues, transport, defence, diplomacy, science and technology, and so on, is increasingly only a fragment of a more broadly relevant policy area that expresses itself in the external world in ways and for reasons that are only barely comprehensible even to those at the very centre of government. In pursuing so many issues that are immediately relevant to external affairs, in other words, Parliament may be missing the real policy choices that Britain faces in relation to the rest of the world.

Nowhere are all of these problems more immediately expressed than in the question of Britain's relationship with the European

Community. There is a growing recognition throughout Westminster that Parliament is being left seriously behind in the British government's dealings on European affairs. Parliamentarians are schooled on more immediate and domestic concerns and are frankly bored by the details and technicalities of EC business. The select committee on European Legislation has a limited brief to examine EC documents to see if they are worthy of debate either in the House or in committee, but its work does not excite great interest. The Lords Select Committee on the European Communities is noted for its wider brief and its work has an excellent reputation. So too does some of the work of the Lords Select Committee on Overseas Trade, which has tackled more conceptual questions about Britain's approach to the external world and the European Community in some surprisingly trenchant reports. But by definition a Lords committee does not operate at the centre of parliamentary debate and the reports that are produced have little public impact outside a small circle of interested observers, however good they are. In the Commons, on the other hand, formal debates on EC issues tend to be after midnight in front of a thin attendance in the chamber. It all appears to be highly specialist: almost a dialogue for the *cognoscenti*. Another prevalent feature is that by the time Parliament discusses an EC issue it is normally already agreed and packaged between the government and Community. Parliament is often presented with a *fait accompli* and the choice either of complete acceptance or complete rejection. This, as a number of MPs have observed, tends to suit the government, but it pushes parliamentary influence further to the margins. More importantly, the present situation disguises the fact that some vitally important issues of principle, not to mention of Parliamentary sovereignty, are wrapped up in the detail of these nocturnal debates: issues concerning broadcasting regulations, border controls, industrial policies, and so on. In failing to recognise the real nature of what is at issue in such matters Parliament has effectively abdicated responsibility for some of the major political questions about Britain's future external relations and left the definition of British interests effectively in the hands of Whitehall officials. In the words of MPs George Robertson and George Foulkes, Parliament provides 'woefully limited responses to the amount of material being decided and planned in the EC'.[27] This fear was spectacularly vindicated over the 1989 EC summit in Madrid. The Commons had no discusssion over it beforehand and yet at Madrid stage one of European monetary union was agreed and the EC's social charter was approved.

Two solutions have been offered to this problem: that the House should constitute a 'European Grand Committee' along the lines of the Scottish Grand Committee; and that there should be a European select committee system in the Commons which might join forces with that in the Lords. In the light of the disquiet over the Madrid summit, the Procedure Committee stated that 'The Way the House was treated ... represented a serious breakdown in scrutiny'. It provided a welcome touch of indignation but it was difficult to believe that there was any meaningful scrutiny arrangement that could have broken down. Nevertheless, the Procedure Committee suggested that no less than five special standing committees should be established as 'pre-legislative scrutineers' to cover specific areas of European legislation – finance, agriculture, transport and the environment, trade and industry, and general matters.[28] Neither the proposal for grand committees of the whole House, still less for a tier of policy-*influencing* scrutiny committees has met with much favour, not only because a government does not relish intervention in the policy-formulation stages, but also because of the very interdepartmental nature of EC issues. For any parliamentary scrutiny on such issues to be effective it would have to range across most or all of the 14 departmental select committees and would throw their work into some disarray. Select committees can normally only effectively tackle one or perhaps two issues at a time, and yet EC monitoring demands an ability to hold several issues in contention simultaneously, such is the nature of EC internal politics. Above all, any effective device for detailed scrutiny of EC issues would require access to some of the material that flows *between* Whitehall ministries and departments, rather than merely within them; and successive governments have steadfastly refused to countenance such access.

Just as external relations are on the frontiers of constitutional evolution,[29] so parliamentary influences on external relations are on the frontiers of executive-legislative relations. As we outlined in the previous chapter, the executive in Britain handles European Community issues very efficiently, but may be failing to cope with them in a deeper political sense. In the same way, Parliamentary thinking is inextricably bound up with that of the government and may be failing to cope with the EC in a different way, but for the same reasons.

The press and broadcasting

If Parliament risks becoming a declining institutional influence over external relations, the 'media' has become an ever-increasing one in recent years. In most previous studies of British foreign policy-making the role of press and broadcasting has been recognised as part of the domestic environment in which policy is made, and debate tends to centre on the ways and extent to which it can be seen to affect policy. There is a very interesting literature, for example, on the ways in which the 'political press' – and more commonly the 'quality press' – appears to have affected policy in the past: in supporting appeasement during the 1930s; in criticising the Suez operation in 1956; in taking particular positions over the Arab-Israeli conflict, and so forth.[30] The focus is generally on the way in which the press has acted as a channel for influential opinion to express itself, and to a lesser extent, of leaders' awareness of the potential power of the media as a political weapon, and on the use that diplomats and officials make of the media as a two-way process of communication. There is a wealth of more or less anecdotal evidence of the role of the press and broadcasting in the external policy process. It has frequently been observed, for example, that the BBC, and in particular the BBC External Services, enjoy a privileged status thanks to supporters in Parliament who can always be relied on to leap to their defence, even when the Conservative Party seems to hold the BBC in general disfavour.

Similarly, the chorus of criticism which greeted the famous Central Policy Review Staff Report into overseas representation in 1977, and which effectively sank it, was based more on the Report's handling of the relatively peripheral roles of the BBC and the British Council, than on the meat of the investigation itself.[31] Or again, the 1980s were characterised by a series of public disputes about the rights of official disclosure that the media should assume. Between 1979 and 1987 the government was involved in legal action against the *Guardian, The Observer, The Independent* and the BBC over what it interpreted as breaches of security and confidentiality. Two individuals were imprisoned, other prosecutions were dropped or lost, two officials were dismissed, and disciplinary action was taken against others. There were three (inconclusive) inquiries by MI5 against leaks appearing in *The Times, The Sunday Times* and *The Economist*, while intense political displeasure was provoked but no action was taken over at least three other cases of breaches in security involving book publishing, ITV programmes and pro-grammes on Channel 4. Appendix 7 offers a list of the most notable cases, and indicates how unsuccessful the government generally was during these years in employing legal action against the press and broadcasting organisations. Such competitions within the policy process will always be of interest, for it reflects the cutting edge of the delicate relationship between modern government and the media. And the controversies of the 1980s, for all their drama, have not indicated that the government has bent the media to its will. Indeed, there is no reliable evidence that the media is either more or less influential in particular cases of policy-making than it ever was.

The media as a policy arena

In the 1990s, however, the mass media is more accurately seen not so much as a channel of opinion and information to and from political leaders, or as a battle for the control of information between officials and journalists, but increasingly as a policy arena in itself. It can be regarded as an arena partly because of the multinational nature of modern media organisations. Like most multinational companies, media organisations straddle both national and product boundaries, operating in several countries with a range of media and non-media products and services which cross-subsidise each other. The second reason for regarding media organisations as policy arenas in external affairs is that they are, in themselves, issues in external relations. They not only have ubiquitous effects on the domestic societies on whose behalf external relations are conducted, and thereby on the policy processes, but the presentation of policy in the world's media is a major instrument of foreign policy in its own right. When the output of so much foreign policy is essentially declaratory, seeking to establish positions and advertise commitments, the ability of states to appear in the media in the way they would wish goes far beyond the calls of mere vanity.

Multinationalism

The effects of modern technology and contemporary political and market conditions on the media can be discerned in a number of ways. Firstly, the multinational nature of media organisations is perhaps their most obvious modern characteristic. Between 1986 and 1989 around $70 billion was pledged to media take-overs. By the mid-1980s it was possible to discern seven companies in Britain alone who between them controlled almost half of all book sales and TV transmissions, almost two-thirds of video rentals and record and cassette sales, and over three-quarters of all daily and Sunday newspaper sales. In addition, the same seven companies also held a wide portfolio of other interests which ranged from transport and leisure companies to property and finance, contruction and extractive companies.[32]

Rupert Murdoch's News International offers one of the most clear-cut examples of the new species of media group, for it owns *The Times*, the *Sun*, *Today*, *The Sunday Times*, and the *News of the World*, which gives it a 35 per cent share of the daily newspaper market and a 38 per cent share of the Sunday paper market. In 1989 Murdoch owned over 60 per cent of the Australian newspaper market, had a 50 per cent stake in the company that controlled 50 per cent of the New Zealand press, owned other papers such as the *Boston Herald*, the

San Antonio Express and Star, the *South China Morning Post*, a number of papers in Oceania, and had a share in Reuters, Reed International and Pearson. He owned all of Twentieth Century Fox and part of Fox Network; he owned TV stations in New York, Chicago, Washington DC, and Los Angeles; was the largest magazine publisher in the United States behind Time Publishing; owned Collins publishers; had voting shares in London Weekend Television and was the owner of Sky TV. His News Corporation, operating world-wide, had annual revenue of around £4 billion. Such an immense concentration in media ownership set several alarm bells ringing during the 1980s, particularly as some of the 'media dukes' – more powerful than the 'press barons' of an earlier period – seemed prepared to acquire and hold on to newspapers and TV channels against their commercial instincts. Other observers took a more relaxed view: the media market-place was becoming more diverse and 'Most of these media dukes are driven by nothing more pernicious than megalomania'; they would get their free-market comeuppance.[33]

From our perspective, however, the importance of the emergence of such media groups is not whether they are, or not, an affront to democracy, but the way in which the press and media are no longer strictly national institutions in the sense that they were, and have generally been seen to be in most previous accounts of the media and foreign policy. Though individual newspapers and TV channels still serve essentially national markets, they are more than ever driven by international market forces, and are increasingly organised and produced on an international basis. Newspaper circulation revenue, and TV programme domestic sales, for example, are far less relevant factors in their economic health than their ability to attract advertising and to lower production costs – both of which are increasingly multinational calculations. More significantly, the fall in real costs in media operations has encouraged the penetration of domestic media markets by foreign interests. In the cheap satellite broadcasting world of the 1990s we will hear much more of pan-European media groups such as Compagnie Luxembourgeoise de Télédiffusion, Bertelsmann, Siemens, Hachette and Bouygues. British commercial television companies acknowledge that they have better chances of winning and keeping franchises if they link themselves with European partners, and European media groups are keen to exploit a deregulated British industry to get a solid grip on the English-speaking media, wherein the widest audiences in the world are to be found. Indeed in 1991, when British TV listings were deregulated, the top competitor to *Radio Times* and *TV Times* was a publication (*TV Quick*) printed in Cologne by the Bauer company of Hamburg. The concentration of ownership has not, however, prevented the emergence of a greater diversity of smaller media operations, particularly in film and television, whose lifeblood is their ability to occupy international niche markets for their output.

The upshot of this is that however much the media focus their output on narrow national questions and domestic concerns, their own interests are significantly more multinational. Rupert Murdoch may well have used his personal power and influence to support the Conservative governments of Mrs Thatcher, and to have intervened in the running of the newspapers that he owned to that effect.[34] But the effects of personal influence in the old style of the Beaverbrooks and Rothermeres pale beside the economic logic which has kept his media empire in front of most of the competition. If the *Sun* claims to 'speak for Britain' it is because that is its target market, not because, as was the case only 20 years ago, it assumed itself primarily to be part of the institutionalised political dialogue within British politics.

Diversity of the press

A second phenomenon in the contemporary media is the diversity of its commitment to the coverage of external affairs. There is little reliable information on the amount and nature of press coverage of foreign affairs. A two-year survey, undertaken for this study at the end of the 1980s, attempted to establish some quantitative and qualitative assessments. All the trends identified in the survey, reproduced in Appendix 8, have been highlighted over the last two years, when international affairs have scarcely been off the front page. In the early 1970s it had been determined that the quality press devoted about 20–25 per cent, and the tabloid press about 10 per cent, of their coverage to international affairs.[35] The survey undertaken for this study, however, indicates that the quality press does rather more now and devotes around 40 per cent of its news coverage to international affairs, the mid-market tabloids give it perhaps 15 per cent, and the other tabloids offer, at best, 5 per cent, even on a liberal interpretation of what sort of news stories could be regarded as 'international'. Such diversity is reflected throughout the survey. As newspapers become cheaper and easier to produce so the quality press has tried to offer a good deal more in sheer quantity of newsprint, since this is a vehicle for efficient production and better advertising turnover. As a result, the quality press offers four or five times more newsprint than the popular tabloids, over ten times more international news, and gives anything up to ten or twelve times more of their total column inches to international features. To this must be added an awareness that the tabloids now devote increasing amounts of space to competitions, special offers, selling campaigns and advertising for related companies. Clearly, the difference between the tabloid and the quality press is now not only in writing style and respective readerships. It is rather in the species of publication each represents.

The diversity of the press is intimately bound up with the influence of television as a provider of information. An overwhelming majority of the population get their political information, and in particular, their information about international affairs, from television. And they give more credibility to television news, in contrast to the press, and generally regard it as non-partisan. This has encouraged newspapers to become more partisan as a way of emphasising their own role.[36] Since newspapers cannot compete with the power of television to present news information, they have had to concentrate on their ability to provide background and longer features. Quality papers have done a great deal to differentiate themselves from television by developing their own identities. The *Guardian* and *The Independent* have used their feature coverage to try to give themselves a particular stamp: *The Daily Telegraph* is known for its comprehensive news coverage; *The Times* for being a newspaper of record. The popular tabloids, however, have not tried to assert a separate newspaper identity in the traditional sense at all but instead have overtly become entertainment publications. Indeed, they have fed off television for an increasing proportion of their news and feature coverage, and often serve as a vehicle for the other activities of their parent media companies. In a sense, they have integrated themselves with their television opposition and seem decisively to have turned away from the provision of traditional news and comment altogether. The coverage of entirely foreign news in the popular tabloids – material that does not have either a British or a human interest angle – is negligible as a proportion of the whole since the tabloids find it so difficult to present foreign news for its own sake. In one typical example where it did cover inherently foreign news – in the case of a US naval build-up after a new twist in the Lebanese hostage problem – the *Sun* could only bring itself to report the event under the headline, 'Make My Day, Zap An Arab Today'.[37] Even the Tiananmen Square massacre in June 1989, happening on a Saturday afternoon in front of the cameras of the world in the most cinematic possible way, failed to dislodge sex scandals from the front pages of the Sunday tabloids. Their particular identity has become unshakably that of 'the sabbath aphrodisiacs' as Hugh Cudlipp describes them.[38] The mid-market tabloids, the *Daily Mail*, the *Daily Express*, and *Today*, have a difficult time drawing a line between the two ends of the newspaper market: *Today* is noticably more TV-derivative than the other two, for instance. But all three offer some specialist news pages on international affairs but try to balance their hard news coverage with human interest foreign material. They gave a good deal of coverage to events in South Africa, for instance, though almost always via the personal stories thrown up by the situation. The *Daily Express* characteristically covered the problem of East German refugees fleeing to the West in September 1989 by sending a reporter to the border between Austria and Hungary to find a typical family of refugees.

Press coverage

The third phenomenon that characterises the contemporary media world is the variety of ways with which international affairs are handled and the weight that they are accorded. One of the more obvious developments is the way in which the press seems unable to escape from a traditional frame of reference in its coverage of international events. As the survey in Appendix 8 indicates, daily newspapers tend to concentrate at least 60 per cent of their foreign news coverage on Western Europe, North America and the Middle East, though in the last two years they have given a good deal of coverage to developments in the socialist world. This concentration is not surprising: it is not substantially different from the pattern of coverage analysed in the early 1970s, to which we have already referred, and may be regarded as wider coverage than would normally be found, say, in daily papers in the United States. More surprising, however, is the general failure of all of the press to deal with international events and phenomena outside the framework of national news. International news even in the 1990s, in other words, is mainly that which comes out of other nations: international phenomena are recognised only as reflections of national politics. Like Parliament, the media tends to follow the political agenda as expressed by national politicians. After seven years of reporting on the war in the Persian Gulf, the British press was still taken as much by surprise when the war began to involve external powers as were the politicians themselves.[39] Or again, there is no shortage of economic and business news in the press. Even the tabloids devote space to business matters as share ownership in Britain has grown. But the coverage of such an inherently international subject is, in fact, nationally based – in some cases extremely insular. (The great exception to this is *The Financial Times*, which scores as an excellent newspaper on almost every count, but is excluded from this survey since it does not quite class as a general daily paper.) The nature of the world economy, or of world economic actors within it, or of global trends deriving from it, are not the stuff of the daily papers' economic reportage or feature-writing. The 'international economy' is seen to be a function of the economic policies of national governments and even the business news pages of the quality dailies are dominated by economic news viewed through a national policy prism. Another example is that the quality press displays great intellectual inventiveness in its feature coverage of social and domestic trends. Quality papers run broadly-based feature sections that offer innovative perspectives on domestic society or culture – 'science and technology', 'living', 'agenda', 'society tomorrow' – and so on. But only a small proportion of such features involve international or foreign material, and though all of the quality press give explicitly political international features a prominent editorial place in their papers, the nature of the coverage is not very thematic. Many of the political writers are extremely good, but their terms of reference are not noticeably inventive. As one leader writer commented, what the British papers lack is 'both a historical and an international perspective'.[40] And at the other end of the market the popular tabloids do not even have genuinely national terms of reference to offer, but rather a predictable mixture of personality politics and quite risible national stereotypes.

Television and radio

Television and radio operate a little differently. The electronic media has come to political news rather late. Only since the 1960s has it grown into a role as an independent news media, with a right to present the news as it sees it and to investigate policies as it thinks fit. Its news coverage is, by law, technically 'balanced' in that it offers equal time to the different interests of the main political parties and both radio and TV have established a high reputation for their standards of reporting. Whitehall officials privately admit that it is pretty easy to get round most of the British press: by feeding the tabloids what they want and by treating the quality press to the privileges of 'the lobby' which blunts commentary in return for a little access. Television producers are felt to be more independent, however, and have the enormous power of presenting images on top of official statements: images of the politician making the statement, or images of something else which belies it. Officials undoubtedly fear broadcasters a good deal more than they fear the press. The main BBC and ITV evening news programmes are together watched by over 15 million people every night and their balance between domestic and foreign reporting varies greatly with the nature of the day's news. They have more resources to devote to foreign news if they so wish and can provide background reports from a TV reporter in any part of the world. It was with some smugness that the BBC's man-on-the-spot in Puerto Rico was already filing his second report on Princess Anne's visit, on the day in 1989 that her marriage was declared to be over, while the tabloid 'ratpack' was still scrambling into Puerto Rico by the planeload. In the case of television news, no less than with the press, there is a similar contrast between the 1970s, when just under 40 per cent of airtime went to foreign affairs reasonably regularly, and the late 1980s when the BBC (which devotes more resources to foreign reporting than ITV) allocated anything from 25 per cent to 80 per cent of its airtime to foreign stories from all over the world. ITV's evening news seldom gives more than 50 per cent of its time to international items and is more inclined to link them specifically to events in Britain.[41] The importance of the emergence of television as the public's main provider of news cannot be overestimated. For it offers a genuinely mass news and information service that has repeatedly demonstrated its political and social power within society. On the other hand, it is driven by pictures and images as much as by information and is probably the single most potent instrument for the shaping of public attitudes towards the international world which, by definition, is unfamiliar to most of the population. In a conceptual sense, radio is a long way ahead of television in its ability and willingness to reflect some of the more abstract aspects of the international world, certainly in its feature programmes, but television has more of the audience for more of the time, and is by far the greater influence.

All of this contributes to a complicated media arena in which the government's external policies have to exist. It is in some ways more critical and well-informed than two decades ago: there is more background on offer on foreign issues and government policies and media organisations can summon impressive international resources to their aid. The government can still use the D-notice system whereby the press censors itself on any particular issue subject to a D-notice. But the D-notice system has undergone some heavy political weather in recent years. While it was extensively and successfully used by the Wilson Governments in the 1960s, it was seen as increasingly anachronistic during the 1980s. More to the point, the terms of reference concerning the categories of national security that are to be protected by the system have become more difficult to apply, and the whole system in any case only apples to the mainstream national press. It does not cover the foreign press or what might be called the 'radical' press in Britain. So it is virtually impossible for the government to prevent information being published in the foreign press, which can then be referred to, if not reproduced, in domestic newspapers.[42] Indeed, as was amply demonstrated by the British government's disastrous campaign to ban the publication of Peter Wright's *Spycatcher* book – and the various press and TV reports derived from its text – it is almost impossible for a single national government to guard even the most secret forms of secret if the journalists – and owners – of the international media organisations decide there is something worth pursuing. The multi-national media groups certainly raise potential problems for demo-cratic societies, but they also have the capacity to act as a sort of international fourth estate within national societies, as indeed they have done within socialist societies throughout the world. The effects of the international media have been credited in part with turning a Peking student hunger strike in 1989 into a national opposition movement in China.[43] The media has done a great deal to keep environmental issues in the forefront of the popular agenda throughout the West: it has showed itself able to harness inter-national concerns over famine and disasters in the underdeveloped world, and it can have decisive impacts on particular issues or political images, as the leaders of the Soviet Union clearly showed they had understood during the 1980s. At the same time, however, the media also lends itself to the creation of narrow national conceptions of the external world, even to xenophobia. As it becomes less of a political institution and more a part of the entertainment and leisure industries, the media has the power to narrow and reinforce images just as much as to expand and question them. Cinema and television images of foreign societies or political events, for example, are taken very seriously by politicians who presumably feel that such images have some real bearing on public attitudes. The British government showed itself to be constantly anxious about the portrayal of friendly Arab states in popular films and television, since they had discernible political effects on both public attitudes and foreign relations. It is not clear quite how the xenophobic shorthand of the tabloid press which interprets the international world as a series of personal clashes between cartoon character nationalities – even its 'just a bit of fun' stories about Huns on holiday beaches and Wop bottom-pinchers – may or may not affect public attitudes. Some observers are confident that the public knows quite well what it is reading in the tabloids and is not so gullable in the face of crass journalism: it knows entertainment when it sees it. Nevertheless, the tone and style of reporting have been observed to affect the opinions of their readers. Readers of News International papers, from *The Times* to the *Sun* have been shown to have significantly more negative opinions than non-readers of these papers about the BBC and ITV television networks, thus reflecting the opinions of News International's owner and the campaign to promote his Sky Channel satellite television.[44]

During the 1980s the British government showed itself more aware than ever before of the complex nature of this arena of influence. It understood that it was no longer only a two-way channel of communication between governors and governed. The activities of the Central Office of Information, of ministerial press officers, and of the lobby briefing system, in keeping the media informed of government policies was seen as clearly inadequate to the task. The Conservative Party of the 1970s had learned the value of a pro-active attitude to public information and image-making and it applied it vigorously whilst in government. Between 1983 and 1986, thanks mainly to the influence of Lord Young, it increased its advertising budget from around £20 million to over £100 million per annum, and by 1990 to £168 million, making it one of the British advertising world's top ten big spenders: so that, as one observer noted, 'advertising and marketing techniques have entered the mainstream of departmental thinking'.[45] Press and public relations were brought increasingly under centralised control by Bernard Ingham, Mrs Thatcher's long-serving Chief Press Secretary, and given a rather more assertive edge. The Conservative government had a particularly poor relationship with the BBC and the Independent Broadcasting Authority (IBA) as it disapproved of the way in which television news coverage and drama treatment tended to contradict governmental information over events such as the Falklands War – with its 'unctuous "impartiality"' according to Norman Tebbit: its nuclear relationship with the United States, its handling of the death of IRA bombers in Gibraltar, the existence of the *Zircon* surveillance satellite, and the 'oxygen of publicity' it believed broadcasters were giving to Sinn Fein and the IRA.[46]

From the point of view of external policy-making, however, the arena should not be seen as merely a struggle between the government and the broadcasters. There was certainly a struggle between the Conservative Party and the broadcasters. Meanwhile, for most of the 1980s, Mrs Thatcher's press office at Number 10 effectively hijacked both newspapers and television in a remarkably successful and sustained feat of image-maintenance, while the FCO, the MoD and the DTI had to acknowledge frankly that their public image was rather poor. Throughout the decade, Mrs. Thatcher dominated the media arena in a way that her government did not. As she became more her own foreign secretary, she was seen on foreign trips dealing with issues that were scarcely of prime ministerial weight, but gaining a full measure of prime ministerial coverage. Number 10 was blessed with an unfailing sense of photo-opportunism. In the same way, the Prime Minister was successfully presented as 'taking on' foreigners, particularly within the European Community, and standing up for old-fashioned British interests in debates over key political choices. It was typical of the complexities of the media's relationship with government that the more the personal image of the

Prime Minister was burnished, the more sceptical the public and parliamentarians seemed to be about the role of government ministries. Attacking the civil service was, after all, one of the Prime Minister's own hobbyhorses. Throughout the decade, external relations were increasingly employed by Mrs Thatcher as a weapon in the media arena, whilst her civil servants tried to employ the media as a weapon in their external relations arena. By most reckoning, her efforts were more successful than theirs. As an institutional influence on foreign policy the media has proved itself to be a very broad and important institution indeed.

Organised interests and external policy

There are many different types of organised interest or pressure group that have some bearing on external policy. They range from highly specific, 'one-issue', pressure groups – such as the Friends of John McCarthy, which was concerned to keep the case of a particular British hostage taken in Lebanon on the public agenda – to what is commonly known as 'the City', comprising an extremely influential collection of interests which exist at the very core of day to day external relations. They can be described in many different ways: as 'insider' or 'outsider' groups, depending on their access to Whitehall; as 'politicised' or 'non-politicised', depending on their overlap with the work of political parties; as 'interest', 'promotional' or 'pressure' groups, depending on the range of their concerns and the ways in which they go about their business; or as 'pluralist' or 'undemocratic', depending on how the observer assesses the strength of the British constitution at a given time. It is easier to think of different groups, however, than to assess their effect on various aspects of external policy. For though it is possible to list and classify different groups, their numbers, activities and effectiveness will vary from year to year according to circumstances. There is, to be sure, an interesting literature in Political Science that looks at the phenomenon of pressure groups (which, as a shorthand term encompasses interest and promotional groups), but it is not easy to apply in a specific sense.[47]

In the case of British external relations, however, we can offer two generalisations about pressure groups and organised interests in the process of policy-making. The first is that it is less useful to try to assess the way in which given pressure groups may affect particular policies, than to consider the role that pressure groups in general have played in creating the domestic conditions in which external relations exist. In particular, organised pressure groups have played a bigger role in external relations than either they, or other observers, have normally appreciated, since they have done a great deal in the past to shape the terms of debate about Britain's role in the world and the definition of essential national interests.

Second, it is clear that either the nature, or in some cases the importance, of the most prominent groups has altered during the 1980s. Debates about the role of pressure groups in the policy process have always reflected implicit views about the nature of British government, and as several writers have pointed out, comparatively little attention has been paid to pressure groups acting in an external context, or on behalf of an external interest, though there are many examples of such groups. But perceptions of pressure group activity is changing as the nature of their activities change: in particular, as they become in some way more international. Though the majority of pressure groups remain domestic and comparatively limited in their aims, an increasing number of formerly 'domestic' groups have a significant international dimension, and a number of inherently international pressure groups have become more intrinsically influential in the British policy process.

For the future it seems that the most influential pressures and interests on British external relations will not be the more obvious ones that we have lived with for most of the post-war period, but will instead be rather informal and disparate collections of interests, who represent themselves in individual and varying ways according to their particular circumstances. The next chapter considers the non-institutionalised and more disparate influences on external relations which seem likely to prove more powerful in the next decade than most of the traditional 'peak groups' analysed in this section. Nevertheless, we should consider here how it is that the most obvious peak groups – whose role has been to represent collections of related interests and provide institutionalised channels for them to government – are in process of decline or transformation, and what effects they have had in the past on definitions of British national interest.

Overt pressure groups

The most obvious – though not the most powerful – pressure and interest groups bearing on external relations are those that advertise themselves as such: Amnesty International, the Anti-Apartheid Movement, the British Red Cross Society, the Council for Education in World Citizenship, the Catholic Institute for International Relations, the Fabian Society, Pax Christi, Oxfam, the Muslim Institute, Christian Aid, the United Nations Association, the Overseas Students' Trust, the British Council of Churches, Friends of the Earth, the Campaign for Nuclear Disarmament, the Safer World Project, and so on, and so on. In any given year, the FCO alone will deal with well over a hundred such groups. They come and go as matters of public concern alter and it is clear that within Whitehall both the FCO and the MoD, at least, take more trouble to keep open channels of communication to and for such groups than has been the case in the past. Both ministries have become aware of a need to improve their general image and convey the nature of their work more forcefully to the public: the MoD is anxious to show that it is not a war ministry, and the FCO that it is not an 'old pals' club. Thus the degree of contact between outsiders and Whitehall and the amount of information generally available to the public is now greater than at any other time. The MoD has made the annual Defence White Paper a glossy publication, the first volume of which is intended for widespread public consumption, and it produces generally available statements on current British defence policy, and periodic material from the UK Delegation to NATO about Britain's contribution to the Alliance. The FCO produces quarterly reviews of arms control and disarmament, as well as a succession of generally accessible 'Background Briefs' and 'Foreign Policy Documents' that are available on limited distribution or in libraries. It also produces several series of 'Documents on British Policy Overseas'. Both ministries participate in a number of outside seminars, as well as running their own sessions to take advice from outside groups. The Secretariat (Policy Studies) in the MoD is charged with the job of maintaining academic liaison and each of the three armed services has a liaison officer who is of a senior rank and whose job is specifically to maintain contact with as many relevant public groups and organisations as possible. In the FCO, the Policy Planning Staff and Research and Analysis Department, and the Historical Branch of the Library Records Department, maintain regular contacts with the interested public outside Whitehall.

The British goverment as an institution, of course, could hardly be regarded as 'open'; in fact within the developed world it is one of the governments most closed to its public. Then too, official secrecy and the classification of documents has become more a fetish than a practice throughout British government.[48] Quite harmless documents are routinely classified, even when copies of them are freely available, say in Brussels, Washington, or even in non-governmental offices in Britain. And outsiders have to contend with a civil service attitude which, in a collective sense, is unswervingly patrician. It is an attitude that is in a curious way also unscholarly, for there is a sense that the intensity of day to day pressures of government and the intrinsic importance of it relieve the patrician of the need to think more deeply about the nature of the work itself or the assumptions behind it. Nevertheless, both the MoD and the FCO are as responsive to particular requests as they are able to be within the general constraints and the prevailing attitudes which underpin the existing system and they give increasing proportions of their officials' time to dealing with members of the public. When activists, or academics, complain these days that they have got no information from Whitehall on some aspect of external affairs, it is usually because they have not genuinely asked for it.

Thus the relationship between self-advertised pressure groups and the external policy-making establishment is in many respects easier now for the campaigners than during the past, though there are, of course, always particular exceptions – such as when the MoD established unit DS 19 in 1981 explicitly to counteract the existence of the 'peace movement' and MI5 investigated them with its full panoply of anti-subversive measures.[49] The most notable feature of the modern relationship between government and interest groups, however, is more in the growth of international contacts in the way such groups work. Friends of the Earth or Greenpeace, for example, derive a good deal of their influence from their ability to operate internationally and present relevant information from international sources. CND always remained an essentially national campaigning group, but one of the reasons for its effectiveness in influencing opinion in the 1980s and at least keeping nuclear issues on the national agenda was that it was able to derive a lot of accurate information about the British nuclear deterrent from American sources available under the Freedom of Information Act. In the same way, Oxfam, the European Movement, or Amnesty International are not only concerned with international issues in themselves but increasingly operate in a more international way. Government ministries now find themselves facing internationally orchestrated pressure group campaigns. This means that pressure groups have the capacity to be more sophisticated, and that in responding to such groups governments have to be aware that there is no longer any such thing as a purely 'domestic' statement. Anything said by an official or a minister – indeed very often anything said in a *Times* editorial – will be noted by foreign audiences and taken to be an expression of government policy. Officials thus have to be extremely careful what they say to the more internationally-based pressure groups, such as anti-apartheid campaigners, environmental groups, European integration groups, campaigns against certain regimes around the world, and in some respects campaigns to promote disarmament or to control the arms trade. Few of the most signifi-cant, as it were 'permanent', pressure groups have remained essen-tially national in their operations. Those that have remained curious-ly national, and therefore have had a diminishing impact, have included campaigns on behalf of aid for the underdeveloped world, anti-Soviet pressure groups and campaigns to promote the United Nations, or particular approaches to world order or international law.

Institutional interest groups

The CBI, the TUC and the City constitute more organised aggregations of interests which have had some powerful indirect effects on British external relations, and all of which seem destined to play a somewhat different role in the 1990s.

The Trades Union Congress

The Trades Union Congress (TUC) has a long history of expressing the Labour Movement's views on international issues and this may have added to the weight of international opinion from time to time. But the TUC's real effect on external policy has not been in performing this role; rather, it has been in exercising an effective power of veto for a long period in the 1960s and 1970s over government economic policies, and in strengthening an essentially parochial view of national economic interests during this period. From the early 1960s British governments reacted to recurrent economic problems by becoming more interventionist in the economy and the institutional connections between government and trade unions greatly expanded. As governments reacted to events in the international economy over which they had little practical control – particularly during the 1970s in the teeth of a world economic crisis – they found it increasingly difficult to reconcile external pressures with domestic interests. In reality, the TUC and the trade unions were never as effective a power over Labour governments as their own rhetoric and the alarm of the Conservative opposition made them seem. There were, however, undoubtedly periods in the late-1960s and mid-1970s when the trade unions were able to cast an effective veto over government economic policies and limit its room for manoeuvre in international economic negotiations and in dealings with multinational companies. The TUC took a remarkably limited view of the nature of British interests and of the protection of trade union interests within them. This was partly due to the TUC's own remit, to protect the interests of its members in an economy that was in a state of structural change. It was also because as one arm of the Labour Movement in Britain, the TUC shared the general 'little Englander' attitudes of the political Left and was instinctively suspicious of the forces of international capitalism. In the crises of the 1970s the TUC represented an influential voice that supported 'beggar-thy-neighbour' economic policies and strengthened the hand of those within the government whose instinct was to dash for national solutions to international problems.

The Confederation of British Industry

The influence of the Confederation of British Industry (CBI) worked in a similar direction over two decades though for different reasons. The CBI was formed out of three different associations in 1965 and was not immediately particularly effective or influential with government. It did, however, enjoy better fortunes during the 1970s: it developed improved channels of influence to different Whitehall ministries, and to government-appointed administrative or consultative bodies – QUANGOS – and it established a reputation for the quality and relevance of its research work.[50] But the CBI suffered from some structural weaknesses in the 1970s whereby it reflected the state of British industry rather more accurately than it reflected the state of industry in Britain. It was not as powerful an organisation as it may have seemed because it was in some ways too broad in its purposes: it was trying to do too much in being an umbrella organisation for so many different economic interests and it was regarded by some of its members has having to make too many compromises in the presentation of positions to government.[51] More importantly, it did not necessarily represent the growing body of multinational foreign firms establishing themselves in Britain during the 1970s and 1980s, many of which preferred to keep a low political profile and did not, in any case, necessarily share the CBI's views of what was in the interests of British industry. Nor has it kept pace in the range of its representation with the growth of the service sector, or of small businesses, both of which became a significantly greater part of the economy in the 1980s. Though it has wide networks of representation to all sectors of the economy, the CBI is dominated by large, British, manufacturing enterprises. And as we saw in Chapter 3, these represent declining areas in Britain's economic picture. It is not that the CBI takes a parochial view of British interests in the way that the TUC has traditionally done, but it is clear that it has become impossible for one organisation to represent adequately so diverse a set of interests as presently constitute industry in Britain. Its most effective role has been in lobbying for the big manufacturing battalions who have been fighting the international forces of keener competition, growing non-tariff protectionism, and inflationary cost-pressures. Such problems, however, have not universally afflicted all of the different sorts and sizes of companies operating in Britain. The big battalions were intermittently protectionist: they were ambiguous about Britain's joining the European Community, but then became very protectionist within the EC framework against

Third World manufactures; they have looked for government subsidy to help them modernize their industries but have then been reluctant to give it up. Fighting the corner for such interests is not necessarily the same as arguing for British economic interests in general, however, and in this sense, the CBI has represented an economically nationalist voice in a world of growing economic internationalism. It has, of course, always recognised the need for international economic strategies and understood the value of protecting world trade. But the weight of the interests the CBI has represented reinforced traditional, rather than modernising, interpretations of Britain's external economic interests. There was a widespread feeling among informed observers in the 1970s that government had become too much concerned with the 'metal-bashing' industries to the detriment of more profitable economic sectors: a point not lost on the Thatcher governments of the 1980s who were implacably opposed both to national protectionism (though not always EC protectionism) and government subsidy to older industries. The CBI is an instinctive supporter of Conservative governments, but its relations with Thatcher governments were never easy during the 1980s as it tried to stand up for the metal-bashers who were suffering so severely throughout the decade. The new Conservatives were determined to distance themselves from institutionalised economic interest groups: true Thatcherites regarded the CBI with some suspicion as part of the economic coalition of the 1970s that had prevented economic reform, and who were hostile to the transformation of British industries. The CBI worked hard to try to counteract this image, but the fact remained that, curiously, the CBI had less influence over Conservative external economic policies in the 1980s than it had exercised under Labour governments of the 1970s.

The City of London

The City of London constitutes a major economic (and general) external interest in its own right. It developed its own form of interest articulation quite separate from the other avenues of economic representation, thanks partly to the astonishing degree of social homogeneity among the individuals who traditionally operated in it.[52] The role of the Bank of England gives the City uniquely privileged access to government which is both direct and informal and draws its most impressive strength from the natural consensus on business matters that exists between financiers and government officials. Thus the City for years helped maintain a collective interest in British government, shared by most politicians and industrialists, that the external value of sterling must be maintained and that the flow of capital in and out of London should not be subject to government controls.[53] And it successfully defended its unique position against any attempt to rationalise or redirect it. When the Central Policy Review Staff initiated in 1972 an investigation of the City's relationship with government with a view to a more challenging future – a study sub-contracted to researchers from the commercial banks – the City and the Bank of England reacted with barely disguised hostility to the investigation and the report, when it appeared had a good press but no discernible effect whatsoever.[54] Unlike the CBI or the TUC, the view of the City has an immediate relevance to government which no minister can afford to ignore, since the collective view in the City of what is in Britain's best economic interests has an immediate effect on the currency and share prices. Governments can, of course, influence City thinking and there is a constant interaction between the views of the Treasury, the Bank of England and the major firms operating in the City: but the final reality is that whereas the government can stand against the views of the TUC or the CBI, it would court disaster to stand against the City since capital follows the capricious god of confidence all the way around the world.

Changing effects on external policy

The effects of such institutionalised interests on external policy have changed in the 1990s, like so many other elements in the external picture. If the TUC, CBI, the City and some of the more powerful single-issue interest and pressure groups of the last two decades have reinforced a consensus that upholds a relatively narrow view of British influence in the world, and a particularly national view of the appropriate framework for the articulation of economic policies, they have now either changed their focus, or been undermined by the articulation of more particular interests. The TUC's influence as the voice of organised labour has probably declined the most. This has been due to the fall in trade union membership, down from some 13 million to less than 9 million workers and from over 450 separate unions to just over 300 in the decade up to 1989; indeed in the wake of successive privatisations there are now considerably more shareholders than trade unionists in Britain. The TUC's decline is also due to the swing of opinion against the trade unions after the industrial crises of the 1970s and the determination of Thatcher governments explicitly to deprive the TUC of influence in government policy-making. It is also due to the fact that trade unions all over Europe have simply been less effective in their negotiations with an increasingly internationalised business community. Trade unions find it far more difficult to deal effectively with service industries, small businesses and multinationals, all of whom have great mobility in their capital, than with the traditional managements of the old heavy industries. The TUC had always been overtly opposed to Britain's membership of the European Community and accepted the fact of membership with a sullenness during the first fifteen years after 1973. Only at the end of the 1980s, with the prospects offered by the Single European Act of a greater 'social dimension' to the EC did the TUC become genuinely interested in developing representation at a European level, since it saw in this a way of winning back some of the territory from which it had been so summarily ejected in 1979. It has a longstanding association with the EC's Economic and Social Committee (ECOSOC), but the work of this body is limited, and not likely to be the main driving force behind the attempts to create a powerful 'social dimension' to the post-1992 European Community. In short, the TUC finds itself diminished in stature by its declining membership, expelled from national policy-making and regarded with deep scepticism within Establishment circles, and a newcomer to the international scene where it might usefully have involved itself at least two decades ago.

British business interests in the 1950s and 1960s were slow to see the potential contained in the evolution of the European Community. They did not constitute a unified interest either pushing for British membership of the EC or for opposing it: if anything there was a general indifference to the EC that lasted well into the late-1960s and which only changed slowly after that.[55] The CBI's immediate predecessor, the Federation of British Industry, had not originally favoured the European Community, but came round to the idea by 1961 when Britain first applied for membership, and may have helped to ease the government's path in making the first application. The CBI, therefore, inherited a favourable disposition towards the European Community and has long had an office in Brussels and maintained active contacts with its counterpart organisations elsewhere in Europe, mainly through the Union of Industrial and Employers' Confederations of Europe (UNICE) which has been in existence since 1958 and includes members from 22 different countries. Indeed, the CBI is now pro-actively 'European' and has put a good deal of time and effort into preparations for the 1992 single European market. Nevertheless, the problem of the generality of its representation has meant that other organisations and individual companies have targeted their own campaigns on those more particular aspects of the EC or the arrangements for 1992 that are of interest to them. In a sense, the CBI is struggling to keep up in a more diverse and vigorous arena of international campaigning among the wider range of British economic interests. The Institute of Directors, with its 33 000 members, and the Association of British

Chambers of Commerce, for example, represent competitors to the CBI who are narrower in their range but often more effective in campaigning on those issues that matter most to them. Meanwhile, the leading European industries are increasingly dominated by a small number of giant multinational companies who have their own campaigning resources and their own particular channels of access to domestic and foreign governments. It became common during the 1980s for very senior figures in government to move into director-ships of multinational or international companies when they left the government. Lord Prior became chairman of GEC: Lord Armstrong was on the board of BAT Industries; Lord Rippon worked for Britannia Arrow; Edmund Dell held a directorship of Shell (as also did Lord Armstrong), and many former ministers are involved with banking firms. George Younger became the director of the Royal Bank of Scotland when he lost his job with the government in 1989; Sir John Nott became chairman of Lazards merchant bank; Christo-pher Chataway became a director of Orion Royal Bank, and so on. There is nothing new in this, though the extent of the present list and the immediacy with which former members of the government join major companies has been the object of comment.[56] But the degree to which former government ministers and officials are in demand within industry, particularly those individuals with international business and political experience, especially experience of dealing with the bureaucracy in Brussels, illustrates a certain determination on the part of industry and the City to advance their interests individually, dealing simultaneously at a national and an inter-national level. It is also not without significance that the major companies direct very little of their energy towards attempts to influence either MPs at Westminster or MEPs at Brussels or Strasbourg. The most effective channels are the informal ones that exist at government level and former members of the executive may provide both access to them and invaluable knowledge about them.

Since the deregulation of the City of London in 1987 that too has become 'an institution' which operates more effectively than before at an international level. The City, of course, is by its nature a collection of international interests, but deregulated financial markets have created a genuinely global arena in which City business is now done by an international financial elite. One of the consequences of this is that the Bank of England is not in as good a position as a decade ago either to control the City or to resist its pressures in the pursuit of national economic objectives. The more limited role of the Bank is already somewhat politicised, depriving it of some of the informal influences. In the opinion of one commentator, 'Rule by the governor's eyebrows is a thing of the past – the City is very legalistic these days': in particular, any domestic financial institution which respects 'guidelines' or 'understandings' intimated by the Bank of England which are not consistent with the international financial consensus, simply risks losing business to international competitors.[57] It becomes increasingly difficult, in fact, to imagine the interest articulation represented by the financial elite in a national context at all.

In essence, the relationship between almost all interest/pressure groups and government is in process of major change. The majority of individual single-issue groups have realised that they can be more effective by operating simultaneously at a national and an international level: and certainly in the European context there are many useful forums other than that of national governments in which they can operate. Business and labour interest groups, meanwhile, are having to reappraise their role both in relation to government and to the international environment in which they operate. In the 1960s it was common to speak of 'the corporate state' as consisting of a coalition between government and aggregated interest groups. The Thatcher era explicitly contradicted such thinking as the government distanced itself from those groups that had become corporatist, reduced the numbers of QUANGOS that had proliferated in the 1970s, and showed distinctly less enthusiasm for the international coordination of domestic policies that had been a growing characteristic of its predecessors. 'Corporatism' was, in any case, somewhat alien to the political culture of Britain and the individual cultures of business and labour groups.[58] The result of all this was that such groups appeared to be essentially weak in relation to government during the 1980s. On the other hand, corporatism was not snuffed out by Thatcherism. Instead, after a dose of Conservative radicalism in the early 1980s which disrupted many of the relationships that had built up around government, Britain has witnessed the growth of what might be termed a neo-corporatist form of economic management. It is 'neo' insofar as purely national corporatism makes little sense in the 1990s, and economic management depends much more on the contruction of stable international regimes to regulate monetary relations, investment, industrial policy, research and development, and so on. Such regimes consist of the institutionalisation (though not necessarily within formal institutions) of international business interests, international capital, governments, sub-national authorities, and international organisations. Thus governments *do* enter into partnerships with various interests in a form of corporatism, though it is a more vague and international corporatism than anything identified in the 1970s. At this stage, for example, labour groups in many European countries are simply unequal to the task of making up one part of the old triumvirate of government, business and labour interests. And an explicit acceptance of any neo-corporatism came hard to Thatcher governments that had placed so much faith in economic recovery through independent national action. Nevertheless, during the 1980s British governments discovered the severe limitations of their various attempts at national economic solutions, and forms of neo-corporatism were clearly emerging at the end of the decade as the government reacted to international financial and economic pressures.

This is the context in which pressure and interest groups and their relation to external policy have now to be seen. The relation between articulated interests and governments is more diverse and subtle and it exists at both a national and an international level.

International institutional influences

We outlined Britain's position in the network of international institutions in Chapter 3. Some institutions, however, have more influence on Britain than others and the most prevalent patterns of institutional influence, like everything else in the 1990s, are changing rapidly. To put it simply, the well-understood institutions that have most affected British external relations are giving way to new institutional arrangements, whereby a variety of different types of co-ordinating behaviour – involving new issues and different players – now take place. The international institutions that have most deeply affected Britain in the past have probably been NATO, GATT, the IMF and the OECD. They are the most important of the international organisational pillars of the post-1945 western economic and political order, and they still reflect a powerful consensus on certain basic attitudes.

NATO

The influence that the various institutions of NATO have exerted on British external relations, for example, is greater than most accounts of them imply. In contrast to the influence of the European Community, for example, it is clear that, even under the influence of major reforms in Eastern Europe, British membership of NATO effectively ruled out discussion of first order questions about the purposes of the institution in the scheme of Britain's essential interests. It would be simply unthinkable for the British government to oppose unilaterally a collective NATO decision, or to threaten to renegotiate its relationship with the alliance. When the Labour opposition adopted a defence policy that would have involved such dissent within NATO in the mid-1980s it caused explicit alarm throughout British defence circles: such a policy was regarded as irresponsible and unrealistic. Yet the government regularly expressed dissent in this way in its dealings with the European Community; it was certainly prepared to hold out in isolation to the other members and to threaten to play a spoiling role in negotiations, and Whitehall did not react with outrage when the domestic political debate about the EC was cast in terms of the first order questions – whether in essence it is, or is not, a good thing. It is one of the basic contentions of this study that Britain's involvement in the EC has changed greatly in recent years, but certainly for the first quarter century of the EC's existence, and for the first decade of Britain's membership of it, debate about the institution was certainly a first order political question within Britain. This has never been the case with NATO, even at the time of the founding of the alliance. In other words, Britain's membership of NATO is not only more traditional to the country in historical terms but is also more deeply in tune with British political instincts than is its membership of the EC.

For Britain, NATO is, as David Allen has pointed out, 'much more than a purely military alliance', since it involves extensive networks of national and cross-national consultation that profoundly affect several areas of British government.[59] And it is founded on ideas of European 'collective security' that were British in origin and absolutely consistent with the immediate needs of British defence policy in the post-war era. Moreover, NATO may be regarded as having been an excellent bargain for Britain, institutionalising a status that the country held in the late 1940s for many years after, and acting as a major vehicle for British diplomatic influence. Evidence of such influence does not mean that the government responds positively to every suggestion made at NATO headquarters in Brussels: the NATO staff only wish that it would, since it is in the nature of their work that they spend their time trying to harmonise the detail of the various national defence policies of the member states. Nor does NATO constitute an influence in the sense that a pressure group or a section of parliamentary opinion is an influence on external policy. 'NATO' is not adequately portrayed only by what goes on at its headquarters in Brussels or its military headquarters at Mons: it is an impressive institution in organisational terms but it is also a powerful political abstraction – a symbol of unity and a commitment to collective defence. The importance of NATO as an influence on external policy, therefore, is partly that it constitutes a major package of tangible and intangible commitments which are part of the daily fabric of policy-making in many areas of Whitehall – the MoD, the FCO, the DTI, the Treasury, the Cabinet Office, and within the individual organisations of the armed services, not to mention the defence industries whose future is tied up with the alliance. It also constitutes an influence simply because its existence helps define the range of acceptable political choices available to elected leaders. Of course, commitments come in all shapes and sizes, and all commitments ultimately rest on a perception among political leaders of their intrinsic importance. But in the case of NATO, its institutional existence as an organisation – so much more tangible than the treaty alone – adds great weight to the influence it perpetually exerts on policy-making since it enshrines in its routines and bureaucratic procedures the limits of what are generally regarded as realistic policy options. In particular, it affects the allocation of the defence budget and influences the detail of how it is spent. There is room to doubt whether NATO is the institution that requires Britain to maintain its independent nuclear deterrent. It is always cited by the government as the irreducible commitment that makes spending on the nuclear programme necessary, but most observers do not regard this as wholly convincing. On the other hand, there is little room for doubt that the NATO alliance constituted a very powerful framework for the expensive maintenance of a major land and air commitment on the continent. There are many conceivable ways in which Britain might contribute to collective defence and security in Europe, but as critics from both the Left and the Right observed for over 20 years, the institutionalisation of the British Army of the Rhine and RAF (Germany) made it virtually impossible to conduct a serious debate within government circles about an alternative allocation of defence resources, even in a time of great economic stringency.[60] The mere existence of NATO as it was, and still is, constituted rules out of the official Whitehall mind radical defence reviews of this kind. Though defence has been much-reviewed since 1945, it has always been at the level of second order questions, which do not tackle the most fundamental issues.

The IMF, GATT and OECD

The same is broadly true of the influences represented by the IMF, the GATT and the OECD. For these organisations also give tangible expression to values and behaviour that are essentially in tune with British economic thinking and therefore exert an institutional influence over policy by codifying certain commitments and con-straints on policy choices. They express the values of international free trade, which has always been a rallying cry in Britain, and a particular one during the years of the Thatcher governments. The IMF and, in a more indirect way, the GATT were born out of a series of wartime negotiations between Britain and the United States over the economic system for the post-war world. They therefore embody common strands of Anglo-American thinking about the world economic order, as well as having specialised interests to safeguard – good international banking practice, free market policies for lenders of international capital, and the pursuit of international free trade – which constantly affect governmental thinking. The OECD has a more general remit than the IMF or the GATT and it probably exercises a more general and pervasive influence. It has no direct powers over its members, and its only tangible output is its well-respected statistical information and occasional statements. Nevertheless the *Annual OECD Surveys* have become standard measures by which members 'submit to the critical attention of their inter-dependent colleagues'.[61] And since the OECD represents a powerful negotiating forum between the economies of its 24 members and as economic co-ordination is essential in an interdependent world, the views expressed within the forum of the OECD and the consensus positions that emerge from its myriad committee discussions have a powerful, indeed almost ingrained, influence on the making of British external relations: 'a subtle discipline' as a former British representative to the organisation described it.[62] Britain's commit-ments to these economic organisations are regarded by officials and politicians as simply unavoidable – a pragmatic and necessary response to the imperatives of the international economic system. And so they are. But as many writers have pointed out, they are also expressions of an ideological consensus on the nature of global economic activity and the relationship of the state to such activity.[63] 'The identification with the prevailing liberal economic order', says Roger Tooze, 'becomes, in effect, a process of reinforcing the international economic structure in such a way as to use it to achieve domestic economic goals.'[64] It is not our purpose here to analyse how this has come about or, indeed, to assess the degree to which governments can successfully use the international arena to achieve domestic economic goals – though they increasingly do in response to the contemporary pressures they face. It is clear, however, that where international institutions express and reinforce common ideological beliefs, they have a pervasive influence within the policy process that goes well beyond the particular commitments that membership of them involves.

Other international organisations

Outside the web of highly influential institutions that we have defined, there are other international organisations, of which Britain is a loyal member, which have less natural influence over British governments even though they are important to it on particular issues. British governments have a lot to say at the United Nations, and at the UN Conferences on Trade and Development, for instance, or in the UN Law of the Sea Conference, the World Health Organisation, in the International Maritime Consultative Organisation, or in the Conference on Security and Co-operation in Europe (CSCE), or the Commonwealth. In its membership of an institution such as the International Labour Organisation, Britain has undertaken an extensive series of commitments over the years, and is likely to take on more rather than less of them in the future. British governments engage in active diplomacy in all of these forums and they have real interests to defend. But the influence that such international institutions have on the conduct of external relations is a different class of input to the policy process as compared, say, with the OECD or NATO.[65] Whereas the most influential institutions are noted for the degree to which their presence is felt in a number of Whitehall ministries, the majority of other international institutions, though their work frequently crosses departmental boundaries, do not loom large in the thinking of more than one ministry at a time. The FCO handles most of the relevant issues and keeps a watching brief to co-ordinate responses on all necessary matters. It does this, for example, with the work of the Food and Agriculture Organisation with whom the Ministry of Agriculture, Fisheries and Food (MAFF) primarily deals. More importantly, as Susan Strange has pointed out, international institutions embody a range of ambiguous and sometimes blatantly contradictory objectives, yet Britain subscribes to virtually all of those for which it is eligible.[66] It is inevitable, therefore, that many institutions which formally are committed to the same ideals as the GATT, the IMF or NATO do not carry the same weight with policy-makers since they do not represent deeper commitments that are perceived by leaders to be both essential *and* ever-present in British external relations. The GATT, for example, was built on a recognition of an essential and ever-present reality in the British context, namely the underlying power of the United States in the world economy of the 1940s and 1950s. It was not just that the GATT expressed the virtues of international free trade, but also that it was backed by the power of the United States to manipulate its provisions, even against the free trade principle, in order to promote political and economic growth among its allies. In the early days of the GATT its non-discrimination provisions were interpreted by the United States in such a way as to allow its allies to operate various trade restrictions against US goods – particularly for Britain in retaining discriminatory exchange controls within the sterling area – as a device to promote economic recovery. For Britain, belonging to the GATT was, and still is, a way of hooking up to the US economic locomotive, as well as signing up to a series of free trade principles. Britain's membership of so many institutions and what is normally characterised as its 'web' of formal commitments to them, in other words, does not take account of the underlying power and interests that back up some and not others. The United Nations, the Commonwealth, the CSCE, and those various institutions that we have characterised as having a secondary influence on policy-making, deal with issues that are important to Britain, but unlike the institutions that have primary influence, the negotiating frameworks that they create and their own continued existence in the international arena do not in themselves constitute perennial and essential British interests.

Changing patterns: the European Community

However we define the most prevalent international institutional influences in British external policy-making over the last 40 years, the indications are that the pattern of influence is now changing fairly rapidly. One vital change is that the European Community has become a major institutional influence on British external relations in its own right. More than that, as was pointed out in Chapter 3, it constitutes a new type of international commitment – even a subversive one – which fully intends to have a lasting effect on wide areas of British society and policy. Though Britain has been a member of the EC since 1973, it is true to say that the Community has only come to represent a ubiquitous institutional influence during the last decade. The Community has strengthened its authority over areas in which it was already intrinsically involved, it has extended its authority to areas that were previously peripheral to it, and the Single European Act of 1986 put some of its existing responsibilities on a more legal footing and extended the use of majority voting in decision-making within the Council of Ministers. Though the British policy process does not automatically mesh with the EC, as it did with NATO and the original OEEC, and though the EC does not naturally fit into a British ideology of international relations, as the IMF and the GATT did, the fact remains that during the 1980s the EC came to be less a matter of political choice for Britain and rather more a perennial institutional framework of prime importance to British policy. By the late 1980s it was clear that the EC had emerged in the British external policy process as an institutional expression of the boundaries of acceptable policy options: less natural to Britain than NATO, but increasingly powerful nevertheless. The attitude of Mrs Thatcher towards the European Community went against this trend, especially in her famous Bruges speech of 1988, where she threw open the question of the extent to which national interests and EC interests were necessarily compatible. In a sense, the Prime Minister was struggling to keep open first order questions about Britain's membership of the Community.

Nevertheless, in terms of the policy process and the day to day activities of Whitehall, it is clear that the relevant questions are increasingly second-order since the EC framework is essential to effective policy *implementation* in a widening range of areas, whether or not it is 'natural' to British officials' thinking. In the average year the European Community will issue around 4000 regulations, 500 decisions and 100 or more directives.[67] Directives are the more politically important outputs of the Community and normally come from the Council of Ministers: regulations and decisions deal mainly with technical and administrative issues and are chiefly the business of the Commission. But the sheer ubiquity of the output of regulations and decisions – not the more publicised policy arguments over directives in the European Council or national reactions to them – constitutes a powerful influence on the policy process, for it constantly shapes and reshapes the implementation framework within which British officials have to operate. Britain's mission to the Community, UKREP, has been characterised by Hugo Young and Anne Sloman as 'the hidden arm of Whitehall'. It is hidden not because the effect of British membership of the Community is a secret 'but because hardly anyone understands how deeply this fact has imposed itself on the way our governing classes spend their time.'[68] In a way that was scarcely anticipated in 1973, the routines of the EC – as opposed to the policies of it, as such – have come to constitute an important new institutional influence in the realm of practical choice over how policies can be put into practice.

EPC

The influence of the European Community as an institution is very evident in matters directly related to diplomatic aspects of external policy – the issues that are dealt with in the political co-operation procedure (EPC). Ministers and officials constantly make it clear that co-ordination within EPC is an essential prerequisite to the adoption of any policy stance. Indeed, their anticipation of Community reactions is an important influence in the more formative stages of policy. It has applied with particular force, for instance, in the CSCE process, where, as FCO officials themselves express it, the 'context of the Nine was absolutely basic to the positions we took'.[69] It is to be expected that the EC would have a natural influence in such overtly foreign matters. But the day to day routine of the EC also constitutes a significant influence in most major areas of economic external policy, since trade, investment, monetary stability, even the availability of primary resources, or aid to the developing world, are matters that clearly exist within an EC framework. Bilateral action on all such matters is possible, but only to a certain extent. The 12 members of the EC constitute a sufficiently potent economic grouping to provide a framework within which the realistic policy choices on external economic relations lie, and the work of Community institutions creates a bureaucratic routine which structures the timing of decisions and the manner of their implementation. Thus, British policy in relation to the Uruguay Round of the GATT, or to negotiations for a new Lomé Agreement – which between them cover almost all of Britain's trading partners – has its detailed agenda and its timetable settled for it within the context of the Community. And the specifics over which the negotiations in GATT and Lomé take place, such as the application of 'rules of origin', to take just one example, are articulated within the Commission, which harmonises views and definitions, provides relevant statistics and monitors compliance. Thus, whether or not British officials are 'Euro-minded' and regardless of the major political debates about Europe that go on over their heads, it is clear that whatever Britain's trade policies might be, they have to be implemented within a pattern of activity that is structured in Brussels. As has been described above, this was 'naturally' the case for years in relation to NATO's institutional influence over the practical implementation of defence policies; it is now less naturally, but nevertheless just as obviously, the case in relation to most aspects of economic external policy.

Defence and security ˙

Something similar is even beginning to apply to issues that were previously the preserve of NATO. As matters of defence and security increasingly become economic calculations: about the preservation of defence and high-tech industries, international collaboration, or 'economic detente' between East and West instead of merely 'diplomatic detente', so the EC framework has become more appropriate as a forum in which to discuss such issues. The implication of this is not that NATO is being undermined, for it will always have its own particular concerns. But the detail of such issues – the impact of conventional arms cuts on high-technology industries, or the degree and manner of trade access that should appropriately be offered to Eastern bloc countries, or the degree of official support that should be given to collaborative research and development – increasingly falls under the remit of the EC. Ministers may hammer out their policies for economic detente with the East in a NATO-centred forum, not least because they will then be developed around the essential core of the United States's attitude, but any agreed economic policy will have to be implemented through the mechanisms of the EC. It is clear, therefore, that NATO and the EC will not be able to remain as functionally separate in the 1990s as they have customarily been. More importantly, the British affinity for NATO politics and its natural official reserve in the face of EC politics, must somehow be reconciled. The political arena of the EC does not work in the way that the domestic arena, or even the NATO arena, works. It has been shaped by politicians and officials who come from a different cultural background and who do not see the Anglo-American approach to world affairs as inevitable, or merely an expression of a fact of international life. It is built around coalition politics, which is not strange to most continental countries, and it conducts its affairs in a political language that employs different codes and symbols to those with which most British officials were brought up. The influence of NATO and the Atlantic relationship on British policy seemed entirely appropriate to officials and politicians in the 1940s, but the influence of the EC has never been felt in this way. Yet the functions for which the Atlantic Alliance has been responsible are becoming shared, and British policy-makers face great uncertainty as they try to assess the appropriateness of new diplomatic practices within the EC that originated from a series of initiatives in which Britain originally took no part. In this respect the Western European Union may have a useful role to play here, at least an an enabling device to help governments and officials reconcile their different working practices as between the Atlantic Alliance and the European Community.

Changing patterns: institutionalised behaviour

The second way in which patterns of international institutional influence are changing is that formal institutional influences are being replaced by the growing influence of *institutionalised behaviour*, which is not quite the same thing. In a sense, the institutional influences flowing from the external world have become somewhat disaggregated. Organisations such as the IMF or the GATT are less capable than any time in their history of managing alone their traditional areas of concern. The IMF, for example, is certainly not capable by itself of managing international debt and liquidity or of stabilising balance-of-payments problems around the world. The GATT has lost its pre-eminence in the matter of guaranteeing international free trade, as protectionism has taken so many particular and local forms. Rearguard actions against growing and ever more ingenious protectionism are pursued through a number of more limited organisations and patterns of bilateral and multilateral behaviour which have become effectively institutionalised. Equally, the role of NATO in Britain's security environment is less exclusive than it used to be. Apart from the functions that have begun to overlap with the competence of the EC, NATO has become characterised by a so-called 'European pillar' which has revolved around related institutions such as the Independent European Programme Group, the 'revitalised' Western European Union and, perhaps most significantly, a series of bilateral relationships between various allies – to develop common weapons programmes or initiate joint exercises – that have now become noticeably institutionalised.[70] NATO, the GATT, the IMF, and the OECD rather than being management mechanisms from an era in which the coherent western world order allowed them the scope, by and large, to manage, are increasingly becoming 'umbrella' organisations which try to give coherence in a less coherent world order to the actions of a series of other institutions and multilateral arrangements.

Effects on external policy-making

The effect of these developments on British external policy-making is that international influence, translated into demands and constraints on policy-makers, now comes from more diverse sources. Such influences are more difficult for politicians and officials to interpret, since they do not necessarily appear as part of the well-understood routines of the major organisations. Nor do they always take a recognisable form that the policy machine can easily handle. In September 1989, for example, the British government found itself having agreed to a toughly-worded draft charter from the World Health Organisation (WHO) on environmental issues. This was thanks to the Department of Health and Social Security (DHSS) which dealt with the WHO and which reacted to pressures from environmentalists, the United Nations and the government of the Federal Republic, which was anxious to appease its green voters. Yet the draft charter seemed bound to act as a spur to the EC Commission to propose expensive new directives on environmental protection to which the British government was frankly opposed. The Department of the Environment and the FCO suddenly found themselves with an unwelcome implicit commitment because they had not recognised the implications of the DHSS's work on the issue, and the DHSS had not assumed that it was dealing with a highly politicised external problem.[71] In fact none of the international institutions through which Britain has traditionally defined its commitments are capable of representing the breadth of environmental pressures that now bear upon the government.[72] Like many new international issues of the 1990s, environmental requirements are hard to define within the existing institutional structure that has previously provided British policy-makers with their sense of what constitutes the demands and constraints of the outside world. If the government reacts to domestic and international pressures to do more to combat the trade in narcotics, for example, it will get little feel for the problem unless it is prepared to handle it within the EC and the UN and to allow those institutions to be the filter for international demands and constraints: in a word, to give them more political weight than Whitehall has habitually done. Equally, if Britain is to react to the new pressures that have arisen with the transformation of Eastern Europe then it will have to regard 'security' as something not exclusively the preserve of NATO and be prepared to work through a series of institutions, such as the UN Economic Commission for Europe, the CSCE, and again, the EC, where its expectations have normally been rather limited and its attitude on East-West matters has tended towards a wary scepticism. It is not that the traditional pattern of well-understood institutions has become irrelevant to British policy, but that the new issues that now affect external relations are 'new' in a conceptual sense and cannot be expected to show up early in the routines of such institutions. The net of relevant institutional influences that flow from the external environment has become both wider and less formal.

Conclusion

All of the influences that have been analysed in this chapter are profoundly affected by the new context of British external policy that has been outlined in the first two chapters. But they have not been affected in the same way. FCO officials have privately observed that while they are trying to come to terms with an external world in which most of the old premises appear to be changing, they also perceive a general disaggregation of domestic institutions in Britain in relation to external affairs. No longer do Whitehall, Parliament and the Press form a natural consensus that transfers itself to a public which is in any case consensual in the matter of foreign relations. Whitehall does not, indeed cannot, leave external affairs primarily to the FCO or the MoD: while Parliament and the press have become significantly more adversarial in their treatment of foreign issues.

As an institution, Parliament appears to have narrowed in relation to the government's handling of external affairs. That is, Parliament retains all the formal authority that it has always had in relation to government and there is no indication that this has fundamentally altered. On the other hand, such formal authority applies to a rather smaller area of governmental activity in external relations. The institutional power of Parliament in relation to the executive is no less than it ever was but it is proving itself inadequate to the task of performing its constitutional role in relation to contemporary external relations.

The role of the traditional interest and pressure group has also narrowed as business and labour interests have proved more difficult to aggregate. The City's role has expanded as international finance has figured more prominently in every state's domestic economic environment. The CBI and the TUC have declined, at least as interest groups in relation to government, since any meaningful direct influence over national economic management has been taken out of their hands by government, and then almost taken out of government's hands by the forces of international capital. The more traditional 'explicit' pressure groups, such as the Anti-Apartheid movement or Oxfam, are neither more nor less powerful than before, as their influence depends on individual circumstances. They too have been affected by the internationalisation of European politics, but in a sense, the class of such groups are not especially important in an analysis of external policy. They will always exist, they will adjust their methods to the circumstances around them, and they will be successful to a greater or lesser degree depending on time and chance.

The press and broadcasting organisations, on the other hand, have visibly expanded their institutional role in relation to external policy-making. 'The media' does not merely consist of press and radio and television broadcasting any more. It is a multinational and multiform institution that has both expanded in scope and become a more deeply entrenched part of the political and international environment. Indeed, it may be a mistake to regard the media as an institution at all, since in the last twenty years it has become so ubiquitous and is now on the verge of truly global expansion. Certainly, it may no longer be sufficient to regard the media as one of the elements of national politics, in the way that the legislature or the executive is. The media has become a political element that transcends national politics, even though it appeals to generally parochial interests within them. If this suggests that a great deal more work needs to be done to understand such a phenomenon for the coming years, it also offers an indication of the fact that some of the most potent influences on the external policy process are not to be found in the formal and institutional categories into which they are normally put. These more subtle, essentially non-institutionalised pressures and influences, and the newer forms of institutionalism they are beginning to take, are examined in the next chapter.

6 Non-institutional Influences on External Policy-making

In contrast to the influences we have analysed in the previous chapter, the non-institutional forces that bear on British external policy-making are much less easy to define or even to list. In some respects it is an overstatement to regard these influences as 'non-institutional', since most things in political life have some sort of institutional base. Indeed, in the case of law – analysed in this chapter – the concern is explicitly to uphold political institutions. Nevertheless, the distinction is useful since it distinguishes between the accepted, stable, political and constitutional influences and those newer and more disparate influences whose impacts on the external policy-making process, and the channels through which they are exercised, are a matter of some dispute, though they undoubtedly exist as powerful undercurrents. Given what we have said about the changing context in which British external relations now exist, it is entirely likely that such influences will prove to be of growing importance since they represent some of the more dynamic and subtle elements in the environment with which policy-makers have to deal.

In this respect, external relations display the same symptoms as other aspects of British politics. Sources of power and influence in Britain appear to be changing. Good analyses of contemporary politics are well aware of the limited utility of formal 'power maps' to explain the way in which policies operate and the influences that bear upon them.[1] Even Marxist and neo-Marxist analyses that see Britain as locked into 'the politics of a weak capitalism' where economic and political power remain concentrated, nevertheless accept that the forces acting upon British policy-makers have become more diffused and anonymous.[2] By definition, it is difficult to be precise about the nature and strength of these influences on external policy, since the relevant evidence tends to exist in the form of examples, anecdotes and speculation. While it is possible, for example, to measure the amount of parliamentary scrutiny there may be over external relations and ascribe some weight to it, it is a different matter to gauge the depth of economic interdependence or measure its influence on the policy process. We can illustrate such phenomena but not measure them.[3] Nevertheless, the examples that exist of the power and subtlety of what are defined here as 'non-institutional' influences offer *prima facie* evidence of their growing importance to any analysis of Britain's contemporary external relations.

Economic influences

Given the way that transnational economic influences have become so prevalent for Britain, the question arises as to what significance this development has for the practicalities of policy-making. Traditionalists may argue that transnational economic influences really pose few conceptual problems for the student of external policy-making. Governments have never controlled more than the tip of their economic circumstances, even if they have on occasion pretended to, and as long as economic activity *is* taking place within the territory of the legal government, the fact that such activity is increasingly transnational may be regarded by traditionalists as a complicating factor but one that hardly makes it fundamentally different. There are, however, several ways in which Britain's modern economic circumstances create new sources of influence on the policy-making process.

We have outlined in Chapters 2 and 3 some of the ways in which world markets have changed and how Britain may be affected by the new circumstances in which it finds itself. Without repeating that analysis we may summarise the changing trends as falling into three categories. First, the western world's economy is becoming significantly more *integrated* as firms find it profitable to manufacture and operate across national borders. As the Department of Trade and Industry told British manufacturers in 1989, they must appreciate the increased relevance of the state of the world market and the volatility of international exchange rates rather than becoming too focused on the state of the British domestic market. They should be 'prepared in many cases to see a total change in the way the business needs to perform'.[4]

Second, the world market is on the verge of a new revolution in *competitiveness*, whereby cheap production may be less profitable than efficient and sensitive production. Successful companies, in other words, are those which are able to respond most quickly and appropriately to shifts in demand and taste. 'Low cost/high quality' competition is giving way to the 'knowledge-based competition' of customised and differentiated specialist goods and services.

Third, in response to these trends, there is a much greater *multinationalism* throughout the manufacturing and service companies of the Western world. This has taken the form both of greater acquisition – as markets become dominated by fewer, bigger multinationals – and more recently by greater inter-company collaboration. In trying to respond efficiently to more sensitive markets, where manufacturers become providers of a complete service above and beyond the manufacture of the product, and where service industries increasingly differentiate and diversify their services, companies who have no motives to merge nevertheless find it profitable to collaborate on design, development and servicing of particular products. And where efficient production depends on sensitive subcontracting, logistical services and component supplies become vital to the competitiveness of even highly transnational production operations.

All these trends are strongest in the European context. During the 1980s the more integrated world market encouraged expansion and collaboration outside as well as inside Europe. To some extent, this is bound to continue throughout the 1990s and beyond, and certain industries are naturally more suited to genuinely global, as opposed to regional, production patterns. But world economic growth is unlikely to continue at the pace it achieved in the 1980s, and if slower world growth becomes the norm for the coming decade, the European market, encompassing both East and West European states and still far and away the largest and most sophisticated of the world's markets, will come further to dominate the corporate strategies of British and other European companies.

Such developments translate into new influences on the British policy process in both particular and general ways. In a particular sense, such economic trends have tended to disaggregate and change the economic influences to which governments are subjected. One of the dynamics of the more integrated world economy is the growth in mergers and co-operative ventures as all major industries undergo a restructuring process. The European Community expects some 40 to 50 mergers every year during the coming decade between 'major' companies (where the joint world turnover of the merged companies exceeds £3 billion). Of these, around 10 to 15 are thought likely to involve British companies.[5] More significantly – since it is a comparatively novel innovation – there has been a rapid growth in the number of companies engaged in joint ventures. Partnerships between companies are often more promising than mergers since they can be selective, covering only some of their products, and may not trigger the monopoly regulations of their governments. Cross-shareholdings, joint ventures or particular co-operative agreements open up prospects that companies will achieve greater flexibility and sensitivity in their output and marketing. In the final quarter of 1989 almost 700 corporate partnership deals were concluded by European companies; over 50 per cent of which were within Western Europe, some 36 per cent with Eastern Europe, and around 10 per cent outside the continent.[6] This represents something of a boom in commercial partnerships, reflecting a greater awareness of the post-1992 market in Europe as well as the desire of the new governments in Eastern Europe to integrate their economies with Western Europe (for which joint partnerships are a particularly appropriate mechanism). It is likely that this rate of corporate co-operation will continue to grow in Europe until the late 1990s when a period of consolidation is generally expected.

For Britain, such developments have affected both the traditional and the new industries. In the high-technology industries, aerospace and electronics have led the way, while the pharmaceuticals and telecommunications industries began a restructuring only in the late-1980s. At the other end of the industrial spectrum British construction companies entered a joint venture boom during the same period, as did the engineering industry which desperately needs some share in the new products developed by its foreign competitors. But the same also applies, for instance, to accountancy firms who recognise how underdeveloped the European market has been in the past, or to advertising and other service firms who likewise see the advantages of transnational operations during the 1990s.[7]

British governments therefore find themselves lobbied by major multinational concerns who are not merely 'foreign' multinationals, but may be mixtures of British and foreign concerns, which complicates their already powerful impact upon the British economy. Where firms collaborate or merge, or where foreign firms invest heavily in Britain, the government has found itself defending foreign commercial interests as an expression of its own judgement of what is in the public interest. When Rover and Honda began to collaborate fully on car production in 1986, for example, the British government found itself defending Honda's claims against Italian objections that the cars being produced in Britain could not be treated as British: in 1989 it was having the same argument against French objections to Nissan's car production in North East England. Or again, when the British electronics firm, the General Electric Company (GEC) formed a partnership with Siemens of West Germany, it was not long before they were in a position to take over Plessey, who produced so much in the defence electronics sector. The Ministry of Defence originally opposed this acquisition, on the grounds that it would be unhealthy to allow a transnational group such a monopoly, but was forced eventually to accept certain safeguards and agree to the acquisition. Within a year GEC had taken over Ferranti's defence systems sector in order to rescue it, and in the process had become an even more dominant producer in defence electronics. On this occasion the British government was pressured to acquiesce in the growing GEC/Siemens defence electronics monopoly because the

German government had threatened to withdraw its support for the Ferranti radar to be installed in the new European Fighter Aircraft (EFA). The GEC deal kept alive both the Ferranti radar development, and, at the time, the EFA project itself.[8] The British government had accepted that it could not halt what appeared to be a steady progression towards a defence electronics monopoly – a transnational one at that – after a decade of preaching the virtues of open competition in defence procurement.[9]

Nor is there yet any discernible pattern to this phenomenon since every case is different. We cannot simply assume that the more institutionalised influences on the policy process outlined in the previous chapter – the Confederation of British Industry (CBI), the Trades Union Congress (TUC) and the institutional powers of the City, for instance – are being replaced by analogous new institutions beginning now to form in the melting pot of the 1990s. For it is in the very nature of such transnational commercial influences that they are not aggregated into any permanent channel of institutional influence to which the government can respond.[10] And it is in the nature of the international market-place from which they draw sustenance that they cannot easily be institutionalised at a national level. Many of the joint transnational ventures that have sprung up in recent years, for instance, are individual arrangements to address particular contracts. The British company, Taylor Woodrow, was involved in three separate international consortia in 1989 to win major European construction contracts; whilst John Laing and Tarmac were in two different international consortia both bidding for the contract to build a new River Severn crossing.[11] The Channel Tunnel is built by an international company formed especially for the purpose, as are the British rail-links from it. Major international contracts in all sectors are increasingly becoming feasible propositions only for appropriately balanced and financed consortia of companies, but since each contract makes different demands, few of the consortia are entirely appropriate to more than one of them. There have, therefore, been a series of *ad hoc* issues during the last decade, some attracting more publicity than others, in which the British government has had to respond to commercial and industrial pressures that are a constantly shifting mixture of foreign and domestic business and social interests. This phenomenon will undoubtedly increase as the implications of post-1992 Europe are felt. The European Community is making some real inroads into the previously restrictive realms of public procurement. For the future, more government-awarded contracts above a certain value will have to be made genuinely available to international competition.

There is, therefore, no common institutional framework through which these transnational commercial arrangements are channelled to government, or through which their interests are represented and understood, save that of the market itself. The European Community has aspirations to provide institutionalised channels for such influences, and for official reactions to them, through its industrial and competition policies. It aims to provide a common framework within which European industries would operate, both inside and outside the Community. It is likely to be some time, however, before it is able to make a contribution that is both sufficiently potent and generalised to offer a coherent institutional framework through which member governments can deal with multinational concerns in anything other than an *ad hoc* manner.

Transnational networks

In the absence of any clear framework emanating from governments or from the European Community, transnational economic interests have begun to develop their own networks and specialised interest groups whose relationships with governments are vague, at best. Albert Bressand has discerned the growth of corporate 'networks' in the European economy, a mixture of 'infrastructures' and 'infostructures' as European-based firms strive to achieve the most effective market strategies. He has defined four types of network: 'intracorporate', 'transcorporate', and more visibly, 'intercorporate' and 'metacorporate' networks, 'intended to influence the corporate environment through lobbying, standard setting, etc.' [12] In these respects, he says,

> The physical elimination of custom houses is an almost narrow symbol of the deeper and more complex ways in which corporate strategies are reshaping the new phase of economic integration...[which] go a long way in accounting for the discrepancy between traditional political visions of Europe and the unexpected renaissance of regional integration.'[13]

Ron Smith has made a similar point:

> There is a real sense in which the MNCs have been more successful at creating truly European institutions, integrated on a continental scale like Ford Europe, than have the European political bodies. Ford centralises European R&D, strategic planning, and finance; the EC has not been able to coordinate, let alone centralise any of these functions.[14]

The practical effect of such networks is to encourage and facilitate the development of corporate lobbying in international as well as national arenas. The Secretary General of the European Commission has recorded the fact that the Commission has daily contact with industry and labour organisations of all kinds, much of which is (deliberately) not channelled through EC member governments.[15] Nor do such economic interests only consist of the major industrial and multinational concerns. The 1980s saw a significant growth in the number of transnational interest groups representing smaller businesses as well as professional groups who previously had operated in a restricted national context. Needless to say, none of this presents a consistent trend. Such networks pursue their interests by national and international contacts, and by lobbying some of their 'own' nationals working in international organisations – notwithstanding the fact that such officials are international civil servants.

Professional networks

Developments in the operations of professional associations as international interest groups are particularly instructive. The 'professions' are normally considered to consist of the more traditional occupations such as law, medicine, accountancy, and so on; and they have protected their interests by regulating entry into the occupation, by effective discreet lobbying, and by developing and diffusing a 'professional ideology'.[16] There are also a number of newer 'professions', such as planning, information science, advertising, or certain branches of applied engineering, whose status is based upon a shared expertise in a specialised area of knowledge. Most of these professions, the traditional no less than the newer ones, are in some sort of process of deregulation or internationalisation. The older professions are coming to terms with more deregulated market conditions in Europe. Investment bankers and stockbrokers responded to the pressures which led the City of London towards deregulation in the 'big bang' of 1986. The same pressures have led the legal, insurance and accountancy professions in exactly the same direction. There has been a merger boom in British law firms – over 100 a year since 1987, as compared with less than 100 for the previous twenty years up to 1987 – as they acknowledge the de facto internationalisation of the legal business. Like other professional bodies, the Law Society found itself under intense pressure to respond to the rapid restructuring of the legal profession in order to allow firms to become multidisciplinary and thus part of 'supermarket companies' of accountants, architects, surveyors, and so on, that would be capable of competing effectively in the Europe of the 1990s. German law firms, rather than the German government, have pressed for a more deregulated European market in legal services. While only six of the twelve EC member states do not currently operate monopoly practices for their lawyers, it is entirely likely that legal deregulation will continue to grow – albeit unevenly.[17] The older professions, in fact, are moving into their own multinational networks since they cannot help but acknowledge their place in the modern service sector as European service industries respond to the needs and the opportunities provided by the growth of multinational industry throughout Europe.

Meanwhile, most of the newer professions – information science, management consultancy, advertising, and so on – have been less tightly regulated and are more naturally 'internationalised' since they have tended to grow up as a component of the modernisation of major industries. Their international networks have already become significant factors in the world economy since they are closely concerned with the setting of common international standards for their activities.[18] Contrary to popular belief, the European Commission has not played an arbiter's role in the harmonisation of technical standards; it has rather been a medium between different national and professional requirements that have been rapidly driven towards convergence by market conditions. Thus, one can point to the emergence in 1990 of the non-regulatory European Accounting Forum in an attempt to harmonise national accountancy practices; the European Telecommunications Standardisation Institute of 1988, the European Cockpit Association of 1990, which ultimately aims to embrace all EC flight crew unions, or indeed to the renewed vigour with which small firms in Europe, particularly in the service sector, have together attacked the restrictive technical practices of their large competitors and appealed to the mechanisms of national and EC law to achieve more effective competition through greater technical standardisation.

The international 'market'

The more general way in which developments in the international economy have created diverse and less institutionalised influences on the British external policy process emerges from the more ubiquitous influence of 'the market' which has proved stronger than any attempts by individual governments either to regulate it or to control its effects on domestic society. It is unlikely that the 'New Right' governments that came to power in many Western countries in the early 1980s committed to an acceptance of 'the market' really appreciated how great its power could be. Certainly, international market conditions have become more pervasive since 1980 than at any other time in this century. In international arenas they are not regulated by a Bretton Woods system or even by a clear politico-economic system of hierarchical or hegemonic power. In domestic arenas market forces are no longer filtered through the structures of the 'corporate state', which reached a high point in Britain in 1972 and declined steadily thereafter.[19] Still less are market forces successfully filtered through the 'centrally-planned' socialist state. But if this appears to vindicate the views of the New Right during the 1980s, it is remarkable how little thought the Right has given to the implications of this for the external policies of a country such as Britain. If the 1980s witnessed the 'triumph of the market' in international politics it would be unrealistic to suppose that such a triumph would not have the effect of deepening interdependence even further. The traditional belief of the Right in the efficacy of the market is not necessarily compatible with an equally traditional belief in the efficacy of the state as the central organising device of international politics, *particularly* in the conditions of a modern transnational market. Social democrats, meanwhile, have had to accept the raw power of the international market-place which has asserted itself after the collapse of the Bretton Woods system. European social democracy in the 1990s – and Western Europe still *is* a region of social democracies, notwithstanding more than a decade of New Right governments – 'starts with an acceptance of the free market, private property, the price mechanism, and the various other accoutrements of capitalism, and ends with some redistribution of income through taxation and welfare'.[20] And while social democracy has generally been more internationally-minded than other political ideologies, it has not always put its internationalism into practice and is, in any case, facing a completely new situation whereby the 'free market' and so on, and attempts to organise 'some redistribution' have become matters of transnational, if not international, concern.

The effects of the ubiquitous market forces of the last two decades, in other words, go some way beyond the paradigms with which politicians of both Left and Right normally think about the nature of external affairs. This has been particularly the case in Britain, not only because of a certain natural insularity in comparison with its European partners, but also because the political polarisation between Left and Right since the effective decline of the corporate state naturally took the form of intensely domestic debates.[21] The Left in Britain wanted to regain the domestic economic control it felt it had lost immediately after the first post-war government; the Right wanted to release the domestic economy from all the constraints it felt had shackled it for 30 years. Neither was much interested in analyses which implied the diminution of the relevance of national economies.

Politicians have characteristically overestimated, and certainly overstated, the power they have to harness market conditions to national purposes. Nevertheless, it is possible to look back to a period after 1945 where the structures of world economic order and the growing powers of corporatism in the major domestic economies of the West offered governments a set of national and international levers by which they could manipulate the effects of the international market. The fact that Western economies worked in so many different political and ideological ways for a quarter of a century is some testimony to the success of governments in designing their own strategies. Since 'the international market' has become a genuinely global market, however, rather than merely an extension of the highly regulated Western market of the Bretton Woods era, it has taken many politically sensitive choices out of the hands of politicians and in many cases has reduced governments to the role of powerful lobbyists rather than authoritative arbiters.

The international marketplace is not only important because it is ubiquitous but also because it has moved so swiftly towards international market integration in those sectors most vital to the economies of the developed countries. For by the late 1980s economists were beginning to suspect that such changes had major implications for the techniques of domestic economic management. International market integration had expanded much faster than trade (at 20 per cent per annum, foreign direct investment had grown four times faster than trade from 1983–88[22]). An individual country's exchange rate management, therefore, was a much less effective economic policy instrument in the 1980s than had been the case a decade earlier since it could only have a direct effect on trade and could have opposite effects on the flow of investment. The western world, it was observed, had paid a high price for the floating exchange rates of the 1970s and 1980s. Exchange rate management structures that pursued stability through measured adjustments, such as the European Monetary System, therefore became progressively easier for governments to join as they realised how limited a national policy instrument they would be relinquishing in giving up exclusive control of exchange rates.[23] International economic coordination of microeconomic matters has begun to emerge, in itself, as a more effective economic policy instrument than many of the traditional national instruments used by governments. It is not just the European Community that forces Britain to coordinate its microeconomic policies with its partners – regulations, competition policy, tax law, and so on – but the international market itself.

Governments have very little precise idea of the ways in which the ubiquity and character of the international market affects them: what type and strength of influence it constitutes on the policy process. The approach of governments to the external economic world is overwhelmingly reactive and even governments' statistical knowledge of the forces of the international marketplace is extremely sketchy compared with the statistical material available on the domestic economy. The strength of international economic phenomena are normally measurable only insofar as they can be assessed from aggregates of domestic data. Trade flows can be measured and company assets, employment, or turnovers can be valued, but this gives governments only a very general idea of the degree to which their societies are affected by transnational investment, or of the strength of international markets in any particular sector. International phenomena such as the annual arms trade, the international narcotics market, or the size of the Euro-currency markets can only be guessed at with margins of error of up to 30 or 50 percent. As DeAnne Julius points out, the analytical models that have been applied to foreign direct investment, to take one example, have tended to reflect single-country experiences and 'have been sadly inadequate for the 1980s and may be dangerously misleading for the 1990s.' Some of the questions that arise from a more genuinely international analysis concern whether we are 'misinterpreting the linkages between the real and the financial markets at the international level? Are the channels of policy influence more diffuse than we realise?'[24]

The defence-industrial base

One of the best examples of the important but mysterious ways in which market forces influence external policy-making is provided by recent trends in the defence-industrial base (DIB), from which the government must procure the weapons it needs for its armed forces. The defence market is at once both politically important and reasonably discrete as a domestic economic sector. It is also a high-technology sector and may therefore be regarded as symptomatic of the most recent manufacturing trends. It thus offers a good test case of the strength of international market forces. The Ministry of Defence had been seized in the past with the need to ensure that it spent its money more efficiently. Between 1963 and 1969 it went through a series of exercises to try to drive tougher bargains with its defence contractors, and would claim to have this matter constantly on the agenda. Nevertheless, Conservative governments in Britain during the 1980s were absorbed with the task of getting better value for money from their defence equipment budget, and under the Chief of Defence Procurement, Peter Levene, appointed in 1985, it clearly had some success. Certainly, the contractual terms on which firms performed work for the Ministry of Defence and the way in which the contracts were monitored over the long periods in which weapons systems were developed, left a great deal to be desired in the pre-1979 era, and Peter Levene was able to make a considerable impact by imposing a more cost-effective regime. By 1987 the

Procurement Executive claimed to have made savings of around 10 per cent in the £9 billon equipment budget.[25] In this respect, the growing influence of the international marketplace suited the government's purposes as it strove to introduce more competition into its defence procurement, and though some 95 per cent of the Ministry of Defence's orders went to British industry, the government was determined that this should not be regarded as automatically the case where foreign suppliers could be more competitive in supplying a product which met the right specifications. In fact, the list of around 100 firms with whom the MoD annually placed significant equipment orders remained remarkably stable throughout the 1980s.[26] The government had, therefore, managed to bring some value for money into the procurement business, not so much by opening up competition (except among the smaller and newer British suppliers), but rather through *threatening* greater competition and driving much tougher bargains with the major firms it has always dealt with: British Aerospace, Rolls Royce, GEC, Lucas, British Shipbuilders, and so on. This constitutes a generally successful policy that was roughly consistent with a belief in the value of market forces and represents the responsible attitude of a government that regarded itself as fulfilling a duty to maintain a broad and autonomous DIB (something that not all of Britain's NATO partners invest with the same importance).[27]

On the other hand, despite the scale of the government's annual equipment spending, international market forces have rendered somewhat tenuous the power that British policy-makers have over the DIB, and created a series of contradictory defence market influences on government that strain the power of officials and observers even to comprehend them. For one thing, the component suppliers and the subcontractors to the major defence firms loom increasingly large in the DIB. Though the Ministry of Defence lists around 100 major contractors, it is estimated that there are some 800 firms in Britain which make equipment designed specifically for military use.[28] As the component suppliers and the software elements loom larger, so the DIB becomes increasingly indistinguishable from civilian industry. Second, this trend has been strengthened by the natural market expectation among private firms that defence contracting is too risky a business to rely heavily upon. Costs and development times are too great; the chances of cancellation increase in direct proportion to them; and the successes of arms control and detente in the late 1980s effectively put a 'peace blight' on a number of major defence projects. The result has been that major contractors have been working hard to shift their strategies away from a heavy dependence on military production and to 'civilianise' their business.[29] Thirdly, as we have already observed, major firms are involved in a boom in acquisitions and joint ventures. Britain's DIB is becoming significantly transnational and its capacities to produce certain ranges of equipment conforms increasingly to what the international market demands and not necessarily to what the British government may want.[30] Independent military aircraft production, for example, is already beyond the scope of the British DIB acting alone, regardless of how much the government might be prepared to pay for it.[31] Indeed, the internationalisation of the DIB may well work even against the government's basic drive for efficiency through greater competition. For the European, and to a lesser extent the 'transatlantic' DIB, moved decisively towards concentration in the late 1980s: government's choice of prime contractors for defence requirements became increasingly limited (even though the competition between sub-contractors increased). Finally, the British DIB reacted belatedly, but rapidly, to the implications of the Single European Act which was '... just as momentous for the defence sector as the breaching of the Berlin Wall'.[32] For it changed the industrial environment in which the defence industries, as part of essentially civilian multinationals, would henceforth have to operate. It also created the prospect that defence industries would in future be subject to increasing numbers of EC regulations which supercede national regulatory structures.

The practical results of these market-orientated shifts are that defence officials in Britain have become aware of how little they know about Britain's effective DIB, beyond their longstanding knowledge and contacts with the traditional major British contractors. The relationship between government and DIB at the beginning of the 1980s was well-established and was based on an expectation that they would continue to produce front-line weapon systems that were state-of-the-art: the grand technological weapon system approach. From the government's point of view, the DIB was a hierarchy of established companies that had some tangible institutional existence. From the perspective of the market of the late 1980s, however, the DIB became increasingly structured in a horizontal fashion, and characterised by more transitory relationships between old and new companies, not to mention the skeleton companies who are established to operate various consortia arrangements. The scope of the DIB, therefore, its strength and extent, its transnationalism, and above all, the directions in which it is moving, are more than ever matters of estimation and guesswork.[33] The essential political choice – whether the established British objective of maintaining a broadly-based and independent British DIB is best served simply by a reliance on market forces, or whether it would be more appropriate to adopt different objectives for a market-led DIB – had scarcely been addressed by 1990.[34] The British government appeared to be ambiguous as to whether or not it was content just to allow the DIB to be one sector of a high-technology market, and unsure how it could affect it if this was not regarded as desirable. Given the nature of the DIB these uncertainties are not surprising, but it is nevertheless ironic that such a nationally sensitive area should be in the forefront of decentralising economic trends. As Trevor Taylor has pointed out, there is an interesting conceptual paradox in the spectre of governments upholding their sovereignty by pursuing defence procurement policies that rely on the complex forces that shape International Political Economy: 'if nothing else, developments on the defence industrial front seem to undermine the contribution of Power Politics thinking to our understanding of defence policy, a broad area where such thinking has been traditionally dominant'.[35]

Social influences

Society's influence on foreign policy is, in its nature, very broad. It may express itself indirectly as a form of continuity among a social elite who articulate the prism through which Britain views the external world. One interpretation of such influence is that the very indirectness of elite influence is the source of its power: channels of consensus and mutual support among members of the elite flow across all the boundaries that normally separate policy-makers from the rest of society and exist independently of the accepted channels of official influence. The result is characterised as 'government by moonlight'. Few would dispute the power of elites in any analysis of social influences on foreign policy, though attempts to document the indirect nature of such power normally add up to a circumstantial conspiracy thesis.

The more direct impact of society on foreign policy is normally interpreted as the power of social elites to express their attitudes and opinions through the established channels of influence that already exist, such as the political parties, the media, interest and pressure groups, all of which constitute institutional influences of some kind on external relations. There is, however, a more general level of social influence on the policy process that might be expressed as that of the 'general public' as distinct from the 'informed' and 'interested' (that is, the 'elite') public. Conventional wisdoms about the role that the general public plays in external relations normally hold that social influences reveal themselves as 'public opinion' which acts as a permissive influence on policy. It therefore only expresses itself strongly on prominent issues: it can establish the outer boundaries of acceptable government action and is capable of turning against governments for behaviour over particular issues that is regarded as unacceptable. For the remainder of the time, however, public opinion in Britain is not greatly interested in international affairs and reflects a traditional mainstream consensus in British society in favour of pragmatic conservatism.[36] Certainly, 'foreign relationships' and 'defence' are normally perceived by electors as having 'small impact' on their voting intentions, and what impact they have on party politics normally reflects a caution that has been demonstrated to work overwhelmingly to the advantage of the Conservative Party.[37] Even in the elections of 1983 and 1987 when defence issues were prominent in the campaigns, the main impact was caused less by defence arguments as such than by the effect they had on the public images of the opposition parties. Partly for this reason, there is a dearth of detailed information on the general public's attitude to external relations, particularly outside election campaigns, and to the source of such attitudes. Opinion poll organisations in Britain do comparatively little on the public's reactions to foreign issues and have only given systematic coverage over a period of years to some of the more obvious public opinion questions such as the public's reaction to the superpowers, their trust in world leaders, their support for nuclear weapons or their varying expectations of the likelihood of war. Similarly, analysts of political behaviour have seldom addressed attitudes to external issues as an important political phenomenon to be explained.[38]

The view that the general public is an essentially consistent element in British foreign policy was probably never as accurate a characterisation as it has been presented in most accounts of foreign policy. There have been many examples of occasional public protests and vigorous public debates over British foreign and defence policies, during the years of pacifism and appeasement between the wars, over relations between Britain and the United States during the Korean War and later during the Vietnam War, during the Suez crisis of 1956, and the start of the anti-nuclear public protests in the late 1950s. Dissent over foreign policy is by no means unknown in Britain. On the other hand there is now a vigorous debate among analysts of domestic politics as to whether British society demonstrates an underlying structural continuity as opposed to disintegrative trends, and the effects this might have on political participation and attitudes to policy.[39] Some, such as Andrew Gamble and Tom Nairn, see Britain in a state of economic and political decline that necessarily leads to social disintegration; others, such as Colin Crouch, perceive an underlying strength in Britain's economic and political institutions.[40] There is no disagreement about the fact that British society has changed a good deal in the last forty years; the debate is rather over the direction and extent of such change. But the analyst of external policy is concerned now with a slightly different question, for it is evident that assumptions of an underlying continuity in public attitudes to foreign issues have to be reappraised as we come to terms with what has been called 'The creeping internationalization of Britain'.[41] It is not that the British population has suddenly become 'international' in its tastes, beliefs and behaviour, even though there are significant elements of this in elite sections of the population. There are, however, other good reasons to believe that the basis on which the 'foreign policy consensus' has been assumed to rest is in process of change and that its structure has become significantly more volatile, partly as a result of developments in the international world.

Multiculturalism

In the first place, the composition of 'the British public' is undergoing a series of significant changes which can be expected to affect the way in which it is likely to react to the international environment. Britain is already a multicultural society wherein some 5 per cent of the total population is made up of non-white ethnic minorities – over 2½ million people, of whom more than half originated from the Indian subcontinent. The rise of multiculturalism is no longer primarily a matter of immigration stemming from the Nationality Act of 1948. Since the early-1960s successive governments have been involved in restricting the rights of citzenship and settlement previously granted, and in the last decade there has been a new British Nationality Act of 1981, and an Immigration Act of 1988 which created a series of new restrictions involving probationary periods for dependants, visa requirements and penalties for airlines who carried passengers lacking the correct documentation.[42] In the mid-1970s immigrants numbered perhaps 80 000 per annum, but by the late-1980s numbers were around 45 000 per annum and in most years were matched or exceeded by numbers of emigrants. Instead, multiculturalism is promoted by the fact that over 40 per cent of peoples now defined as ethnic minorities were born in Britain and the age structure of such minorities will promote significantly higher growth rates than exist within the white community with its lower growth rate and ageing population structure. Multiculturalism will also be promoted by the freer movement of peoples within the European Community of the 1990s. Already, there are between 8 and 15 million non-EC immigrants and migrant workers inside the Community, plus at least 1 million illegal imigrants. Though restrictions are placed on the freedom of such groups to move completely freely around the Europe of the 1990s, they undoubtedly will become more mobile – both legally and illegally – in the coming decade, and the numbers of people in this position will be supplemented by immigrant workers in European countries that subsequently join the EC, and by the growing press of cheap labour in North Africa and from the East that is struggling to find work in Europe. It is entirely likely that the EC will adopt ever more stringent immigration controls during the 1990s, but the pool of migrant foreign labour is already high and it will tend to flow towards areas of manual labour shortage. [43]

Socio-economic changes

Secondly, the socio-economic pattern of the population is in process of change for the same mixture of reasons that apply in other industrialised countries. Manual labourers now account for considerably less than the half the British work-force, for the first time in 150 years. Some 70 per cent of Britain's 30 million workers are in public or private service industries; only 30 per cent are now employed in manufacturing.[44] Over 45 per cent of the work-force are women, more than half of whom are concentrated in only three service sectors.[45] Women, in fact, make up a higher proportion of the British working population than in most other developed countries, except the United States. During the 1980s, the number of private shareholders in Britain grew to an astonishing 12 million, due mainly to Conservative governments' privatisation policies, easily outnumbering the 9 million trade unionists. In one important respect there is an essential continuity in the socio-economic make-up of Britain, namely that 'the family is still the main agency through which individuals orientate themselves to the world'.[46] But if the family remains the most important source of political attitudes in Britain and though the growing number of women in the work-force has not weakened the traditional nature of family units, it is nevertheless the case that the socio-economic circumstances of the family have changed somewhat in recent years. It represents a more mobile and adaptable institution that has become surprisingly sensitive to instrumental, as opposed to traditional, political and social preferences. The occupational structure of the traditional family has become more responsive to changing employment and residence patterns as manual labour has declined; its consumption pattern has become more independent as the private sector has been given greater responsibility for social provision.[47] Moreover, the long-term trend throughout the twentieth century towards the private ownership of homes is now set to have significant effects on the distribution of family wealth in Britain. An ageing population is on the verge of inheriting between 1½ and 2 million houses from the 5 million who will die by the turn of the century. This will put up to

£100 billion (depending on the trend in house prices) into the hands of middle-aged people who will tend to be more comfortably off, and who will spend or invest it as a windfall. Added to this is the fact that the 1980s, in particular, were characterised by the limited abilities of government to control domestic credit and the general availability of extra purchasing power to just such wealthier sections of the population. Socio-economic trends such as these are generally discussed in terms of their effects on the distribution of wealth or on the pattern of party political allegience in Britain.[48] But for our purposes they also point to a greater degree of physical and financial mobility and independence among an increasing proportion of the population who, in the nature of the economic circumstances that Britain faces in the 1990s, are likely to become ever more aware of how international developments affect their economic and social well-being. Only the admittedly large number of British people hovering around the poverty line (perhaps 10 million), few of whom have settled employment, are *directly* unaffected by the potency of international economic forces.[49]

International mobility

Thirdly, this is coupled with a greater mobility of people and ideas created by the knowledge revolution in modern industries. The necessity for growing numbers of managers to travel internationally, and for more workers to rely on international information networks in the course of their normal occupations may be expected to have some impact on their positive (and negative) attitudes to the external world. Certainly, there is some evidence that attitudes towards Europe and Britain's participation in it are affected by the sheer penetration of European affairs in British economic life over the last two decades. Even those members of the public who dislike the European Community now regard it as a necessary part of Britain's political environment.[50]

These trends are likely to work in different directions on public perceptions. Inequalities of wealth have become greater and the multicultural pattern of Britain coincides with such inequalities. An international management class has been created which is set to grow and may therefore further heighten existing inequalities. On the other hand, poorer workers are constantly affected by international networks, and take foreign holidays in generally increasing numbers, while minority groups are more able than ever before to maintain their contacts with those foreign countries and groups that contribute to their own sense of personal and family identity. By 1990 over 100 newspapers and magazines were published by ethnic minorities in Britain. It is clear, in other words, that social and demographic trends in Britain now display a greater complexity, particularly in relation to the external world, than at any previous time.

Effects on policy-making

It is difficult to be precise about how such complexity may be directly translated into influences on the policy process, though some good pointers are offered by Farrands, who suggests that such social complexity makes it more difficult to define national interests, affects the image of Britain abroad – however partial the image might be – and, most importantly, has an impact on the ability of a government to gain legitimacy for its policies.[51] There is contemporary evidence to support all these propositions. The existence and growing consciousness of black minorities in Britain, for instance, raise questions about the definition of national interests, and certainly about the legitimacy which resulting policies may be accorded by prominent minorities. Black minorities in Britain are noted by students of political behaviour for being less interested in foreign affairs and defence issues than the rest of the population.[52] Important caveats, however, now have to be entered to this generalisation. One is provided by the awareness of black electoral power within the Labour Party. By 1989 black minority groups formed more than 15 per cent of the population in over 58 parliamentary constituencies and more than 10 per cent of the population in more than 100. Since 1980 the rate of voter registration among such minorities has doubled to around 80 per cent which puts it on a par with registration levels across the whole country. The voting intentions of black minority groups during the 1980s were overwhelmingly in favour of the Labour Party.[53] Of the 58 constituencies with the highest concentration of black minority voters, between 15 and 30 can be regarded as marginal seats where such a distribution of votes, for the first time in British electoral history, could have significant effects on the outcome of general elections. The election of 1987 brought the first four black MPs since the war into the Labour opposition and the late 1980s witnessed a series of persistent demands for a distinctive 'black section' within the party, all of which reflected a politicisation of black consciousness that was essentially directed at domestic issues and the persistence of racial inequality. Black minorities do not put 'defence' and 'foreign policy' high on their political agendas, mainly because they identify such terminology with the Conservative Party's agenda. But they do give distinctly higher priorities to immigration, nationality questions, discrimination and law and order.[54] And all of these issues are either acquiring transnational dimensions or else have an attitudinal relevance to other mainstream international issues, such as the Hong Kong settlement for 1997, reactions to change in Southern Africa, or to particular regional conflicts during times when they become major news items.

In particular, the British Muslim community provides a direct link to foreign policy concerns. The community has grown considerably since the early 1970s and is the biggest non-Christian religious group in Britain. The 850 000 strong community of Muslim believers makes up some 10 per cent of all religious adherents in Britain, which is more than twice the size of the Jewish adherent population and amounts to almost 60 per cent of the 1.5 million adherents of the Church of England.[55] Particular British interests in the Middle East and official attitudes to certain Middle East countries, as the Salman Rushdie affair of 1989 demonstrated, were significantly affected by concerns to preserve racial peace in Britain. Perhaps more important for the long term, the existence of a sizeable Muslim community in Britain appears to have sensitised majority opinion (both for good and bad) on international attitudinal issues. According to opinion polls, the late 1980s witnessed a growing belief among the British public as a whole that the country had become significantly more divided both by economic class and by race and indeed that Muslim/Christian differences in the international environment had become easily the most likely source of future international conflict.[56] With the formation of a Muslim political party in 1989 and the presence of significant and concentrated Muslim minorities in certain electoral constituencies, it is reasonable to assume that 'Muslim interests' – where they are articulated as such – may replace Jewish interests as the most powerful and visible minority religious pressure group in Britain, though in this case the power of such a pressure group will be all the more apparent because of differences in colour.

Equally, Britain's social complexity can be seen, as Farrands suggests, to have a discernible impact on the image of Britain abroad. The concept of 'class' in Britain has been of declining relevance to political scientists in explaining the trends of British electoral politics, but the image of Britain as a class-based, unequal society struggling to contain its social unrest and adapt itself to an essentially classless Western world, provides the single most common explanation of British politics both to internal and external external observers, even among the majority of foreign diplomats in London. Certainly, professional foreign observers, it is claimed, have been inclined to draw a harsh distinction between what they took to be Britain's self-image as a prosperous international actor and 'custodian of moral and liberal values' and 'the often squalid reality which struck those who ventured outside Belgravia'.[57]

Such observations do not, however, provide much illumination on the effects of social complexity on particular cases. It is not clear whether issues as dramatic as the Salman Rushdie affair, for example, should be regarded as tips of an iceberg or simply as nasty diplomatic accidents, or indeed whether the persistent inequalities of wealth and race in Britain have a systematic or merely a random effect on the definition of political issues, still less those which affect external relations. Most of the sources of social complexity that have been identified express themselves most powerfully in the domestic arena, even if they do not originate from it. Nevertheless, there is evidence that some of the consequences of Britain's much greater social complexity has begun to have an impact on the public's general attitude to external affairs. If it is impossible to second-guess reactions to particular events, it is still possible to discern broad movements in the level and direction of public support for traditional concerns of foreign and defence policies.

Changes in public opinion

No direct empirical links can yet be convincingly established between the greater social complexity of Britain and the general public's 'opinion' about external affairs. This is not necessarily because such links do not exist but because there is as yet comparatively little polling information on external affairs. There is, however, at least a circumstantial case to be made that social change is beginning to reveal itself in a greater potential volatility in attitudes to external affairs. This potential volatility can be analysed from reliable polling information.

'Reliable' polling information consists of polls professionally conducted among at least 1000 people, asking comparable questions, or a range of different questions that point up the same underlying attitudes, over a sufficiently long period to allow for trends to be discerned over a number of years. Single poll findings are notoriously vulnerable; but in the last two decades cumulative poll results have established a reputation for surprising degrees of accuracy. Certainly, public opinion polling has become a major tool of modern political analysis – if only because politicians themselves take it seriously – and while a healthy scepticism is appropriate in analysing polls, the critics who dismiss polls do not generally dispute the fact that 'public opinion' requires some explanation, but only have anecdotal evidence and guesswork to offer.[58]

The broad attitudes of the British public towards external affairs reveal a complex mixture of stability and potential volatility. Public opinion remains relatively stable in matters that are expressed at a high level of abstraction. In this respect the old 'consensus' still exists. As Appendix 9 demonstrates, the public is very clear that Britain is a committed member of the Western alliance with a strong tradition of anti-communism. NATO has been consistently popular with the public, as has been the United States, which is regarded as culturally (and uniquely) close to Britain. There is a consistent belief in the efficacy of strong deterrence and defence policies and in the proposition that Britain should remain a nuclear power as long as other nuclear powers exist in the world. The public is also consistent in its attitudes towards assertions of British sovereignty. There is an attachment to the notion of independent action and a consistent wariness at the machinations of 'Brussels' where they threaten British independence. Throughout the 1980s Mrs Thatcher was regarded as a major world figure and an asset to British diplomacy through her reputation for strong leadership. In these respects public opinion could be interpreted as offering a stable consensus for a foreign policy based on a traditional view of world politics and a conservative approach to Britain's role within them. When issues are presented to the public as 'foreign policy' matters, in other words, the reaction is consistent and predictable.

On the other hand, where issues are presented in more particular ways, and the symbolism is less obvious, public reactions indicate a far more discriminating set of attitudes; some of which are volatile, many of which are inconsistent with the trends of the 'conservative consensus'. Appendix 9 also offers some examples of those issues that have been frequently – and comparably – polled during the last decade or more. The selection is necessarily narrow since few questions directly relevant to external relations have been consistently asked of the public. Nevertheless, in almost every area polled, the underlying trends offer evidence of changing attitudes on specific issues and it is reasonable to suppose that this would probably apply to other particular areas if they were polled more systematically. Certainly, there is no convincing evidence that different attitudes towards external affairs are accountable through generational, gender or class differences among the British public. The greater volatility and sense of discrimination applies to the full cross-section of the British public: variations according to age or gender are very slight.[59]

Attitudes to the superpowers

Expectations of war and international conflict are always volatile, and the public's agenda of the most relevant external issues is normally a reflection of those items that have been in the news in the immediate past. More significantly, the public's image of Britain in the world has been somewhat more modest than that of its governments during the last decade. The perception is of a Britain that is less influential in the world than it was, despite the prominence of Mrs Thatcher as a leader. There is a prevailing sense of fatalism and cynicism about the nature of world politics. While the public is quite clear that it much prefers the United States to the Soviet Union as *societies*, for example, the 1980s witnessed a dramatic turnaround in the attitudes towards particular policies and the policy-makers of the two superpowers.[60] In the early 1960s the British public expressed a great deal of faith in the wisdom of American presidents, but that faith was in steady decline throughout the 1970s. During the Reagan presidency of the 1980s the public's trust in US policy-makers fell to very low levels and was easily exceeded by their growing trust in the new generation of Soviet leaders who came to power after Brezhnev's death in 1982. Soviet leaders were more trusted 'to deal wisely' with world problems. More particularly, the Soviet Union was regarded as having less militaristic aims than the United States, as being more likely to honour its arms control agreements, as intervening outside its sphere of interest to less harmful effects than the United States, and as being less likely to initiate a nuclear war. Any one of these perceptions may be suspect in the way it has been polled and all are partly the outcome of the muddled threats and bizarre assertions made by the Reagan presidency over eight years. But the underlying trend is clear: the public no longer regards US *policy* as morally or politically superior to that of the Soviet Union. There is an underlying cynicism about the role of the superpowers in the modern world. They are regarded as being more or less equally responsible for the (peaceful or conflictual) state of the world and equally likely to start a war in Europe. This is all the more remarkable since there is no comparison between the ability of the United States to explain itself – and be understood – by the British public, as opposed to the abilities of the Soviet Union to affect the public's attitudes to it. In spite of all the natural sympathy of an Anglo-Saxon culture and a generation of Cold War, the British public is either unsure about Soviet policy or sees it as no worse, and often better, than that of the United States. Britain has been seen as powerless to play a significant part in superpower relations, whether to prevent the United States launching missiles sited in Britain against British wishes, to affect the Soviet invasion of Afghanistan or even the US invasion of Grenada.[61] The public, for example, was constantly confused by the United States's strategic defence initiative, and was consistent only in its view that Britain would have no influence over its development and was unlikely to derive any defence benefit from it, even if there was more support for the notion that Britain should participate in SDI research if offered the chance.[62]

Attitudes to nuclear deterrence

Apart from reactions to the superpowers, nuclear deterrent issues have been the most frequently and consistently polled over recent years. On this issue there was always a majority in favour of nuclear deterrent policies and the weapons systems necessary to back them up. Establishment views commanded a stable majority for over 30 years. But, again, there were important subtleties. It was not an absolute majority. Opinions generally divided into a three-way split whereby 40 per cent of the public agreed solidly with the traditionalist view of the efficacy of nuclear deterrence: 25 per cent resolutely opposed it; and 25 per cent were uneasy about deterrence and could be critical of it, but felt unable to throw in their lot with the avowedly leftist 'peace movement'. Only 10 per cent regarded themselves as 'don't-knows', which is a surprisingly small proportion on an issue of such complexity and sensitivity.[63] Thus, during the height of nuclear protests after 1981, the government could win on every nuclear issue, but it had to fight them all. As the years went on the increasing strain of 'uphill success' – certainly in comparison to the previous years of the nuclear age where the government barely had to explain its most important decisions even to Parliament – took its toll both on future nuclear decisions and on other related defence issues. Government could not rely on the loyal 40 per cent to smooth its way and it failed to marginalise the peace movement as an expression of leftist entryism into mainstream British politics, even though a determined effort was made in the early 1980s. Opposition to the siting of Cruise missiles in Britain, for example, fluctuated between 38 per cent and 61 per cent in eight polls conducted between 1981 and 1983, the highest opposition rating apparently uniting those who opposed Cruise missiles because they were nuclear, those who opposed them because they were additional weapons, and those who opposed them because they were American weapons on British soil.[64] In the same way, a belief in the efficacy of deterrence did not automatically translate into an acceptance of the need for new nuclear systems to maintain it. The same gut reactions that led the majority opinion to see deterrence as a matter of 'common sense' also led to an equally 'common sensical' distrust of ever more sophisticated technologies.[65] In this respect the civil nuclear disaster at Chernobyl, though a quite different class of technological problem to that posed by nuclear weapons, was identified with nuclear safety in a way that became a body blow to the prospects of nuclear modernisation in Europe. It was suspected as early as 1983 by Pentagon and Ministry of Defence officials that Cruise and Pershing 2 missiles would be the last deployment of wholly new nuclear systems in Europe, given the opposition they had aroused.[66] Chernobyl confirmed that suspicion.

The final twist in the trends of public opinion on nuclear issues shows that the consistent majority of support for British nuclear weapons is also balanced by an equally consistent and far stronger majority (60–70 per cent) who do not believe that they should ever be used, no matter what the circumstances. Indeed when specific scenarios are offered, those advocating 'use' fall to negligible proportions: only 10 per cent agreed to nuclear use in the event of the fall of Britain's closest allies to a *conventional* attack (80 per cent did not); and only 20 per cent agreed in the event of a direct attack on Britain itself (70 per cent did not). The greatest proportion advocating the use of Britain's nuclear deterrent was probably polled by the National Opinion Poll (NOP) in 1981 at the height of the resurgent Cold War. In the most extreme case of a clear-cut 'nuclear attack on Britain' by Russia and its allies, a majority advocated nuclear retaliation, though at just over 60 per cent it was less resolute than might have been imagined. Throughout all of these 'nuclear' polls the vast majority (70–90 per cent) did not believe that nuclear weapons could be used by Britain without occasioning nuclear retaliation and in that event the overwhelming consensus was that Britain would be destroyed. In the case of Londoners, a one-off poll confirmed the general impression when a similar majority said that they neither expected, nor wanted, to survive a nuclear exchange.[67] Throughout the last 20 years, in fact, the British appear to have accepted the rationale of nuclear deterrence rather than to have actively supported it. A sense of fatalism and detachment has produced a picture that is more fickle than it first appears, whereby the independent deterrent is seen as a necessity occasioned more by Britain's inability to affect the other nuclear arsenals of the world, rather than as a positive centrepiece of British defence policy as such. The British public want leaders who talk convincingly about nuclear weapons but who will not, in the event, use them. And after the collapse of the socialist bloc in 1989, the public displayed even greater scepticism about the particular circumstances to which nuclear deterrence would be applicable. In 1983 Capitanchik and Eichenberg produced a valuable survey of British public opinion on defence issues and were impressed by the general stability over major issues.[68] They could not have known that so many specific defence issues were to arise in the decade following their poll findings, and though they hinted at some of the volatility that was to emerge during the 1980s, the contrast between their findings and those indicated in Appendix 9 are a testimony to the shift in underlying public attitudes in a comparatively short time.

Attitudes to the European Community

The third major area in which public attitudes have been consistently monitored is in reactions to the European Community. Again, traditional attitudes appear to be relatively stable where they are expressed in general terms. The British will not easily give up their sovereignty or autonomy to Brussels and throughout the 1980s there was general support for the uncompromising stances taken by Mrs Thatcher towards the European Community. But on more specific aspects of this stance, in the enforcement of environmental legislation, or the acceptance of the EC as a major political arena in the East-West equation, for example, the public appears to be remarkably comfortable with the work of Brussels. Even on relatively symbolic issues such as proposals to scrap sterling, or abolish frontier controls, majorities against are not overwhelming (under 60 per cent) and are matched by the combined totals who agree or are uncertain. In other words, if 'the EC' is expressed as a foreign policy issue, then the attitude is traditional; but if the 'policy sectors' with which the EC deals is expressed as a functional issue, then the attitude is more discriminating.

In 1989 the International Social Survey Programme published the first major comparative study of social attitudes in a series of developed countries, both within and outside the EC, aiming to explore national attitudinal differences throughout the developed world.[69] Comparisons revealed that British attitudes to a range of social issues were far more 'European' than distinctively 'British'. In almost every respect, in patterns of work, attitudes to the state, the family and social and political issues, British attitudes and social statistics put the British public squarely in the middle of European trends. Britain was truly distinctive only in being significantly more secular and more monarchist than its European partners, and even these characteristics did not apply uniformly when Scotland and Wales were taken into account. Polls taken in the later years of the 1980s suggest that the public remained confused and uncertain about the EC as a political institution. But Britain had become an essentially Europhile country. The findings of the International Social Survey Programme were supported by the EC Commission's own *Eurobarometre* surveys, which revealed a distinct switch in majority opinions in favour of the EC during 1988 and 1989.[70] There was an acceptance that Britain's future lay with the European Community – part of the image of Britain as less of a world power in the traditional sense – and that developments towards the single market of the

1990s and even the expansion of the EC to involve Eastern European states, did not offer Britain a realistic scenario of opting out. Campaigns by elite groups in Britain, such as those urging membership of the European exchange rate mechanism, or that businesses 'get ready for 1992!' appear to have reinforced the public sense that the logic of specific issues all pointed in one direction. Indeed, in 1989 a clear majority in two polls were of the opinion that a United States of Europe would exist by the year 2000.[71] Though the political significance of this would run up against Britain's attachment to its particular view of sovereignty, as discussed in Chapter 1, the sense of functional inevitability of the development of a united Europe – still fanciful to most students of politics – is evidence of how shallow public backing for the Conservative government's 'Euro-scepticism' had become by the end of the decade.

The evidence suggests, therefore, that public opinion has become a complex informal influence on external policy. The old consensus still exists but only at a certain level of abstraction. 'Sovereignty' issues show that public support can be gained for the old consensus, but the anti-nuclear movement of the 1980s also shows that large sections of the public can be mobilised to support stances that are quite at variance with prevailing official norms. More nuanced views of the traditional consensus always perceived that 'shifts' in public opinion were often shifts in informed and elite opinion rather than among those of the wider public. For this reason, even vitriolic disputes over external affairs tended, in the past, to be contained within established channels of public debate and influence. The situation for the 1990s, however, suggests that shifts in elite opinion will react in a more sensitive, and perhaps exaggerated, way to the greater volatility that underlies the attitudes of the wider public. Taken together with the greater influence of the media, and the ability of the media to present instant news and images from any part of the world, it is difficult to avoid the conclusion that contemporary public opinion affects policy-making by being more sensitive than ever to the presentation of policy. Whereas in the past, as we have noted, the public certainly proved capable of expressing violently divergent views on major issues of international affairs, such as the Suez crisis, perhaps the most important feature of the contemporary British public is that it seems capable of expressing divergence not just in times of crisis, but on the basis of day to day external issues which increasingly impinge on its consciousness.

New legal influences

It may seem strange to classify legal pressures as anything less than highly institutional influences on Britain's external relations. Legal frameworks are generally regarded as being very stable in Britain and have seldom even figured in modern British Political Studies since they have not generally been regarded as one of the more interesting and dynamic elements of political discourse. But legal matters have moved high up the agenda of external relations and constitute not merely a more potent influence than hitherto, but a profoundly evolutionary one. Whereas previous accounts of British foreign policy could largely ignore legal questions, save in relation to some highly specialised constitutional matters, any contemporary account must consider not only the ways in which British constitutional and administrative law is changing in response to international developments, but also the way in which such changes have opened up new channels of influence on the policy-making process.

Traditional views

There is a powerful line of argument which maintains that the independent British legal tradition is just as powerful as it always was: that where law changes it does so within a constitutional framework based on the sovereignty of Parliament which, *by definition*, constrains the effects of any change within the existing framework. This undoubtedly held true from at least 1689 (if not earlier) until 1972, when the European Communities Act was passed, and has remained a conventional wisdom for many observers since 1972 as the implications of Britain's membership of the EC continues to be debated. This view is based on three essential propositions.

First, that as a sovereign state Britain can choose to join or leave any organisation that it wishes. While it is a member of an international organisation it may be required to alter its domestic law in order to meet its membership obligations. Britain has enacted important enhancements to domestic law in several cases in order to give effect, for instance, to its membership of such organisations as the UN's International Labour Organisation (regarding minimum employment standards), the European Social Charter of 1962 (on the right to strike), the COCOM rules (enshrined in the Export of Goods [Control] Order 1985), GATT (on provisions to guarantee free trade) and, most significantly, the European Community. But in all of these cases, Britain retains the right to withdraw from the organisations and redefine its domestic legal provisions.

Second, British sovereignty is based upon the sovereignty of

Parliament and it is logically impossible for a sovereign Parliament to 'entrench' any legislation, either constitutional or administrative. Entrenchment is therefore impossible in English law, so that no Parliament can enact legislation that is necessarily binding on its successors. Whatever Parliament enacts it can – by definition of the fact that it is a true Parliament – repeal. Any supranational law, therefore, 'is ranked in respect to national law by a decision taken according to national constitutional norms' which thus have legal primacy.[72]

Third, in English law, 'Clear and unambiguous precedents' are the 'main tenets of the legal profession'[73] and the precedents and practice of English domestic law in relation to international obligations have tended to uphold these constitutional principles. In fact, as a matter of political good sense, Parliament has always adopted a permissive attitude towards the obligations that Britain has entered into as a result of its international agreements. There is a presumption that Parliament will not legislate in a way that is inconsistent with its international obligations and that the judiciary will regard international conventions and agreements as 'guides to interpretation' of domestic law. Nevertheless, the application of international standards of law has remained largely indirect to Britain. International norms are only directly enforceable in Britain if they have been expressly legislated by Parliament.

The supremacy of Parliament, for example, rules out the possibility that international human rights legislation could be directly applied in the British legal system. Britain is a co-signatory of the European Convention on Human Rights and has recognised the jurisdiction of the European Court of Human Rights since 1950. But it is the only co-signatory who has not incorporated the Convention into its domestic law. British individuals do not themselves have recourse to the European Court of Human Rights: they can make a complaint to the Human Rights Commission, who must then decide whether there is a case for the government to answer and whether all possible domestic remedies have been tried. It is ultimately the Commission, rather than the individual, who challenges the government before the Court.[74] Since 1960 the Court has handed down over 200 judgements, almost 40 of which have involved Britain, which is the most frequent defendant before it, and which has lost in the vast majority of cases.[75] It has normally adjusted British law and practice to avoid repetition of the offences. But it has not generally used the European Convention on Human Rights as a guide to interpretation in any analogous cases and has certainly not used it as a criterion by which other official and administrative Government action could be judged. When Lord Donaldson in the Court of Appeal rejected a challenge by journalists in 1989 against the banning of Sinn Fein statements on British radio or television he 'unhesitatingly and unreservedly rejected' the argument that discretionary power should be exercised in a manner consistent with the Convention. This, he said, would impute to Parliament 'an intention to import the Convention into domestic law by the back door, when it has quite clearly refrained from doing so by the front door'.[76] In the same spirit Lord Fraser, the judge in the Government Communications Headquarters (GCHQ) case (*Council of Civil Service Unions vs. Minister for the Civil Service*, 1985) declined to consider the relevance of international labour conventions to the case because they were 'not part of the law in this country' and Lord Diplock put the principle succinctly in *British Airways Board vs. Laker Airways Ltd.* in 1985:

> the interpretation of treaties to which the United Kingdom is a party but the terms of which have not either expressly or by reference been incorporated in English domestic law by legislation is not a matter that falls within the interpretative jurisdiction of an English court of law.[77]

International conventions can, and do, influence the law, but they do not command it. In the interpretation of the traditionalists this is as true of the innovative European Community Act of 1972 as it was of any other of the international treaties to which Britain has become a party.

'Evolutionary' views

There are, however, more impressive arguments that can be seen increasingly to operate in the opposite direction and which indicate that the law is not only in process of a rapid evolution in response to essentially international pressures, but that it is also a growing direct influence on the process of external policy-making. This is the case both in matters of practice and in principle, and though the traditionalist arguments above are based largely on principle, British constitutional and administrative law has always been a subtle mixture of practice and principle and is capable of radical alterations in relatively brief periods.

Politicisation of the law

On a practical level, the salience of the law as a political issue has been greatly heightened during the last decade for a number of reasons. Conservative governments of the 1980s were far more inclined than their predecessors to use the law as a direct instrument of policy implementation, and since they were prepared to invoke the law more freely, so governments found themselves open to legal challenge by individuals and organisations who opposed them politically. More significantly, the Conservative governments' policies of devolving civil service powers to independent agencies, of which there was a plethora in the late 1980s, required extra legal provision to empower them to deal directly with the public. And since the public accountability of such agencies no longer flowed directly through Parliament via ministerial responsibility, public redress against this burgeoning sector of 'privatised' central and local government lay within the civil law. Then, too, British society appears to have become more litigious in recent years. In this respect, it is following a general trend in the OECD world which shows no sign of abating. The European Commission on Human Rights, to take only one example, has considered less than 20 petitions brought by government since it was founded, but no less than 10 000 individual petitions. Finally, it has to be admitted that the present generation of the judiciary have not shrunk from assuming a politically interpretative role somewhat akin to a 'checks and balances' constitution. A government that invokes the law in pursuit of its policy, in effect, invites the judiciary to play such a role, since it establishes the need for legal interpretation on a range of party political matters which are necessarily sensitive. The judiciary cannot, of course, rule on constitutional issues in these cases, as the US Supreme Court does. In a state where there is no written constitution it is inconceivable that the judiciary would become a 'supreme court'. But while this supports a traditionalist explanation of the increasing political role of the judiciary, it also supports an evolutionary analysis, since in holding the government to a strict interpretation of its own legislative rules, it is also upholding the rights of those individuals and organisations affected by them in a way that, in effect, writes constitutional rules as it goes. The fact that this role expanded so much during the 1980s – some said that the judiciary was compensating for the inadequacy of Parliament in holding the government accountable – emphasised the evolutionary power of British law and diminished the influence somewhat of those trenchant critics of British law who characterised the judiciary as little more than the Tory party in fancy dress.

International harmonisation

These developments, however, were not merely the fashions of a particular political decade. They were also responses to deeper trends. It became clear, for instance, that Britain had much greater need of international legal harmonisation during the 1970s and 1980s. The most obvious problems, though arguably not the most important, concerned the need to increase legal harmonisation between countries in respect to terrorism and international crime. In 1977 European countries agreed to a European Convention on the Suppression of Terrorism which entered into force the following year and deals, among other things, with the harmonisation of law on extradition for terrorist offences. It was designed to dovetail into the domestic Suppression of Terrorism Act of 1978, which, taken together constitute an extensive legal code to cope with modern European terrorism. Non-terrorist international crime, however, raises more interesting political questions. As an indication of what is now implied by the term 'international crime', it should be noted that in addition to the existence of drug barons, the mafia and triad gangs, the term must also encompass the growth of crimes such as forgery, from being a criminal cottage industry to its status now as a major, high-technology multinational concern, forging passports, vehicle registration certificates, travellers' cheques, Eurocheques, and, most important of all, almost every type of official and commercial validation document.[78] Meanwhile, the advanced economies found themselves in 1990 still grappling with the problem of assessing the scale of, and dealing with, a decade's growth in major computer crime, and of the utilisation of computer crime to assist other forms of offence, such as the dispersal of profits from international narcotics operations. Though all this does not constitute a fundamental development in the principles of law, it is clear that British law is, of necessity, becoming more internationally harmonised as a result of the transnationalism of crime. It is no coincidence, for instance, that 'judicial co-operation', 'terrorism', 'consular affairs' and 'human rights' make up four of the thirteen functional working groups within the European Political Co-operation machinery.

More significant than anything that happens in relation to criminality, however, is what happens to the law in relation to commerciality. Major companies throughout the developed world became less concerned with securing state aid in the late 1970s and more concerned to secure conditions of 'fair competition' (a matter of personal judgement in itself) in the markets that were important to them. This has been particularly strong in Europe, though it applies throughout the OECD world. Thus, companies have challenged national law everywhere to further their own interpretation of 'market liberalisation' by appealing to international legal norms. The European Court of Justice, says Bressand, 'is the least mentioned, yet indeed a key actor, in the overall liberalisation process'.[79] The growth of integrated markets has given multinational companies a very powerful stake in operating within a compatible, if not a common, legal framework in relation to company law, contracts, competition policy, health and safety, consumer protection, and so on. This sort of commercial pressure tends, in fact, to bypass governments and their judiciaries, since companies are adept at creating suitable arrangements between themselves where governments fail to provide them; arrangements which often contradict other aspects of national or international law and in turn stimulate governmental action to counteract such cartel arrangements. But as John Pinder has pointed out, 'That does not make the juridical framework within which business is done any the less important: on the contrary, the firmer the legal framework the less need there will be for business people to go to law.'[80] The use of European Community law, in particular, to secure appropriate market conditions has developed in a number of areas, in particular, in respect to free competition, the freedom of movement for workers and goods, and sex equality within Community countries.[81] Everything that is implied by the development of a single European market during the 1990s will increase the pressure towards ever deeper legal harmonisation between the member states. Already, about half of all legislation enacted in Britain originates in the European Community. On the basis of existing trends, this proportion will rise to around 80 per cent by the end of the 1990s.[82]

The area that has become most sensitive to the requirement for a harmonisation of laws is that of transborder data flows (TBDF). This was a phenomenon unrecognised until 1974, but during the 1980s it became a ubiquitous feature of the international economy and Britain has figured very largely in it. Thanks to its universal language, and its penetration by international investment, Britain originates around two-thirds of all data traffic between Europe and the United States and one-quarter of all the transborder data traffic within Western Europe.[83] Most governments have responded to the legal problems posed by TBDF by introducing data protection laws to safeguard privacy. This has created a jungle of national legal regulations that are uneven in their scope – some countries have many, others have none – and also in the severity of their regulations and their degree of enforcement. Britain's 1984 Data Protection Act therefore has potentially important implications for the international regulation of data, even though it was encouraged by some highly parochial pressures from British industry. Most important, data flows are regulated, as they have been in Britain, according to the principles of individual privacy: they are the outcome of concerns for the individual and have been promoted by civil liberty lobbies throughout the EC. But around 90 per cent of TBDF is non-personal, economic information. This has proved to be a severe handicap to the increasing number of major multinational corporations who want access to data that had hitherto been regarded as common property, who have made information technology one of their most highly invested resources, and who are establishing their own on-line international data networks and private telecommunication systems. Companies therefore find themselves infringing national laws merely by transferring information within their own corporate organisations. Data protection legislation is also regarded as a potential non-tariff restriction on trade which has led many multinational comapnies into a series of bitter protests.[84] The present network of national regulations, therefore, are under some pressure both from multi-nationals, who see in them unfair commercial restraints which they are prepared to test in the courts, and from international organ-isations, such as the OECD and the EC, who see in them a general restraint on economic growth and political progress.[85]

EC law

The question still arises, of course, as to whether the practice of increasing regulatory commercial law, either through international organisations or through the harmonisation of national legal codes, affects the principles of law. In this respect, the law of the European Community represents a key issue in any discussion of the future of law in Britain and the way in which law and external affairs have become intimately related. To what extent, in other words, does EC law have – or has gained over the last two decades – legal or political supremacy over domestic law? The answer is not obvious since, in the classic phrase of de Smith the European Communities Act of 1972 was 'a wilful manifestation of legislative schizophrenia... The United Kingdom Government has seated Parliament on two horses, one straining towards the preservation of parliamentary sovereignty, the other galloping in the general direction of Community law supremacy.'[86] Debate among legal analysts has been fierce during the last twenty years over the precise constitutional implications of the original 1972 Act, the European Assembly Elections Acts of 1978 and 1981, and the European Communities (Amendment) Act of 1986 which gave effect to the decision to create a single European market for the 1990s.[87] The view that domestic law remains superior to EC law flows from the traditionalist principles outlined above based on a view of Parliamentary sovereignty expressed in the most eloquent and trenchant form by Dicey.[88] Parliament remains sup-reme. The government has specified in some detail in which areas it is prepared to accept the jurisdiction of EC law and to further this, in the words of Sir Geoffrey Howe, 'Parliament intends to refrain (as is required by the treaties) from exercising its own legislative power.'[89] Indeed, though Parliament intends not to legislate (or uphold previous legislation) in a way that is inconsistent with British treaty obligations, it is nevertheless conceivable that it could legislate in an inconsistent manner. One legal interpretation of such a situation is that the job of the judiciary would be to decide whether or not the inconsistency was intentional, and if so, uphold it. Britain would then be in breach of its treaty obligations and would presumably renegotiate or withdraw from them.[90]

During debate over the Referendum Act of 1975 the clear presumption was that Parliament reserved the right to repeal anything it had agreed to three years previously if the country willed it, and under Section 6 of the 1978 European Assembly Elections Act, Parliament inserted a unique clause to ensure that no further treaty intended to increase the powers of the European Parliament could be ratified by the United Kingdom unless approved by another Act of Parliament.[91] In both cases Parliament acted in unique and extraordinary ways, in the first, by introducing a constitutional novelty which departed from British constitutional practice but reinforced the doctrine of parliamentary sovereignty; in the second by choosing to exercise unprecedented constitutional power, constraining the ability of the executive in the ratification of an international treaty.

Arguments opposed to traditionalist views, however, do not regard any of this as immutable and there is good reason to believe that EC law represents a significant constitutional and legal departure for Britain. In the first place the legal supremacy of Parliament is less absolute than it first appears. There is no such thing as British law, but rather three separate legal entities consisting of the law for England and Wales, Scottish law, and that for Northern Ireland. Some EC legislation has been enacted in three separate forms. As Gregory points out in a very useful introduction to the matter, 'Britain may not exist as a single legal entity in respect, of, for example, company law.'[92] More importantly, the notion that 'entrenchment' – the impossibility of repealing legislation once enacted – is incompatible with Parliamentary sovereignty is not beyond challenge. Entrenchment may be thought to be impossible in English law, but it is not clear that this applies to the law of Scotland. It is entirely likely that the Union Agreement of 1707 between Scotland and England has to be regarded as entrenched. It is difficult to imagine that the 1707 Act of Union could be repealed by a Parliament that – as the first Parliament of the United Kingdom of Great Britain – was created by it. In Scotland the 1707 Articles of Union were regarded as 'fundamental and unalterable...a rudimentary framework of a written constitution', and this interpretation, according to de Smith, 'remains largely intact'.[93] The implications of this are potentially very great, as Lord Cooper expressed it in 1953, 'The principle of the unlimited sovereignty of Parliament is a distinctively English principle which has no counterpart in Scottish constitutional law.'[94] The same is true of the Statute of Westminster of 1931 which limited the powers of Parliament to legislate for the Dominions. It is impossible to believe that Parliament could re-assume powers over the legislatures of the former Dominions, still less over former colonies, now republics, who have been granted Acts of Independence since the 1960s which expressly renounced legislative power over them. In 1982 the Statute of Westminster was further developed in relation to the Canadian constitution. For the 1931 statute had preserved the old method of amending the British North America Acts of 1867–1930 which were the basis of the Canadian constitution. Any constitutional amendment in Canada, therefore, could only be made by the British Parliament at the request of the Canadian Parliament. The Canada Act of 1982 recognised both political reality and common sense by granting legal power to Canada to amend its own constitution.[95] It is politically inconceivable that this Act could be revoked. Absolute doctrines of parliamentary sovereignty, in other words, which maintain that the judiciary must uphold Dicey's interpretation of Parliament's un-limited competence to legislate on any matter, at any time, without restriction, fly in the face of the legal tradition that law should also reflect political practice and constitutional developments. If some-thing is politically inconceivable the judiciary follows the principle of presuming it to be also legally inconceivable.

Entrenchment, therefore, may well have occurred already in several constitutional developments and on the basis of such precedents the European Communities Act of 1972 is regarded by some as 'semi-entrenched'.[96] This is partly based on the extent to which EC law has become directly applicable within Britain. Community law is defined as those obligations contained in EC treaties, and in its regulations, directives and decisions. An EC regulation is directly applicable in its entirety in all member states. Regulations apply directly to individuals and organisations within the state with the full force of law in national courts. British judges must uphold the provisions of a regulation though they have not been re-enacted by Parliament. They are therefore primary rather than delegated legislation (though his is referred to as 'secondary legis-lation') and redress against their effects can only be granted at the level of the EC itself. De Smith is quite clear that they represent 'a major constitutional innovation'.[97] EC directives, on the other hand, are binding only in respect to the results that have to be achieved and member states can choose how to give effect to them and what national legislation they may have to enact to do so. An EC decision applies only to the agency or individual to whom it is directed and simply requires that they comply with their EC obligations. The view of the Community in operating these legal requirements, and certainly of its European Court of Justice (ECJ), has tended to be expansive. The ECJ maintains a monistic theory of the relationship between national and Community law and claims that the EC constitutes a 'new legal order'.[98] All EC law, therefore, whether primary or not, takes precedence over domestic law since it is now the superior element of a single system. The ECJ concedes that Community law is distinct from national law and exists beside it, but shall prevail wherever they happen to conflict. Moreover, the ECJ claims the power of judicial review, whereby it can require a change in any existing domestic laws it regards as incompatible with EC law, even though a conflict between them may not, in fact, have arisen.

The areas in which EC law applies in Britain are significant, not only in their extent but also in the increasing depth and technicality of the EC's legal competence. Taxation law has long been integrated with Community law. Legally enforceable rates of customs duties and agricultural levies applicable in Britain can be varied directly through EC regulations, and 1 per cent of British value added tax and 90 per cent of all proceeds from customs duties are legally due to the Community in the same way.[99] Similarly, it has long been the case that EC nationals have legal rights regarding their movement, employment and dependants that are directly enforceable through EC regulations, backed up by directives re-enacted in domestic law. Since the entry into force of the Single European Act on 1 July 1987, however, the direct and indirect applicability of EC law has been extended to many more such technical areas. Article 100A of the Single European Act extended the principle of qualified majority voting within the Council of Ministers – overriding the effective veto of any member state – to most of the measures designed to create and sustain the single market in Europe. This had the effect of extending EC regulations and directives to legal sectors that had previously been the preserve of domestic legislation. It may not be surprising that EC legislation applies to environmental and health matters, safety at work, or food labelling. But it is significant that it has come to embrace, for instance, motoring legislation on speed limits, seat belts, alcohol levels and tyre tread depths.[100] The Single European Act has led the EC to initiate a great deal of extra legislation in new policy areas. The legal adviser to the House of Commons Foreign Affairs Committee in 1989 was of the opinion that Article 100A 'could be used in a manner which would encroach on areas ordinarily falling outside Community competence', and in evidence to the committee some observers were very clear that the EC Commission had made it plain that they intended to interpret their brief in this respect as widely as possible.[101] As the committee concluded in a delphic turn of phrase, 'It is clear to us that the

Community now developing is very different from the Commnity that the UK joined in the 1970s'.[102]

For Britain the judicial adjustment to EC law has gone surprisingly smoothly. In the earliest cases where EC law figured in legal judgements a series of dramatic statements were made which seemed to indicate the ease with which the primacy of EC law was accepted by the judiciary. Lord Denning likened EC law to, 'an incoming tide. It flows into the estuaries and up the rivers'.[103] But the practice of law since the 1970s has not produced any major contentious cases where the relationship would be seriously tested. This may be regarded by traditional analyses as the good luck of a conflict postponed, or by evolutionary analyses as evidence of the real influence of EC law on British society. Lord Denning's later estimation in 1979 probably expresses best the ambiguous truth: EC law, he said, 'is not supplanting English law. It is part of our law which overrides any other part which is inconsistent with it.'[104]

If such arguments appear as legal niceties, they have nevertheless come to constitute an important influence on British external policy. They have become important 'non-institutional' influences because they are self-evidently evolving in a situation where the realities of economic interdependence require sensitive legal judgements on a range of particular issues that have great potential importance to external relations. The integration of the world economy brings with it a host of important legal issues and in responding to this, EC law is continuing to grow at a pace which easily outstrips the growth of domestic law. All legal traditions evolve, but the EC legal tradition has evolved faster than most. Nor is it merely the ubiquity of relevant legal judgements that constitutes such influence on external policy, for the form of such judgements is also changing. British judges find themselves having to apply and interpret EC law which, in the continental tradition, has a rather different emphasis to English or Scottish law. For one thing, it tends to be phrased in a more general way, requiring overtly politicised judgements on behalf of the interpreter. English law is based upon the principle that judgement has to be guided not by the merits of the effect of the law, but rather by the correctness of its application. In continental legal traditions, however, the practice of judicial review, doctrines of natural law and of 'proportionality' are a more prominent part of the tradition. Judicial review has become increasingly prevalent throughout the Community since the beginning of the 1980s. Moreover, the concept of proportionality maintains that judgement on a law must balance the good it may do society against the harm it may have on groups who will be disadvantaged by it. The law must be judged on its merits as much as its correct application. This is a profoundly political, and un-British, judicial task but it has been noted that the

British legal tradition is moving towards the acceptance of such a principle.[105]

In short, it is difficult to escape the conclusion that the British judiciary are quietly but steadily emerging as a more influential political force in British policy-making during the 1990s. This has got very little to do with the 'liberal-capitalist' consensus – even the 'establishment conspiracy' – so prevalent in many standard analyses of British politics. It is driven by the imperatives of Britain's external environment which so deeply affects its domestic environment. If anything, this increase in the politicisation of the judicial function is likely to move in anti-establishment directions since the trends of international legislation are towards deregulation, the establishment of common social standards and protection of the individual. Old-boy networks are being broken up in modern Europe, and though there is no guarantee that they will not be replaced by new-boy networks, they will, of necessity, be wider and more international.

7　The Politics of External Relations

Little mention has been made so far about the politicians who deal with Britain's external relations. This is partly because a study of the nature of British external policy-making in the 1990s is necessarily concerned with the underlying determinants of policy and will therefore tend to concentrate on the institutions, the structural factors, and on general trends within the world of officialdom. Moreover, many analysts, not to mention many officials, consider that the politicians who preside over external affairs simply make very little difference to policy. Most of the existing literature on British foreign policy-making makes only passing mention of the role of different politicians and parties on the policy-making process. Personalities and political parties matter, of course, and may have critical effects on particular issues. When leaders change, at the very least, a new set of personality characteristics comes into the reckoning. But most previous accounts of British foreign policy-making have found little that could usefully be said about the effects of different political leaders and of changes of government on the nature and conduct of the external policy process.

This view has to be challenged in the 1990s, though there is still a legitimate and unresolved debate over the extent to which politicians matter. Nevertheless, the party political arena has changed somewhat in the way it deals with external relations. Most significantly, more than a decade of Thatcher governments naturally raises the question of the degree to which political leadership can influence the policy process. The sheer longevity of the Thatcher premiership, coupled with the distinctiveness of Mrs Thatcher's views on foreign and defence affairs – not to mention on the civil service which administers them – have made the 'Thatcher era' an inevitable test case for the thesis that external policy-making has become party politicised since the 1970s.

Party politics

The problem of bipartisan consensus

There is certainly *prima facie* evidence that the last decade and a half has witnessed a breakdown in the traditional bipartisan consensus that had marked the party politics of external relations in the past. Accounts of bipartisanship in some of the older analyses of British foreign policy may seem to belong to a bygone age. They normally observed that the real party political argument takes place not between the respective front benches on the floor of the House of Commons but rather between the front and back benches in the various forums of intra-party debate. This was where Left and Right wing views, traditional and radical views, 'little Englander' and 'world role' views, would really compete for prominence. The party leaderships would tend to agree with each other and Opposition leaders would certainly not make the political mistake of being seen to attack the country in front of foreigners; their task was to contain and mollify the various species of political wild men on their own back-benches. Indeed, the unity of the government in external relations, or the suitability of the Opposition as an alternative government, often seemed to depend on the success with which they could do this.[1] In the decade after 1945, for example, Clement Atlee, no less than Anthony Eden, made frequent statements whilst in opposition on the need to promote bipartisan support for the government's foreign policy. In so far as the front benches disagreed on external policy, it was in matters of emphasis over a small range of issues. On all the major premises of Britain's post-war foreign and defence policy there was no disagreement, and bipartisanship was preached extensively in an effort to disarm critics on the back-benches or within the party rank and file.[2]

This bipartisan consensus appeared to rest on several factors. One was the very nature of external relations, wherein events tended to move at a glacial pace and were less susceptible than domestic issues to political influence. Another was the fact that front bench political leaders tended to have some experience in external affairs and were acutely aware that they would likely inherit the problems for themselves after an election. Then too, a certain national style and the habits of consensus politics were seen to promote an agreed view of what was in the 'national interest'; particularly in a country in a state of retreat and decline where major foreign policy choices appeared to be limited. Finally, there was the traditionally low salience of foreign affairs in British political debates, which meant that for party leaders there was little electoral credit to be won in taking distinctive stances on external issues, but a great deal to be lost from an appearance of disunity or even of disloyalty. The result, as Frankel pointed out in 1975, was that the motivations of the political parties in foreign affairs were clearly different, but not their essential objectives.[3] Even radical explanations of post-war British politics attest to the power of a foreign policy consensus – as part of the corporatist economic consensus – that was sustained by the special relationship with the United States and the adoption of a post-imperial world role.[4]

The basis of this consensus could be seen to lie behind the somewhat arcane foreign policy arguments that the front benches had with their subordinates. The Labour leadership, both in and out of government, spent much of the decade from the mid-1960s arguing with its left wing about the Government's stance over the Vietnamese War, over defence policy and over the decision to apply for membership of the Common Market. The Conservative Party, in the same way, spent a great deal of energy during those years arguing with the vocal remnants of its old imperial wing about the withdrawal from East of Suez and also about the Common Market. On all of the major foreign issues of the period – British post-imperial withdrawal, unwillingness to identify too closely with the United States in Vietnam, the commitment to an independent nuclear deterrent, to joining the Common Market, even the attitude towards rebel Rhodesia and to South Africa – the front benches shared the same essential objectives and differed chiefly over tactics and emphasis. The only distinctive alternatives to these policies were offered by political fringe elements on the back-benches in alliance with small groups of what Vital called their 'ideological associates' outside Parliament.[5]

It is clearly not difficult to argue that both the underlying conditions of this bipartisan consensus and the manifestations of it since the mid-1970s have altered considerably. The underlying conditions can no longer be taken for granted. As we have pointed out throughout this study, the international context in which Britain finds itself in the 1990s moves at anything but a glacial pace and is clearly all too susceptible to the influence of political leadership as a new Europe – indeed a new global order – takes shape. Nor is it necessarily the case that the consensus is promoted by the fact that front bench leaders tend to have some common experience of international affairs. The first Thatcher government in 1979 was able to draw upon a certain reserve of foreign and defence policy experience, but the new Prime Minister was almost entirely innocent of any familiarity with the subject. Her interest in it was low, though her instincts about it were strong and uninhibited by inexperience. She rapidly came to distrust the advice of the acknowledged Conservative Party specialists in external relations and tried to supplant them instead with those in whose instincts she trusted. So the experience of Thatcherites in external relations was not great during the early period. The Labour Party, meanwhile, was embarked upon more than a decade out of power which eventually left its front bench team completely devoid of any first-hand experience of foreign or defence matters at cabinet level.

Another aspect of the 1980s that undermined the conditions of the traditional consensus was the very ideological vigour of the new government. Mrs Thatcher set herself against the promotion of 'consensus' and 'corporatism' in British politics and was determined to take a more assertive view of Britain's national interests, while the Labour Party shifted to the left in opposition and the centre parties enjoyed another brief renaissance at Labour's expense. Foreign and defence policies became parts of increasingly polarised arguments between the parties during the 1980s, so much so that even the apparently inescapable reality of British decline and withdrawal from a global role became a matter of party political debate as the Conservative government asserted that Britain was now conducting its policy once more from a position of inherent strength. Finally, the proposition that foreign affairs has a low salience in British politics was also questionable in the 1980s as the scope and depth of *external* relations – as defined in Chapter 3 – made decisive impacts on British domestic politics and 'internationalised' British society in some of the ways described in the previous chapter.

The experience of party politics since the mid-1970s would appear to bear out these shifts in dramatic ways, since the party battle has encompassed some of the most sensitive of foreign and defence policy issues. Indeed, a hint of the vehemence to come was provided by Mrs Thatcher's first visit to the United States as Conservative Party leader in 1975. Going out of her way to break the convention which maintains that politicians do not criticise the government when abroad (a convention that has been oft-broken since) she criticised socialist Britain as an 'eleventh-hour nation' being ruined by the 'relentless pursuit of equality'.[6] It was an approach that was to become familiar in different guises as Mrs Thatcher in government committed herself to what has been described as an 'intensely nationalistic foreign policy' that was 'in clear contrast to the internationalism of all her post-war predecessors, with the possible exception of Anthony Eden at Suez'.[7]

Of particular note in the early years of the 1980s was the attitude of the new Conservative government to defence issues, and reflected in that, to the role of the United States, the Soviet Union and Eastern Europe. The value to Britain of the special relationship with the United States had never previously been seriously questioned between the parties. There had always been a Gaullist element in the Conservative Party that had a curious counterpart with the far left in the Labour Party who each argued against the restrictions that so close an Anglo-American relationship seemed to impose on Britain. But there was never a significant front bench argument about this: James Callaghan, as a Labour Prime Minister, was as close to his American counterpart as the Conservative Macmillan had been to his, 20 years previously. Perhaps more surprisingly, it was impossible to detect much difference in the traditional attitudes of the front benches towards the Soviet Union. There were, of course, marked differences of ideological emphasis over attitudes to the communist world, but remarkably few differences emerged over the tactics that each party should adopt in dealing specifically with the Soviet Union and Eastern Europe. Labour governments were more willing to open up expansive trade deals with the East, as was demonstrated in 1975, but in truth, both parties 'dealt' with the Soviet Union largely by ignoring it. Anglo-Soviet relations were adversarial and tenuous and for that reason absorbed very little diplomatic or political capital and generated minimal controversy in the party arena.[8]

The defence debate in the 1980s

Defence issues, however, became a touchstone in the 1980s for a complex set of arguments over relations with both adversaries and allies which seemed decisively to break the old front bench consensus: setting the Conservative Government on a road that was divergent from the traditions of Heathite and Macmillan conservatism, even though it reaffirmed the commitment to an independent British nuclear deterrent; leading the Labour Party into an antinuclear stance that had a major impact both on the general image of the party and on its own attitudes to the superpowers and Britain's diplomatic partners. Even the re-emergent centre party alliance between the Social Democrats and the Liberals was punctuated by differences between the partners over defence policy, and partly foundered on such differences in the aftermath of its 1987 electoral disaster. It was a revealing irony of the time that the Social Democratic Party (SDP) – formed mainly from the right wing of the Labour Party – was a good deal more conservative on defence issues than its Liberal Party allies, who at some times during these years found themselves driven towards positions that were effectively indistinguishable from those of the Labour Party.

For the decade from 1975 to around 1985 the Thatcherite Conservative Party – notwithstanding the presence of traditional Conservatives within it – adopted a hostile and uncompromising stance towards the Soviet Union and its allies, assuming the *détente* of the previous years to have been both unrealistic and unproductive. The Soviet invasion of Afghanistan at the end of 1979 confirmed all the worst fears of the Thatcherite Conservatives. There was thus no alternative in this view but to maintain strong defences, and subsequently to agree the deployment of the new Cruise and Pershing II nuclear missiles in Britain, and to begin the process of replacing Britain's Polaris nuclear submarine force with the American Trident system. As John Nott, the Defence Secretary, expressed it to the Conservative faithful in 1981, Labour's unilateralist nuclear defence policy amounted to 'the lunatic demand that Britain should abandon its allies, shut ourselves out of Europe and emasculate our defences and adopt a policy of craven appeasement to the Soviet Union'.[9]

After the Falklands War in 1982, no one doubted the defence commitment of the Conservative Party that lay behind such rhetoric. This coincided with a new assertiveness in United States defence policy during the final years of the Carter Administration and a notably more aggressive interpretation of the United States's own world role during the first Reagan Administration. Thus the close identification of the Thatcher governments with the Reagan Administration which came into office in 1981 became another symbol of a powerful set of instinctive defence and security commitments on the part of the Thatcherite Conservatives which were maintained through thick and thin and which frequently established the targets for the opposition parties to attack. President Reagan's espousal of the Strategic Defense Initiative (SDI) in March 1983 encapsulated the phenomenon. It was a self-evidently unrealistic scheme, certainly in the way President Reagan conceived it, and despite privately sharing all the reservations of any sensible observer, the Prime Minister continually supported it in public and identified her government boldly with the most risible and slow-moving of all the anti-nuclear targets. It was a gift to the Opposition who openly pledged to reverse the Anglo-American Memorandum of Understanding on the SDI of December 1985 and sought to present the Government as a dangerous henchman to an even more dangerous American master.[10]

The Labour Party had always been significantly more sympathetic to the disarmament movement, and during the late 1970s increasing numbers within the party and around a quarter of all Labour MPs identified themselves closely with the resurgent Campaign for Nuclear Disarmament (CND). On the basis of the strength of CND within some of the trade unions, particularly that of the Transport and General Workers Union, and in almost all of the constituency parties, the Labour Party became significantly more radical on defence and nuclear issues.[11] The 1970s had witnessed a growing disparity between the attitude of the majority of members at successive Labour Conferences and the Wilson/Callaghan leadership towards defence. The latent anti-Americanism within the Labour Party's rank and file had found expression in calls for the closure of the US Polaris bases at previous Labour Conferences of

1972 and 1973 and in the two election manifestos of 1974, though the leadership seems never to have felt seriously constrained by this. By September 1981, however, with the party in a state of crisis following the 1979 election defeat, the Conference repeated its feat of 1959 by passing a unilateralist anti-nuclear motion at the Annual Conference. It went on to strengthen this in 1982 by passing similar motions with the necessary two-thirds majority to make it mandatorily party policy. By the time of the 1986 Conference, the party had repeatedly and consistently adopted a non-nuclear strategy, involving the removal of American nuclear bases from Britain. By 1986 these resolutions were passed by a series of very large majorities. In 1959 the flirtation with unilateral nuclear disarmament had immediately become a struggle for the very soul of the party: Hugh Gaitskell had pledged himself to 'fight and fight again' to preserve the party he loved, and managed to get the unilateralist resolution reversed the very next year. In the 1980s, however, though the unilateralist policy was also arguably part of a more complex and protracted struggle for the soul of the party, its passage and retrenchment was more than just a tactic in the struggle for control, and its adoption was no mere flirtation with unilateralism. It represented a decisive break in the defence consensus and the Labour Party fought and lost two successive elections with a non-nuclear defence policy – and all that it implied for British relations with its allies – as part of its platform.

The centre parties, too, expressed a similar break in the old consensus. The Liberal/SDP alliance struggled to define a workable 'less-nuclear' policy that might be made acceptable to the allies and make a contribution to getting East-West arms control restarted. The Liberal/SDP Alliance, while it lasted, was determined to distance itself from the Thatcherite identification with some of the defence excesses of Reagan's America, and prove that the government was constantly ignoring chances to improve the atmosphere with the Soviet Union and East European states. But the Alliance was never quite able to manage the differences between the partners over what to do about Britain's independent nuclear deterrent. Two of the founders of the SDP – David Owen and William Rodgers – held trenchant views on nuclear issues and cited defence as one of their prime reasons for breaking away from the Labour Party. David Owen in particular, emerging as the single leader of the SDP, espoused a personal commitment to Britain's nuclear deterrent that seemed to grow stronger as the controversy mounted. This position became impossible for the leadership of the Liberal Party to maintain in the face of its own grass roots membership, and some of its MPs, a number of whom were explicitly unilateralist. Like the Labour Opposition, members of the Liberal section of the Alliance simply could not swallow the lofty assertions of Thatcherite nuclear statements in the name of the 'national interest'. And they certainly could not resist attacking some of the more obvious political targets that the right-wing governments of the 1980s offered as the world seemed to be slipping back into the most threatening days of the Cold War. The US invasion of Grenada, the attack on Libya, the embarrassment of the Iran-Contra scandal, the muddled US involvement in the Persian Gulf, were all grist to the political mill and provoked vehement exchanges between the party leaderships in some intriguing three-cornered fights.

By the time of the 1987 General Election, therefore, the defence consensus between the parties appeared to be a thing of the past. The Conservative Government went into the election sticking – quite literally – to its guns. The Labour Party articulated a non-nuclear defence policy that was argued through and presented in more detail than any defence policy that had ever been presented in a General Election; though it has to be said that its leaders argued it out during the campaign with less conviction than such a radical departure required. And the Alliance came up with a less detailed set of compromise defence proposals designed to keep Britain's nuclear options open well into the 1990s, which nevertheless had the virtue of being backed up by some of the most sophisticated reasoning that it is possible to present to the public in an election campaign: there could be little doubt that the Liberal/SDP Alliance represented the most internationalist of Britain's political parties. By 1987 the British defence debate had apparently become, therefore, a choice between genuine defence alternatives, so much so that US defence officials went out of their way to comment ominously on the implications of a Labour election victory. In the event, the consistency of the Conservative approach to defence appeared to be more persuasive to the electorate than the alternative challenges. The status quo won the argument.[12]

But the ground was already shifting under this debate by 1987. The East-West confrontation began to dissolve after 1986 with the growing influence of Gorbachev on the international scene and the declining influence of President Reagan. In December 1987 the Treaty on Intermediate Nuclear Forces was signed and Cruise, Pershing II, SS4, SS5 and SS20 missiles – the focus of so much of the defence controversy in the early 1980s – were to be phased out and completely destroyed. A new beginning was to be made on strategic arms reductions and even on the imbalance of conventional forces between NATO and the Warsaw Pact. It was not just that a new impetus had been given to arms control, but rather that the negotiation process was dramatically changed after December 1987 so that arms control, instead of merely seeking to alleviate the conditions of the strategic status quo, suddenly became a major agent of changing such conditions. It was a symptom of the fact that a new era was manifestly opening in the relations between East and West.

All this had a curious impact on the party political defence debate in Britain. On the one hand, both the Government and its critics drew different lessons from the remarkable changes in the international context. The Government claimed that it vindicated the tough conservative approach of Britain, the United States and the NATO allies. They had proved to the Soviet Union that the transatlantic allies would remain united and that there would be no easy political victories for Moscow or opportunities to blackmail the West. Faced with such resolve, the Soviet Union had bowed to the reality of power and recognised its own bankruptcy. Just as George Kennan had predicted in 1947 – and as Karl Marx might have, had he been able – the internal contradictions of the Soviet state had finally caught up with it. In this sense Kennan's 'containment' could be seen to have worked. The critics of the British government, however, drew different lessons from this turn of events. For them, it proved what they had always maintained: that it was possible to deal co-operatively with the Soviet Union, whose defence policy had been a mixture of defensive aggression and paranoid reaction. Given the first taste of sensitive leadership, the Soviet Union had powerful motives to engage in arms control and a reorientation of its defence policy. Moreover, the critics observed, contrary to the Government's analysis, the Soviet Union was willing to give up far more than the West across the whole spectrum of negotiations in which it was then engaged. To those on the left who had been so effectively attacked by the Conservative Party for the dangerous foolishness of being 'unilateralist' in their anti-nuclear stance, there was the grim satisfaction of observing that arms control was now in danger of being superceded by a plethora of unilateralist actions on the part of the superpowers, most notably by the Soviet Union itself. Far from upholding the wisdom of the Conservatives' approach, the events of the late-1980s were seen on the left to vindicate their attack on the concept of nuclear deterrence and expose the short-sightedness of failing to grasp the opportunities that were rapidly opening up.[13]

On the other hand, however, the Conservatives, no less than the opposition parties, desperately needed this dramatic change in the international context to get them off a series of difficult political hooks. The Conservatives were anxious to show that they were not one-dimensional anti-communists and that the Conservative Government was capable of dealing straightforwardly with both the Soviet Union and the governments of Eastern Europe. Indeed, much capital was made out of the openings to Eastern Europe that Mrs Thatcher had personally made in 1984 and her friendly personal relationship with the ascendant Mr Gorbachev. By 1987 the anti-nuclear battles, and the embarrassments of being so staunchly pro-American at a time when Soviet diplomacy constantly wrong-footed Washington and won friends across Europe, had taken their toll of the Conservative Party. A new identification as the party of effective negotiation was needed and in this respect the dramatic caving in of the Soviet diplomatic position after 1987 provided a welcome vehicle for a Conservative change of emphasis.

The opposition parties, meanwhile, drew from the experience of the 1987 election the lesson that nuclear unilateralism simply could not be sold to the British public. In truth, it is arguable whether this really was a lesson of the 1987 election, and by the turn of the decade unilateral reductions in armaments seemed to be an idea whose time had come, certainly in Washington and Moscow. Nevertheless, the Labour leadership made it abundantly clear that nuclear unilateralism could not be part of the new-look Labour Party for the 1990s. As Neil Kinnock put it to the National Executive Committee in 1989 with astonishing honesty and clarity: 'I am not again going to make that tactical argument for the unilateral, independent abandonment of nuclear weapons without getting anything in return.'[14] Changing international circumstances, it was said, made the old defence policy irrelevant and it was necessary to address the new defence issues that would arise in the early 1990s. The independent nuclear deterrent was now accepted, at least insofar as the first Trident submarine would already be built by the time of the next election. A future Labour government would accept this until it could be negotiated away and the party explicitly put its faith in arms control and security negotiations now that multilateral disarmament approaches appeared to be set to bear unprecedented fruits. Having dropped the unilateralist commitment of the 1987 election, the Labour Party did its best to avoid explicit discussion of the details of defence policy, feeling instinctively that defence issues remained a potential death-trap for the left in Britain. The Liberal/SDP Alliance disintegrated very soon after the 1987 election, to leave the Liberal Democrats holding what was left of the electoral centre ground. The Liberal Democrats too, revised their radical defence policy in the light of new circumstances and put their faith in attacks on the Conservative Party for being narrowly nationalist and insufficiently sensitive to the nature of security negotiations in the new Europe.

So the effect of the breakdown in the traditional defence consensus was never resolved. Both sides of the defence argument could fairly claim some vindication for their views and were able to escape from what had become a stark intellectual and political confrontation over a set of issues that had not previously been matters of genuine interparty conflict. Whatever the future of these arguments in the 1990s, the fact remains that they represented a party battle over both specific nuclear issues and matters of general orientation in defence and foreign policy that was historically unique in its duration and intensity.

Southern Africa and the Commonwealth

The debate over the future of Southern Africa was another important example of an external issue that followed a similar pattern in these years. As with defence issues, the front benches had faced a mixture of pressures on Southern Africa's problems over the years. Macmillan's Conservative Party had to adjust itself to the withdrawal of South Africa from a changing Commonwealth in 1961. The Wilson Government had faced a series of delicate cross-party pressures over Rhodesia's Unilateral Declaration of Independence in 1965, operating with a parliamentary majority of just one.[15] And Edward Heath had faced bitter attacks from many sides in response to his decision to resume arms sales to South Africa. Of course, there were consistent party political elements in all this. The Labour Party always identified itself strongly with the ideals of the multi-racial Commonwealth that began to develop in the 1960s. Immediately on taking office in 1964 Harold Wilson, even before his first cabinet meeting, had announced an immediate ban on arms sales to South Africa.[16] Heath was pushed by Conservative Party commitments into a controversy on the issue as soon as he won the 1970 election and eventually reversed the ban in February 1971.[17] Wilson immediately reimposed it again on taking office in 1974. Vehement party differences were therefore not new on the South Africa issue, but differences were over means rather than ends; there has never been a front bench defence of the principle of apartheid. Indeed, the fundamentals of British policy towards South Africa were laid down by the British Labour Government between 1947 and 1951: apartheid was opposed, as was any extension of Afrikaner influence northwards, but continuing contact was regarded as vital both for strategic reasons and to encourage internal reform. This approach remained substantially intact throughout changing governments for the next 30 years.[18] Moreover, while differences over South Africa have been fiercely argued out in the country at various times and have always been the subject of vigorous domestic (and international) lobbying, they have never figured as an election issue, even in 1966 in the aftermath of the Rhodesian UDI.[19] South Africa, as the essence of the Southern African problem, therefore, represented a curious issue. It would be wrong to say that there was ever a clear front bench consensus on South Africa, as there had been on defence. It had been a highly visible and controversial moral and political issue since at least 1960, but it was not politically divisive and did not appear to hold the key to other vital external issues.

This situation changed, however, in the late-1970s as the British approach to South Africa took on the aspect of a more important party political conflict. In some measure this was because the issue itself became more stark after 1976. Not since the Sharpeville Massacre of 1960 had there been a major outbreak of mass violence in South Africa, but in 1976 the township of Soweto erupted and though the internal pressures on Pretoria subsequently waxed and waned, this marked the beginning of the thread of violence that was to bring the Republic to the State of Emergency in 1986. It was also the period in which the Gleneagles agreement of 1976 laid down Commonwealth rules over sporting links with South Africa and in which the United Nations, in 1977, introduced a mandatory ban on the sale of arms to South Africa. It was also the period in which the Conservative Party under its new leader began to redefine its perspective on international affairs. The same assertiveness that infused its views of defence and security policies also found expression, more slowly but no less effectively, over policies towards South Africa.

As with defence issues, the South Africa policies of the Conservative Government that came into office in 1979 became a touchstone for a much wider and vehement party political debate over other international issues. In a regional sense, South Africa was the linchpin in the politics of rebel Rhodesia, disputed Namibia and in the policy that the West might adopt towards the Marxist states of Angola and Mozambique. In a deeper sense, however, the Conservative government's South Africa policy became an argument over its attitudes towards the usefulness of the Commonwealth, of the United Nations and of the respect it accorded to Third World countries. It was an issue that set it apart from the rest of the European Community and which identified it further with Reaganite America. And it was an issue that served both as a symbol and a test case of the Conservative approach to morally difficult international problems.

The Thatcherite Conservatives were instinctively sympathetic to the dilemmas faced by the white minority in South Africa; instinctively disapproving of the Moscow-backed African National Congress (ANC) who would not eschew the use of violence to achieve their aims. Apartheid was indefensible but could best be reformed by a process of constructive engagement that offered both threats and inducements. The obverse of this positive approach, however, was that the Conservative Government found itself standing against both international and domestic trends that came more and more to favour an increase in all possible pressures on the Pretoria government, especially in respect to sanctions. In particular, the Conservative approach – to be distinguished from the prevailing approach of most government officials – became deeply antithetical to what was seen to be the hypocrisy of Third World states in the UN and especially in the Commonwealth, who called for sweeping measures more readily than they ever gave effect to them and whose definitions of racism could be highly selective. What the Conservative approach claimed to be an important difference over tactics, its more radical opponents claimed to be implicit support for the principle of apartheid itself. On this charge the Thatcherite response was to hit back directly. As Mrs Thatcher herself put it,

> I find nothing *moral* about people sitting in comfortable circum-stances with good salaries, inflation-proof pensions, good jobs, saying that we, as a matter of *morality* will put x hundred thousand black people out of work, knowing that this could lead to starvation, poverty and unemployment, and even greater vio-lence.[20]

Such contempt extended to the other members of the European Community who also argued for sanctions, though a compromise position was eventually reached which held until the internal situa-tion in South Africa changed with the arrival in office of President de Klerk.

The Conservative Party did, however, as in the case of defence, have a natural ally in the Reagan Administration. President Reagan effectively reversed the orientation of the Carter Administration on Southern Africa, being much exercised by the Marxist regimes of Angola and Mozambique. This provided support for the more assertive British position at exactly the appropriate moment and also offered some diplomatic shade, as international attention naturally focused on debates taking place in Washington.

Again, the Thatcherite Conservative Party had set up the targets for the domestic opposition to attack. The Government's argument with the Commonwealth was in principle the same that Edward Heath had had a decade before, and in reality few other Western governments were doing more than Britain to isolate South Africa.[21] But the level of rhetoric rose considerably in the 1980s and the British government defended its attitude with an assertiveness that was backed by a certain casual arrogance in the new Conservative Party at a time when the international consensus on sanctions was greater than it had ever been. Both the substance and the style of this British policy, in the eyes of the Labour Party, was therefore doing enormous damage to Britain's international reputation.

The acrimonious Commonwealth Conference in 1985 at Nassau appeared to be the pivot of Britain's isolation. Mrs Thatcher had gone out of her way to stress how small was the significance of the sanctions that had been agreed to: she had offended most of the Commonwealth in doing so; the meeting sent an 'eminent persons group' to Southern Africa which subsequently came out unanimously in favour of concerted economic sanctions; and the Foreign Secretary was sent on a fruitless mission to the capitals of the region where he was alternately snubbed and insulted in retribution for Nassau. Opponents of the Conservative approach perceived in all this an instinctive Thatcherite paranoia when dealing with any forces sympathetic to Moscow. They perceived a dangerous closeness to the United States which identified Britain with reactionary forces in the world, and an almost perverse desire to back the inevitable losers in the eventual outcome of the struggle for power in South Africa. Mrs Thatcher's willingness to entertain President Botha on a visit to Britain in 1984 was regarded by the opposition parties as the height of diplomatic folly and an expression of the Conservative Party's real stance on the matter of racism. Labour leaders openly identified themselves with the cause of the growing anti-apartheid movement in Britain and with the ANC in South Africa, notwithstanding its associations with violence, but recognising it as the legitimate voice of black politics in the Republic. It supported the views of most of the Commonwealth and the European Community partners against the British position and professed to be embarrassed, on behalf of the British people, at the reactionary isolation of the Conservative Government. The opposition parties, in effect, accepted a Conservative invitation to judge its attitudes to the developing world in general by reference to this particular issue.

As in the case of defence, however, a satisfying resolution of the argument was thwarted by the process of internal change in Southern Africa itself which offered justification for both sides. In a sense, the Conservatives could already point to a notable early success in the Rhodesian settlement at Lancaster House in January 1980, though ironically, this was achieved against the grain of the new Conservative approach and represented a triumph of Foreign Office thinking, skillfully grafted onto a personal and brave commitment on the Prime Minister's part to engineer an agreement. If Mrs Thatcher had not then been in power for so short a time it seems likely that the Foreign Office would have been a good deal less influential. Nevertheless, the diplomatic victory of Rhodesia was eventually followed by a turning of the international tide in Southern Africa. The Marxist regimes began to turn in economic desperation to the West and in 1989 the Soviet Union openly supported a co-operative superpower settlement in the region along the lines of Western thinking. This, coupled with the sheer cost to South Africa of its wars of destabilisation and its unfavourable economic prospects, finally unlocked the Namibian impasse, and the accession to power of President F.W. de Klerk in South Africa in August 1989 initiated an official acceptance that genuine internal reform had become both inevitable and urgent. So again, the ground shifted under the political argument and allowed both the Government and the Opposition to claim some vindication for their views in the light of the progress that had been made across the whole of Southern Africa. Though there had never been a party political 'consensus' on South Africa to break, the 1980s had nevertheless witnessed a unique degree of party politicisation over it, reflecting a deeper difference both of philosophy and style in the approach of the major parties towards external affairs.

Acrimonious political debate

The tone of Thatcherite Conservatism since the late 1970s, and the internal struggles that all of the opposition parties underwent during the same time, illuminated a number of other issues in external affairs in which essential bipartisanship appeared to have broken down. The opposition parties found it difficult to criticise the general nature of the Government's response to the invasion of the Falklands: indeed it was pointed out at the time that only the Bennite group within the Labour Party offered a genuinely alternative analysis of the policy of sending a task force to retake the Falklands. But the Government came under heavy immediate pressure over its decision to order the sinking of the *General Belgrano* – a pressure that dogged Mrs Thatcher's premiership for some considerable time – and over the efficacy of its Falklands policy prior to the invasion, which had undoubtedly encouraged the Argentinian leadership to embark on its dangerous adventure.[22]

The Conservatives also ran into vitriolic criticism over the Westland crisis of 1985–86. Westland plc was Britain's only helicopter manufacturer and sought to escape from its production and financial problems by forming an association with the American aerospace company, Sikorsky, which also included the Italian company Fiat, as a junior partner. Michael Heseltine, as Defence Secretary, sought, as he put it, to offer Westland a choice, and began to lobby vigorously for a counterproposal through the European National Armaments Directors which would associate it instead with a European consortium of aerospace companies.[23] The issue spiralled out of control in the final weeks of 1985 so that it was not at all clear what was really at stake. The matter seemed to resolve itself into three issues: a strategic choice concerning the degree to which Britain should lean towards European as opposed to transatlantic co-operation in its weapons procurement; the highly ambiguous attitude of the government towards intervention in the defence industrial market; and most important in the light of the resignations of both the Defence and the Industry ministers within two weeks of each other in January 1986, an investigation into the propriety of the government's behaviour. On 27 January Mrs Thatcher faced the House of Commons and was attacked by the Labour leadership for her 'incompetence, ruthlessness and dishonesty'. Indeed, even with her majority of over 140 seats, Mrs Thatcher reportedly remarked as she left for the House that 'I may not be Prime Minister by six o'clock tonight'.[24] It was not that she was facing defeat in the Commons, as such, but rather that she was facing a loss of political credibility in that particular debate which might easily have led to a defeat within the ranks of the Conservative Party. She escaped such a fate because, not for the first time, the indignation she excited in the Opposition overcame its tactical good sense. The debate became a predictable, ill-tempered dogfight along party lines and the position of the Prime Minister was thereby preserved.

Nor was there any shortage of evidence during the 1980s of increasingly acrimonious interparty debates on external issues wherein the difference between the Government and the Opposition was essentially tactical: over the handling of British hostages taken in the Lebanon; over the granting of British passports to selected members of the community in Hong Kong, prior to its handover to the People's Republic of China in 1997; or over individual cases such as the unwitting delivery driver of some of the components of an Iraqi 'supergun' who was arrested with his cargo as it made its way through Greece.

On these sorts of issues the tone of party debates, both inside and outside Parliament, has been noticably more strident over the last decade than might otherwise have been expected. Governments are not merely questioned in an attempt to elucidate their attitude or to obtain more facts. Increasingly during the 1980s the opposition parties sought to criticise not just the Government as such, but rather the Thatcherite Conservatives' approach to external issues, and the underlying philosophy that informed their sense of the national interest. In the characterisation of the opposition parties, the Conservative government lacked personal compassion in external matters just as it did in domestic; it held an excessively shallow and short-term view of what was in Britain's national interests; it increasingly isolated Britain from its partners in Europe by refusing to accept the logic of increased European interdependence; it marginalised Britain from the redrawing of post-Cold War Europe because the Conservative approach could not really accept that the Cold War was over; and it linked Britain too closely to the excesses of Reaganite American foreign policy in a way that diminished both Britain's policy options and its reputation.

The New Right

A large part of the reason for this growing party politicisation of external affairs is to be found in the approach of the parties themselves throughout the last decade and a half. With the election of Mrs Thatcher as leader of the Conservative Party in 1975 the influence of the New Right was in the ascendant. New Right thinking was a mixture of liberal individualism and some of the more traditional conservative values that stressed legitimacy and structures of authority. There is a legitimate debate about how 'new' such thinking really was, but there is no doubt that the New Right assembled such elements into a package of coherent views that could fairly lay claim to being an ideology, on the grounds of its internal consistency and its ability to provide an explanation, however contentious, of the world it wanted to change.[25] Mrs Thatcher never admitted to being an ideologue, but she made no bones about the fact that she was a 'conviction' politician and if her convictions had any intellectual roots then they were in the New Right. The influence of the New Right within the Conservative Party ebbed and flowed throughout the next 15 years and it was, in itself, an evolutionary doctrine that changed over the years of government.

In the heady early days of the Thatcherite Conservative Party, however, the New Right quickly articulated its distinctive views on external issues in the 1970s, though they were not at the heart of the corpus of thinking. The view was sceptical of European unity, suspicious of the Soviet Union and the communist world, unimpressed by multilateral negotiations and inclined to place its faith in a reassertion of the Anglo-Saxon concert of powers as the guarantee of political and economic freedom for Britain.

More important than its views, however, the New Right drew great vitality by being significantly more inclined than in the past to use external affairs as a weapon in the party battle. The Conservative Party has always been noted for the degree to which it employed its reputation for experience and reliability in foreign policy as a positive asset that the other parties could not match.[26] By the 1980s, however, that claim had been transmuted somewhat as the Thatcherite Conservatives appeared to break with the old Macmillan tradition in dealing with external affairs. For now the Conservatives claimed not only that the opposition parties were not fully competent to deal with foreign matters, but also that their approach was all part of a flaccid legacy of the 'consensus era' in which Britain's real national interests were consistently compromised for lack of a sufficiently hard-headed analysis of the real benefits to be derived. Labour Governments, for example, were portrayed as having been consistently duped by the Soviet Union over the £1 billion trade deal of 1975 or the negotiations that established the Conference on Security and Co-operation in Europe. The Helsinki Declaration of 1975 had legitimised Soviet control over Eastern Europe and in return had made only a series of vague commitments to human rights in the Eastern bloc that were easily flouted. It was obvious, in the words of Mrs Thatcher in early 1976, that the Soviet Union was 'bent on world dominance' and exercising its growing power in Vietnam, Angola and even Portugal.[27] Or again, the Seven Power summits between the major developed economies had merely involved Britain in a series of vague economic commitments that either had little effect or else served to restrict the Government's own freedom of manoeuvre in such matters. On the basis of a noticably more assertive and limited interpretation of the national interest, the new Conservatives attacked their opposition unmercifully for their naivety in dealing with foreigners, especially socialist ones.

The Labour Party

From the Conservative point of view, the Labour and centre party opposition could not have reacted to these intellectual assaults more helpfully. The Labour Party moved distinctively to the left in the immediate aftermath of defeat. In itself, this need not adversely have affected either its competence or its image in dealing with external relations. Shifts towards the ideological wings of a party are common in opposition and since all of the major premises of the new Conservatives' approach to external affairs in the 1970s proved essentially unfounded by the end of the 1980s, there is no reason in principle why a leftist interpretation of Britain's external relations could not have been sustained throughout the decade, to be vindicated by the turn of events in so many areas at the end of it. But the party's shift to the left and its subsequent rehabilitation to the centre ground under the leadership of Neil Kinnock was not informed by any clear vision of external policy that took sufficient account of the nature of the international context in which Britain now found itself. Instead it was a protracted bloodletting; an intra-party revolution carried out by the left, followed by a Kinnockite counter-revolution and a series of national and local party purges. The Labour Party allowed itself to be cast as a party that did not understand the *realpolitik* of the external world, could not offer leadership on foreign issues, and was frankly dangerous in its handling of defence. In truth, this was an unfair characterisation and owed much to the injection of confidence that the Conservative leadership enjoyed after the Falklands war. But in such circumstances the longstanding insularity of the Labour Party finally caught up with it during the 1980s.

Throughout its internal power struggle the Labour Party ignored the realities of the growing integration of the world economy and dealt with external events in a confused and vacillating way that lacked either skill or real conviction. This was never more true than over defence. Thatcher governments set the agenda of issues – and targets – and the Labour Party lost no opportunity to attack them, but the vehemence of its attacks never managed to suggest that there was a decisively better agenda available or to reverse the traditional impression that the Labour Party was not at home with foreign or defence affairs. Nor did it manage to convey the impression that it was dealing with defence issues strictly on their merits; defence always appeared to be part of the struggle for dominance within the party. This was demonstrated by the fact that while it was working out its radical defence policies between 1982 and 1987 the Labour Party made very little effort to explain itself to the governments of allied countries who would be intimately affected by them. Nor did it try to integrate its policies even with those of the sympathetic political parties in other European countries so as to present an international socialist alternative to the right wing policies it so opposed. The result was all too predictable. During the opening shots of the election campaign in March 1987, Neil Kinnock visited Washington to put his views on defence to the Americans, while Mrs Thatcher went to Moscow to present hers to Mr Gorbachev. Kinnock spent 30 minutes with President Reagan and failed to convince him; Mrs Thatcher spent 13 hours with Gorbachev, and also failed to convince him. But the Labour leader's trip was regarded as a humiliating political failure while the Prime Minister's was interpreted as a triumphant exercise in power brokerage.

The centre parties

The centre parties, too, had much the same problem. Though they were heirs to a more internationalist tradition in British politics and tried repeatedly to shift the ground of debates in the 1980s to more fundamental issues of foreign and defence policy, they failed to maintain their own unity or to wrest the initiative from the Conservatives.[28] Again, defence and external relations appeared to be matters that divided the two political allies as much as they united them. The influence of David Owen, as a former Foreign Secretary, strong supporter of nuclear deterrence and a believer in the strength of the Anglo-American relationship, constantly clashed with many of the more radical instincts of the Liberal Party, who were distinctly less enthusiastic about nuclear weapons and more attached to a vision of European unity in which the American connection did not loom so large. In the light of the collapse of the Liberal/SDP Alliance, it was not surprising that some of their support should go to the emergent Green Party and even to the Scottish Nationalists. Here were two minor parties that, for different reasons, had uniquely internationalist outlooks: the Greens because environmentalism simply cannot work on a national basis, and the Scottish Nationalists because nationalism on their scale is only feasible in a more devolved version of the European Community. Neither party, however, was able to make any impression on the Conservatives' domination of the external policy agenda.

For all of these reasons, therefore, it is apparent that the 1980s witnessed a consistent erosion in the traditional consensus that is assumed to exist between the two front benches on matters of foreign and defence policy. This should not, however, be overstated. Certainly, changes have occurred but it is entirely possible that such trends may turn out to have been products of the particular circumstances of the parties during the 1970s and 1980s rather than long-term changes in the nature of British party politics. The rhetoric of the party battle in the Thatcherite era also disguised some long-standing consistencies between the two leaderships. The Labour Party in government, for example, despite its distaste for the business of defence, has been characterised by its programmes of higher defence spending in 1947, 1950, and again in 1978; whereas Conservative governments, despite their identification with national security, have been noted for reducing defence programmes in the 1950s, particularly after 1957, again in the early 1980s, and again after 1989.[29] But these trends are not consistent with the public image of the parties. Thus, in the 1987 election campaign the Conservative Government had entered a period where it proposed to restrain further defence expenditure, while the Labour Party pledged itself to reorder defence priorities and spend more money on conventional forces. The public perception, nevertheless remained that voting Labour meant voting for defence cuts and vice versa.[30]

European unity

Party attitudes towards European unity, likewise, appeared to emerge as a front bench tussle in the late 1980s, but in reality the rhetoric tended to disguise underlying similarities. In the period prior to 1975 it was very clear that once the party leaderships had become converted to the idea of British membership of the European Community – the Conservatives in 1960–61, the Labour leadership in 1963 – the political arguments were fundamentally intra-party debates that crossed all the political and ideological boundaries. Anti-marketeers and pro-marketeers joined forces across party lines in some remarkable political alliances and EC issues offered a prime example of the consensus between front benches who devoted most of their political energy on the issue arguing with their backbench colleagues. After 1975 the Thatcher leadership in some respects appeared to mark a change in this, since she brought to the Conservative front bench and then the Government itself a brand of 'British Gaullism' that echoed many of the concerns of the anti-marketeers of a decade previously. This produced a degree of ambiguity and confusion within the Conservative front bench that did not diminish throughout the 1980s. But ironically, this did not really mark a break with the front bench consensus, since in reality it mirrored rather closely – though for different reasons – the ambiguity and confusion of the Labour front bench towards the EC throughout the same period.

During the period of the first Thatcher government when the new Prime Minister was strident in her scepticism at the EC, the Labour Party turned explicitly against the Community as part of its shift to the left. Pro-EC sentiment was only to be found among the Tory 'wets', increasingly relegated to the back-benches, among the disaffected Labour members who were in the process of breaking away to found the SDP, and in the longstanding support for the Community within the Liberal Party. During the late 1980s the ambiguities were compounded. The Thatcher leadership never relaxed its wary scepticism of the European Community and indeed, entered into something of a renewed Gaullist crusade to keep the EC a community of fully sovereign states with Mrs Thatcher's famous Bruges speech of 1988. As a matter of necessity, however, Thatcherite governments were drawn ever more deeply into the thickening webs of European unity so that the Prime Minister presented the spectacle – not as unusual as popularly thought during the 1980s – of being backed half-unwillingly into the further development of the European Community, well beyond the bounds of what she would have regarded as acceptable during the early 1980s. The Labour leadership, meanwhile, after 1987 appeared to rediscover the value of a more positive commitment to European unity in all respects, not merely through the European Community itself but also through its Confederation of Socialist Parties, through which the Labour leadership intended to form links with non-member states, prove itself at last to be a modern European socialist party, and help the emerging democracies of Eastern Europe. Even some Labour left-wingers came, by 1990, to accept the logic of a European currency union, partly for its own sake and partly as a device to criticise Mrs

Thatcher's 'shrivelled view' that preached nothing but 'a seventeenth century version of sovereignty'.[31]

On the face of it, therefore, Britain's attitude towards the European Community seemed to have crystallised by the end of the 1980s into a party political battle that embodied some of the elements present in the debates over defence and South Africa. The Conservative leadership was hanging on to a Gaullist vision of Europe; the Labour leadership had developed an enthusiasm for further European integration. In reality, however, the domestic debate over the European Community remained what it had always been; a cross-party issue that raised problems of intra-party management for both front benches. After the election campaign of 1983 most members of the two front benches and certainly the leaders of the minor parties agreed on the essentials of most EC issues. They supported the signing of the Single European Act and generally subordinated their own particular opposition to some aspects of the EC to a more basic realisation that Britain could not afford to be excluded from the general direction of European politics. In so far as the political argument had crystallised, it had resolved itself into a debate between a predominant group of 'accepters' of the EC – some of whom were enthusiastic, others simply fatalistic – and a minority group of 'resisters' who were determined to oppose what they perceived to be a slide away from the sort of organisation that Britain had originally joined towards a federal Europe. Resisters were a vocal but diminishing band by the late 1980s and were to be found in both major parties in roughly equal proportions, numbering no more than about 50 MPs across all parties.

The *appearance* of front bench struggle was created more than anything else by the character of Mrs Thatcher herself. Her personal commitment to a distinctively Anglo-Saxon view of Britain's role in the world; a frankly conservative interpretation of the changes that have taken place in Britain's international context; and Mrs Thatcher's uncanny ability to take a personal stand on particular issues which served to dramatise the debate and supply her adversaries with irrestible political targets, certainly stimulated vigorous clashes between the Prime Minister and the Opposition. Her stance also gave prominence in the mid-1980s to the 'European Reform Group' of 72 Conservative MPs and then later to the 'Bruges group' of 16 Conservative resisters inside – and a great many more outside – Parliament. This was at a time when the Labour Party's resisters chose to keep quiet so as not to detract from the appeal of Labour's policy review process. But these debates in Parliament were altogether more personal than they would have been in the event of a genuinely inter-party argument. The EC provided much to disagree with in the 1980s, but the fact of its existence and that Britain remained one of Europe's 'big four' powers rendered it an aspect of political reality that effectively elevated it above party political ideologies. It was the character of the Prime Minister and her personal diplomacy that was the real issue between the two front benches, not the EC itself, as was revealed in the combination of factors which led to Mrs Thatcher's resignation in November 1990. Even in the early 1990s when accepters constituted the great majority, it was clear that both front benches would still have to accommodate their respective bands of resisters, who were likely to become more truculent as the evolution of the EC appeared to speed up.

A volatile consensus?

The general question, therefore, as to whether the old consensus between the parties on foreign and defence affairs has now broken down, still remains open. The consensus is certainly subject to more rapid fluctuations and may well exhibit some spectacular discontinuities, as in the case of defence in the early 1980s. But the context in which party debates about external affairs has taken place since 1980 is too complex to allow for easy generalisations. In the first place, a great deal of the debate on most external issues remained a matter of emphasis rather than substance. One of the personal talents of Mrs Thatcher was to make matters of emphasis appear to be matters of substance and to commit herself, in a courageous though populist way, to achieving certain short-term goals. Much of the opposition to government external policies of the 1980s was driven by the fury she excited in those with whom she disagreed. Second, it was one of the paradoxes of the decade that in a curious way these arguments were not all due to Mrs Thatcher's particular style. The ground was shifting under all of the major external issues during these years. Ironically, the debates about her leadership were, albeit half-consciously, debates about Britain's future orientation. In a sense, the differences of emphasis *were* major issues in themselves, since they tended to point towards some fundamental choices that Britain was likely to have to make in the 1990s – how much to value the American connection if it conflicted with all-European aspirations, how to maintain influence as a major power at a time when the value of military force appeared to be declining in the OECD world, how to manage the new diplomacy of complex interdependence, and so on. But if these issues were implicit in some of the party debates of the 1980s, they were seldom made explicit or allowed to emerge as more than short-term, tactical arguments. Third, the fact that the international context was changing so dramatically on almost all fronts effectively changed the terms of debate even on short-term issues in ways that British political parties found difficult to assimilate. With the end of the cold war, the move towards reform in South Africa and the collapse of the explicit Marxist challenge in the region, the dynamism of the European economy, and the rapid erosion of the East-West division in Europe, all of the parties struggled to redefine their objectives over the great issues that had divided them in the 1980s. Britain's imperial legacy and its traditional ability to deal on a world scale had generated a certain indifference to post-war European affairs and to the politics of interdependence. This was reflected for over three decades in the various attitudes of all the political parties. In the 1980s such indifference was exposed as a problem of sheer insularity which prevented any of the parties from coming properly to grips with the new world that was taking shape around them.

The politics of Thatcherism

The development of party politics during the late 1970s and the 1980s, in external relations no less than any other policy area, was dominated by the personality of Mrs Thatcher and the development of what came to be known as 'Thatcherism'. If there is a case for the argument that individual politicians are critical to the nature of external policy-making, then Thatcherism ought to provide it. To what extent, therefore, has there been a 'Thatcherite revolution' in British external policy?

Over three successive terms of Thatcher governments beginning in 1979 the language and appearance of a Thatcherite revolution grew progressively. The most obvious claims that a revolution was under way came from the Prime Minister's camp itself. As leader of the Opposition from 1975 to 1979 Mrs Thatcher in fact made very few statements on international affairs and was clearly more interested in domestic matters. Her statements on international matters were nevertheless revealing, and they reflected a combination of instinct and calculation that chimed in perfectly with the preoccupations of the ascendant New Right within the Conservative Party who were determined to revolutionise British politics. Her instincts leant towards narrowly focused patriotism that was deeply antithetical to communism, infused with a belief in the desirability of Anglo-Saxon power and diplomacy, and sceptical of the ability of entrenched government bureaucracies to stand up honestly for the interests of the nation. In this sense, her instincts were self-consciously Churchillian even though she lacked the wider vision and imagination that informed Churchill's statesmanship. Her calculation, rightly, was that the Labour Government of the time was electorally vulnerable to the charge that it was internationally naïve; duped by the Soviet Union into supporting detente and cutting back on defence, duped by the European Community into paying too much into the Community budget, and duped by the new Commonwealth countries into a fruitless guilt over Britain's imperial heritage.[32]

There were only three significant Thatcher statements on international affairs in the 1975–9 period. In July 1975 it was necessary for the new Leader of the Opposition to take a position on the Helsinki Agreement due for signature in August. With the help of the historian Robert Conquest she drafted a speech that set a characteristic tone in dismissing with some scorn the Labour Government's approach to detente.[33]

The second, and undoubtedly most significant, statement on international matters did not appear until the following year. On 19 January 1976 in Kensington Town Hall Mrs Thatcher offered a general review of Britain's position in the world that attacked all the favourite targets of the New Right. She revealed here the embryo of one source of her uniqueness among post-war political leaders in being simultaneously both anti-Commonwealth and anti-European. But the emphasis of her speech directed most attention to the dangers Britain faced from the communist world. The Soviet Union was only one of her targets, but it was clear that this provided the leading edge of her attack, and it earned her the first and most persistent of her 'revolutionary' images. The Soviet ambassador lodged an official protest about the anti-Soviet content of her speech and *Krasnaia Zvezda* dubbed her the 'iron lady'. She relished the title and declared that she was happy to live up to it. In retrospect, both she, and we, have reason to be thankful for small mercies since other Soviet publications depicted her as a cartoon witch and penned verses about 'Mrs Thatcher, Trouble Hatcher', 'Tory Leader, Cold War Pleader' and, from *Komsomolskaya Pravda*, even the 'militant amazon'.[34] Having indicated through the controversy which followed that she had no time for fuzzy compromise or consensus foreign policy, she returned to the same themes in her third major statement in July 1976 which formed the basis for the publication in October of *The Right Approach*; a document which guided the Conservatives' thinking into the 1979 election.

Like all ideological statements, the Thatcher view and *The Right Approach* was more a systematic reaction to prevailing conditions than a particular initiation of new ones. Mrs Thatcher was not the first leading Conservative to say such things. All of her targets had been individually picked out by other senior party members and both Peter Walker and Julian Amery had already made similar *tours d'horizons*.[35] But by the end of 1976 Mrs Thatcher had established her credentials as the standard bearer for a new departure in external relations. Her Churchillian stance became almost literal, warning of the dangers of appeasement in language that was similarly vivid and determined to emphasise the special role that Britain had to play in helping the United States to fight tyranny.[36] Such Anglo-Americanism was reinforced by the antipathy to the European Community. To be a 'Eurofanatic' was also to be identified with the discredited Heathite wing of the party and to be overly concerned with the problems of 'managing interdependence' was a way of hiding from the realities of power. In future there would be no substitute for patriotic common sense.

On this basis the stage was set for Mrs Thatcher, though she did not initially warm to external affairs, nevertheless to put her own stamp on them. The broad themes of Thatcherite foreign and defence policies were established very quickly. Mrs Thatcher took pride in defending what she interpreted as Britain's interests in the EC, was resolute in maintaining British defence commitments, took clear decisions on nuclear matters, both over the British independent deterrent and over NATO's intermediate nuclear forces, and re-mained staunchly anti-communist in thought, word and deed. She argued through defence policies that she had, in fact, inherited from the previous government – to increase defence expenditure, to support NATO'S dual track nuclear decision, and to proceed with Polaris replacement – in such a way that they seemed to be very much her own policies; argued out on the grounds that 'our way of life' would be put at risk without them, since, 'a bully always goes for the weakest' and the Soviet Union was 'the greatest threat since Munich in 1938'.[37] In 1982 the Falklands War provided more proof, if any were needed, of her resolve to defend British interests. But the Falklands also marked a new strand in the Thatcher approach. As the conflict developed, the rationale for retaking the islands shifted somewhat from defending the Falklanders towards the need to stand up to aggression on behalf of the Western powers. Alexander Haig thought it was 'very evident' that Mrs Thatcher increasingly felt that the issue was a test of Britain's reputation in the world and that she aimed specifically to avoid 'a major setback once again of a western democracy in the eyes of the totalitarian east and the Soviet Union'.[38] The respect accorded by the rest of the world to the Prime Minister after the victory – and the second term in office it delivered to her – in fact became the springboard for the development of her growing seniority among the world's leaders. Reinforced by her deepening sense of partnership with the Reagan Administration, Mrs Thatcher was increasingly inclined after 1983 to travel and to 'speak for' the Western world.

Nowhere was this more evident than in relation to the Eastern bloc. Before 1983, in the words of Hugo Young, 'Moscow played little part in the prime minister's thinking than that of the useful idiot whose manifest wickedness and incompetence supplied the butt she needed'.[39] Now, however, the Thatcher Government was prepared to differentiate between some communist powers and others and to foster better relations with reformers. At this stage there was still an instinctive wariness in her attitude to the Soviet Union. In 1982 she had not attended Brezhnev's funeral. In 1984 she attended Andropov's but did not make any attempt to speak, nor even shake hands, with his successor, Chernenko. Not until Chernenko's funeral in March 1985 was the occasion used for an hour's summitry. This was undoubtedly facilitated by the fact that in December 1984 Mrs Thatcher had conducted her first meeting with Mr Gorbachev when he was heir apparent to Chernenko, heading a Supreme Soviet delegation to Britain. She immediately struck up a 'businesslike' relationship with him that became the cornerstone of a new strand in Thatcherite diplomacy.[40] In the mid-1970s she had sounded a Churchillian siren voice of warning about the perils of totalitarianism. A decade later she had become the most senior statesperson of the western world and was now Churchillian in a different sense; the power-broker who could engage in *realpolitik* diplomacy between tough leaders who commanded strong domestic support. On more than one occasion Gorbachev made a point of cultivating Mrs Thatcher as a way of aiding communication with a Reagan Administration that was frequently in desperate chaos, and Mrs Thatcher certainly did not shrink from arguing Western positions in Moscow that were unpopular with her hosts, or from reminding Washington of its responsibilities to the European allies. Indeed, in the personal rapport that was seen to develop between Gorbachev, Reagan and Mrs Thatcher in the two and a half years from mid-1985 to late 1987 the ghost of the old Grand Alliance made some intriguing appearances. As with all such apparitions, no one was quite sure whether they had really seen it and in any case it had little to do with reality. Nevertheless, it demonstrated a curious strength that Mrs Thatcher, for a while, displayed: she was a major world leader of a less major world power, commanding a diplomatic status somewhat more exalted than that of the country she represented.

The impact of the Thatcher leadership

It is perhaps understandable, therefore, that Mrs Thatcher was inclined to take an expansive view of her impact on British diplomacy and the politics of the Western world. Whether in opposition or in government she had always spoken in terms of 'Britain's destiny' and of the international environment as a 'battle of ideas'. With the revolutions in the Eastern bloc many of her instincts appeared to have been vindicated. During her visit to Japan in September 1989 she addressed the International Democratic Union on the subject of 'the true revolution of the 1980s', in which she claimed some considerable credit for the new world taking shape about her. Her election in 1979, she said, not only put a stop to the winter of discontent in Britain, but helped initiate a process that led to the rise of Gorbachev and the reform of communism – and it was not finished yet. 'As a history lesson', said one journalist who accompanied her, 'it gained in passion what it lost in accuracy'.[41] Two months later she spoke just as passionately in London about the difference between merely 'containing communism' and actively promoting 'the spread of freedom'. The importance of the latter – to promote individual freedom – was as intrinsic to the task of burying socialism in the world as to building the right sort of European Community, or pursuing the proper tenets of free trade.[42] 'The liberal economy is the back-up to political freedom', she repeated yet again in an interview in December 1989, and 'without the liberal economy you would not have the political freedom...its best expression in the English language is set out in the American constitution'. As one of her interviewers commented, she was 'guided by her head towards the commercial significance of the EC, but by her heart to the political/social ethos of the United States.[43] In short, a democratic and economic revolution was taking place throughout the world in which both she and her country were part prototype, part prophetess and part initiator. It was a claim, sincerely made, that ran through Mrs Thatcher's Bruges speech just as consistently as it ran through her speeches on Eastern Europe or her valedictory speech in Westminister Hall for the outgoing President Reagan. There can be no doubt that the Thatcher leadership, from the very beginning, made no apology for claiming to be in the business of revolutionary change.

Another body of evidence that the Thatcher leadership made a dramatic difference to British external policy lies in the administrative reform of the policy-making process that marked the Thatcher governments of the 1980s. Believing in the need to push back the frontiers of the state, the new prime minister began immediately in 1979 to address the question of reducing the size and role of the civil service. Inevitably, this became less a discrete policy than an endless crusade which evolved through a number of different forms, three at least of which represented something of a cumulative strategy. The first was that the public sector should be reduced directly through programmes of privatisation. Between 1979 and 1989 at least 22 major concerns were privatised, from minor components of British Rail to all of the ten Water Authorities. Interestingly, many of these privatised concerns were intimately connected with Britain's external interests – British Airways, British Aerospace, Britoil, Royal Ordinance, Rolls Royce, and so on. Though this did not directly reduce the civil service establishment that handled external relations, it did put beyond the direct control of the government many bodies who would have an important regulatory role in the evolving diplomacy of international economic networks.[44]

The second innovation was the effort to devolve blocks of civil service responsibility directly to newly-created executive agencies. This culminated in *The Next Steps* programme of 1988 under which some 50 individual 'executive agencies' were to be established by 1991 that, in effect, privatised the work of around 200 000 civil servants – around 30 per cent of the total number.

Third, there was a continuing effort to introduce 'managerialism' into Whitehall, 'for those parts of the public sector that could not be privatised or subjected to the sanitizing forces of the market'.[45] Such managerialism encompassed a number of initiatives: the scrutiny of Derek Rayner's Efficiency Unit – 'Rayner's raiders' as Whitehall knew them – who conducted some 266 reviews between 1979 and 1985; the Management and Information System for Ministers and Top Managers (MINIS) which was introduced first into the Department of the Environment in 1980, and then into the Ministry of Defence, as a way of isolating and assessing objectives for every section of a big ministry; and the Financial Management Initiative, launched in 1982, which tried to encompass the range of previous reforms in an effort to devolve financial responsibility and management down to the lowest practical level within each department. None of these initiatives should be regarded as short-term political expedients; they were all built on the premise that the organisation of government was being remoulded for the long-term future. *The Next Steps*, in particular, was regarded by politicians and civil servants alike as a timeless innovation that would probably be adapted, but certainly retained, by any future government.[46]

None of the ministries closely involved in external relations were immune from these reforms. The big spenders such as the Department of the Environment and the Ministry of Defence had large programmes that were ripe for renewed scrutiny, and the politically senior ministries such as the Treasury and the Foreign and Commonwealth Office were regarded by many as long overdue a process of reflection on their own performance. Ministries that were neither big spenders nor intrinsically senior, such as the ministries that were merged into the Department of Trade and Industry in 1983, found themselves in a political vortex whereby they pursued the managerial philosophy but without a settled consensus on the nature and extent of their political responsibilities within a shrinking central government. The Ministry of Defence in particular, as the biggest single centralised spender, felt the smack of managerial government in a series of reforms that tightened the civilian organisation of the ministry by diminishing the powers of the separate armed services, getting a better grip on the extensive procurement budget and cutting staff by almost one-third between 1979 and 1988. Senior civil servants acknowledged that such reforms have been broadly successful, though the MoD was set to be tested to the limits of its management and flexibility by the outbreak of European peace of 1989–90.[47]

Perhaps the most telling body of evidence, however, pointing to the impact of Thatcherism on policy-making was the explicit intention of successive Thatcher governments to produce an *attitudinal* change, not only in the way that government was conducted, but also in the expectations that citizens should have of it. Many writers have observed that Mrs Thatcher displayed an instinctive suspicion of all institutions. Her reputation will forever have to bear Julian Critchley's comment that 'She cannot see an institution without hitting it with her handbag'.[48] But her attitude toward the civil service was more subtle than this. It was, in Hennessy's words, that the civil service 'fell prey to her version of the "guilty men" theory. In Mrs Thatcher's demonology, it is the protagonists of the failed Keynes-Beveridge consensus who have brought Britain low'.[49] The attitudinal revolution has been much discussed by both academics and officials. Few would quarrel that one of its manifest results was to reassert 'the overall primacy of Ministers in relation to the Civil Service'.[50] The Thatcher years saw ministers enacting many policies that officials and interest groups would have argued out of court in the era of consensus. Beyond this, others claim to see the beginnings of a long-term trend that will politicise the civil service by socialising it in the doctrines of the market-place, separate the civil servant from the automatic protection of the responsible minister, and gradually dismantle the class of officialdom that has existed since the Gladstone era.[51] Still others claim to discern a process of *party* politicisation not just in the appointment of sympathisers to head semi-official agencies and Quangos but also within the mandarin class of senior civil servants. After all, the sheer longevity of Thatcher governments saw a complete turnover of permanent secretaries and deputy secretaries throughout Whitehall by 1985. By 1990 the Thatcher leadership had lived through two generations of those senior civil servants in whose appointment the Prime Minister is directly involved. It is inevitable in this situation that such appointments would in some way reflect the leader's preferences.[52] It has to be said, however, that such claims do less than justice to the professionalism of the civil service. Attitudinal change there certainly was; indeed after three terms of Thatcherite government it would be an indictment of British democracy if there had not been. But hard evidence of party politicisation within the civil service is very difficult to find.

The public, too, were urged to understand that their attitudes would have to change after 1979. Companies dealing with the Ministry of Defence should realise that the disciplines of the market *could* be introduced into defence procurement. Businessmen should realise that the government would not win orders for them, even if other governments, and on occasion the Prime Minister herself, tried to do so. The burgeoning number of British travellers abroad would have to learn that in reality there was little the government's consular services could do for them in the event of trouble; the chief responsibility lay with the firms and agencies who sent them. And industries suffering from fair foreign competition would have to become more efficient or die. The government constantly argued that it had a patriotic duty to fight against unfair competition, but an ideological duty to accept the challenges posed by fair competition. Just as the Thatcher leadership claimed some credit for the dramatic changes in international politics, so it made it quite clear from the outset that the new Conservatives were in the business of 'turning Britain around' from its relative decline by reawakening the enterprise culture upon which, it was assumed, British power had originally been built.

Notwithstanding this body of evidence, however, most observers are not convinced that there has been a genuine Thatcherite revolution in external policy or policy-making any more than in any other area. The rhetoric of revolutionary change attaches more to the personal style of leadership displayed by Mrs Thatcher during the 1980s, while the substance of policy was a good deal more pragmatic than Thatcherites would have the public believe. For an academic observer such as David Howell, Thatcherism in office represented 'blind victory' – the obsession with method over substance.[53] For an ex-Permanent Under Secretary at the Ministry of Defence, the language is different but no less forceful: the MoD was left 'leaner, tauter and fitter' by the Thatcherite approach but after seven years of managerialism still with 'remarkably little in the way of defence policy'.[54] If there is a generally accepted interpretation of Thatcherism, it is that the personal leadership of Mrs Thatcher undoubtedly revived the fortunes of the Conservative Party and may have changed the nature of British conservatism. The New Right has given the party fresh impetus during those periods when it needed a boost. But there is considerable scepticism as to whether the same can be said for the country. Quite simply, too much of the

Thatcherite phenomenon relied on the personality and style of the leader.

The personal style of Mrs Thatcher presiding over British external relations is a difficult phenomenon to disentangle, and like that of many leaders, cannot be regarded as particularly consistent. Much of the difficulty arises from the fact that Mrs Thatcher's professed beliefs in personal and economic liberty were frequently counteracted by her (rather stronger) didactic instincts. 'For someone supposed to be engaged in rolling back the "nanny state",' it was observed, 'she suffers from the disadvantage that she is temperamentally one of nature's nannies'.[55] Her style of cabinet government was notably personal, since she was known to conduct as much business as possible with her cabinet colleagues on a bilateral, rather than a collegiate, basis. The role of the staff at Number 10 itself, in the Private Office, the Press Office and the Political Office took on a steadily increasing significance throughout the 1980s. Meanwhile, cabinet reshuffles, both voluntary and involuntary, left the Prime Minister by 1989 with only one of her former cabinet colleagues of 1979. In the event, Mrs Thatcher proved to be critically isolated from her own supporters in the party. Throughout her years in office the role of personal advisers to the leader – the 'inner circle' of friends, party gurus, cabinet colleagues and trusted close officials that all prime ministers have – loomed ever larger in the process of policy-making. Mrs Thatcher had always displayed an aversion to the establishment of Royal Commissions; she abolished the Civil Service Department in 1981, the Central Policy Review Staff in 1983, and came to rely for independent advice more on her own Policy Unit within the Number 10 Political Office, and on the work of trusted think tanks in the private sector. Think tanks, in particular, were seen to have some real influence on the Prime Minister, since they provided an intellectual energy outside the framework of the consensus-minded civil service and university sectors. They floated ideas, provided the leadership with the possibility of 'deniability', and offered reinforcement to many of Mrs Thacher's own instincts. Mrs Thatcher also took to convening task forces on particular subjects, and personal seminars with small numbers of academic specialists, though there was no definite policy rationale to such meetings.

None of this should be regarded as constitutionally unusual, however. All prime ministers tend to behave in such a way, and since Mrs Thatcher established such political longevity and was a self-confessed 'conviction politician', the personalisation of her leadership simply became a more assertive version of what might have been expected in any other premiership that went beyond one continuous term. She certainly increased the influence of the 'inner circle' and was temperamentally inclined to take more notice of it than some of her predecessors, but the circle did not become noticeably more extensive during the 1980s and despite some departmental closures, Mrs Thatcher was no constitutional reformer. There was no attempt to mould the machinery of government more closely around Number 10. What effect she had on government, she had as a result of her personal and political strength and not through any systematic change in the nature of the cabinet system.

She was, in any case, a good deal more pragmatic than her 'iron-lady' image admitted. Though Mrs Thatcher showed herself determined to carry through certain difficult key policies in both the internal and external spheres, and normally did so, she nevertheless also spent a good deal of political energy drawing back from the brink of certain policies, or else moving quickly to counteract some of their effects. She was a prime minister who suffered an astonishing number of tactical defeats at the hands both of her colleagues and her circumstances – though almost never at the hands of her opponents – and yet retained the image of the victor for over a decade. She had the political courage to commit herself personally to the solution to various problems both large and small; from the Falklands War or the determination to break the power of the trade unions, or to get 'my money back' from the EC, to her personal interventions to secure some Bosporus Bridge contracts for British firms, or to persuade the United States to buy a British battlefield communication system instead of the French one they intended to (and eventually did) buy. Indeed, in 1980 it was only with some difficulty that she was dissuaded from taking personal charge of the 'Yorkshire Ripper' murders enquiry when the police seemed to be getting nowhere.[56] Such reckless bravery did not harm her strong image during the 1980s. Her victories won respect and her defeats were generally borne by others. She personally announced very few of the many policy reversals her governments engaged in, appearing less than any other prime minister of recent times in the House of Commons to do battle with the Opposition. Her attitude to Parliament – not without some justification – suggested the high-handedness of the school matron who ventured into the boys' dormitory only to remind them of the time.

Thatcherism and external relations

The Thatcher style in government can be seen to have had two general effects on external policy. The first was that relations between Number 10 and the Foreign and Commonwealth Office – and to a lesser extent the Ministry of Defence – were unpredictable and stormy throughout the 1980s. Mrs Thatcher did not trust the

FCO. 'To her the Foreign Office is like the BBC, full of doubters', remarked Peter Riddell.[57] This was indeed the case and it was immediately apparent that the new leader preferred to define her own attitudes to most external issues. She took the opportunity of the outbreak of the Falklands War to lay a good deal of the blame for British vacillation over the issue at the FCO's door, though the Franks Report of 1983 made it very clear that this was not a sustainable view.[58]

The Ministry of Defence, too, appeared to be remiss at the time for not controlling more effectively its spending plans. For a while after 1982 Mrs Thatcher appears to have toyed with the idea of establishing some sort of Prime Minister's Department that would have circumvented much of the combined bureaucratic weight of the FCO and the MoD, but the idea was quickly dropped.[59] Mrs Thatcher was not really interested in such major structural changes. In some respects relations with Number 10 improved after this, though it was clear that they could not continue on the low level they had reached. They improved partly because both the FCO and the MoD made specific attempts to improve their public and parliamentary images. Both ministries acknowledged that they did not always communicate effectively with the rest of the political world and addressed the problem with some vigour. Relations also improved for the more general reason that the civil service *is* obedient to its political masters and made some of the adjustments in attitude that the government seemed to desire. Nevertheless, differences in emphasis towards important policy goals still remained and as the European Community began to move into a new era in the late 1980s, the 'attitude to Europe' became the focus of more strain, in particular between Number 10 and the FCO, though the Treasury also found itself at odds with the centre on a number of important European issues.

Three people, in particular, seemed to enjoy the trust of the Prime Minister in external policy matters, to the extent that outside observers came to regard them as *de facto* policy-makers on important matters of detail and emphasis: Bernard Ingham, her press secretary; Charles Powell, her private secretary dealing with foreign and defence affairs, and Sir Percy Cradock, her special adviser on foreign affairs. Both Ingham and Powell were deeply involved, presumably on the Prime Minister's behalf, in the final act of the Westland affair in 1986.[60] In 1987, the Foreign Secretary had to battle for a place on the trip to Moscow when Mrs Thatcher made her visit: she intended only to have Powell and Ingham with her for her meeting with Mr Gorbachev, and even then the Foreign Secretary was not included in the select group who met Mr Gorbachev for a private dinner.[61] Later that year some significant differences emerged in the attitudes of the FCO and the Number 10 staff towards South Africa, for example towards the Kagiso Trust, established by South African churches to channel EC money to anti-apartheid organisations. EC officials believed that Charles Powell was, in effect, interpreting British policy toward the Trust over the head of Lynda Chalker, the responsible FCO minister of state.[62] It was Powell, too, who drafted Mrs Thatcher's Bruges speech, which though not necessarily inconsistent with the view taken in the FCO, nevertheless expressed some important differences of emphasis.

As the external issues facing Britain became more critical with the turn of the decade, so the Prime Minister appeared to turn, in adversity, more determinedly to the inner group of advisers whose judgement she had always trusted more than that of the traditional foreign policy establishment. Under the foreign secretaryships of Geoffrey Howe and then Douglas Hurd, the FCO could claim some credit for softening and nuancing those natural instincts of Mrs Thatcher towards external affairs which frequently excited foreign hostility. Indeed, for a time between 1984 and 1987, particularly in relation to the Soviet Union and the conclusion of the Single European Act, it appeared that the FCO had established a more settled and constructive relationship with Downing Street which the Prime Minister greatly valued. The initiative to exploit a new diplomacy with the East had paid off well for the Prime Minister and in the early-1980s it had been British diplomacy that helped restart the European Community on the road to deregulation and increased the status of Mrs Thatcher in European circles. This proved, however, to be only a temporary respite in a constant seesaw of influence at the centre of government. The FCO, the Treasury and the MoD were not overawed by Number 10 and in many ways gained a new ascendancy during 1990 in the battles over the government's attitude to the EC. But the FCO-Downing Street relationship, in particular, remained inherently difficult. Throughout the 1980s the Thatcher premiership created intermittent confusion in the institutions charged with co-ordinating external relations, which on several occasions transmitted itself to the substance of policy.

The second and more important effect of the Thatcher style on the conduct of external relations concerned the instinctive attitude of the Prime Minister toward the external world. Her instincts contained strands that were at once intellectually consistent and temperamentally inconsistent. It has often been observed that Mrs Thatcher represented a characteristic anomaly of the New Right in being a radical reformer in domestic matters but a very conservative Conservative in international affairs.[63] Domestic crusades were directed towards achieving economic modernity, but international crusades were intended to further a revolution that would reestablish the older international order of the mid-twentieth century. In one sense, however, this was a consistent intellectual strand of thought. The international revolution for which Mrs Thatcher claimed some credit in 1989 and 1990 was, in her view, achieved through the domestic example set by the conservative Western democracies during the 1980s. The nineteenth century radical liberalism from which the New Right drew such inspiration, held it as axiomatic that international affairs were no more than a reflection of domestic ones. Peaceful international relations were built on the diplomacy between democratic, free trading countries; and countries could only be truly democratic through the interaction of the economic and political freedom of the individual. If the theories behind Thatcherite politics were predominently concerned with domestic political economy, they were nevertheless also implicit theories of international relations.[64]

On the other hand, the consistency of the theoretical basis underlying Thatcherism should not be overestimated. There was very little in this nineteenth century radicalism that could accommodate the imperatives of modern interdependence, or the contradiction between individual liberty and the integrative forces of contemporary capitalism. Instinctive patriotism frequently clashed with intellectual liberalism in the Thatcherite scheme of things and left the Prime Minister responding in an ad hoc manner to a number of issues that challenged classical liberal assumptions. Above all, Mrs Thatcher's perception of the 'revolution' in international affairs was narrowly focused. It was an anti-communist revolution that seemed to vindicate her natural inclination to uphold post-war atlanticism. But her focus could not easily come to grips with the new realities which thereby took centre stage. The growth of international institutionalisation, the changing role of the state in relation to economic management, international production patterns, or the changing utility of military forces in relations between developed countries, all exposed glaring inconsistencies in the Thatcher view of the world and reduced the 'conviction' politician to the more familiar role of the survivor who drifted from issue to issue somehow keeping the ship afloat each time. The Bruges speech may have represented a vision of Britain's future in the world, but it did not represent an attempt to come to grips with the changing *nature* of world politics, or encapsulate a philosophy that would offer guidance on short-term problems in the reconstruction of a new Europe. Mrs Thatcher was, in any case, too prosaic a leader to spend much time theorising. She knew whose instincts she naturally trusted and placed great faith in her own power of intuition and strength of personality.

To her supporters, the Thatcher style itself provided the element of consistency. Her instincts were to be trusted and the strength of her personality ensured that a hard-headed realism would infuse British policy. For her opponents, the very reverse was the case. Britain's role in the world of the 1990s was rapidly becoming that of an 'Island Kingdom ... drifting on a raft poled into the sunset by a mad queen whose shouts grow gradually fainter.'[65]

In all, it is difficult to conclude either that Thatcherism or Mrs Thatcher herself revolutionised the substance or the making of external policy during the 1980s. The decade was certainly colourful and British external relations would undoubtedly have been different had Mrs Thatcher not enjoyed three consecutive terms in office during those years. There were indeed changes in the rhetoric and the general approach, with many overtones of revolutionary rejuvenation, but the reality of Thatcherism was no more than radical reformism. In some policy areas genuine reform did take place; in others – including most areas of foreign and defence policy – reformism amounted to little more than some much-needed good housekeeping. Moreover, it was good housekeeping carried out in the guise of something rather more fundamental by a conviction politician, and the price paid for it in terms of disruption, internal struggle and the effect on civil service morale, was regarded by some as too high.[66] During the Thatcher era British external relations enjoyed the benefits of a strong political leader, but not necessarily of strong political leadership.

Conclusion

In every other chapter of this study it has been noted that all the most important determinants of British external relations are in process of great change. This is not obviously true in the case of the political leadership given to external relations. It is no surprise that there is certainly evidence of greater volatility in the political climate at almost every level: bipartisanship can no longer be taken for granted; some external policy issues have taken on the character of sensitive touchstones for a series of other attitudes; and for the last two decades there has been a genuine battle of ideas in British politics that has served to polarise inter-party argument. British political debate has certainly taken on a more ideological character.

Nevertheless, the key differences that the politics of the last two decades have made to external relations appear to lie in the tone and style of the parties' stances and in their expressions of internal confusion over some of their long term objectives. Such volatility may, of course, be the prelude to a new era, but it seems more likely that it represents an interval between regular electoral cycles in Britain's stubbornly two-party political system.

The optimistic conclusion is that this indicates a certain stability in the British approach to the external world. Britain might be thankful to have been saved the confusions and swings of intellectual fashion which seem unduly to influence the policy process in the United States, or even to an extent, in Germany. The virtue of the British cabinet system, it could be said, is precisely that it allows a Mrs Thatcher to remain in power for over a decade, to maintain the crusading impetus of a strong leader, and yet to mould Thatcherite foreign policy to the realities of Britain's changing context. And the virtue of the two-party system, it might be added, is that it is based on a political culture which excludes from power a Labour Party that has departed too far from the underlying consensus which still lies at the heart of Britain's view of the world. The 'bipartisanship' described by Vital, Frankel and Barber is still, despite everything, alive and well.

The more pessimistic conclusion, however, is that the major parties have not returned to the old consensus so much as failed to keep pace with Britain's changing circumstances. There is a coincidence in the parties' inability to get properly to grips with Britain's external relations which may pass for underlying convergence but which is better characterised as simply a vacuum. Neither of the major parties has had a clear international perspective over the last two decades. They have reacted to external events and defined appropriate attitudes where necessary. But it cannot be said that either Thatcherism or the socialism of the Labour Party have treated the international environment as anything more than a peripheral concern to their mainstream policies. The early expression of Thatcherism was frankly naive about the real nature of international affairs and the more mature Thatcherite approach of the late 1980s was based upon the actions and experiences of Mrs Thatcher as prime minister. Thatcherism in external policy was seldom more than a series of short-term rationalisations. The stand that Mrs Thatcher took in the Bruges speech – to be an enthusiast of co-operation but not of integration – is regarded by some as revealing a consistent view of the nature of international politics that has kept open a vital strand of argument at a time when Europe is rebuilding itself. But even this is a view that has not shown itself capable of detailed elaboration in the face of reality; the behaviour of Thatcherite governments was always less consistent than the sentiments expressed at Bruges and there is evidence that this issue still opens up deep fissures up to the very top of the Conservative Party.

Meanwhile, the Labour Party has never taken a view of the international environment as something intrinsic to the task of building democratic socialism in Britain. This may seem more strange in the case of a socialist perspective and reflects the fact that the Labour Party had such hybrid and peculiarly domestic beginnings. It never tried, and probably would never have been able, to become an internationalist socialist party.[67] Its conversion to the importance of the international economic environment of the 1990s has been very recent and does not yet overcome suspicions that the Labour Party still feels itself to be on weak electoral ground in dealing with external affairs. The Labour Party attacked the Conservative government whenever it calculated that the government was vulnerable on external issues, but there were no significant examples of the Party voluntarily leading any of its campaigns on an external plank.

Both major parties, therefore, even in a period characterised by a world leader of the status of Mrs Thatcher, have revealed themselves as parochially 'British'. The Labour Party is attempting to become more like a European socialist party, loosening its ties with the trade unions, and embracing more enthusiastically the concept of the free market and international institutions, not least those of the European Community. The depth of such commitments to 'market internationalism' is still in doubt, however, since it is the product of the Kinnockite attempt to divest the party of some of its more entrenched interests, and the party presently has almost no experience of operating within the institutions of Europe. If the Labour Party's links to the forces of international socialism are somewhat tenuous, however, the Conservative Party has become quite unique in Europe. Christian democratic parties in Europe do not view the prospects of neo-corporatism as an intrusion of socialism by the back door; 'but rather accept the case', in Helen Wallace's words, 'for social partnership to go hand in hand with sound economic policies'.[68] All other European Community conservative parties accept the general thrust of the EC's Social Charter, for example, which leaves the British Conservative Party without any significant soulmates in Europe on the most critical issue which defines the state in relation to its own economy and to that of its neighbours.

It is difficult to resist the conclusion that Britain's party politics have not evolved as quickly as the context in which external policy exists, and that there is a considerable time lag between the impact of a rapidly changing reality and political debate about it. More than that, British party politics has been insular by nature, but now is in danger of becoming insulated from major arguments that will have a profound effect on British society. This is chiefly because British politicians find it so difficult to tune into mainstream political debates in continental Europe, and increasingly, in the United States and the wider Anglo-Saxon and Commonwealth worlds also.

8 Conclusion

The attempt to offer a conclusion to any study that is trying to identify trends for the future is necessarily misstated. 'Conclusions' suggest that answers are possible on the basis of the foregoing analysis, but in that case the only conclusion we could draw here would be that British external relations in the 1990s are replete with paradox: the present international context of external relations reinforces old as well as new influences in policy-making; it supports traditional realism as well as modern behaviouralist perspectives; it reinforces both balance of power politics and integrationism, and so on. Given that striking paradoxes can be identified in the confused reality of any state's foreign policy at any time in its history, such a conclusion may be regarded as less than helpful.

Nevertheless, just as the influence of contradictory forces has underpinned so much of the analysis presented here, the prevalence of paradoxical trends suggests that we should at least reconsider some of the basic questions that lie at the heart of the study of policy-making in the 'external relations' field. For the sake of clarity it is possible to organise the relevant questions into those that are predominantly *conceptual*, dealing with our interpretation of the nature of British external relations; those that are *methodological*, being concerned with the study of external relations; and those we can classify as *policy* questions, being concerned with the future choices faced by British policy-makers. In all three categories, the same ghosts of the past and spectres of the future haunt each analysis, albeit in a different range of costumes.

The nature of British external relations in the 1990s

The nature of what we mean by 'foreign policy', 'defence policy' or now by 'external relations' is a fundamental question that has been frequently asked and well-answered by students of the discipline over the years.[1] The answers, however, can never be definitive, for, as we have already observed, foreign policy is at the frontier of constitutional evolution. As the modern state continues to evolve, therefore, the nature of its external relations will reflect that evolution. To understand external relations in the 1990s, therefore, we have to try to identify the key questions relating to the current evolution of the British state as an international actor. Of all those that could be asked, two are particularly relevant to our concerns.

European social integration and national sovereignty

The first question concerns the degree to which European societies – including British society – may be drawing closer and becoming more integrated than the governments which represent them. This issue has been most eloquently raised over the years by William Wallace, who formulated a rhetorical question in 1976 that has run throughout the literature on British foreign policy since: 'how foreign is foreign policy?'[2] For it was clear that in the light of the circumstances of the late 1960s, terminology such as that applied to foreign policy in the developed states could not be used without important caveats. Under the pressures of interdependence and the increasing links between peoples and government officials of different nations, Wallace contended that it was necessary to reformulate the distinction normally made between domestic and foreign societies, particularly within the OECD world. The power of interdependence was pulling people and economic forces together, particularly within Western Europe, and governments were failing to perform adequately because they were running behind the trend. 'Over the whole range of British foreign policy', Wallace had said in 1975, 'established assumptions continued to determine the direction of policy long after the international environment to which they related had been transformed...'[3] His contention was that governments had to grapple with the increasing unity of internal and external political forces. This meant not only that governments must organise their policy-making machinery differently in order to cope with the new range of policy concerns, but also that they must begin to conceptualise their external relations in a different way in order to appreciate what is really at stake in contemporary economic or social policy. It is a theme to which he has adhered with some consistency ever since.[4]

Critics of the Wallace view have pointed out, however, that such pressures of interdependence proved not to work all in one direction. Though the domestic/foreign boundary was crossed much more frequently, it was not always diminished by the crossing. Indeed, frequent 'boundary crossing', in some respects, encourages governments to intervene with regulatory powers and 'nationalise' any transnational phenomenon that appears to be politically significant. Moreover, the right-wing political mood in the leading Western democracies during the 1980s, as we have seen, strengthened the view that the independent nation state was still the most potent form of political – and hence economic – organisation even in an interdependent world. The growing together of societies, after all, was fine where there were no serious differences of opinion. Once differences arose, however, it was by definition the job of governments to clarify the interests of their society and to express those differences. The Wallace view that foreign policy as we had for so long known it was fast disappearing, was therefore challenged on a number of grounds. For one thing, it had been demonstrated in the 1980s that interdependence could not be managed without at least the passive support of nation states. For another, as Wallace himself observed, conditions of interdependence stimulated bilateral as well as multilateral diplomatic contacts which, in many respects, made old-fashioned diplomacy more important than before.[5] Above all, as Alan James has pointed out, even the growing integration of an organisation as potent as the European Community has not diminished its essentially inter-state nature; nor the fact that the members of the Community are still regarded as fully sovereign by other states outside Europe.[6] In other words, the traditional conception of the state – which by definition had to have a foreign policy – was alive and well even in the midst of the interdependence that had so impressed Wallace during the 1970s and 1980s.

The evidence of this study offers empirical support for both these positions, though the nature of the trends described here are likely to provide increasing vindication throughout the 1990s for the position that William Wallace first articulated in 1975. If he was not obviously right then, or if he seemed perhaps too sanguine that the trends of the 1970s and 1980s were all moving in a consistent direction (of which he approved), his analysis nevertheless has turned out to be remarkably appropriate for the 1990s. None of the developments of the last 20 years can be seen clearly to have divested any of the OECD states of their sovereignty. Nevertheless, the deepening complexity of interdependence can be regarded as a quantitative trend that has begun to have the qualitative effects on the existence of sovereignty and the exercise of foreign policy that Wallace outlined. When Wallace wrote about the tensions between British sovereignty and interdependence in 1986, and then about the nature of contemporary European society in 1990, he was able to recognise many of the contradictions and diverse trends of the previous decade without compromising the essential consistency of his erstwhile argument that British society had become a good deal more integrated with its European neighbours than the British government – or the British political elite – cared to recognise.[7]

Over the last decade, therefore, both Wallace and his critics have crystallised the argument over the degree to which economic, social and demographic change in Europe have not only altered the context in which the British state exists but have altered the nature of the British state itself. In 1990 and 1991 the debate was both current and heated as Britain appeared to face some of the very political choices in its attitude to the European Community that were implied in the academic debate. On one side of the argument is the proposition that if the economic and social interests of Britain are to be defended, then the attachment to a peculiarly British version of national sovereignty must be abandoned in favour of a more flexible – and continental – conception of the doctrine which does not equate sovereignty so closely with national identity or political freedom.[8] On the other side is the proposition that this is no more than another approach to European federalism, which is not an inevitable or even desirable development. Europe is witnessing a post-Cold War era in which national identities are stronger than ever, and in a world of such international complexity, national sovereignty is precisely that legal claim which alone can safeguard political and economic freedom for a people.[9] The fact that both these arguments are a mixture of the empirical and the normative merely reinforces the point that these debates exist on the frontiers of the most basic of questions for the future of Britain.

Sources of international political power

A second fundamental question concerning our perception of the nature of British external relations in the 1990s is the degree to which we think that the sources of international political power have changed. Both traditional state-centric realists and a new generation of theorists more concerned with structures of interdependence would probably agree on the prima facie importance of most of the evidence offered in this study. There would be little dispute, for example, that there has been a great diffusion of political power within the international system, as described in Chapter 2. A similar process has taken place within British society, as evidenced in Chapters 5 and 6, not merely by coincidence but in part because the same processes of change affect domestic as well as international society. We can generally agree with Joseph Nye, therefore, that 'power' in the contemporary world is widely distributed by the complexities of interdependence; is determined less by the application of military force and rather more by the magnetism of economic strength, the influence of knowledge and the employment of information to particular ends. More characteristically, it involves financial transactions, investment decisions, and the ability to create regulatory structures.[10]

Where analysts disagree is in the significance of such trends for the state. One view is that the state is bound to be adversely affected by a gradual shift in the manifestation of international political power. For knowledge, information and financial control – unlike military force or legitimate domestic policing – are not activities over which the state has a monopoly, or in which it has even shown great expertise in most societies. Political power, in other words, may have become so intangible and diffused that the state can no longer command a significant preponderance of it in its relations with other internal and external actors.

Against this proposition, Nye himself and, for example, Susan Strange – who must also be counted as one of the most acute analysts of interdependence – have pointed out that at least the United States is still well placed to take advantage of such a transformation in the nature of political power. In the realm of financial and informational power, for example, Strange contends that the United States still possesses 'structural' power within the system: the ability to affect the structure of finance itself by its own independent action. Against this, even a state as financially dominant as Japan, regardless of the fact that it is a net creditor while the United States is the major debtor, can only exercise 'relational' power in its dealings with other actors.[11] Nye's most recent analysis, that the United States is 'bound to lead' in the next century, runs along the same theoretical lines.[12] Even if we posit a development as significant as a transformation in the nature of political power in the international world, therefore, the ability of the United States to continue to act independently in the world is not compromised since it is in a position still to dominate the structures through which political power is manifest.

For Britain, however, as for any European country, there may indeed be a sense in which a transformation in the nature of power leaves it struggling to compete with other actors and trends. Not possessing a high individual degree of 'relational' power in the areas that matter (as Japan undoubtedly does in the area of investment) and finding it impossible to affect the structures of power, except in a collective endeavour, any given European state may be a political entity more different from the United States than has traditionally been assumed. The relational power of the German economy may be quite considerable, as may the British economy in the promotion of financial services. As a group of states, the West Europeans may assume a degree of structural power through their influence in the OECD, the GATT or through the presence in so many diplomatic and economic arenas of the European Community. Even within a collective entity, however, individual European states could not be described as the most important determinant in the exercise of the more subtle and consequential expressions of political power in the contemporary world. Through collective action they may become part of the 'primary structures' of power that Strange has described.[13] But this reinforces the point that such influence may only be possible in such a collectivity. Moreover, these collectivities are historically unprecedented. They are not merely modern expressions of balance of power or alliance politics which would have been familiar to Bismarck or even Churchill, but rather, as this study has indicated, they are part of a new sort of institutional*ism* in Europe that is a mixture of governmental and non-governmental, public and private, activities. For governments that represent some of the 20 most powerful states in a total of more than 160, it is significant that the Europeans cannot exert more individual power in the world.

A hybrid form of sovereignty?

Both of these questions – about the nature of the modern European state and the significance of the transformation in the manifestations of political power – go to the heart of the problem of how we should characterise British external relations in the 1990s. If we tend towards traditional answers to these questions then we will view British external relations as a more complicated expression of foreign policy but nevertheless 'foreign policy' in a recognisable sense: where the state retains sufficient power over its internal and external environment to remain a key determinant in both and a gatekeeper of the distinction between them. The task for the traditionalist is therefore to be sufficiently sensitive to the complications of the modern era and to see through them to the heart of the process whereby the British government still has to safeguard certain values and interests in relation to the external world.

The less traditional view – to which this study leans – is that we may have to reassess the nature of external relations for a state such as Britain in the Europe in which it now finds itself. The defence of values, the articulation of interests, the implementation of policies, and so on, are coming to exist in an arena in which politics at the national level will be only one variant of authoritative policy-making – and in many cases not even the most important. The 'political system' for Europeans (even including the newly-liberated East Europeans) cannot be satisfactorily defined predominantly by the geographical boundaries of the state, or even by a group of states, but must include the evolving institutions of Europe and the more institutionalised behaviour of the OECD world in general and the effects of that on the wider international system. Though this transformation of the salient 'political system' has manifested itself more gradually in the case of Britain for a number of geographical and historical reasons, the evidence of this study suggests that this interpretation is now very difficult to resist. Both pro- and anti-

European integrationists acknowledge the significance of European political structures on our own political processes. The significance for external policy is that as we understand better the relations between highly dynamic societies in Europe, as opposed to those between its governments, our understanding is likely to alter what we consider to be 'internal' and 'external' to our political system.

This interpretation, however, immediately raises the question of sovereignty, as outlined in Chapter 1. According to the logic of most studies of International Relations, sovereignty is indivisible: a state either retains sovereignty by retaining the ultimate right of independent action; or it gives it away and is no longer a sovereign entity since ultimate power lies in other hands. The suspicion grows, however, that a division of sovereignty is precisely what is happening to contemporary states in the Western part of Europe, and that it is tolerated more comfortably by states other than Britain because, as we pointed out, theories of sovereignty are supported by a different constitutional tradition in other countries. Britain may be one of the 15–20 states in the world – all of them European – which are beginning to experience a hybrid form of sovereignty that both adds to their capacity for action but decreases their individual legal authority. This may place them in a more advantageous – and powerful – position than other OECD states such as Canada, or even Japan; but raises questions about their individual legitimacy that non-EC states do not face.

There are several attributes of this hybrid form of sovereignty. First, while a state such as Britain remains the primary focus for the cultural identification of its people, it is not automatically the main focus for their economic interest articulation, their legal redress, or – in certain circumstances – even their personal or moral loyalty.

Second, the collective power of the European states in the world enhances the individual importance and influence of any given European state in its relations with other states and actors. Britain is, therefore, a more influential state in the world within the European Community and as a member of the network of European and OECD institutions than it would be were it not in the EC or were it less deeply enmeshed in the other forms of institutional collectivity. Yet within this deepening network of interdependence – particularly in Europe – there can be little doubt that Britain has surrendered significant governmental powers over taxation, monetary management, transfer payments, and has consented to the effective entrenchment of an external legal code of laws.

Third, Britain can exercise its sovereignty in a very traditional sense in relations with states in the non-OECD world. Its membership of the EC is simply one facet of its bilateral relations with India, for example. But within the EC Britain does not exercise sovereign choice in the same way and can be held to collective decisions it did not vote for, and can be examined by international courts over the propriety of its actions.

Finally, Britain could, whatever the cost, still withdraw from the European Community. In this respect the traditionalist can claim that Britain retains the indispensable element of sovereign choice; no matter that such a choice would now be exceedingly difficult to effect. On the other hand, in or out of the European Community, Britain would discover, like most non-EC European states, that the sheer economic magnetism of the EC group and the rapidly changing nature of all European societies creates *de facto* legal and economic frameworks within which a British government would have to operate and in which British authorities have less than complete political choice.[14]

The European Community is an association of states and is likely to remain so for the foreseeable future. It complements the power of its member governments in the external world while diminishing their legal entitlements to exercise statehood within the Community itself. It is a unique political arena that could not have existed but for the fact that post-war Europe has been in a state of remarkable social and economic evolution. We may now be witnessing the evolution in political thinking that can reasonably be expected to follow such social and economic change. Though sovereignty may, in logic, be indivisible, the political context in which British sovereignty is now set suggests that the logic is deeply compromised. Theories of sovereignty may remain completely valid since they are concerned with the destination of ultimate authority. But such theories have become a poor explanation of the nature of the international world in which Britain finds itself. One of our problems in the study of International Relations is that we have insisted that the theory of sovereignty should also be an explanation of the world as it is, when we have imposed that obligation on few other theories in the discipline.

For the student of British external relations, therefore, the comforting thought is that the nature of the subject is still comprehensible by reference to the traditional texts on foreign policy where we are dealing with Britain's relations with peripheral states and international actors on the fringes, or outside, the OECD world. The disturbing thought is that within the core of Britain's interests, the definitions of our relevant political community, the policy-making arena and the nature of state as opposed to non-state interests have all to be established afresh. Nor will this be a once-and-for-all reorientation of our thinking, since the evidence suggests that the rapid evolution of the influences on external relations has got some way to go yet and that different policy communities, decision-making structures and interest articulation processes will arise in response to different issues.

The study of British external relations

If the nature of our characterisation of British external relations is very much at issue then so is the way in which we should study it. Again, there is comfort here both for the academic traditionalist and the more radical thinker, since the existing basis of foreign policy methodology is vindicated and in some ways deepened, while at the same time it is evident that the methodology should be applied to deeper sets of questions.

Decision-making theories and foreign policy analysis

Existing methodologies for the study of external relations have grown from the development of decision-making theories and then from the more recent articulation of foreign policy analysis.[15] Decision-making and foreign policy analysis have been concerned primarily to develop alternative explanations to state-centric realism and to the characterisation of foreign policy-making as 'rational action' – both of which have had a powerful, if less than precise, influence on academic thinking about foreign policy throughout the twentieth century. Decision-making analysis offered alternatives to state-centric/rational actor conceptions by trying to differentiate between international actors. It was concerned to explain why states differed from other types of important international actor, and why they differed from each other, by much greater reference to the political pressures that bore on state decision-making in foreign policy. States could not be assumed to behave in a certain way merely because they were defined by the observer as a single class of international phenomenon commonly called 'a state' and sharing certain common attributes of other entities called states. An analysis of how politicians make their decisions on behalf of the actor called the state was therefore a vital part of any explanation of the international system.

Decision-making analysis also established a critique of rational actor assumptions in studies of foreign policy that has been developed to a point of some sophistication by the subdiscipline of foreign policy analysis.[16] Traditional conceptions of foreign policy action had been dominated by notions of 'rational action' which were based on an (often implicit) assumption that foreign policy decisions were made by those politicians formally responsible for them as a deliberate and purposeful choice between alternative courses of action.[17] Whether or not the outcome of a 'rational' decision could be regarded as 'right', it was regarded as rational in so far as it was goal-directed action, sanctioned by those political authorities whose job it was to make such choices. Though this obviously describes a major part of any foreign policy process it is far from being the whole story. Foreign policy analysis, therefore, has undertaken a number of critiques of rational action assumptions to expose their limitations when applied to the confusing reality of foreign policy problems. From such critiques it has tried to articulate other models of decision processes which account for those aspects of policy which are clearly not particularly purposeful or which are not undertaken by those politically responsible for foreign policy. It has developed a series of models of policy-making drawn from a number of sources which look at administrative and bureaucratic forces that influence the process, the nature of 'decision' itself in a world of routine action, the problems of policy implementation, and the extent of meaningful choice that is open to senior politicians even when they are aware that important decisions have to be confronted.[18] Chapters 4 and 7 offer a good deal of material that would fit 'non-rational actor' models of policy-making. Perhaps most important, foreign policy analysis has also gone some way towards an understanding of how these models should be used in relation to each other. For though they are characterised as 'alternatives' to rational actor decision-making, foreign policy analysts do not assume that rational actor models are 'wrong' or that any other model of policy – organisational politics, incrementalism, or whatever – is more 'right'. They are all facets of a complex reality and the trick for the student of foreign policy is to be able to employ a combination of them in order to ask the most perceptive questions according to the type of policy issue under discussion. Some issues will be more explicable in terms of rational actor assumptions, other in terms of bureaucratic politics assumptions; others will be explicable by both models at different stages of the policy process. The sensitive policy analyst must keep all the alternative models available all of the time.

None of this effort is wasted in analysing British external relations in the 1990s. The pluralism of the more modern approaches is greatly to be welcomed, as is the fact that it has been built on an attempt to make explicit a series of assumptions that had previously been left implicit. Modern approaches acknowledge their own limitations and – mercifully – do not become embroiled in fierce methodological arguments for the soul of the discipline. The simplistic debates of the 1960s and 1970s between 'traditionalists' and 'behaviouralists' which confused methodological with substantive arguments in a sterile struggle for predominance, have given way to a more mature discipline in which it is generally acknow-ledged that the contradictory nature of international politics demands a large degree of theoretical pluralism. For these reasons foreign policy analysis and decision-making theories have proved to be particularly appropriate to the study of Britain in its modern inter-national context. As Richard Little, among others, has pointed out, the study of contemporary British foreign policy and the questions that both analysts and policy-makers choose to ask about it, bears directly upon the major political choices that Britain now faces.[19] To understand that British policy-making in relation to economic issues in Europe is becoming less explicable as 'rational actor' choices and is increasingly disaggregated, for example; or to attempt a char-acterisation of the nature of the European interdependence of which Britain is a part, is both an academic and a policy issue of some importance. The foreign policy analyst can be congratulated for being both modern and relevant in the 1990s, and policy-makers – socialised into polite scepticism at the usefulness of academic debates – would do well to take more notice of what they have to offer.

The need for an interdisciplinary approach

On the other hand, the study of British external relations in the contemporary world also demands that the insights developed by foreign policy analysis and decision-making studies be applied to new and deeper issues. The questions raised by the material presented in this study all suggest that an interdisciplinary approach is necessary to provide adequate answers. Some understanding of economic analysis, legal and institutional studies, social studies, sociology and political geography, even applied technology, as well as the relationship between political studies and international rela-tions will be increasingly necessary to an understanding of British external relations. Interdisciplinary analysis, of course, represents something of a rallying cry throughout the humanities. Few acad-emics would argue against interdisciplinary approaches: that would be like arguing for a narrowing of knowledge. But few of us possess the personal capacities to operate easily within so many disciplines and few have been able to make interdisciplinary approaches work satisfactorily. It is relatively easy to accumulate *multi*disciplinary perspectives on an issue but extraordinarily difficult to integrate them into a genuinely *inter*disciplinary whole that is more than the sum of its parts. Nevertheless, the insights to be gained from the promising development of traditionalist, and less traditionalist, methodologies outlined in Chapter One and of foreign policy and decision-making analyses mentioned here, are only likely to remain relevant if they can address some rather new questions.

If the nature of 'British external relations' and even of 'sovereignty' is at stake, then one key question concerns the way in which we delimit the decision-making system to be analysed. It is not sufficient to regard it as the national government, albeit heavily influenced by its external environment. This study suggests that on many issues – though not all – the politicians charged with taking decisions for Britain are not all British, and the 'system' to which they relate is not all national, or even an accumulation of national systems, since it also involves a high degree of international institutionalisation. The foreign policy analyst, in other words, cannot be merely a student of British politics who happens to adopt the 'foreign' area of governmental activity as a speciality, or even a student of international relations who happens to concentrate on Britain.

Second, the analyst must be prepared to study economic, social and legal structures at national and international levels in order to appreciate the nature of the decisions that are being analysed and the composition of the decision-makers – both politicians and officials. Foreign policy analysis has always recognised the importance of such structures as part of a more complex 'environment' in which modern decision-making takes place. But this is predicated on the notion that the 'decision' to be taken is still essentially national. For the 1990s this is likely to be true in a smaller proportion of cases. Decisions that affect Britain are increasingly both 'international' and 'intersectoral' decisions which have to be arrived at by an international group of politicians and officials and which are intrinsically matters that cannot be characterised as simply 'economic', 'legal', 'social', or 'regional', and so on. British politicians and officials have an input to these decisions, of course, but if the analyst is looking for the precise point of decision, or the main channel for the flow of policy, or the mechanism of effective implementation, then it will not automatically be found within the constitutional framework of national government. What used to be 'the environment' of policy-making for a European state such as Britain is increasingly coming to represent the policy-process itself.

A third set of questions that must be confronted concerns the way the analyst defines what external relations issues are about. If William Wallace is correct in his analysis that European societies are moving together without necessarily generating a federal structure, then several key concepts have to be re-examined.[20] If Wallace is wrong, then the present agenda of foreign policy definitions would continue to apply. Or if Europe *did* move to a genuinely federal structure, then the same definitions would continue to apply at a higher level of government. But Wallace suggests an untidy reality, with which this study is in accord, that we are facing a new sort of political process throughout Europe. Some redefinitions are already on the public agenda. 'Defence policy' is now regarded as more intimately connected with the concept of 'security' which has wider and more diplomatic and institutional overtones. Defence policies are commonly regarded as national responsibilities – even 'NATO defence policy' was a harmonisation of national positions – whereas 'security policy' is more difficult to define and certainly wider in scope. The analyst of British security for the future has to concentrate on a number of European and international structures in order to give the term some sensible meaning. The values underlying concepts of security are also more contestable than those which underpinned concepts of defence.

Another redefinition on the public agenda is the meaning of the terms 'integration' or 'integrationism'. It was conceptually easy for Britain to stand aside from the original establishment of the European Community since the founders spoke so clearly about the federal Europe they envisaged, which was anathema to Britain at the time. The argument throughout the 1970s and 80s within Britain about its relationship with the EC was carried on in very much the same terms. But it is now clear that 'integration' in Europe is neither what the founders wanted nor what the British in the 1950s feared. It is a rather different political *and social* process which intimately affects our relations with other societies and cannot be satisfactorily defined by reference to the concept of integration as developed so far.[21]

Other redefinitions appearing on the public agenda concern the relationship between 'environment' and 'economic development'; or between the role of the 'international market' and the concept of 'social democracy' in Europe; or over the definition of 'public accountability' in a system where national authorities are already being bypassed on a regular basis; or over how accurate it is now to classify institutions into 'sub-national', 'national', and 'international', when so many of them operate in the same policy arenas. To tackle any of these problems requires an appreciation of the external relations of British society that takes account of different intellectual disciplines. If we are to understand the implications of, say, security policy, environmental policy, or social policy in the European context of the next decade then we have to cast our intellectual net far more widely than in the case of policies formulated outside the context of the European/OECD world.

These conclusions may appear to place impossible burdens on a generation of students interested in British external relations. Too much has become relevant and the capacity of any researcher is necessarily limited. Nevertheless, the fact that we cannot scale a mountain does not invalidate our appreciation of its size or the reality of its presence as we survey it from ground level. More to the point, an awareness of the fact that we are moving into an era in which foreign policy analysis will face critical tasks of redefinition, driven as much by European social as by political evolution, constitutes at least an optimistic roping-up for the attempt.

British policy-making in the 1990s

Finally, this study also suggests a series of policy questions that have arisen with greater force over recent years. Our concern here is not to address a 'policy agenda', which in any case will alter from year to year, but rather to indicate some of the underlying questions that the 1990s pose for policy-makers, their reactions to which will condition the range of credible choices likely to be perceived when they do face their immediate agendas. It is eloquent testimony to the Janus-like nature of British external relations that whereas the conceptual and methodological sections above suggest that new questions have to be faced, debate over more specific policy matters raises time-honoured questions, but now suggests that, for the first time in half a century, dramatically new answers are possible and necessary.

After the Cold War

One major issue concerns the reaction of British policy-makers to the ending of the Cold War in Europe. This is more important for Britain than for most other European states apart from Germany. For the Cold War not only provided a unifying assumption that underlay so many of the international organisations in which, as we have seen, Britain has had so much of a stake. Given that Britain's conception of security has revolved more around matters of defence and the provision of military force, the politics of the Cold War provided an effective vehicle for British influence that often exaggerated the real power of the country. In both war and peace, from Korea in 1950 to the new *détente* with Eastern Europe in 1984, Britain's status as a staunch but skilful player in the politics of the Cold War enhanced its international reputation and strengthened the domestic consensus behind its defence and foreign policies.[22] In particular, the Cold War provided a bedrock rationale for the Anglo-American 'special relationship' which was such a prerequisite for the success of British diplomacy. The Cold War also simplified for Britain its attitude towards European institutions. Britain was a completely loyal founder member of all the relevant security organisations in Europe and as such was committed to the collective defence system that had evolved around them. It reserved the right to exercise large measures of discretion in its attitudes to all other economic and social organistions in Europe.

Each of these stances reinforced the other; the Anglo-American relationship made it imperative to safeguard collective defence arrangements and raised serious questions over the wisdom of Britain's participation in any institutions that appeared to embody 'French Europeanism' which might undermine transatlantic relations. Similarly, the organisational structure of Western Europe which upheld such a clear distinction between security and economic/social institutions played to British strengths in reinforcing the special relationship with the United States, since security issues were naturally more consensual than economic matters.

The future of European security

The ending of the bipolar Cold War (even if there is no guarantee that other forms of Cold War will not arise) poses fundamental questions in both of these areas. In the first place, British policy-makers have to confront a Europe in which the institutional boundaries are now very soft and permeable. British policy-makers have a natural predeliction to hang onto NATO. This they can do, but the fact remains that NATO will probably play a more specific – and quite possibly smaller – role in the security of the continent in the future. If, as we have pointed out in Chapter 5, security in Europe is likely to involve the pursuit of economic goals to a much greater extent then the institutional boundaries between NATO, the Western European Union and the European Community, backed up with some of the diplomatic authority of the United Nations and the Conference on Security and Co-operation in Europe (CSCE), will have to overlap to an extent that, in the past, has tended to make British policy-makers nervous. The political debate in Britain has looked at the future of Europe as a matter of stark choice. On one side is a Thatcherite view of a Europe as a modern balance of power; a Europe that 'should be *free*, politically and economically. And it should be *open*.'[23] On the other side is an argument that we must use the European Community as the only vehicle capable of shaping an integrated security approach to such a complex future as we face.[24] But British policy-makers face a future in which balance of power security politics are very likely to make a reappearance, particularly now that Germany is united, satellite states are free of communist control, the Soviet Union has withdrawn from its position in Eastern Europe and the United States has reappraised its security interests in

Europe. In a multipolar Europe there is bound to be a sense in which some individual powers are 'balanced' against others. On the other hand, this will be a balance of power that works through an unprecedented degree of institutionalisation within the region, which is driven by economic rather than military power, and in which countries, other than the United States, already find it virtually impossible to engage in unilateral action on any major security issue.[25] The evacuation of one's own nationals stands as the only likely example of effective unilateral action in the security sphere of the 1990s, and even this is probably best achieved multilaterally.

British policy-makers, therefore, have to try to define an attitude to the institutional development of new European security that somehow preserves what is best within NATO without inhibiting the evolution of other organisations and structures. This is not easy to imagine, since commitment to NATO, with its inherently trans-atlantic basis, makes it difficult to express as enthusiastic a commit-ment for other forms of organisation in which transatlanticism does not figure so largely. If NATO was an alliance that 'entangled' the United States in Europe, and if one assumes that the active involve-ment of the United States is necessary to any future European security order, then the prevailing British approach is probably right in fearing that the United States will not be so easily or cheaply 'entangled' in anything that emerges from this post-Cold War Europe. On the other hand, the European political agenda has been moving at breakneck speed in the last decade and does not seem likely to take a breather for a while yet. If European political institutions are regarded as *capable* of bearing the substantial economic, military and diplomatic burdens of European security; if a hybrid can be devised which marries together some of the func-tions of NATO and the EC and anchors them to the political legitimacy that could be derived from the CSCE or UN structures; then it would be a mistake to try to preserve the neat distinctions between security and economic organisations that Britain has hitherto understood. British policy-makers have to question whether they can play for both outcomes at once: preserving NATO as far as possible in an effort to 'wait and see' what else transpires. At root, this may reflect an inherent British discomfort at the prospects of the growing European institutional*ism* we have described, as opposed to the discrete security institutions within which Britain has operated so effectively.

Anglo-American relations

This question is intimately connected to the second problem: the response of British policy-makers to the future of the Anglo-

American relationship. The political debate on this matter in Britain over recent years has been generally sterile and has revolved around assertions of whether it does, or does not, or still does, or ever did, exist. It is evident that there is a distinctive relationship between Britain and the United States, but it exists at the top and bottom with very little in between. At the top, the common language and a degree of shared friendship and culture between leaders has clearly provided Britain with some extra diplomatic leverage with US policy-makers. At the bottom, there is a degree of detailed co-operation and understanding between the armed services of the two countries and their intelligence organisations. It is difficult to pinpoint anything else, however, that would indicate that Britain is consulted more frequently on a day-to-day basis, or that it enjoys concessions not available to others, or that it possesses more diplomatic influence on European issues than it is entitled to, given the natural importance of Germany.[26] It is difficult, in other words, to detect quite how the Anglo-American relationship translates into general practice, though it has the capacity to be reasserted at certain times and over rather particular issues, as happened in the military deployments in the Gulf during 1990–91.

For British policy-makers, however, the question is not whether or not a special relationship exists, or indeed what effects it may have, but rather how they perceive the future role of the United States in Europe, not only from security, but also from economic and social, points of view. Again, the realistic choice may not be to attempt to hold on to the traditional Anglo-American relationship in the way that Mrs Thatcher tried to, as if it still represented one pillar of a global orientation for Britain that offered an alternative to a more European orientation. In a post-Cold War world, the realistic choice is more likely to be between the different ways in which Britain should pursue its relationship with the United States from within the structures of European institutions. In this way, the intangible elements of the Anglo-American relationship – the very things that make it an elusive political phenomenon – can be a source of strength. For in the situation of complex interdependence we have described, the art of successful diplomacy depends on the ability to create management structures which can span security, economic and social arenas, encompass such complexity and channel it to collective purposes. Success is therefore dependent on the ability of governments to generate a high degree of mutual trust, effective communication, tacit understanding, and co-operation at a low political level. In other words, the management of interdependence puts a premium on the less formal political processes that the Anglo-American relationship has generally embodied. Given the dynamic nature of European interdependence which draws Britain further into its web, the Anglo-American relationship – whether 'special' or not – has the potential to be one of the vehicles for the effective political management of the transatlantic elements of modern interdependence. For this to be the case, however, British policy-makers would have to take an explicitly integrative, rather than a separatist, view of the future of Anglo-American relations within a strengthened European Community, and be prepared to try to diversify the working practices of the relationship away from military and intelligence issues.

Britain and European politics

The ending of the Cold War has plunged Britain more deeply into the various arenas of European politics than at any time in its modern history. The politics of European defence co-operation, for example, for over 30 years were concerned to improve the management of NATO. Defence co-operation in Europe was an intra-allied issue at which Britain was a useful player. Since 1987, however, it has become one of the key variables in the attempt to construct a new all-European security order; an aspect of security management for the whole continent rather than a matter of good housekeeping within the alliance. Or again, the reassessment by the superpowers of their interests in Europe has placed the emphasis on their economic relationships within the continent. This, too, embroils Britain in the more general debates over the future of European integration, since its hitherto stable relationships with both superpowers are becoming less militarily-based. Security in Europe after the Cold War goes to the heart of what we mean by 'Europe' as a political, and even a geographical, entity.[27] The Cold War gave Europe a very specific definition. The ending of it raises disturbing questions about the definition and strength of British interests in the continent that will emerge during the 1990s.

Policy-making and international economics

The ending of the Cold War represented a dramatic change and posed manifestly important problems for British external relations. This study also suggests, however, that the internationalisation of economic forces has raised equally profound questions for the policy-maker. Chapter 7 described the way in which the approach of Thatcher governments to the relationship between the domestic and international economies was consistent only in a tenuous and vague sense. In most specific respects it was marked by great uncertainty and vacillation which translated eventually into political weakness both for the country and its leader. British politicians, therefore, have to address yet again the matter of the most appropriate relationship between government and the economy and the government's responsibilities for providing the appropriate economic infrastructure. But in the 1990s the influence of the external world on the government-economy relationship is more marked than it ever was in 1979. There is far less scope for politico/economic experiment, from either wing of British politics, and the realistic choices lie in the debates that take place among Britain's international partners regarding the role of government in modern economies. Industrial or regional policy, for example, are explicitly internationalised within the European Community and to a lesser extent within the frameworks of the Group of 7 or the GATT. More illuminating, education policy is a national responsibility and is likely to remain so, but it is a policy that will be tested in the international arena. Any British government has now to bear in mind that its population will be in direct economic competition with other educated populations in a world in which the power of information and applied knowledge looms ever larger.

This is not to make any particular recommendations as to Britain's most appropriate economic policies. The point is rather that policy-makers have to articulate their choices within an international trend of thinking among governments and powerful economic actors where consensus has so far proved elusive. Other governments have also been ambiguous about their relationships with the economy. Nor have they many answers to the problems of international debt, to the sudden collapse of so many socialist economies at once, or to the deepening problems of the poorest countries of the world who have so little influence with the rich. Policy-makers face the dual problem of confronting an international economy which is at once immensely powerful and yet lacking in political direction. It has the innate power to veto and spoil national economic solutions to problems, as the socialist states and so many Third World countries have discovered to their cost, without offering obvious alternatives.

Policy-makers who have to deal with the workings of the British economy, therefore, must begin by facing a series of questions regarding, first, the degree of regulation, encouragement, protection, or intervention that should be applied to international capital; and second, the most appropriate political organisations through which they should be implemented. Without the Cold War, or the Bretton Woods system underpinned by its Keynesian principles, and without the economic leadership of the United States (at least since the early 1970s), it is not clear what political purpose the international economy is to serve. The relationship between economic growth and distribution is not clear, nor is the definition of economic growth itself. The failed socialist economies are desperate to create a market, while the successful market economies are concerned about the abilities of the free market to deliver politically desirable goods and services.

In this situation policy-makers should be forgiven for feeling highly constrained and unable to do more than react on a very short-term and *ad hoc* basis. Nevertheless, as an economy that depends more on international trends than most, Britain has a high interest in trying to promote something akin to the consensus among the 15 or so powerful economies of the world that existed during the Bretton Woods era. The Thatcher approach which boasted of a deregulating economic revolution represented a somewhat shaky convergence of separate views among like-minded Western leaders in the conservative 1980s that was, in any case, based on separate national perspectives. Policy-makers could choose to continue in this vein, since it allows them to survive in an uncertain world and a great deal of the form of inter-governmental co-ordination can pass for the substance.

The minimalist approach of British governments of the 1980s towards the further integration of Europe was an example of this trend of thinking: the Single European Act was a useful measure as long as it was concerned with free trade and deregulation. But it was inappropriate insofar as it became a vehicle to extend the competence of the European Community over other economic and social matters. In the 1990s, however, whether for good or ill, the EC has taken upon itself the task of trying to provide some of the deeper consensus on the purposes and procedures of international economic management that had been lacking for a decade and a half. British policy-makers may or may not agree with the direction it is taking. To regard the debate as illegitimate, however, would be simply self-defeating for a country that is intrinsically part of the European Community. If the collapse of the Cold War has pitched Britain into the rough and tumble of an all-European security debate, the triumph of capitalism has done the same in relation to an all-European economic debate. Britain does not have a realistic choice of theoretical or ideological detachment from it. Europe of the future will be an untidy spectacle. An EC with 15 or more members is bound to be a multi-tiered organisation, however much it protests the reverse, and the EC does not represent the totality of European economic management in a 'liberated' Europe of 30–40 states of vastly different size. The diversity of states is already overshadowed by the scope and diversity of institutions in Europe, and for economic purposes, the United States has to be regarded as a European power, albeit outside the EC. Nevertheless, the EC represents a core of politico-economic thinking that will influence such debates throughout the developed world. Its rhetoric is far more grand than its achievement, but it is addressing those particular underlying questions concerning the relationship between government and the economy that had become acute at the end of the 1980s and which Thatcherism had effectively ignored by placing an implicit and excessive degree of political faith in the economic market.

Britain's world role

A final question that policy-makers have long faced and which now confronts them anew is the problem of defining a 'role' for Britain in the world. This is more than an academic parlour game since the self-perception of an external policy elite will play a part in its view of the issues with which it deals, and is a vital ingredient in the support that both native and foreign publics will accord to policy. Having taken the decision to withdraw from East of Suez in 1967 and concentrate on the European arena of its foreign and defence relations, the British role that emerged in the 1970s was one that might be described as an 'Atlantic manager'. Having entered the European Community in 1973 the Foreign and Commonwealth Office and the Ministry of Defence could take some pride in their ability thereafter to represent a special sort of Western power; both transatlantic and European, understanding the politics of collective defence and rapidly mastering the politics of European bargaining; able to operate effectively in a number of different negotiating arenas simultaneously. It was a congenial self-image to have and a useful international role to perform, even if it sometimes ran into a certain amount of party political opposition from the anti-EC left and the pro-Empire right.

This conception of a role came under severe scrutiny in the 1980s, however. One reason was the scepticism of Thatcher governments at the ease with which the external policy elite had slipped into the European aspect of the role. There was considerable suspicion among those around the new Prime Minister as to whether such a conception was sacrificing tangible British interests in the pursuit of a comfortable abstraction. The result was a decade of great uncertainty in the general orientation of British diplomacy where the political leadership tugged in one direction and the force of events pulled inexorably in another. As we pointed out in Chapter 4, the policy-making process never let slip its grip on the details and the co-ordination of external policy but there was a deeper hiatus that lasted for several years as to the real direction of British diplomacy. Second, this conception of a role also became more difficult to sustain as international events increased the convergence between the business of NATO and the European Community and increased the diplomatic and economic influence of other European powers with the United States. By the end of the 1980s there was no discernible agreement as to the British role in the world, either inside or outside the country. For some, Britain had reverted to being a minor world power under the assertive leadership of Mrs Thatcher and was keeping open the argument for national freedom against European federalism. For others, Britain had become an obstructive power in Atlantic politics, magnifying European differences and preventing the Europeans from dealing with the United States from a position of unity. For others, Britain was simply an over-extended, pragmatic power that had become lost in the new Europe of the 1980s.[28]

All of these positions were magnified by the events of 1989–90. With so much more to play for – a new 'Balance of Power' Europe of 35–40 states, a 'widened and deepened' European Community, or a new approach to 'world order' based on the co-operation of the superpowers – the conception of an 'Atlantic manager' role could be regarded as both too narrow and frankly anachronistic. Just as it was not clear what international role Germany, France, Japan, or even the United States would adopt in the politics of the post-Cold War world, so Britain suffered from similar uncertainties, while at the same time showing greater tentativeness over the international context in which it expected to operate. An 'Atlantic manager' role is still conceivable for Britain and it possesses considerable attributes with which to play it, but the institutional ground has shifted so much that it would have to be played in a different way and could not be based essentially on the NATO experience, supplemented by greater involvement in European economic management. If anything it would have to work on the reverse principle.

In the 1950s Britain 'lost an empire' but had 'not yet found a role'. In the 1970s, Britain accepted the loss of the empire and 'found a role'. The danger is that in the 1990s we would have to conclude that Britain had lost an empire, found a role, and then lost that role.

Notes

1 INTRODUCTION

1. Good modern expressions of realist thinking can be found in Hedley Bull, *The Anarchical Society*, (London: Macmillan, 1977); Martin Wight, *Power Politics*, 2nd edn, (Harmondsworth: Penguin Books, 1986); Kenneth Waltz, *Theory of International Politics*, (Cambridge, Mass.: Addison-Wesley, 1979); John Garnett, *Commonsense and the Theory of International Politics*, (London: Macmillan, 1984).
2. There are a wealth of behaviouralist and process approaches to contemporary world politics. Some of the more explicitly theoretical such works of recent years are, Robert O. Keohane and J.S. Nye, *Power and Interdependence: The International Sources of Domestic Politics* (Boston: Little Brown, 1977); Richard W. Mansbach and J.A. Vasquez, *In Search of Theory: A New Paradigm for Global Politics*, (New York: Columbia University Press, 1981); Gavin Boyd and G.W. Hopple, (eds), *Political Change and Foreign Policies* (London: Frances Pinter, 1987). The most recent formal behaviouralist expression is that by Michael Nicholson, *Formal Theories in International Relations*, (Cambridge: Cambridge University Press, 1989).
3. See, Alan James, *Sovereign Statehood: The Basis of International Society*, (London, Allen & Unwin, 1986).
4. Wolfram Hanreider, 'Dissolving International Politics: Reflections on the Nation State', *American Political Science Review* 72(4), (1978), pp. 1276–87.
5. Hedley Bull, *The Anarchical Society*, op.cit., p. 279.
6. James, op. cit., pp. 266–7.
7. Basil Williams, *The Whig Supremacy 1714–1760*, 2nd edn, (Oxford: Oxford University Press, 1960), p. 8. For a distinctively more modern view of the same phenomenon see Paul Langford, *A Polite and Commercial People: England 1727–1783*, (Oxford: Oxford University Press, 1989), pp. 700–25.
8. For a good discussion of the development of sovereignty in British political philosophy see Ellen Kennedy, 'The State and Sovereignty' in Lawrence Freedman and Michael Clarke (eds), *Britain in the World* (Cambridge: Cambridge University Press, 1991).
9. Enoch Powell, 'Towards a Europe of Sovereign Nations', *The Independent*, 6 September 1989, p.12.; Richard Ritchie (ed.), *Enoch Powell on 1992*, (London: Anaya, 1989).
10. Dahrendorf, Ralf, *On Britain*, London, BBC Publications, 1982, p. 133.

11. Paulo Cecchini, *The European Challenge*, (Brussels: European Community, 1988).
12. On the historical development of sovereignty see F.H. Hinsley, *Sovereignty*, 2nd edn (Cambridge: Cambridge University Press, 1986). Also Edmund Morgan, *Inventing the People: The Rise of Popular Sovereignty in England and America*, (London: Chatto, 1989).
13. On the relationship between Britain's present conditions and the concept of sovereignty see, William Wallace, 'What Price Independence? Sovereignty and Interdependence in British Politics', *International Affairs*, 62(3), (1986), pp. 367–89.

2 DIVERSITY AND HOMOGENEITY IN WORLD POLITICS

1. See, Henry Kissinger, 'East Asia, the Pacific and the West: Strategic Trends and Implications', in *East Asia, the West and International Security: Prospects for Peace*, Adelphi Paper 216(1), (London: International Institute for Strategic Studies, 1987), pp. 3–4.
2. An international 'regime' may be defined as a set of institutional and non-institutional arrangements, among both governments and other organisations, which regulate some aspect of international life according to a consensual notion of common interests. Examples of international regimes in action would include the air traffic control regime, the nuclear non-proliferation regime, or what might be termed as the international financial regime. Clearly, some regimes are more effective and all-embracing than others.
3. Compare for example, Robert Gilpin, *The Political Economy of International Relations*, (Princeton: Princeton University Press, 1987), pp. 364–78; Susan Strange, 'The Persistent Myth of Lost Hegemony', *International Organization*, 41(4), (1987), pp. 551–74.
4. Paul Kennedy, *The Rise and Fall of the Great Powers*, (London: Fontana Press, 1989), pp. 601, 681.
5. 'The Times 1,000, 1988–89', *The Times*, 17 November 1988, p. 28. Companies are measured by size of turnover.
6. Gilpin, op. cit., pp. 386–8.
7. Seyom Brown, *New Forces, Old Forces, and the Future of World Politics*, (Boston: Little, Brown, 1988), pp. 161–3.
8. Susan Strange, *States and Markets*, (London: Frances Pinter, 1988), p. 82; Gilpin, op. cit., pp. 252–3.
9. Stephen Wilks, 'Industry in Western Europe', *Europe 1989*, (London: Europa Publications, 1988), p.34.
10. *Sunday Times*, 12 April 1987, pp. 1, 4. See also Juliet Lodge, 'British Local Authorities and the European Community', *Talking Politics* 9(2), (1989), p.38.
11. Kenneth Clark, *Civilization: A Personal View*, (London: BBC and John Murray, 1971), p. 347.

12. One of the best reviews of the debate about the fate of the West, in particular that of America, in the post-war era is, Paul Kennedy, 'Fin-de-Siècle America', *The New York Review of Books*, 37(11), 28 June 1990, pp. 31–40.

13. See, Ali Mazrui, 'Changing the Guards from Hindus to Muslims: Collective Third World Security in a Cultural Perspective', *International Affairs*, 57(1) (1980), pp. 1–20.

14. See, James P. Piscatori, *Islam in a World of Nation-States*, (Cambridge: Cambridge University Press for the Royal Institute of International Affairs, 1986).

15. A.D. Smith, *Nationalism in the Twentieth Century*, (London: Martin Robertson, 1979).

16. Strange, *States and Markets*, op. cit., p.164.

17. On invisible trade see British Invisible Exports Council, *Invisible Trade in the World Economy 1972–86* (London: BIEC, 1988); Phedon Nicolaides, *Liberalising Trade in Services: An Overview of Issues and Difficulties*, Discussion Paper 3 (London: Royal Institute of International Affairs, 1988), p.2.

18. Strange, *States and Markets*, op. cit., pp. 75–6.

19. Harold Lever and Christopher Huhne, *Debt and Danger: The World Financial Crisis* (Harmondsworth: Penguin Books, 1985), p.11. The 1989 figures are quoted from the World Bank in Peter de Groot, 'The Ties That Bind the Third World', *New Scientist*, vol 125 24 February 1990, p.62.

20. Brown, op. cit., p. 193.

21. William Rees-Mogg, 'Wasps, Wimps and a Tradition which Lost Confidence in Itself', *The Independent*, 2 August 1988, p.12.

22. Strange, *States and Markets*, op. cit., p. 134.

23. Nigel Swain, 'The Global Information Technological Revolution and Political Legitimacy in Hungary', in The Open University, *Global Politics*, Block III, Part 2 (Milton Keynes: Open University, 1989), pp. 59–95; 'All the World's a Dish', *The Economist*, 21 August 1988, p.9.

24. Steven L. Canby, 'Military Reform and the Art of War', in Asa A. Clark, *et al.* (eds), *The Defense Reform Debate: Issues and Analysis*, (Baltimore, Mass.: Johns Hopkins University Press, 1984), pp. 127–9.

25. On summit meetings, see Robert D. Putnam and Nicholas Bayne, *Hanging Together: Co-operation and Conflict in the Seven-Power Summits*, (London: Sage, 1987).

26. 'Civil Aerospace: A Survey', *The Economist*, 3 September 1988, p.7.

27. Ibid., pp.7, 22.

28. *The Financial Times*, 13 April 1988, special report, p.III.

29. *Marxism Today*, October 1985, p.5.

30. 'Ford Strike Casts Shadow over Europe', *The Independent*, 9 February 1988, p. 23.

31. See, 'Multinational Companies and European Integration', *Journal of Common Market Studies Special Edition*, 26 (2), (December 1987).

32. Michael Artis and S. Ostry, *International Economic Policy Coordina-*

tion (London: Royal Institute of International Affairs/Routledge, 1986), p.4.

33. James P. Hawley, 'Protecting Capital from Itself: US Attempts to Regulate the Eurocurrency System', *International Organization* 38(1) (1984), p.155. See also Strange, *States and Markets*, op. cit., p. 105; Gilpin, op. cit., p. 315.

34. *Business Monitor: Quarterly Statistics*, Overseas Travel and Tourism, Quarter Four, 1988, CSO, MQ6, (London: HMSO, 1989), Tables 4A, 8A. *Atlantic Outlook* 3, 3 May 1991, pp. 5–6.

35. David Churchill, 'Europe's Growing Hotel Appeal', *Financial Times*, 10 July 1990, p. 18.

36. Roderick Rhodes, *European Policy-making, Implementation and Subcentral Governments: A Survey* (Maastricht: European Institute of Public Administration, 1986).

37. Christopher Tugendhat and William Wallace, *Options for British Foreign Policy in the 1990s* (London: Royal Institute of International Affairs/Routledge, 1988), p. 30.

38. Per Kleppe, 'EFTA and EC Moving Closer', *The European*, 1 (3), (1987), p. 36.

39. *The Financial Times*, op. cit., 13 April 1988, special report.

40. David Marquand, 'The Fading Role of National Sovereignty in Europe After 1992', *The Independent*, 10 August 1988, p. 12.

41. See, Helen Wallace, 'Negotiations and Coalition Formation in the European Community', *Government and Opposition*, 20(4) (1985), pp. 453–72.

42. John Palmer, *Europe Without America?*, (Oxford: Oxford University Press, 1987), pp. 133–6. The Eureka programme was devised by France partly as a European civil response to the challenge posed by the American Strategic Defense Initiative (SDI) programme, to undertake initiatives and promote development of the high-technologies that the SDI would nurture within the United States. The Eureka programme involves EC members along with Norway, Austria, Finland, Switzerland and Sweden.

3 BRITAIN IN THE CONTEMPORARY WORLD

1. Christopher Tugendhat and William Wallace, *Options for British Foreign Policy in the 1990s* (London: Royal Institute of International Affairs/Routledge, 1988), pp. 35–59. For a contrary opinion, see a review of this by Tessa Blackstone, 'Leaning Inwards, Looking Outwards', *International Affairs*, 65(2), (1989), pp.305–7. See also, Malcolm Rutherford, 'A Lucky Country', *The World Today*, 45(1), (1989), pp. 15–6.

2. Nicholas Henderson, *Channels and Tunnels: Reflections on Britain and Abroad*, (London: Weidenfeld & Nicolson, 1987), pp. 113–20.

3. 'United Kingdom', *Europa Yearbook 1989*, (London: Europa Publications, 1989), p 518.

4. Ibid. See also, Phedon Nicolaides, *Liberalizing Trade in Services: An Overview of Issues and Difficulties*, Discussion Paper 3 (London: Royal Institute of International Affairs, 1988); Andrew Glyn, 'Extraordinary Contrasts', *The Financial Times* 8 November 1989, p. 27.

5. Phedon Nicolaides, *Liberalizing Service Trade* (London: Royal Institute of International Affairs/Routledge, 1989), p.23.

6. *Europa Yearbook 1989*, op. cit., p. 522. See also Samuel Brittan, 'The True External Position', *The Financial Times*, 23 November 1989, p.28.

7. Grahame Thompson, 'United Kingdom Economic Autonomy', in *The Open University, Global Politics*, IV(2), D312 IV, (Milton Keynes: The Open University Press, 1989), p. 19.

8. DeAnne Julius, 'Britain's Changing International Interests: Economic Influences on Foreign Policy Priorities', *International Affairs*, 63(3), (1987), p.385.

9. Tugendhat and Wallace, op. cit., p. 37. See also *The Economist*, 30 January 1988.

10. *Europa Yearbook 1989*, op. cit., p. 521.

11. Thompson, op. cit., p.22.

12. *Britain's Top 1000 Foreign Owned Companies 1988*, (Bristol: Jordan and Sons, 1988) pp. A7-A8.

13. An excellent review of the scope of Britain's commitments and responsibilities can be found in John Baylis, *British Defence Policy*, (London: Macmillan, 1989).

14. Tony McGrew, 'Security and Order: The Military Dimension', in Michael Smith, Steve Smith and Brian White (eds), *British Foreign Policy: Tradition Change and Transformation* (London: Unwin Hyman, 1988), pp. 102–3.

15. *Statement on the Defence Estimates 1989*, vol. 1 (London: HMSO, 1989), pp. 14–21.

16. Ibid., p. 38. This calculation should not be confused with the defence budget as a whole. This is the proportion of the 55.2 per cent of the total defence budget for 1989–90 that the MoD estimates goes to meet 'defence commitments'.

17. See, for example, John Baylis, '"Greenwoodery" and British Defence Policy', *International Affairs*, 62(3) (1986), pp. 443–58. Expenditure figure from *Statement on the Defence Estimate 1990*, vol. 1 (London: HMSO, 1990), p. 44.

18. Sixth Report of the Defence Committee, 1987–88, *The Future Size and Role of the Royal Navy's Surface Fleet*, HC 309, (London: HMSO, 1988), pp. XIV-XVI. This claim is disputed by the MoD which maintains that it can keep modern gas turbine ships at sea longer and that as of 1990 there were 48 ships in this category, 42 of which would be 'available for operations' immediately or at short notice (private communication with the MoD).

19. Christopher Coker, *British Defence Policy in the 1990s*, (London: Brassey's, 1987), p.7.

20. Lawrence Freedman, *Britain and Nuclear Weapons*, (London: Macmillan, 1980), p. 47. This is not, of course, official information, but it was for many years undenied.
21. Richard N. Cooper and Ann L. Hollick, 'International Relations in a Technologically Advanced Future', *Economic Impact*, 54(2), (1986), pp. 69–77: Margaret Sharp and Claire Shearman, *European Technological Collaboration*, (London: Royal Institute of International Affairs/Routledge, 1987), p.5.
22. *The Economist*, 2 September 1989, p.92.
23. Mario Pianta, *New Technologies Across the Atlantic*, (London: Harvester Wheatsheaf, 1988), pp. 65–81.
24. Sharp and Shearman, op. cit, pp. 11–12.
25. Pari Patel and Keith Pavitt, 'Is Europe Losing the Technological Race?' *Research Policy*, 1 (1987); OECD, *OECD Science and Technology Indicators: Resources Devoted to R&D*, (Paris: OECD, 1984); Philip Gummett, *UK Military R&D: Report of a Working Party, Council for Science and Society*, (Oxford: Oxford University Press, 1986); *Annual Review of Government-Funded R&D, 1990*, (London: HMSO, 1990).
26. Michael Kenwood, 'The Decline and Fall of British Technology', *New Scientist*, vol. 115, no, 1577, 10 September 1987, pp. 28–9.
27. Derived from Sharp and Shearman, op. cit., p.109.
28. Margaret Sharp, *The New Biotechnology: European Governments in Search of a Strategy*, (Brighton: Science Policy Research Unit, University of Sussex, 1985), pp. 76–94.
29. Tugendhat and Wallace, op. cit., p. 53; see also William Wallace, *The Foreign Policy Process in Britain*, (London: Royal Institute of International Affairs, 1975), pp. 144–9.
30. Ibid., p. 54.
31. David Butler and Gareth Butler, *British Political Facts 1900–1985*, 6th edn, (London: Macmillan, 1986), pp. 459–60.
32. By Sir Anthony Acland, in Fourth Report of the Foreign Affairs Committee, 1984–85, *Overseas Programme Expenditure 1985–86*, HC 295, (London: HMSO, 1985), p. 117.
33. Raif Dahrendorf, *On Britain*, (London, BBC Publications, 1982), p. 138.
34. An excellent general analysis of economic organisations after 1971 can be found in Robert Fraser, *The World Financial System*, (London: Longmans, 1987), pp. 181–200.
35. On this ambiguous attitude see, David Allen, 'Britain and Western Europe', in M. Smith, S. Smith and B. White, op. cit., pp. 181–4.
36. Stephen George, *Politics and Policy in the European Community*, (Oxford: Oxford University Press, 1985), p.22.
37. See, Philip A. Daniels and Ella Ritchie, *Relaunching the European Communities: The Responses of Britain, France and Italy to the Institutional Reform Proposals in 1985*, (Brussels: European Community, 1989).

38. Butler and Butler, op. cit., p. 467.
39. Susan Strange, *States and Markets*, (London: Francis Pinter, 1988), pp. 145–6.
40. Sharp and Shearman, op. cit., pp. 69–73. Other non-EC states in the Eureka scheme are Norway, Austria, Finland, Switzerland, Sweden and Canada.
41. See David Allen, R. Rummel and W. Wessels, (eds), *European Political Cooperation*, (London: Butterworth, 1982); Christopher Hill, (ed.), *National Foreign Policies and European Political Cooperation* (London: Allen & Unwin, 1983).
42. Allen, 'Britain and Western Europe', op. cit., pp. 179–80.
43. For the SEA text see, European Community, *Treaties Establishing the European Communities* (London: HMSO, 1989).
44. Foreign and Commonwealth Office, *The Foreign and Commonwealth Office and the Diplomatic Service 1987, Basic Facts and Figures* (London: FCO, 1987); Fourth Report from the Foreign Affairs Committee, 1984–85, *Overseas Programme Expenditure 1985–86*, op. cit., p.91.
45. Fourth Report from the Foreign Affairs Committee, 1986–87, *Cultural Diplomacy*, HC 24 (London: HMSO, 1987), p.2.
46. Ibid., p. 102. In 1990 the Government announced a 3-year funding programme of £501.6 million for the BBC World Service from 1991–2.
47. Fourth Report from the Foreign Affairs Committee, 1987–88, *FCO/ODA Expenditure 1988–89*, HC 429 (London: HMSO, 1988), pp. 66–9. See, also, Central Office of Information, *Britain 1989: An Official Handbook* (London: HMSO, 1989), p.2.
48. Ibid., pp. 95,98.
49. Tugendhat and Wallace, op. cit., pp. 84–9.
50. Central Policy Review Staff, *Review of Overseas Representation* (London: HMSO, 1977), p. XIII. See also Michael Clarke, 'The Foreign Office and Its Critics', Millennium, 7 (1), 1979, pp. 222–36.
51. Foreign and Commonwealth Office, *Foreign and Commonwealth Office and the Diplomatic Service: Basic Facts and Figures 1986*, (London: HMSO, 1986), pp. 5–7: Fourth report from the Foreign Affairs Committee 1984–85, *Overseas Programme Expenditure 1985–86* op. cit., pp. 90–1.
52. Fourth Report from the Foreign Affairs Committee, 1987–88, *FCO/ODA Expenditure 1988–89*, op. cit., pp. 45, 69n.
53. Gareth Williams, *et al.* (eds), *Readings in Overseas Students Policy* (London: Overseas Students Trust, 1987), pp. 21–3.
54. Tugendhat and Wallace, op. cit., p 89.

4 POLICY PROCESSES IN A CHANGING WORLD

1. David Vital, *The Making of British Foreign Policy* (London: Allen & Unwin, 1968); Joseph Frankel, *British Foreign Policy 1945–1973* (London: Oxford University Press, 1975); James Barber, *Who Makes*

British Foreign Policy? (Milton Keynes: Open University Press, 1976); William Wallace, *The Foreign Policy Process in Britain* (London: Royal Institute of International Affairs, 1975); Lord Strang, *The Foreign Office* (London: George Allen, 1955); Lord Morrison, *Government and Parliament*, (London: Oxford University Press, 1954). See also the older, but still useful collection of papers by Robert Boardman and A.J.R. Groom. *The Management of Britain's External Relations* (London: Macmillan, 1973).

2. Geoffrey Moorhouse, *The Diplomats: The Foreign Office Today*, (London: Jonathan Cape, 1977), pp. 242–5.

3. James Cable, *Political Institutions and Issues in Britain*, (London: Macmillan, 1987), pp. 35–6.

4. *The Observer*, 27 November 1988.

5. Cable, op. cit., p. 38.

6. J. Harvey and L. Bather, *The British Constitution*, 4th edn (London, Macmillan, 1977), pp. 231, 234.

7. Quoted in Peter Hennessy, 'Does the Elderly Cabinet Machine Need Oiling?', *The Listener*, 27 June 1985, p. 8.

8. *Report of the Review Committee on Overseas Representation (1968–69)* (Duncan Report), Cmnd 4107 (London: HMSO, 1969); Central Policy Review Staff, *Review of Overseas Representation* (London: HMSO, 1977).

9. Foreign and Commonwealth Office, *Basic Facts and Figures* (London: HMSO, 1977).

10. Fourth Report from the Foreign Affairs Committee, 1987–88, *FCO/ODA Expenditure 1988–89*, HC 429 (London: HMSO, 1988), p. 2; financial provision includes expenditure for the British Council, the BBC, grants in aid and subscriptions to international organisations.

11. Ibid., p. 2.

12. Ibid., p. 13.

13. For an outline of the work of the British Council, see Fourth Report from the Foreign Affairs Committee, 1986–87, *Cultural Diplomacy*, HC 24 (London: HMSO, 1987), pp. 1–8; Second Report from the Foreign Affairs Committee, 1979–80, *Foreign and Commonwealth Office Organization*, HC 511 (London: HMSO, 1980), pp. 79–80, 83.

14. Fourth Report from the Foreign Affairs Committee, 1986–87, *Cultural Diplomacy*, op. cit., p. 215.

15. Ibid., p. 219; see also Second Report from the Foreign Affairs Committee, 1979–80, *Foreign and Commonwealth Office Organization*, op. cit., pp. 29–30.

16. Memorandum by the Foreign and Commonwealth Office in Second Report from the Foreign Affairs Committee, 1979–80, *Foreign and Commonwealth Office Organization*, op. cit., p. 8.

17. Ibid., pp. 71, 90–3.

18. Roger Tomkys, 'European Political Co-operation and the Middle East: A Personal Perspective', *International Affairs*, 63 (3) (1987), p. 433.

19. 'FO High-flyers are "Oxbridge Reactionaries"', *The Independent*, 3 August 1988, p. 4.

20. Second Report from the Foreign Affairs Committee, 1979–80, *Foreign and Commonwealth Office Organization*, op. cit., p. 4.
21. Ibid., pp. 51, 55, 70, 74.
22. Martin Edmonds, 'Central Organizations of Defence in Great Britain', in Martin Edmonds, (ed.) *Central Organizations of Defense* (London: Frances Pinter, 1985), pp. 85–107.
23. See *The Central Organisation of Defence*, Cmnd 9315 (London: HMSO, 1984); *Statement on the Defence Estimates 1984*, Cmnd 9227-1, pp. 10–18.
24. See Michael Dillon, 'Britain', in G.M. Dillon, (ed.) *Defence Policy-making: A Comparative Analysis* (Leicester: Leicester University Press, 1988), pp. 9–52.
25. See, for example, a list provided by the FCO in Second Report from the Foreign Affairs Committee, 1979–80, *Foreign and Commonwealth Office Organization*, op. cit., pp. 6–7.
26. Information supplied by the FCO.
27. See Peter Hennessy, *Whitehall* (London: Secker & Warburg, 1989), pp. 394–8.
28. Wallace, op. cit., p. 164.
29. Harold Wilson, *The Governance of Britain* (London: Weidenfeld & Nicolson, 1976), p. 87.
30. Anthony Sampson, *The Money Lenders* (London: Coronet Books, 1981), p. 118.
31. Ibid., p. 277. The Bank of England had two senior officials in Algiers when the $5.5 billion deal was made.
32. *The Times*, 7 September 1988.
33. The best example is undoubtedly Peter Hennessy, *Cabinet* (Oxford: Basil Blackwell, 1986), which is acknowledged by insiders and outsiders as being highly accurate.
34. Wallace, op. cit., p. 48; Hugh Heclo and Aaron Wildavsky, *The Private Government of Public Money* (London: Macmillan, 1974), p. 187.
35. Hennessy, *Cabinet*, op. cit., p. 77.
36. Wilson, op. cit., p. 77.
37. See Charles Miller, *Lobbying Government* (Oxford: Basil Blackwell, 1987), pp. 3–7.
38. Extracted from the list offered in Hennessy, *Cabinet*, op. cit., pp. 27–30.
39. Quoted in Hennessy, *Cabinet*, op. cit., p. 188.
40. See Françoise De La Serre, Jacques Leruez and Helen Wallace, (eds), *French and British Foreign Policies in Transition*, (Oxford: Berg Publishers for the Royal Institute of International Affairs, 1990).
41. Hennessy, *Whitehall*, op. cit., p. 404.
42. The best expression of the 'overload' thesis is still probably that contained in A. King, (ed.), *Why is Britain Becoming Harder to Govern?* (London: BBC Publications, 1976).
43. *The Guardian*, 26 July 1989, p. 6.
44. Parliamentary Debates, Commons, 5th Series, QA Written Answers, 6 May 1987; also BBC Radio 4, 12 July 1990.

45. FCO views of its export promotion work can be found in the evidence contained in Fourth Report from the Foreign Affairs Committee, 1987–88, *FCO/ODA Expenditure 1988–89*, op. cit., pp. 16–17.
46. First Report from the Foreign Affairs Committee, 1984–85, *The Abuse of Diplomatic Immunities and Privileges*, HC 127 (London: HMSO, 1985), pp. XXX, XXXVII-XXXVIII.
47. Private meeting during 1988.
48. William Wallace, 'Public Expenditure: The International Dimension', in M.S. Levitt, (ed.), *New Priorities in Public Spending*, Joint Studies in Public Policy, No. 13 (London: National Institute for Economic and Social Research, 1987).
49. Personal interview.
50. Robert Harris, 'Taming the Whitehall Machine', *The Observer*, 21 February 1988.
51. Les Metcalf, 'Institutional Inertia vs. Organisational Design', European Consortium for Political Research, Annual Conference, 1992.
52. See, for example, *The Observer*, 17 September 1989, p. 1.
53. Quoted in *The Times*, 18 November 1988.
54. International Freedom Foundation (UK), *Freedom Bulletin* 8 (1989), pp. 2–3. The IFF is generally regarded as a right-wing organisation but quotes Tony Benn approvingly on this matter. There was an extensive correspondence about this in the columns and letters of *The Times* during November 1988, revolving mainly around articles by David Hart, 'The FO: Road to Reform', 5 November 1988, and Patrick Cosgrave, 'A Too-Exclusive Club', 18 November 1988.
55. Morrison, op. cit., p. 339. For the variety of different views on reform, see the press debate in *The Times* of November 1988.
56. Quoted on Radio 4 'Louder than Words', 10 September 1989; Hennessy, 'Does the Elderly Cabinet Machine Need Oiling?', op. cit., p. 8.
57. On the background to this see Wallace, *The Foreign Policy Process in Britain*, op. cit., pp. 66–7, 78–9.
58. In evidence in Second Report from the Foreign Affairs Committee, 1979–80, *Foreign and Commonwealth Office Organization*, op. cit., p. 107.
59. Private meeting.
60. John Nott, 'Our Defences All At Sea', *The Times*, 5 October 1987, p. 16.
61. Sir Burke Trend, 'Policy and the Public Purse', *Times Literary Supplement*, 16 July 1982, pp. 755–7.
62. See the conclusions in Christopher Tugendhat, and William Wallace, *Options for British Foreign Policy in the 1990s* (London: Routledge/RIIA, 1988), Chapter 7.

5 INSTITUTIONAL INFLUENCES ON EXTERNAL POLICY-MAKING

1. See, Michael Clarke, 'Comparative Politics and International Politics: A Strange Divide', *Politics*, 6 (2) (1986), pp. 3–9.

2. See the discussion on pages 5–8.

3. J. Michael Lee, 'Parliament and Foreign Policy: Some Reflections on Westminster and Congressional Experience', *Irish Studies in International Affairs*, 2(4), (1988) pp. 5–6.

4. Martin Edmonds, 'Central Organizations of Defence in Great Britain', in Martin Edmonds, (ed.), *Central Organizations of Defense*, (London: Frances Pinter , 1985), pp. 103–4.

5. Peter G. Richards, *Parliament and Foreign Affairs*, (London: Allen & Unwin, 1967) p.42.

6. Ian Brownlie, 'Parliamentary Control Over Foreign Policy in the United Kingdom, in Antonio Cassese, (ed.), *Parliamentary Control Over Foreign Policy: Legal Essays* (Alphen aan den Rijn: Sijthoff and Noordhoff, 1980), p.4. For the official statement of 1961 on the Ponsonby Rule see, House of Commons Debates, 5th series, vol 651, cols 940–7, 18 December 1961.

7. *Exchange of Notes Between Britain and France Regarding the New Hebrides*, Cmnd 4997, (London: HMSO, 1972).

8. On Early Day Motions in general see, Hugh B. Berrington, *Backbench Opinion in the House of Commons 1945–55* (Oxford: Pergamon Press, 1973).

9. Information supplied by MoD. See also Peter Hennessy, *Whitehall* (London: Secker & Warburg, 1989), p. 336.

10. Estimates obtained during personal interviews. All politicians and officials interviewed agreed on the general size of the 'interested' group of MPs.

11. Institute for European Defence and Security Studies, *MPs and Defence: A Survey of Parliamentary Knowledge and Opinion*, Occasional Paper 36 (with a commentary by Philip Towel), (London: IEDSS, 1988). The comment is from the preface, by Gerald Frost, p.6.

12. Personal interview.

13. Personal interview.

14. Lord Carrington, *Reflect on Things Past* (London: Collins, 1988), p.371; *Sunday Times* Insight Team, *The Falklands War*, (London: Sphere Books, 1982), pp.53–4; Jock Bruce-Gardyne, *Mrs Thatcher's First Administration* (London: Macmillan, 1984), pp. 110–11.

15. Personal interview.

16. See Third Report from the Expenditure Committee, 1978–79, *Work of the Expenditure Committee During the First Four Sessions of the Present Parliament*, HC 163 (London: HMSO, 1979).

17. Masood Hyder, 'Parliament and Defence Affairs: The Defence Subcommittee of the Expenditure Committee', *Public Administration*, 55 (1977), p. 74.

18. House of Commons Debates, 5th Series, vol. 969, (1979–80) cols 35–6, 25 June 1979. See also, 'The New Select Committees – Constitutional Breakthrough or Marginal Advance?', *Contemporary Record*, 1(1) (1987), p. 17. On the original structure and purposes envisaged for the select committees see, First Report from the Select Committee on Procedure, 1977–78, *Report and Minutes of Proceedings*, vol. 1,

HC 588-I (London: HMSO, 1978).
19. See Gavin Drewry, *New Select Committees* (Oxford: Oxford University Press, 1985).
20. Personal interview.
21. Seventh Report from the Treasury and Civil Service Committee, 1985–86, *Civil Servants and Ministers: Duties and Responsibilities*, HC 92 (London: HMSO, 1986); First Report from the Treasury and Civil Service Committee, 1986–87, *Ministers and Civil Servants*, HC 62 (London: HMSO, 1987); First Report from the Liaison Committee, 1986–87, *Accountability of Ministers and Civil Servants to Select Committees of the House of Commons*, HC 100 (London: HMSO, 1987).
22. *Accountability of Ministers and Civil Servants*, CM 78, February 1987, (London: HMSO, 1987).
23. Ibid., pp. 2–3.
24. Peter Hennessy, 'Dr. John Gilbert – Grand Inquisitor', *Contemporary Record*, 1 (1) (1987), p.19.
25. Andrew Scott, 'Britain and the EMS: An Appraisal of the Report of the Treasury and Civil Service Committee', *Journal of Common Market Studies*, xxiv (3), (1986), pp. 187–201.
26. 'The Bunker Mentality', *The Independent*, 13 January 1989, p. 18.
27. *The Independent*, 20 April, 1989, to the Procedure Committee.
28. Fourth Report from the Select Committee on Procedure 1988–89, *The Scrutiny of European Legislation*, HC.368 (London: HMSO, 1989). See also, Vernon Bogdanor, 'The Need for Scrutiny', *The Financial Times*, 12 December 1989, p.19.
29. See the discussion on pages 75–6.
30. Stephen Koss, *The Rise and Fall of the Political Press in Britain*, vol. 2 (London: Hamish Hamilton, 1984), Ch. XV. See also, P. Elliott and P. Golding, 'The News Media and Foreign Affairs', in Robert Boardman and A.J.R. Groom, (eds), *The Management of Britain's External Relations*, (London: Macmillan, 1973), pp. 305–30; Donald G. Bishop, *The Administration of British Foreign Relations* (New York: Syracuse University Press, 1961), pp. 191–203. A useful summary is provided by James Barber, *Who Makes British Foreign Policy?* (Milton Keynes: Open University Press, 1976).
31. Tessa Blackstone and William Plowden, *Inside the Think Tank* (London: Heinemann, 1988), p. 174
32. James Curran and Jean Seaton, *Power Without Responsibility: The Press and Broadcasting in Britain*, 3rd edn (London: Routledge, 1988), pp. 85–90.
33. *The Economist*, 23 September 1989, p. 14.
34. Curran and Seaton, op. cit., Chap. 7.
35. See *Royal Commission on the Press*, July 1977, Cmnd 6810–4 (London: HMSO, 1977); Yoel Cohen, 'News Media and the News Department of the Foreign and Commonwealth Office', *Review of International Studies*, 14(2) (1988), p. 124; Elliott and Golding, op. cit., pp. 311–20.

36. Kenneth Newton, 'Mass Media', in Henry Drucker, *et al.* (eds), *Developments in British Politics 2*, (London: Macmillan, 1986), p. 318.
37. The *Sun*, 4 August 1989.
38. Hugh Cudlipp, 'The Three Graces in the Street of Shame', *The Independent*, 28 August 1989, p. 12.
39. Philip Robins, 'A Feeling of Disappointment: The British Press and the Gulf Conflict', *International Affairs*, 64(4) (1988), pp. 596–7.
40. David Walker, 'First Rough Draft of History', *Contemporary Record*, 1(1) (1987), p.22.
41. See Cohen, op. cit., p. 123, and Barber, op. cit.,p. 108 for figures relevant to 1971. The present figures are based on the author's own sampling taken on random evenings over a period of six months from May to October 1989.
42. The D-Notice system is overseen by a joint Whitehall-Fleet Street committee. The system has been in operation since 1911. See, Hennessy, *Whitehall*, op. cit., p. 356. See also Maggie Brown, 'Rough Seas for D-Notices', *The Independent*, 9 December 1987, p.16.
43. See, for example, Colina MacDougall, 'Something Will Have to Give', *The Financial Times*, 18 May 1989.
44. Broadcasting Research Unit, reported in *The Independent*, 12 July 1990, p. 8.
45. Torin Douglas, 'Two-Edged Sword Threatening Whitehall Campaigns', *The Independent*, 2 August 1989.
46. Norman Tebbit, *Upwardly Mobile* (London: Futura Books, 1989), p. 248.
47. On pressure groups see, R. Kimbe and J.J. Richardson (eds), *Pressure Groups in Britain* (London: Dent, 1974); Anthony King (ed.), *Why is Britain Becoming Harder to Govern?* (London: BBC Publications, 1976); Barber, op. cit., pp. 66–75.
48. Hennessy, *Whitehall*, op. cit, pp. 344–79.
49. See Gwin Prins (ed.), *Defended to Death*, (Harmondsworth: Penguin Books, 1983), pp. 227–32. This was the subject of the allegations made by Cathy Massiter in a Channel 4 Programme. The programme 'Cabinet' finally made these facts public on Channel 4 when it was eventually screened in a new form on 9 April 1991. Interestingly, Peter Wright, in *Spycatcher* (New York: Dell Publishing, 1987), maintains that CND was regarded 'as largely irrelevant pieces of the jigsaw' (p. 454), but he also claims that there were never less than a staggering 2 million personal files in MI5s Registry, a number that 'began to rise dramatically' in the late 1960s and 1970s' (p.49).
50. QUANGOS is the acronym for quasi-autonomous non-governmental organisations. See also, Michael Moran, *Politics and Society in Britain* (London: Macmillan, 1985), p. 127.
51. Wyn Grant, *Business and Politics in Britain* (London: Macmillan, 1987), p. 125.
52. Moran, op. cit., pp. 168–9.
53. Stephen George, *Politics and Policy in the European Community* (Oxford: Oxford University Press, 1985), p.71.
54. Blackstone and Plowden, op. cit., pp. 142–3.

55. See, for example the conclusions of Simon Burgess, and Geoffrey Edwards, 'The Six Plus One: British Foreign Policy and the Question of European Economic Integration, 1955', *International Affairs*, 64(3) (1988), pp. 393–414.

56. 'A Nice Little Earner Somewhere in the City', *The Guardian*, 26 July, 1989.

57. Bill Robinson, 'No Relief for the Borrowers', *The Independent*, 19 October 1989, p. 29.

58. Moran, op. cit., p. 147.

59. David Allen, 'Britain and Western Europe', in Michael Smith, Steve Smith and Brian White (eds), *British Foreign Policy: Tradition, Change and Transformation* (London: Unwin Hyman, 1988), p. 175.

60. See the summary in John Baylis, *British Defence Policy* (London: Macmillan, 1989), pp. 19–29.

61. Thorold Masefield, 'Co-prosperity and Co-security: Managing the Developed World', *International Affairs*, 65(1), (1988–9), p.10.

62. Nicholas Bayne, 'Making Sense of Western Economic Policies: The Role of the OECD', *The World Today* 43(2) (1987), p.28.

63. See, for example, Barry Buzan, *People, States and Fear*, (Brighton: Wheatsheaf, 1983) pp. 128–55; Roger Tooze, 'Security and Order: The Economic Dimension', in M. Smith, *et al.*, op. cit., pp. 140–5.

64. Tooze, op. cit, p. 144.

65. See, for example, John Vogler, 'Britain and North-South Relations', in M. Smith, *et al.*, op. cit, pp. 201.

66. Susan Strange, *States and Markets* (London: Frances Pinter 1988), p. 182.

67. See an excellent summary by Neill Nugent, 'The European Community and British Independence', *Talking Politics* 2(1) (1988), p. 31.

68. Hugo Young and Anne Sloman, *No Minister: An Inquiry into the Civil Service* (London: BBC, 1982) p.73

69. Michael Clarke, 'Britain and European Political Co-operation in the CSCE', in Kenneth Dyson (ed.), *European Detente* (London: Frances Pinter, 1986), p. 249.

70. See Bruce George (ed.), *Jane's NATO Handbook 1990–91* (Coulsdon: Jane's Information Group, 1990), pp. 195–218.

71. *The Economist*, 30 September 1989, p. 42.

72. On the general issue of environmental policy-making see, David Newsome, 'The New Diplomatic Agenda: Are Governments Ready?', *International Affairs*, 65(1) (1988–89), pp. 29–41; Norman Myers, 'Environment and Security', *Foreign Policy*, 74 (1989), pp. 23–41.

6 NON-INSTITUTIONAL INFLUENCES ON EXTERNAL POLICY-MAKING

1. See, for example, Martin Burch and Bruce Wood, *Public Policy in Britain* (Oxford: Basil Blackwell, 1986); Ian Budge and David

McKay *The Changing British Political System: Into the 1990s*, 2nd. edn, (London: Longman, 1988).

2. David Coates, *The Context of British Politics* (London: Hutchinson, 1984), p.20.

3. See Barry Buzan, 'Interdependence and British External Relations', in Lawrence Freedman and Michael Clarke (eds), *Britain in the World*, (Cambridge: Cambridge University Press, 1991).

4. Department of Trade and Industry, *Manufacturing Into the Late 1990s* (London: HMSO, 1989); 'DTI Calls for a Revolution in Manufacturing', *The Financial Times*, 29 November 1989, p.1.

5. 'Brussels to Vet Large Mergers', *Independent*, 22 December 1989, p.21.

6. In a report by KPMG Peat Marwick McLintock, reported in 'Increasing Number of Firms Form Euro Links', *Independent*, 22 January 1990, p.23.

7. 'Single Market: Battleground of the Future Has Potential', *The Financial Times*, 1 December 1989, p. vii; 'Building on a Decade of Change', *The Financial Times*, 2 February, 1990, p. 26; 'Joint Ventures Become More Popular', *The Financial Times*, 20 November 1989, p.21: 'Packing in More Power Through Strategic Alliances', *The Financial Times*, 2 April 1990, p.21.

8. 'Something for Everyone in Vintage GEC Strike', *The Independent on Sunday*, Business Section, 28 January 1990, p.8.

9. 'Ferranti Deal Aftermath', *The Financial Times*, 25 January 1990, p.6.

10. See Philip Daniels, 'Industrial Policy', in Martin Harrop, (ed.), *Power and Policy in Liberal Democracies* (Cambridge: Cambridge University Press, forthcoming).

11. 'Joint Ventures Become More Popular', *The Financial Times*, 20 November 1989, p.21.

12. Albert Bressand, 'Beyond Interdependence: 1992 as a Global Challenge', *International Affairs*, 66 (1) (1990), p. 59.

13. Ibid., pp. 58–9.

14. Ron Smith, 'The Political Economy of Britain's External Relations', in Freedman and Clarke, op. cit., p. 131.

15. David Williamson, interviewed by Peter Jenkins in 'Louder than Words', Radio 4, 6 August 1989.

16. Michael Moran, *Politics and Society in Britain* (London: Macmillan, 1985), p.135.

17. 'Big Bang for the City's Law Firms', *The Economist*, 9 September 1989, pp. 125–6; 'Difficulty in Defining a European Legal Eagle', *The Financial Times*, 11 January 1991, p. 4.

18. 'European Insurance' (Special Survey), *The Economist*, 24 February 1990, p.4.

19. Walter Eltis, 'The Group of Five', Review of Business Books, *The Financial Times*, 2 April 1990, p.ii.

20. Joe Rogaly, 'Towards the Limits of Capitalism', *The Financial Times*, 2 March 1990, p.21.

21. See Keith Middlemas, *Power, Competition and the State*, vol 2, *Britain 1961–74* (London: Macmillan, 1990).
22. 'Foreign Investment Changing the Structure of the World Economy', *The Financial Times*,9 April 1990, p.3.
23. DeAnne Julius, *Global Companies and Public Policy* (London: Royal Institute of International Affairs/Frances Pinter 1990), pp. 10–13.
24. Ibid., p.2.
25. On the claims of the Levene reforms, see, Peter Levene, 'Competition and Collaboration: UK Defence Procurement Policy', *Royal United Services Institute Journal*, 132(2) (1987); Ministry of Defence, *Value for Money in Defence Equipment Procurement*, Defence Open Government Document 83/01. For general reviews of the reforms see J. Moray Stewart, 'Defence Procurement in Britain', *Royal United Services Institute Journal* 133(4) (1988); Gavin Kennedy, 'Strains and Prospects in Defence Procurement', *Royal United Services Institute Journal*, 134(2) (1989).
26. Trevor Taylor and Keith Hayward, *The UK Defence Industrial Base* (London: Brassey's, 1989), pp. 9–13.
27. Ibid., p.6.
28. Ibid., p. 13.
29. Philip Gummett and William Walker, 'The Industrial and Technical Consequences of the Peace', *Royal United Services Institute Journal*, 135(1) (1990).
30. William Walker and Philip Gummett, 'Britain and the European Arms Market', *International Affairs*, 5(3) (1989).
31. Personal interviews.
32. Gummett and Walker, op. cit., p.1.
33. Frank Cooper, 'Economists and Defence: The Views of a UK Practitioner', *Defence Economics*, 1(1) (1990), pp. 79–82; see also Keith Hartley, Farooq Hussain and Ron Smith, 'The UK Defence Industrial Base', *Political Quarterly*, 58(1) (1987).
34. Taylor and Hayward, op. cit., pp. 140–5.
35. Trevor Taylor, 'Defence Industries in International Relations', *Review of International Studies*, 16(1) (1990), p. 72.
36. For older accounts of the way in which general public opinion reveals a stable consensus see David Vital, *The Making of British Foreign Policy* (London: George Allen & Unwin, 1968), pp. 71–88; William Wallace, *The Foreign Policy Process in Britain* (London: Royal Institute of International Affairs), 1975, pp. 113–17.
37. Ian Budge and David McKay, *The Changing British Political System: Into the 1990s*, 2nd edn (London: Longman, 1988), pp. 91–7.
38. The Gallup Organisation has asked a limited series of international questions over a number of years and assessed attitudes to other nationalities annually. These are recorded in the regular *Gallup Political Index*. The MORI organisation has also conducted similar surveys, though in a less systematic way, and reproduced them in *British Public Opinion*. Other material appears in the European Commission's regular *Eurobarometre* publications which is normally a summary of polls commissioned by the EC from the major polling

organisations. Other polling material covers international issues more sporadically.

39. See, for example, B. Sarlvik and I. Crewe, *Decade of Dealignment: The Conservative Victory of 1979 and Electoral Trends in the 1970s* (Cambridge: Cambridge University Press, 1983); R. Jowell and C. Airey, (eds), *British Social Attitudes: The 1984 Report* (London: Longman, 1984).

40. See, for example, Coates, op. cit.; Andrew Gamble, *Britain in Decline*, 2nd edn (London: Macmillan, 1985); Tom Nairn, *The Break-Up of Britain* (London: New Left Books, 1977). The other views are expressed in Colin Crouch, (ed.), *State and Economy in Contemporary Capitalism* (London: Croom Helm, 1979).

41. Christopher Tugendhat and William Wallace, *Options for British Foreign Policy in the 1990s* (London: Royal Institute of International Affairs/Routledge 1988), p.103.

42. The 1981 British Nationality Act created three categories of citizenship: British Citizenship, British Dependent Territory Citizenship, and British Overseas Citizenship.

43. David Buchan and John Wyles, 'The Intolerance Threshold Nears', *The Financial Times*, 12 March 1990, p.14.

44. Moran, op. cit., p. 25.

45. Namely, the distributive trades, professional and secretarial and miscellaneous services. Coates, op. cit., p.160.

46. Budge and McKay, op. cit., p. 89.

47. European families, for example, are now noted to take a more instrumental and calculated decision on the timing of starting families and are observed to view their parental planning in relation to their economic circumstances. In this respect, European families are notably more instrumental than those in the United States. See Jowell and Airey, op. cit., pp. 143–54.

48. Martin Harrop, 'Voting and the Electorate', in Henry Drucker, *et al.* (eds), *Developments in British Politics 2* (London: Macmillan, 1986), pp. 58–9; D.T. Studlar, 'Non-White Policy Preferences, Political Participation and the Political Agenda in Britain', in Zig Layton-Henry and P. Rich (eds), *Race, Government and Politics in Britain* (London: Macmillan, 1986).

49. The figure of 10 million is offered by Coates, op. cit., p.104.

50. Eurobarometre Poll, reported in *The Financial Times*, 6 April 1990, p.3.

51. Christopher Farrands, 'State, Society and Culture', in Michael Smith, Steve Smith and Brian White (eds), *British Foreign Policy: Tradition, Change and Transformation* (London: Unwin Hyman, 1988).

52. Christopher T. Husbands, 'Race and Gender', in Drucker, op. cit., p. 296.

53. Zig Layton-Henry, 'The Black Electorate', *Contemporary Record* 3(3) (1990), pp.24–5.

54. Ibid., p. 25.

55. In 1987 the numbers of 'religious adherents' in Britain were: Muslims

850 000; Jews 410 000; Sikhs 180 000; Hindus 130 000; Church of England 1 500 000; all Christian churches, 7 000 000.

56. Gallup Poll reported in *The Sunday Telegraph*, 31 December 1989, p.11 and Harris Poll, reported in *The Observer*, 31 December 1989, p.3.

57. Mette MacRae, 'London's Standing in International Diplomacy', *International Affairs*, 65(3) (1989), p.511.

58. David Capitanchik and Richard C. Eichenberg, *Defence and Public Opinion* (London: Royal Institute of International Affairs/Routledge & Kegan Paul 1983), pp. 10–14.

59. Ivor Crewe, 'Britain: Two and a Half Cheers for the Atlantic Alliance', in Gregory Flynn and Hans Rattinger (eds), *The Public and Atlantic Defence* (London: Croom Helm, 1985).

60. Capitanchik and Eichenberg, op. cit., pp. 23–5.

61. See, for example, MORI *British Public Opinion*, 5(9) (1983), p.6.; Crewe, op. cit., pp. 23–6.

62. *Gallup Political Index*, 294, February 1985; 297, May 1985; 300, August 1985; 303, November 1985.

63. Crewe, op. cit., p.32.

64. Ibid., pp. 36–7.

65. Gregory Flynn, 'Images of Security: Deterrence and Deliverance', in Gregory Flynn, *et al.*, *Public Images of Western Security* (Paris: Atlantic Institute, 1985), pp. 61–8.

66. Personal interviews.

67. MORI *British Public Opinion*, 8(9) (1986), p. 4; Crewe, op. cit., pp. 23–6.

68. Capitanchik and Eichenberg, op. cit., pp. 15–25.

69. Roger Jowell, Sharon Witherspoon and Lindsay Brook (eds), *British Social Attitudes, 6th Report: Special International Report* (Aldershot: Gower, 1989).

70. 'Even Brits Learn to Love Europe', *The Financial Times* 6 April 1990, p. 3; European Commission, *Eurobarometre* 1982–89, Brussels. A summary of a decade of Eurobarometre surveys is offered in *The Economist*, 17 February 1990, p. 36.

71. Gallup Poll reported in *The Sunday Telegraph*, 31 December 1989, p.11, and Harris Poll, reported in *The Observer*, 31 December 1989, p.3. See also, Edward Mortimer, 'Is This Our Frontier?', *The Financial Times*, 3 April 1990, p. 21.

72. Paul Taylor, 'The European Communities and the Obligations of Membership: Claims and Counter Claims', *International Affairs* 57(2), (1981), p. 243.

73. Budge and McKay, op. cit., p. 172.

74. Stanley de Smith and Rodney Brazier, *Constitutional and Administrative Law* 6th edn (Harmondsworth: Penguin Books, 1989), p. 428.

75. 'Lost' is being used here as a shorthand to express the fact that judgements have gone in some sense against the representations of the British government, sufficient to require a change in the law.

76. For a list of cases and judgements, see O Hood Phillips and Paul Jackson, *O. Hood Phillips' Constitutional and Administrative Law*,

7th edn (London: Sweet & Maxwell, 1987), pp. 427–9. See also David Pannick, 'Britain Fights Shy on Human Rights', *The Independent*, 20 April 1990, p.17.

77. Hood Phillips and Jackson, op. cit., p.429.

78. 'The Business of Faking It', *The Daily Telegraph*, 9 September 1988, p.15.

79. Bressand, op. cit., p. 50.

80. John Pinder, 'The European Community and the Gaullist Fallacy', *The World Today*, 45(4), p. 56.

81. For a review of cases see, Hood Phillips and Jackson, op. cit., pp. 107–12.

82. Juliet Lodge, 'European Community Institutions', *Contemporary Record* 3(3) (1990), p.7.

83. David Llewelyn, 'The Sale and Transmission of Non-personal Data into England: The Legal Issues', *Computer Law and Practice*, March/April 1986, p. 119.

84. David Bradshaw, 'Around the World in a Way That Pays', *The Financial Times*, 19 January 1990, p. 15; Jill Hills, 'The Telecommunications Rich and Poor', *Third World Quarterly* 12(2) (1990), pp. 72–3.

85. T. Murray Rankin, 'Business Secrets Across International Borders: One Aspect of the Transborder Data Flow Debate', *Computer Law and Practice* March/April 1986, p. 106.

86. de Smith and Brazier, op. cit., p 82.

87. On the legal implications of the SEA for Britain see First Special Report from the Select Committee on European Legislation 1985–86, *The Single European Act and Parliamentary Scrutiny*, HC 264 (London: HMSO, 1986); Second Special Report from the Select Committee on European Legislation 1985–86, [Untitled], HC 400, (London: HMSO, 1986); Third Report from the Foreign Affairs Committee 1985–86, *The Single European Act*, HC 442 (London: HMSO, 1986).

88. A.V. Dicey, *Introduction to the Study of the Law of the Constitution*, 10th edn (London: Macmillan, 1959). See also, Paul Taylor, op. cit.

89. Geoffrey Howe, 'The European Communities Act 1972', *International Affairs*, 49(1) (1973), pp. 1–13.

90. P.F. Smith and S.H. Bailey, *The Modern English Legal System* (London: Sweet & Maxwell, 1984), pp. 224–30.

91. Hood Phillips and Jackson, op cit., p. 100.

92. Frank E.C. Gregory, *Dilemmas of Government: Britain and the European Community* (Oxford: Martin Robertson, 1983), p. 44.

93. de Smith and Brazier, op. cit., pp. 9, 74.

94. Quoted in Geoffrey Lock, 'The 1689 Bill of Rights', *Political Studies* 37(4) (1989), p. 555.

95. For an excellent series of accounts to this issue see First Report from the Foreign Affairs Committee 1980–81, *The British North America Acts: The Role of Parliament* HC42 I and II (London: HMSO, 1981); Second Report from the Foreign Affairs Committee 1980–81, *The*

British North America Acts: The Role of Parliament, Supplementary
Report, HC 295 (London: HMSO, 1981).

96. Lock, op. cit., p. 556.
97. de Smith and Brazier, op. cit., p. 27.
98. Hood Phillips and Jackson, op. cit., p. 79.
99. All customs duties are allocated to the EC but 10 per cent is retained
    for administrative costs.
100. Second Report from the Foreign Affairs Committee 1989–90, *The
     Operation of the Single European Act*, vol. II, Minutes of Evidence,
     HC 82-II, (London: HMSO, 1990), pp. 63,76.
101. Ibid., p. 62; Second Report from the Foreign Affairs Committee 1989–
     90, *The Operation of the Single European Act*, vol. I, HC 82-I
     (London: HMSO, 1990), p. xi.
102. Ibid., (vol I), p. xxviii.
103. Quoted in Gregory, op. cit., p.70.
104. Quoted in Hood Phillips and Jackson, op. cit., p.78.
105. Personal interview.

7 THE POLITICS OF EXTERNAL RELATIONS

1. See, William Wallace, *The Foreign Policy Process in Britain*
   (London: Royal Institute of International Affairs, 1975), p. 93; James
   Barber, *Who Makes British Foreign Policy?*, (Milton Keynes, Open
   University Press, 1976), pp. 78–9, 87; David Vital, *The Making of
   British Foreign Policy* (London: Allen & Unwin, 1968), p.76; Joseph
   Frankel, *British Foreign Policy 1945–1973* (London: Oxford University Press, 1975), p.32.
2. Anthony Seldon, *Churchill's Indian Summer: The Conservative
   Government 1951–55* (London: Hodder & Stoughton, 1981), pp. 409–
   15.
3. Frankel, op. cit., p. 35: Vital, op. cit., p. 74–5; see also, Karl Kaiser
   and Roger Morgan, *Britain and West Germany: Changing Societies
   and the Future of Foreign Policy* (London: Oxford University Press,
   1971).
4. Andrew Gamble, *Britain in Decline*, 2nd edn (London: Macmillan,
   1985), pp. 105–112.
5. Vital, op. cit., p. 76.
6. Hugo Young, *One of Us: A Biography of Margaret Thatcher*, revised
   ed. (London: Pan Books, 1990), p. 120.
7. Martin Holmes, *Thatcherism: Scope and Limits 1983–87* (London:
   Macmillan, 1989), p. 71.
8. See Michael Clarke, 'British Perspectives on the Soviet Union', in
   Alex Pravda and Peter Duncan, (eds), *Soviet-British Relations Since
   the 1970s* (Cambridge: Royal Institute of International Affairs/Cam-
   bridge University Press, 1990), pp. 68–91.
9. Quoted in Peter Jones, 'British Defence Policy: The Breakdown of
   Inter-Party Consensus', in *Review of International Studies*, 13(2)

(1987), p. 117. Conservative Party views on these issues were well summarised by Mrs Thatcher on a number of occasions in *Parliamentary Debates: 1986–87, House of Commons*, 2 April, cols. 1223–4, 1227–9; 12 November, col. 23.

10. Christopher Coker, *British Defence Policy in the 1990s: A Guide to the Defence Debate* (London: Brassey's, 1987), p. 125.

11. Jones, op. cit., p. 113. The development of Labour Party thinking on nuclear issues can be gleaned from, Mike Gapes, *No Cruise, No Trident, No Nuclear Weapons* (Labour Party, 1981); Labour Party, *Defence and Security For Britain*, National Executive Committee Statement to the Annual Conference, 1984; Labour Party, *Britain Will Win: Labour Manifesto 1987*; 'Defence and Arms Control at the 1986 Party Conferences', *ADIU Report* 8(6), (1986), p. 14. The position of the Liberal/SDP Alliance is best summarised in *Britain United: The Time Has Come. The SDP/Liberal Alliance Programme for Government*, (SDP/Liberal Alliance 1987), p.21, though the nature of the dissent within it is well-captured in Brian May, *Is Russia Really a Threat?*, Liberal Challenge Booklet, 7 (Liberal Party, 1986); Brian May, 'Why the Red Card is Never a Trump', *The Guardian*, 22 September 1986. See also the reports of internal alliance arguments on defence in *The Financial Times*, 26 September 1986; *The Times*, 25 September 1986, and an interview with David Owen in *The Times*, 13 September 1986.

12. See Michael Clarke, 'The Debate on European Security in the United Kingdom', in Ole Waever, *et al.* (eds), *European Polyphony: Perspectives Beyond East-West Confrontation* (London: Macmillan, 1989), pp. 121–40.

13. See, for example, Labour's policy review statement in *Labour Party News*, 20 (1990).

14. *The Guardian* 10 May 1989, p.1.

15. Harold Wilson, *The Labour Government 1964–70: A Personal Record* (London: Weidenfeld & Nicolson, 1971), pp. 179–81.

16. Harold Wilson, *Final Term: The Labour Government 1974–1976* (London: Weidenfeld & Nicolson, 1979), p. 58.

17. Wallace, op. cit., pp. 153–4.

18. Ritchie Ovendale, 'The South African Policy of the British Labour Government, 1947–51', *International Affairs*, 59(1) (1982–83), pp. 41–58.

19. James Barber, 'Southern Africa', in Peter Byrd, (ed), *British Foreign Policy Under Thatcher* (Oxford: Philip Allen, 1988), p. 102.

20. Young, op. cit., p. 486.

21. On the moderate reality of international sanctions, see, Martin Holland, 'The European Community and South Africa: In Search of a Policy for the 1990s', *International Affairs*, 64(3), (1988), pp. 415–30; Dennis Austin, 'A South African Policy: Six Precepts in Search of a Diplomacy?', *International Affairs*, 62(3) (1986), p. 396.

22. Lawrence Freedman and Virginia Gamba-Stonehouse, *Signals of War* (London: Faber & Faber, 1990).

23. Lawrence Freedman, 'The Case of Westland and the Bias to Europe', *International Affairs*, 63(1) (1986–87), pp. 1–20.
24. Young, op. cit., p. 454.
25. Norman Barry, 'Ideology', in Patrick Dunleavy, Andrew Gamble, and Gillian Peele, (eds), *Developments in British Politics 3*, (London: Macmillan, 1990), pp. 20–30.
26. Jim Bulpitt, 'Rational Politics and Conservative Statecraft in the Open Polity', in Byrd, op. cit., p. 188.
27. Conservative Central Office News Service. Press Release (Mrs Thatcher's Speech at Kensington Town Hall, Monday 19 January 1976) 42/76, 19 January 1976.
28. Gillian Peele, 'Parties, Pressure Groups and Parliament', in Dunleavy, *et al.*, op. cit., pp. 85–6.
29. Jones, op. cit., p. 112.
30. This voter perception has been a consistent trend throughout recent years, (see *The Guardian* 30 November 1985). For evidence of this in the 1987 election campaign, see the series of questions polled in *Gallup Political Index*, February – June 1987, 318–22.
31. M. Cassell, 'Labour Leader Sees Dawning of a Free Europe', *The Financial Times* 9 February 1990, p. 10; Speech by Brian Sedgemore, *The Independent*, 16 June 1990, p.4. On Labour's conversion to Europe see also, 'Tale of Two Parties', *The Economist*, 23 June 1990, p.36.
32. See Dennis Kavanagh, *Thatcherism and British Politics*, (Oxford: Oxford University Press, 1987), pp. 108–9; Peter Riddell, *The Thatcher Government* (Oxford: Basil Blackwell, 1985), pp. 206–28. See also the later analysis of Peter Riddell, *The Thatcher Decade* (Oxford: Basil Blackwell, 1989).
33. Young, op. cit., p. 170.
34. *Krasnaia Zvezda*, 24 January 1976; *Komsomolskaya Pravda*, 28 January 1976. British reporting of this and the following uproar is to be found in, *The Sunday Times*, 25 January 1976; *The Daily Telegraph*, 29 January 1976; *The Sunday Telegraph*, 1 February 1976; *The Times*, 26 February 1976; *The Sunday Telegraph*, 1 August 1976; *The Economist*, 18 June 1983, p. 34.
35. The speeches by Peter Walker and Julian Amery were reported somewhat after the event by *The Daily Express*, 19 January 1976 and *The Daily Telegraph*, 24 January 1976.
36. Riddell, *The Thatcher Government*, op. cit.,p. 207.
37. *Parliamentary Debates, House of Commons, 1980–81*, 23 July 1981, col. 498; *The Times*, 10 September 1981, p.4. See also the terms of an important speech to the Bournemouth Young Conservatives, 12 February 1983, *Keesings Contemporary Archives 1985* (Longman, 1985), p.33351.
38. Hugo Young and Anne Sloman, *The Thatcher Phenomenon*, (London: BBC Publications, 1986), p. 117.
39. Young, op. cit., p. 389.
40. On the beginnings of this relationship see, Curtis Keeble, *Britain and the Soviet Union 1917–89* (London: Macmillan, 1990), pp. 297–300.

41. By Nicholas Wapshott in his piece 'Thatcher's Messianic Message' for *The Observer*, 24 September 1989, p. 13.
42. Young, op. cit., pp. 561–2.
43. Joe Rogaly, 'Head in Europe, Heart in the United States', *The Financial Times*, 12 December 1989, p.18.
44. Cento Veljanovsky, 'The Political Economy of Regulation', in Dunleavy, *et al.*, op. cit., pp. 291–304.
45. C. Pollitt, quoted in John Greenwood, 'Mrs Thatcher's Whitehall Revolution: Public Administration or Public Management?', *Teaching Politics*, 17(2) (1988), p. 210.
46. Peter Hennessy, 'Testing Time for Reforms Project', *The Independent*, 11 June 1990, p. 5.
47. See Frank Cooper, 'Ministry of Defence', in J. Gretton and Anthony Harrison, (eds), *Reshaping Central Government*, (Berkshire: Policy Journals, 1987), pp. 107–30.
48. Julian Critchley, *Westminster Blues* (London: Futura, 1986), p. 126.
49. Peter Hennessy, *Whitehall* (London: Secker & Warburg, 1989), p. 627.
50. Cooper, op. cit., p. 124.
51. Greenwood, op. cit., p. 222.
52. See the discussion of this question in Hennessy, *Whitehall*, op. cit, pp. 630–1.
53. David Howell, *Blind Victory* (London: Hamish Hamilton, 1986).
54. Cooper, op. cit, p. 125.
55. John Campbell, 'Defining "Thatcherism"', *Contemporary Record*, 1(3) (1987), p.4.
56. Young, op. cit., p.237.
57. Riddell, *The Thatcher Government*, op. cit., p. 207.
58. *Falklands Islands Review* (Franks Report), Cmnd. 8787, (London: HMSO, 1983).
59. Hennessy, *Whitehall*, op. cit., p.645.
60. Young, op. cit., pp. 444–6.
61. *The Independent*, 27 March 1987, p.12; *Independent on Sunday*, 22 July 1990,p.23.
62. *The Independent*, 24 September 1987, p.9.
63. For a useful review of the way in which the literature on Mrs Thatcher has tended to divorce the domestic from the foreign, see David Marquand, 'The Literature on Thatcher', *Contemporary Record*, 1(3), (1987, pp. 30–1.
64. Holmes, op. cit., pp. 3–18.
65. By Neil Ascherson in the *Independent on Sunday*, 15 July 1990, p. 23.
66. Cooper, op. cit., pp. 125–30.
67. James Cable, *Political Institutions and Issues in Britain* (London: Macmillan, 1987), pp. 88–90.
68. Helen Wallace, 'Britain and Europe', in Dunleavy, *et al.*, op. cit., p.166.

8 CONCLUSION

1. For a good summary see Steve Smith and Michael Smith, 'The Analytical Background', in Steve Smith, Michael Smith and Brian White (eds), *British Foreign Policy: Tradition, Change and Transformation* (London: Unwin Hyman, 1988), pp. 3–23.
2. This question was first formulated by William Wallace in a paper to the Political Science Association Conference of 1976.
3. William Wallace, *The Foreign Policy Process in Britain* (London: Royal Institute of International Affairs, 1975), p. 275.
4. Compare, for example, Christopher Tugendhat and William Wallace, *Options for British Foreign Policy in the 1990s* (London: Royal Institue of International Affairs/Routledge, 1988) Chapter 7, with the earlier ideas expressed in Wallace, *The Foreign Policy Process in Britain*, op. cit., Chapter 10.
5. Michael Palliser, 'Diplomacy Today', in Hedley Bull and Adam Watson (eds), *The Expansion of International Society*, (Oxford: Clarendon Press,1984), pp. 382–3. See also William Wallace, *Britain's Bilateral Links Within Western Europe* (London: Royal Institute of International Affairs/Routledge & Kegan Paul,1984).
6. Alan James, *Sovereign Statehood: The Bases of International Society* (London: Allen & Unwin, 1986), p. 249.
7. William Wallace, 'What Price Independence? Sovereignty and Interdependence in British Politics', *International Affairs*, 62(3)(1986), pp. 367–89. For more historical support to the Wallace argument see, Edmund Morgan, *Inventing the People: The Rise of Popular Sovereignty in England and America* (London: Chatto, 1989).
8. William Wallace, 'Time to Surrender Those Victorian Values', *The Financial Times*, 26 April 1989, p 17; John Wyles, 'A More Powerful Voice in the European Chorus', *The Financial Times*, 20 August 1990, p.11. Many of these competing ideas were expressed in a robust exchange of letters in *The Independent* on 6 July, 10 July, 25 September and 27 September 1989.
9. Lord Thomas of Swynnerton, 'Britain's European Choices', *The World Today*, 46 (8–9) (1990), pp. 144–7, offers a balanced critique of different opinions. For more trenchant views see, Kenneth Minogue, 'The Voice That Awoke Europe to its Threatened Freedoms', *The Independent*, 20 September 1989; Richard Ritchie (ed.), *Enoch Powell on 1992* (London: Anaya, 1990).
10. Joseph S. Nye, *Bound to Lead: The Changing Nature of American Power* (New York: Basic Books, 1991), Part III. For an earlier empirical study of interesting evidence on the same theme see, M.P. Sullivan, 'Transnationalism, Power Politics and the Realities of the Present System', in R. Maghroori, and B. Ramberg (eds), *Globalism vs. Realism* (Boulder, Col: Westview, 1982), pp. 195–221.
11. Susan Strange, 'Finance, Information and Power', *Review of International Studies*, 16 (3), (1990), pp. 259–74.

12. Nye, op. cit. pp. 20–22.
13. Susan Strange, *States and Markets* (London: Frances Pinter 1988).
14. William Wallace, *The Transformation of Western Europe*, (London: Frances Pinter/Royal Institute of International Affairs, 1990).
15. Brian White, 'Analysing Foreign Policy: Problems and Approaches', in Michael Clarke and Brian White (eds), *Understanding Foreign Policy* (Aldershot: Edward Elgar, 1989), pp. 1–26.
16. Steve Smith, 'Foreign Policy Analysis and the Study of British Foreign Policy', in Lawrence Freedman and Michael Clarke (eds), *Britain in the World* (Cambridge: Cambridge University Press, 1991), pp. 47–60.
17. Of all the material on rational actor assumptions, a good recent summary is to be found in David Sanders, *Losing an Empire, Finding a Role: British Foreign Policy Since 1945* (London: Macmillan, 1990), pp. 257–72.
18. Clarke and White, op. cit.
19. Richard Little, 'Conclusion', in Smith, Smith and White, op. cit., pp. 245–59.
20. Wallace, *The Transformation of Western Europe*, op. cit.
21. Stephen George, *Politics and Policy in the European Community* (Oxford: Clarendon Press, 1985), pp. 32–3.
22. Not excepting the period from 1978–88 when the domestic consensus on defence was so fractured. Cold War arguments were a crucial ingredient in the defence Establishment's case.
23. Margaret Thatcher, 'My Vision of Europe: Open and Free', *The Financial Times*, 19 November 1990, p.17.
24. A series of statements advocating a step by step approach to such a goal were outlined in November 1990 by Gianni de Michelis, the Italian foreign minister at the end of the Italian presidency of the EC, and supported in a joint statement by President Mitterrand and Chancellor Kohl in early December 1990. See, Robert Mauthner, 'A Common Defence for Europe', *The Financial Times*, 11 December 1990, p.17.
25. See, for example, Barry Buzan, *et al.*, *The European Security Order Recast: Scenarios for the Post-Cold War Era* (London: Frances Pinter 1990).
26. Michael Clarke and Rod Hague (eds), *European Defence Co-operation: America, Britain and NATO* (Manchester: Manchester University Press, 1990).
27. Edward Mortimer, 'Is This Our Frontier?', *The Financial Times*, 3 April 1990, p.21.
28. Sanders, op. cit., pp. 291–4.

APPENDICES

Contents

Appendix 1 The FCO and related institutions

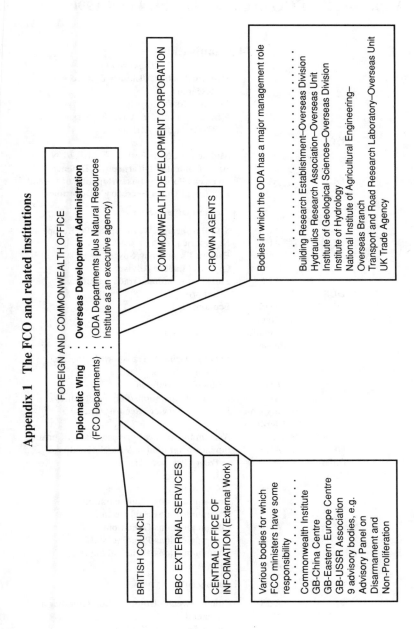

FOREIGN AND COMMONWEALTH OFFICE

Diplomatic Wing : **Overseas Development Administration**
(FCO Departments) : (ODA Departments plus Natural Resources
: Institute as an executive agency)

COMMONWEALTH DEVELOPMENT CORPORATION

CROWN AGENTS

Bodies in which the ODA has a major management role

• • • • • • • •
Building Research Establishment—Overseas Division
Hydraulics Research Association—Overseas Unit
Institute of Geological Sciences—Overseas Division
Institute of Hydrology
National Institute of Agricultural Engineering–
Overseas Branch
Transport and Road Research Laboratory–Overseas Unit
UK Trade Agency

BRITISH COUNCIL

BBC EXTERNAL SERVICES

CENTRAL OFFICE OF
INFORMATION (External Work)

Various bodies for which
FCO ministers have some
responsibility
• • • • • • • •
Commonwealth Institute
GB-China Centre
GB-Eastern Europe Centre
GB-USSR Association
9 advisory bodies, e.g.
Advisory Panel on
Disarmament and
Non-Proliferation

Appendix 2   FCO organisation 1974 and 1990

1974 organisation

PUS			Departments
			Historical Adviser/Library & Records/ Research
			Planning Staff
		AUS	Central & Southern Africa/E. African/ Rhodesian/W. African
	DUS		
		AUS	Middle East/Near East & N. Africa/UN
			Arms Control & Disarmament/Defence
	DUS	AUS	Overseas Police Adviser/Republic of Ireland
			Permanent Under Secretary's Department
			{ Western Organizations*
		AUS	S.E. European/S.W. European/W. European
	DUS	AUS	N. America
			Eastern European & Soviet
			Overseas Labour Adviser
		AUS	Financial Relations/Trade Relations & Exports
	DUS		
		AUS (Chief Economic Adviser)	Economists
		AUS	Energy/Marine & Transport/Science & Technology
		AUS	Protocol & Conference
		AUS (Deputy Chief Clerk)	Personnel Operations/Personnel Policy Personnel Services/Security/Training
			Accommodation & Services/Claims/Consular
	DUS (Chief Clerk)	AUS	Finance/Migration & Visa/Nationality & Treaty/Passport Office
		AUS	Inspectorate
			Communications Administration
			Communications Engineering
		AUS	Communications Operations
			Communications Planning Staff
			Communications Technical Services
		AUS	Latin America
	DUS		{ Caribbean*
		AUS	Commonwealth Co-ordination/Gibraltar & General
			Pacific Dependent Territories
			West Indian & Atlantic
			{ Hong Kong & Indian Ocean*

		AUS	Far Eastern/India Office Library & Records
			S. Asian/S.E. Asian/S.W. Pacific
			Cultural Exchange/Cultural Relations
		AUS	European Integration (Information Subjects)
	DUS		Guidance & Information Policy
			Information Administration/Information Research
			Parliamentary Commissioner & Committees Unit
			News
	DUS	AUS	European Integration (External)
			European Integration (Internal)

PUS – Permanent Under-Secretary; DUS – Deputy Under-Secretary; AUS – Assistant Under-Secretary.

*   Western Organisations Department and Hong Kong & Indian Ocean Department report to *two* Assistant Under-Secretaries and *two* Deputy Under-Secretaries: Caribbean Department reports to two Assistant Under-Secretaries but to the same Deputy Under-Secretary.

Source: William Wallace, *The Foreign Policy Process in Britain* (London: Royal Institute of International Affairs, 1975), p.25.

1990 organisation

┌─────────┐			Economic Advisers
│ PUS │			Planning
└─────────┘			Staff
			(Planning only)
			Research
			Departments
			Policy Planning Staff (West West only)
			United Nations
		AUS	Southern European
			Western European
		AUS	CSCE Unit
Political			Eastern European
Director			Soviet
		AUS	European Community (External)
		AUS	United Nations
		AUS	Commercial Management & Exports
			Economic Relations*
		AUS	Aviation & Maritime
			Environment, Science & Energy
	DUS		Narcotics Control & AIDS
			Security Co-ordination
		AUS	European Community (Internal & External)

	AUS	Claims
		Consular
		Cultural Relations
		Information
		Migration & Visa
		Nationality & Treaty
		News
		Parliamentary Relations Unit
	AUS	Protocol
	AUS	Home Estate & Services
		Medical & Staff Welfare Unit*
		Overseas Estate
		PROSPER
DUS		Personnel Operations
(& Chief		Personnel Policy
Clerk)		Personnel Services
		Security*
		Technical Security
		Training
	AUS	Information Systems Division (Operations)
		Information Systems Division (Projects)
		Information Systems Division (Resources)
		Information Systems Division (Services)
		Library & Records
	AUS	Finance
		Internal Audit*
		Management Review Staff*
		Overseas Inspectorate
		Resource Management
	AUS	Falkland Islands
		Mexico & Central America
		North America
DUS		South America
		South Pacific
		West Indian & Atlantic
	AUS	Far Eastern
		Hong Kong
		South Asian
		South East Asian
	AUS	Central African
		Commonwealth Co-ordination
		East African
DUS		Southern African
		West African
	AUS	Middle East
		Near East & North Africa

		PUSD
		Republic of Ireland
	AUS	International Labour Adviser
		Overseas Police Adviser
		Security Co-ordination
DUS	AUS	Arms Control & Disarmament
		Defence
		Non-Proliferation
		Security Policy
		Service Advisers and Attaches

PUS – Permanent Under-Secretary; DUS – Deputy Under-Secretary;
AUS – Assistant Under-Secretary.
* Joint FCO/ODA departments, September 1990.
Source: Personnel Department, FCO.

Appendix 3   FCO staffing 1990–91

CATEGORIES OF STAFFING IN THE FCO

	%
Geographical departments	13
Functional and public services	19
Advisers and specialists	13
Estate management	15
Personnel management	10
Financial mangement	7
Communication	23

GEOGRAPHICAL DISTRIBUTION OF OVERSEAS STAFF

	%
Western Europe	27.4
North America/Caribbean	11.3
N. Africa, Near and Middle East	10.2
Asia	14.5
Sub-Saharan Africa	13.3
Eastern Europe/Soviet Union	8.2
Latin America	4.7
Far East	4.1
Australasia/Oceania	3.5
Back-up staff	2.8

FUNCTIONAL DISTRIBUTION OF OVERSEAS STAFF

	%
Commercial work	29
Political work	15
Immigration/Visa	14
Consular	10
Head of post	11
Information	8
Aid	6
Economic work	4
Labour/agriculture	3

Appendix 4   ODA organisation chart

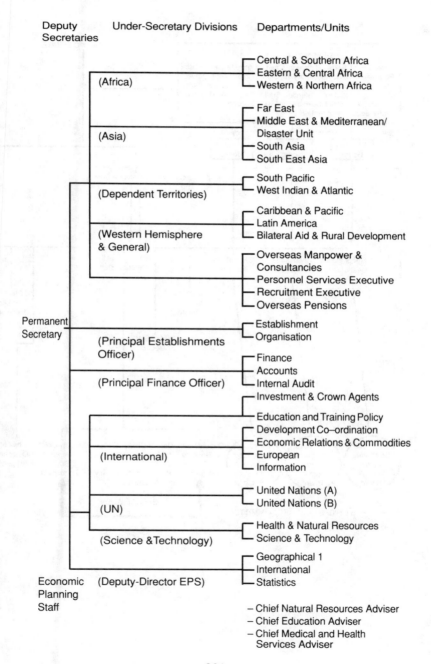

Deputy Secretaries | Under-Secretary Divisions | Departments/Units

Permanent Secretary

(Africa)
- Central & Southern Africa
- Eastern & Central Africa
- Western & Northern Africa

(Asia)
- Far East
- Middle East & Mediterranean/ Disaster Unit
- South Asia
- South East Asia

(Dependent Territories)
- South Pacific
- West Indian & Atlantic

(Western Hemisphere & General)
- Caribbean & Pacific
- Latin America
- Bilateral Aid & Rural Development
- Overseas Manpower & Consultancies
- Personnel Services Executive
- Recruitment Executive
- Overseas Pensions

(Principal Establishments Officer)
- Establishment
- Organisation

(Principal Finance Officer)
- Finance
- Accounts
- Internal Audit
- Investment & Crown Agents

(International)
- Education and Training Policy
- Development Co–ordination
- Economic Relations & Commodities
- European
- Information

(UN)
- United Nations (A)
- United Nations (B)

(Science & Technology)
- Health & Natural Resources
- Science & Technology

Economic Planning Staff

(Deputy-Director EPS)
- Geographical 1
- International
- Statistics

– Chief Natural Resources Adviser
– Chief Education Adviser
– Chief Medical and Health Services Adviser

301

Appendix 5

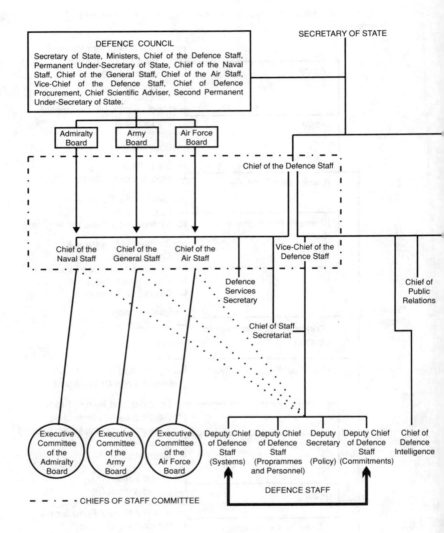

DEFENCE COUNCIL
Secretary of State, Ministers, Chief of the Defence Staff, Permanent Under-Secretary of State, Chief of the Naval Staff, Chief of the General Staff, Chief of the Air Staff, Vice-Chief of the Defence Staff, Chief of Defence Procurement, Chief Scientific Adviser, Second Permanent Under-Secretary of State.

SECRETARY OF STATE

Admiralty Board

Army Board

Air Force Board

Chief of the Defence Staff

Chief of the Naval Staff

Chief of the General Staff

Chief of the Air Staff

Vice-Chief of the Defence Staff

Defence Services Secretary

Chief of Public Relations

Chief of Staff Secretariat

Executive Committee of the Admiralty Board

Executive Committee of the Army Board

Executive Committee of the Air Force Board

Deputy Chief of Defence Staff (Systems)

Deputy Chief of Defence Staff (Programmes and Personnel)

Deputy Secretary (Policy)

Deputy Chief of Defence Staff (Commitments)

Chief of Defence Intelligence

DEFENCE STAFF

– – – · – · CHIEFS OF STAFF COMMITTEE

The higher organisation of the Ministry of Defence

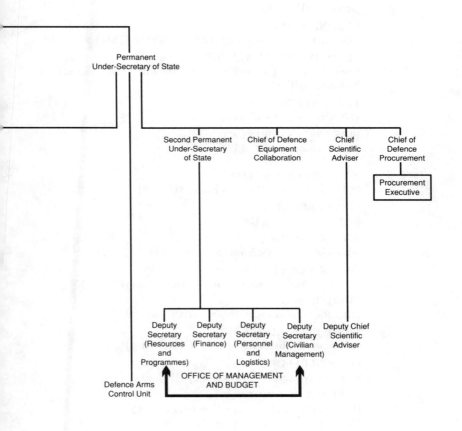

Appendix 6 Defence and Foreign Affairs Committee Publications

Defence Committee publications

1979–80   FIRST REPORT
Ammunition Storage Sites for British Forces
Germany (HC 556)

SECOND REPORT
Statement on the Defence Estimates 1980 (HC 571)

SECOND SPECIAL REPORT
Government Reply to Report on Statement on the Defence
Estimates (HC 816)

THIRD REPORT
D Notice System (HC 773)

FIRST SPECIAL REPORT
Sub-Committees (HC 455)

1980–81   FIRST SPECIAL REPORT
Strategic Nuclear Weapons Policy (HC 130)

FIRST REPORT
RAF Pilot Training (HC 53)

SECOND REPORT
Statement on the Defence Estimates 1981 (HC 302)

SECOND SPECIAL REPORT
Government Observations on Second Report (HC 461)

THIRD REPORT
Sting Ray Lightweight Torpedo (HC 218)

THIRD SPECIAL REPORT
Government Observations on Third Report (HC 473)

FOURTH REPORT
Strategic Nuclear Weapons Policy (HC 36)

MINUTES OF EVIDENCE
Defence Cuts and Defence Estimates (HC 223)
The Royal Dockyards and the Dockyards
Study (HC 362)

MINUTES OF PROCEEDINGS (HC 477)

1981–82   FIRST REPORT
Allied Forces in Germany (HC 93)
Observations presented by the Secretary of State for Defence on
the First Report on the Committee (Cmnd 8571)

FIRST SPECIAL REPORT
Strategic Nuclear Weapons Policy – Government Response to
the Committee's Fourth Report of 1980–81 (HC 266)

SECOND REPORT
Ministry of Defence Organisation and procurement (HC 22)

MINUTES OF PROCEEDINGS (HC 528)

1982–83   FIRST REPORT
The Handling of Press and Public Relations during the
Falklands Conflict (HC 17)

SECOND REPORT
British Forces in Hong Kong (HC 176)

THIRD REPORT
The Future Defence of the Falkland Islands (HC 154)

FOURTH REPORT
Previous Recommendations of the Committee (HC 55)

FIRST SPECIAL REPORT
Positive Vetting Procedures in HM Services and the Ministry of
Defence (HC 242)

MINUTES OF EVIDENCE
Winter Supplementary Estimates (HC 89)

MINUTES OF PROCEEDINGS (HC 389)

1983–84   FIRST REPORT
Statement on the Defence Estimates 1984 (HC 436)

SECOND REPORT
The Physical Security of Military Installations in the United
Kingdom (HC 397–I and II)

THIRD REPORT
Ministry of Defence Reorganisation (HC 584)

MINUTES OF PROCEEDINGS (HC 645)

1984–85   FIRST REPORT
The Use of Merchant Shipping for Defence Purposes (HC 114)

SECOND REPORT
Security at Royal Ordnance Factories and Nuclear Bases (HC
217)

THIRD REPORT
Defence Commitments and Resources and the Defence Estimates 1985–86 (HC 37–I, II, and III)

FOURTH REPORT
The Future of the Royal Dockyards (HC 435)

FIFTH REPORT
The Appointment and Objectives of the Chief of Defence
Procurement (HC 430)

SIXTH REPORT
The Trident Programme (HC 479)

MINUTES OF PROCEEDINGS (HC 602)

1985–86   FIRST SPECIAL REPORT
Defence Commitments and Resources and the Defence Esti-
mates 1985–86: Government Observations on the Committee's
Third Report of 1984–85 (HC 151)

SECOND SPECIAL REPORT
The Appointment and Objectives of the Chief of Defence
Procurement: Government Observations on the Committee's
Fifth Report of 1984–85 (HC 152)

THIRD SPECIAL REPORT
The Trident Programme: Government Observations on the
Committee's Sixth Report of 1984–85 (HC 153)

FIRST REPORT
Further Observations on the Future of the Royal Dockyards
(HC 18)

SECOND REPORT
Statement on the Defence Estimates 1986 (HC 399)

THIRD REPORT
The Defence Implications of the Future of Westland plc (HC
518)

FOURTH REPORT
Westland plc: The Government's Decision-Making (HC 519)

MINUTES OF EVIDENCE
The Defence Implications of the Future of Westland plc (HC
169)

MINUTES OF PROCEEDINGS (HC 611)

1986–87   FIRST SPECIAL REPORT
The Royal Dockyards (HC 15)

FIRST REPORT
Expenditure on Major Defence Projects: Accountability to the
House of Commons (HC 340)

SECOND REPORT (together with SECOND SPECIAL
REPORT)
The Implications for the United Kingdom of Ballistic-Missile
Defence (HC 130/233)

THIRD REPORT
The Progress of the Trident Programme (HC 356)
Government Reply: First Special Report of Session 1987–88 (HC 224)

FOURTH REPORT
Implementing the Lessons of the Falklands Campaign (HC 345)

FIFTH REPORT
Defence Commitments in the South Atlantic (HC 408) Government Reply: First Special Report of Session 1987–88 (HC 224)

THIRD SPECIAL REPORT
The Protection of British Merchant Shipping in the Arabian Gulf (HC 409)

MINUTES OF EVIDENCE
Ethnic Monitoring and the Armed Forces (HC 410)
Memoranda (HC 411)

MINUTES OF PROCEEDINGS (HC 391)

1987–88   FIRST SPECIAL REPORT
Government Replies to the First, Third and Fifth Reports, Session 1986–87, together with minutes of Proceedings (HC 224)

FIRST REPORT
Ethnic Monitoring and the Armed Forces (HC 391) Government Reply: Published with Second Special Report (HC 391)

SECOND REPORT
The Acceptance of Business Appointments by Retiring Members of the Armed Forces and Ministry of Defence Officials (HC 392)

THIRD REPORT
The Progress of the *Trident* Programme (HC 422)
Government Reply: published with the Third Special Report (HC 674)

FOURTH REPORT
The Defence Requirement of Merchant Shipping and Civil Aircraft (HC 476)
Government Reply: Published with the Third Special Report (HC 674)

FIFTH REPORT
The Procurement of Major Defence Equipment (HC 431)

SIXTH REPORT
The Future Size and Role of the Royal Navy's Surface Fleet (HC 309)

SEVENTH REPORT
The Statement on the Defence Estimates 1988 (HC 495)

SECOND SPECIAL REPORT
The Government's Reply to the First Report of Session 1987–88 on Ethnic Monitoring and the Armed Forces (HC 391)

EIGHTH REPORT
British Forces Belize (HC 624)

NINTH REPORT
Business Appointments: Observations on the Government's Reply to the Second Report of Session 1987–88 (HC 622)

THIRD SPECIAL REPORT
The Government's Reply to the Third and Fourth Reports of Session 1987–88 (HC 674)

1988–89   FIRST REPORT
The Future of the Brigade of Gurkhas (HC 68)

SECOND REPORT
Standing Levels in the Procurement Executive (HC 269)

THIRD REPORT
The Working of the AWACS Offset Agreement (HC 286)

FOURTH REPORT
Statement on the Defence Estimates 1989 (HC 383)

FIFTH REPORT
The Progress of the Trident Programme (HC 374)

SIXTH REPORT
The Royal Navy's Surface Fleet (HC 419)

SEVENTH REPORT
Decommissioning of Nuclear Submarines (HC 316)

EIGHTH REPORT
The Procurement of the Tucano Trainer Aircraft (HC 372)

NINTH REPORT
The Availability of Merchant Shipping for Defence Purposes (HC 495)

TENTH REPORT
The Vertical Launch Sea Wolf Missile System and the Type 25 Frigate Command System (HC 409)

ELEVENTH REPORT
The Procurement of the Light Anti-Tank Weapon LAWS (HC 350)

Foreign Affairs Committee publications

(* Refers to enquiries by the Overseas Development Sub-Committee)

Session 1979–80

Reports

FIRST REPORT
Olympic Games 1980 (HC 490)

SECOND REPORT
FCO Organisation (HC 511)

THIRD REPORT
Overseas Students' Fees: Aid and Development Implications* (HC 553)

FOURTH REPORT
Development Divisions* (HC 718 I and II)

FIFTH REPORT
Afghanistan: Consequences for British Policy of the Soviet Invasion (HC 745)

Evidence

Evidence was also published, without a Report on:

HC 362–xiii   Council of Europe
HC 362–xviii   FCO and British Council Estimates
HC 362–xx   Government Response to the Brandt Commission Report

and by the Sub-Committee on:

HC 407–xiii, -xiv   Energy Implications of the Brandt Commission Report
HC 407–xv   Brandt Commission Report: Poorest Countries

Minutes of Proceedings

The Committee's Minutes for the Session were published as HC 843

Session 1980–81

Reports

FIRST REPORT
British North America Acts: The Role of Parliament (HC 42 I and II)

SECOND REPORT
British North America Acts: The Role of Parliament (Supplementary Report) (HC 295)

THIRD REPORT
Turks and Caicos Islands: Hotel Development* (HC 26 I and II)

FOURTH REPORT
Supply Estimates 1981–82 (Class II, Votes 1, 2, 3, 5 and 6) (HC 343 I and II)

FIFTH REPORT
Mexico Summit – The British Government's Role in the Light of the Brandt Commission Report* (HC 211 I and II)

SIXTH REPORT
Zimbabwe: The Role of British Aid in the Economic Development of Zimbabwe* (HC 117)

SEVENTH REPORT
Gibraltar: The Situation of Gibraltar and UK Relations with Spain (HC 166)

Evidence

Evidence was published, without a Report, on:

HC 41–i and v	Foreign Affairs (General)
HC 41–ii	Afghanistan
HC 41–iii	Poland
HC 41–iv	Arms Sales
HC 41–vi	Namibia

and by the Sub-Committee on:

HC 421 i–ii	Overseas Students' Fees: Monitoring Effects on Aid and Development.

Minutes of Proceedings

The Committee's Minutes for the Session were published as HC 482

Session 1981–82

Reports

FIRST SPECIAL REPORT
Government Reply to Seventh Report of Session 1980–81 (HC 374)

FIRST REPORT
British North America Acts: The Role of Parliament (Third Report) (HC 128)

SECOND REPORT
Supply Estimates 1982–83 (Class II, Votes 10 and II)* (HC 330)

THIRD REPORT
Supply Estimates 1982–83 (Class II, Votes 1–6), Spring Supplementary Estimates 1981–82 (Class II, Vote 6) (HC 406)

FOURTH REPORT
The Work of the Commonwealth Development Corporation* (HC 71)

FIFTH REPORT
Caribbean and Central America (HC 47)

Evidence

Evidence was published, without a Report, on:

HC 48 i–iii   Foreign Affairs (General)

and by the Sub-Committee on:

HC 151–i   United Nations Development Programme

Minutes of Proceedings

The Committee's Minutes for the Session were published as HC 533

Session 1982–83

Reports

FIRST REPORT
The Wiston House International Conference Centre (Wilton Park) (HC 117)

SECOND REPORT
Turks and Caicos Islands: Airport Development on Providenicales* (HC 112)

THIRD REPORT
Wilton Park: Supplementary Report (HC 250)

FOURTH REPORT
ODA's Scientific and Special Units (HC 25 I and II)

FIRST SPECIAL REPORT
Government Reply to First and Third Reports (HC 292)

SECOND SPECIAL REPORT
Falkland Islands Inquiry (HC 378)

Memoranda

Memoranda submitted in connection with the Committee's inquiry into the FCO Winter Supplementary Estimates 1982–83 and the Main Estimates 1983–84 (HC 379)

Evidence

Evidence was published on:

HC 31 i–xiv   Falkland Islands
HC 31–xv   Falkland Islands: Appendices to the Minutes of Evidence
HC 123–i   Foreign Affairs in General

and by the Sub-Committee on:

HC 324 i–ii   Supply Estimates 1983–84: Support for Overseas Students

Minutes of Proceedings

The Committee's Minutes for the Session were published as HC 380

Session 1983–84

Reports

FIRST REPORT
FCO and ODA Spring Supplementary Estimates 1983–84 (HC 280)

SECOND REPORT
Grenada (HC 226)

THIRD REPORT
The Forthcoming Fontainebleau Summit (HC 480)

FOURTH REPORT
FCO and ODA Supply Estimates 1984–85 (HC 421)

FIFTH REPORT
Falkland Islands   Vol. I (HC 268–I)
                                       Vol. II (HC 268–II)

FIRST SPECIAL REPORT
Economic and Political Security of Small States (HC 541)

Evidence

Evidence was published, without a Report, on:

Foreign Affairs in General:

HC 251–i	IDA 7th Replenishment
HC 251–ii	Secretary of State for Foreign and Commonwealth Affairs (EEC, Middle East, relations with Eastern Bloc countries)
HC 251–iii	Secretary of state for Foreign and Commonwealth Affairs (EEC)
HC 251–iv	British Council
HC 251–v	Secretary of State for Foreign and Commonwealth Affairs (the Vienna Convention; Hong Kong; and the Secretary of State's recent visit to Moscow)

Diplomatic Immunity: (See First Report 1984–85)

HC 499–i	FCO Officials
HC 499–ii	Sir Francis Vallat GBE KCMG QC
HC 499–iii	Secretary of State for Foreign and Commonwealth Affairs

Minutes of Proceedings

The Committee's Minutes for the Session were published as HC 650

Session 1984–85

Reports

FIRST REPORT
The Abuse of Diplomatic Immunities and Privileges (HC 127)

SECOND REPORT
Famine in Africa (HC 56)

THIRD REPORT
Events Surrounding the Weekend of 1–2 May 1982 (HC 11)

FOURTH REPORT
1985–86 Overseas Programme Expenditure (HC 295)

FIFTH REPORT
United Kingdom membership of UNESCO (HC 461)

FIRST SPECIAL REPORT
The Events Surrounding the Weekend of 1–2 May 1982: Allegations against the Hon. Member of Linlithgow (HC 568)

Evidence

Evidence was published, without a Report, on:

HC 268 – i–iii
FCO/ODA Winter Supplementary Estimates 1984/85

HC 376 – i–iv
UK-Soviet Relations

HC 622–i
The Situation in South Africa

Minutes of Proceedings

The Committee's Minutes for the Session were published as HC 607

Session 1985–86

Reports

FIRST REPORT
Winter Supplementary Estimates: Famine in Africa (HC 123)

SECOND REPORT
UK-Soviet Relations (HC 28–I and II)

THIRD REPORT
The Single European Act (HC 442 (6–iii and iv))

FOURTH REPORT
FCO and ODA Supply Estimates 1986–87 (HC 255)

FIFTH REPORT
The United Kingdom and South East Asia: The Philippines (HC 386)

SIXTH REPORT
South Africa (HC 61–I)
South Africa (HC 61–II)

FIRST SPECIAL REPORT
Government Observation on the Fifth Report from the Committee, Session 1984–85 (United Kingdom Membership of UNESCO) (HC 388)

Evidence

Evidence was published, without a Report, on:

HC 183 – i–iv
ODA's Bilateral Country Aid Programmes

HC 368 – i–iv
South East Asia

HC 600 – i and ii
Cultural Diplomacy

Foreign Affairs in General

69–i and ii	UNESCO: Famine in Africa; ODA's Scientific Units (ODA Officials)
69–iii	European Political Co-operation; UNESCO (Foreign Secretary)
69–iv	The Single European Act (FCO)
69–v	Disarmament: Libya; UK–US relations (NATO) (Foreign Secretary)
69–vi	UK-Soviet Relations (Mr Zamyatin)

Minutes of Proceedings

The Committee's Minutes for the Session were published as HC 616

Session 1986–87

FIRST REPORT
South East Asia and Indo-China (HC 114)

SECOND REPORT
Bilateral Aid: Country Programmes (HC 32)

THIRD REPORT
Cyprus (HC 23)

FOURTH REPORT
Cultural Diplomacy (HC 24)

Evidence

Evidence was published, without a Report, on:

HC 125 – i and ii
South Africa

HC 326 – i and i
FCO/ODA Supply Estimates 1987/88

Foreign Affairs in General
HC 150–i   Disarmament; Japan; South East Asia (Foreign Secretary)
HC 150–ii   UNESCO (FCO and ODA)

Minutes of Proceedings

The Committee's Minutes for the Session were published as HC 395

Session 1987–88

Reports

FIRST REPORT
Famine in the Horn of Africa (HC 297)

SECOND REPORT
Current UK Policy towards the Iran/Iraq Conflict: Report and Minutes of Proceedings (HC 297–I)
Minutes of Evidence and Appendices (HC 279–II)

THIRD REPORT
The Political Impact of the Process of Arms Control and Disarmament (HC 280)

FOURTH REPORT
FCO/ODA Expenditure 1988–89 (HC 429)

Minutes of Proceedings

The Committee's Minutes for the Session were published as HC 724 (1987–88)

Session 1988–89

FIRST REPORT
Eastern Europe and the Soviet Union (HC 16)
Government Reply (CM708)

SECOND REPORT
Hong Kong (HC281–I, 281–II)
Government Reply (CM927)
Further Government Reply (CM1082)

THIRD REPORT
FCO/ODA Expenditure (HC 264)
Government Reply (CM 823)

FIRST SPECIAL REPORT
Recent Developments in the Horn of Africa (HC 63)

SECOND SPECIAL REPORT
Informal Meetings Undertaken by the Committee (HC 21)

Appendix 7 Government actions against press and broadcasting leaks 1979–87

November 1979 *The Sunday Times* publishes cabinet committee documents on privatisation. MI5 investigation. No further action.

December 1979 *The Times* publishes cabinet committee information on British nuclear weapons policy. MI5 investigation. No further action.

March/April 1981 Prior details of defence review appearing in several newspapers. Internal MoD inquiry followed, leading to disciplinary action against several officials.

September 1982 *The Economist* publishes Central Policy Review Staff ideas on future public expenditure. MI5 investigation. No further action.

October 1983 The *Guardian* publishes details of future Cruise missile deployments in Britain. Police enquiry led to the prosecution of Sarah Tisdall, a clerk in the FCO, who was jailed for six months for leaking the offending memorandum from the Minister of Defence.

October 1983 *The Observer* publishes MoD documents on problems with weapons procurement. Police enquiry led to (unsuccessful) prosecution of the newspaper, and (successful) prosecution of Raymond Williams, MoD civil servant, who was jailed for six months.

December 1983 *Time Out* publishes details of a conversation between the Master of the Rolls and a senior civil servant. MI5 enquiry followed. Department of Employment official dismissed.

December 1984 Tam Dalyell, MP, is given information about the sinking of the *Belgrano*. Police enquiry led to the prosecution (unsuccessful) of Clive Ponting, a senior MoD official, under Section 2 of the Official Secrets Act.

June 1986 *The Observer* and the *Guardian* publish some of Peter Wright's allegations contained in his book *Spycatcher*. The government obtained injunctions against any further publications.

October 1986 The BBC includes a programme on the Zircon satellite in its *Secret Society* series. Government obtains an injunction to prevent the screening of the programme (ultimately unsuccessfully) and begins legal proceedings against Duncan Campbell, *New Statesman* journalist. Legal proceedings are subsequently dropped.

April 1987 *The Independent* publishes further details of the Wright allegations. The government prosecutes it successfully for contempt of court on the grounds of the injunctions obtained against other newspapers.

December 1987   The BBC prepares a radio programme, *My Country: Right or Wrong*. The government obtains an injunction, ultimately unsuccessful, to prevent its being broadcast.

During most of this time it should also be noted that the Government was pursuing a campaign, ultimately unsuccessfully, to ban the publication of the Peter Wright book, *Spycatcher*. When the government lost this battle, its successful injunctions against newspaper extracts of the book lapsed.During the same period, Chapman Pincher's book, *Their Trade is Treachery*, which repeated many of the Wright allegations, was also published, though no official action was taken against it. Nor was any action taken against ITV over its *World in Action* programme which interviewed Wright, allowing him to repeat his most serious allegations, or against Channel 4 for its programme *MI5 Official Secrets*, in which a former MI5 officer, Cathy Massiter, alleged misconduct on the part of the security service. On 13 October 1988 the House of Lords ruled finally on the *Spycatcher* case. It upheld all of the actions of the newspapers, with one relatively minor exception in the case of one edition of *The Sunday Times*.

Appendix 8   The British press and international affairs

THE SURVEY

A random selection of the editions of ten national daily newspapers was taken over a period of two years from May 1987 to August 1989. Only editions appearing between Monday and Friday were chosen, on the basis that this would constitute the best average coverage and would exclude some of the considerable variations in Saturday editions. In those editions that were surveyed any supplements or special reports were included if they happened to appear that day.

All parts of the newspapers were included, except sports pages, television and entertainment listings, stock market listings, law reports, letters to the editor, advertising copy and diary columns. The latter category presented some difficulties because many papers, particularly the tabloids, do not make a clear distinction between diary pieces and authored columns, and a good deal of their news is gossip which appears in a succession of small blocks. Gossip columns in the tabloids were therefore included, since this makes up a large proportion of their news and features and becomes impossible to disentangle from other news. Diary pieces such as those by Miles Kington, Peter Simple or Clement Freud were excluded from the quality press, as were agony aunt, cartoon, puzzle or horoscope columns from the tabloids.

The size of the sample covered 127 editions which contained a total of some 86 000 column inches. Fifty one editions covered the four quality papers, *The Independent, The Times, The Daily Telegraph* and the *Guardian.* Thirty-eight editions covered the mid-market tabloids, *The Daily Express, Today,* and *The Daily Mail.* Thirty-eight editions covered the other tabloids, the *Daily Mirror, Sun,* and *Daily Star.*

In surveying the relevant sections of the papers, the author 'allocated' column inches from single items into different categories where this was relevant. In the quality press, this was seldom necessary in the case of news coverage which is clearly structured by its origin. In the case of the tabloid press, however, most international news is a reflection of domestic news ('Maggie slams the Eurocrats') and it was necessary to allocate, say a six-inch column as 3:3 or perhaps 4:2. The same was done for features in both the quality and tabloid press. Some features were unambiguously inter-national ('What future for Perestroika?'). Many features, however, are not directly political but cover social, human interest, arts, fashion, book reviews, travel subjects, and so on. In these cases the article was analysed to provide an allocation of column inches that would reflect the degree of awareness it showed of the external world. Thus, cookery or motoring features proved to be overwhelmingly domestic, while travel, and television or cinema features were predominantly international. Arts and book reviews were an uneven mixture.

The business sections were treated separately throughout. Items of business interest that appear occasionally on the front page are treated as ordinary news. Only that appearing within the designated 'business section' has been analysed under this category. For our purposes, 'business section' has been taken to include 'Money', 'City', 'Personal Finance' sections, and so on, which many of the tabloid press run.

Analysis

This survey was undertaken not just to measure how the press dealt with foreign politics, but rather to assess the degree to which the press was introspective or open to international influences across the range of its coverage. It is concerned, therefore both with political news coverage and also with the awareness of the external world that is contained in the non-news and non-political items in the average daily newspaper.

It is possible to draw quantitative conclusions, based on the data collected, and some more tentative, qualitative conclusions based on some impressions gained throughout the process of analysis.

Quantitative Conclusions

1   News Coverage of International Affairs

The standard wisdom is that quality newspapers devote about 20–25 percent of their news coverage, and tabloid papers around 10 percent of their news coverage, to international affairs. This may have been true in 1971 when those figures were first published, but now there is a much greater spread in the figures. The quality press in this survey devoted some 40 percent of its news coverage to international affairs: the mid-market tabloids devoted 15 percent, and the other tabloids only 5 percent even on a generous interpretation of what constituted international affairs (Table 8A:2a).

2   Feature Coverage of International Affairs

A similar pattern is displayed in the coverage of features. The quality press devoted some 23 percent of its feature coverage to the external world: the mid-market tabloids 7 percent; and the other tabloids barely 3 percent (Table 8A:3).

3   News and Feature Coverage

Feature coverage may be a more telling indication of the level of openness or insularity of the British press than news coverage. News coverage, certainly in the quality press, tends to be structured by the pattern of foreign correspondents that a paper chooses to employ, or the rate at which they normally take material from the international news agencies. Features, however, may reflect greater editorial discretion, and though political features are often given a prominent position, they make up a minor part of the amount of total feature coverage. The degree to which features display an awareness of the external world, therefore, is probably the most telling indicator of the openness of the press. There is no significant difference in the balance between the amount of space given to features as opposed to news as between the quality and the tabloid press (Table 8A:1a)

4 Business Coverage of International Affairs

Given the transnational nature of the modern business world, it is surprising that business pages display comparatively little international material. The quality press devotes 15–20 percent of its business news and features to international business affairs. Figures for the other papers do not conform to any obvious pattern, mainly because the average number of column inches devoted to such matters is so small. All of the mid-market and other tabloids have financial sections, mainly concentrated on personal investment, though some of these only appear on one day of the week (Table 8A:5).

5 Editorial Coverage of International Affairs

The quality press generally operate a consistent policy of ensuring that every second or third editorial piece refers to international events, though the pieces themselves are often shorter than domestic editorial articles. Their average editorial coverage of international topics is just under 45 percent. The tabloids are more variable since they devote few inches in total to editorials and sometimes cover three or four items in six to eight column inches (Table 8A:4).

6 Average Newsprint Per Edition

There is now an enormous variation in the amount of newsprint offered by all the papers. In this survey, *The Times* and the *Guardian* average more than 1 200 column inches every day, about three times as much as the mid-market tabloids and up to five times as much as the average for the *Daily Star*. These figures understate the variation since they exclude sports coverage, various listings, diaries and notice-board items and so on. In all of these cases, including sport, the quality press offers substantially more column inches than the tabloids (Table 8A.1a).

7 Average Column Inches Per Region

Variations between the quality and the tabloid press, expressed here in percentage coverage, are greatly magnified if average numbers of column inches devoted to given regions are compared. An indication of the brevity of some of the tabloid coverage is provided by the fact that, on average, one tabloid column inch contains 30–35 words; one quality press column inch averages 50 words (Table 8A.1b).

8 *Concentration on Certain Regions*

In virtually every case, at least two-thirds of all news coverage is absorbed by news from Western Europe, the Middle East, North America, and the world of the socialist states (Eastern Europe, China, and the individual socialist states around the world). Asia, East Asia, Australasia, Africa, Central and South America together absorb just over a third of all the other quality press news coverage; and a much lower proportion of the others, from a third to a twentieth. Such a concentration may not be surprising, though in the case of the tabloids it seems to become quite severe. There does not appear to be any obvious imbalance between coverage of the Western World and the Socialist World, though in the past, such an imbalance had certainly been noted. The events within the socialist bloc over the last two years, however, appear to be adequately reflected in the amount of news coverage. There was little or no coverage at all of a strictly functional category – the international economy. This was introduced to see how far the press was prepared to deal explicitly in international categories that were not state-centric: in this case with one that assumes an undisputed importance. The evidence from this, and the presentation of the business sections, however, is that the press reflects a strongly state-centric, or personality-based, yardstick for the relevance of news (Table 8A.2b).

Qualitative Conclusions

1 *The Diversity of the National Press*

The press is probably more diverse now than ever before. There are more papers to choose from, they are capable of producing more newsprint, and they offer a wider range of journalistic styles than ever before. Increasingly, there is a gulf between the standards of the quality press and that of the tabloids which may make comparisons relatively meaningless. In this respect, international affairs coverage exposes the greatest diversities, since there is greater editorial discretion in the type and amount of such coverage as compared with domestic affairs

2 *The Quality Press*

The quality press is becoming more structured. Newspapers have a series of discreet sections to deal with different categories of news, different types of features, and so on. International affairs do not figure very strongly in those categories. There are clear foreign news pages and normally a prominent slot for major political articles on foreign affairs. *The Independent*, for example, has adopted a clear policy of putting a high proportion of international articles on its major feature pages. The *Guardian* does this less obviously, but offers a more international flavour to many of its other features and makes special efforts to cover Third World development issues. But, in general, there are few slots in the editorial structures of the quality papers that regularly cover any thematic aspects of international affairs. By contrast, many thematic aspects of domestic affairs are catered for in sections entitled 'Living', 'Media', 'Society Tomorrow', 'Women', 'Motoring' and so on. These sections are not bereft of international perspectives, but their criteria of relevance appears to be intrinsically domestic.

3   The Tabloid Press

Tabloid newspapers are far less structured than the quality press. The midmarket tabloids retain a reasonably regular editorial structure, though there is an inevitable drift in the nature of the material which blurs the older distinctions between news, features, comment and gossip. The other tabloids, the *Daily Mirror*, the *Sun*, and the *Daily Star*, have a clear editorial formula but almost no discernible structure. News drifts into features, comment and gossip, and it is difficult to see any obvious connection between them other than a photograph or a famous name. The *Sun* (16 September 1988) managed to devise a business feature around 'Raunchy Suzy Quatro and Money' and another (15 June 1989) on the notion (with a photograph) that the length of girl's skirts was a reflection of the trend in stock market prices. Most business sections in the tabloids are primarily concerned with personal investment schemes; how to make money. The *Sun* and the *Daily Star*, however, appear to be more concerned in their business sections with how the rich spend it. The *Daily Star*, for instance, has run features on how Jack Nicolson (1 August 1989) and Ivan Lendl (4 July 1989) spend their money. And both the *Daily Mail* (21 January 1989) and *Today* (14 August 1989), for example, have run major feature spreads on the rich and their money.

The lack of clear demarcation lines between types of material extends to editorials, where jokes and puns often make up the substance of an editorial item. The blurring of the boundaries applies more dramatically to advertising. There is no longer a very clear line between newspaper copy and advertising copy. Newspapers' advertising of their own competitions, of their special offers, of their next editions, of satellite television and their parent companies, and of telephone chat lines, increasingly form a seamless web of multi-coloured and frankly confusing copy. The *Daily Star*'s 'Star Finance' section, for example, consists entirely of a page of loan advertisements: the *Daily Mirror*'s lotto competition mixes into its front page story about credit cards (23 August 1989), and entertainment listings and features in some tabloids shade easily into advertising for Sky Television. The survey noted (Table 8A.6) the proportion of the tabloids' copy that was not newspaper copy in the conventional sense at all: news or other material that was simply manufactured by the newspaper itself (much of it concerning soap opera stars or royalty), where it was impossible to discern an event or a development that the item was about. Anything from 8 percent to 50 percent of tabloid copy could be made up of such material.

The effect of all this on international coverage appears to be twofold. First, there are few sections where international material might be expected to appear. The *Daily Express* and the *Daily Mail* run 'World Report' and

'World Wide' sections, but the other tabloids simply mix any snippets of news or particular features into the general melting pot where there seems to be a decreasing amount of space for real news or features that say something about the world outside television. Second, international items tend to be gossip about international personalities or incidents, rather than news as other papers would define it, though this is less so of the mid-market tabloids. This seems to have accelerated the trend towards national stereo-typing in the tabloids. The tabloids tend to build their coverage of international affairs around individual leaders, like Gorbachev or the American president. Where individuals are less prominent or notorious, as in Europe, coverage is built around shorthand national stereotypes. As news, features and comment merge, therefore, so the down-market tabloids have created an international world populated by figures such as Ron, Gorby, Dr K., Charles and Di: or else by 'Euro-crats' (anyone working in Brussels), 'Frogs' (the French), 'Krauts' (Germans), 'Mad Alis' (Iranians) and 'Maggie' (the British Government). Characterisations are therefore very limited and it is difficult to imagine how these tabloids could handle any of the increasing complexity of international affairs.

4 The Purposes of the Press

Given what has been said on the variations in type and amount of content, the essential purposes of the quality and the tabloid press may be more diverse than ever before. Having to take second place to television in the provision of news itself, both the quality and tabloid press try to capitalise on their ability to provide background and features. While the quality press competes fiercely to differentiate itself from television and provide more informative material, the tabloids have stopped competing and embraced their competitor. They seem content to use the potential they have of informing their readers more deeply, merely to entertain more derivatively.

Table 8A.1a   Average column inches per edition

	Inter-national news	Domestic news	Business news	Total news	Features	Business features	Total column inches
The Independent	236	297	143	676	359	53	1088
The Times	224	378	196	798	363	70	1231
The Daily Telegraph	185	367	135	687	292	88	1067
Guardian	231	322	108	661	529	65	1255
Daily Express	35	182	32	249	159	18	426
Today	31	194	51	276	151	19	446
Daily Mail	35	180	40	255	156	32	443
Daily Mirror	8	157	1	166	121	4	291
Sun	10	161	9	180	117	4	301
Daily Star	7	145	4	156	72	12	240

Note: See the analysis on p.319 for the sections not included in this total.

Table 8A.1b   Average daily column inches on regions

	Western Europe	Middle East	North America	Socialist world	Other regions	Inter-national economy
The Independent	48	34	32	36	94	5
The Times	31	32	28	47	84	2
The Daily Telegraph	28	29	24	42	67	0
Guardian	46	29	39	57	57	2
Daily Express	6	4	8	6	11	0
Today	5	3	5	14	5	0
Daily Mail	6	2	15	5	8	0
Daily Mirror	1	0.2	3	1	3	0
Sun	3	0.3	2	3	1	0
Daily Star	2	2	2	2	0.4	0

Table 8A.2b   Coverage of regions as a percentage of all
international news coverage

	Western Europe	Middle East	North America	Socialist world	Other regions	International economy
The Independent	18.7	13.6	13.5	15.1	37.1	2.0
The Times	14.2	14.5	12.3	20.8	37.2	1.0
The Daily Telegraph	15.3	15.6	13.2	22.6	36.2	0.0
Guardian	19.6	12.5	16.7	24.6	24.8	1.0
Daily Express	18.2	11.6	21.4	18.2	30.4	0.0
Today	14.5	9.7	15.5	43.9	16.1	0.0
Daily Mail	7.4	4.3	43.9	13.9	21.6	0.0
Daily Mirror	11.6	1.7	34.2	19.8	32.4	0.0
Sun	31.4	2.3	22.9	28.5	14.2	0.0
Daily Star	24.7	21.3	24.7	23.6	5.4	0.0

Table 8A.2a   Coverage of domestic and international affairs as a
percentage of all news coverage

	Total Domestic	Total International	Western Europe	Middle East	North America	Socialist world	Other regions	International economy
The Independent	55.3	44.7	8.4	6.1	6.0	6.7	16.6	0.9
The Times	62.3	37.7	5.3	5.4	4.6	7.7	13.9	0.4
The Daily Telegraph	66.3	33.7	5.1	5.2	4.4	7.6	12.1	0.0
Guardian	57.8	42.2	8.3	5.2	6.9	10.3	10.4	0.4
Daily Express	83.1	16.8	2.9	1.9	3.4	2.9	4.9	0.0
Today	86.4	13.6	2.0	1.3	2.1	6.0	2.2	0.0
Daily Mail	83.9	16.1	2.6	0.7	7.1	2.3	3.5	0.0
Daily Mirror	95.1	4.9	0.5	0.1	1.6	0.9	1.5	0.0
Sun	93.9	6.0	1.9	0.1	1.1	1.7	0.8	0.0
Daily Star	95.2	4.8	1.2	1.0	1.2	1.1	0.3	0.0

Table 8A.3   Feature coverage*

	Ave daily % of domestic features	Ave daily % of international features
The Independent	80.9	19.1
The Times	76.3	23.7
The Daily Telegraph	77.3	22.7
Guardian	74.6	25.4
Daily Express	90.5	9.5
Today	96.1	3.9
Daily Mail	92.0	8.0
Daily Mirror	97.0	3.0
Sun	98.0	2.0
Daily Star	96.1	3.9

* Includes all features, political, social, artistic, specialist, e.g., tourism or careers but excludes business section features.

Table 8A.4   Editorial coverage

	Ave daily total all editorial inches	Ave daily total int edit inches	% of int edit inches
The Independent	22.2	7.2	32.4
The Times	31.4	18.6	59.2
The Daily Telegraph	12.9	5.4	41.9
Guardian	31.7	13.9	43.8
Daily Express	10.1	0.9	8.9
Today	11.2	2.3	20.5
Daily Mail	11.8	0.2	1.69
Daily Mirror	6.6	2.0	30.3
Sun	9.8	1.2	12.2
Daily Star	4.9	0.5	10.2

Table 8A.5   Business coverage*

	Ave daily business news (inches)	% Domestic	% Internat	Ave daily business features (inches)	% Domestic	% Internat.
The Independent	143	83.3	16.7	53	76.0	24.0
The Times	196	81.1	18.9	70	87.3	12.7
The Daily Telegraph	135	86.7	13.3	88	81.0	19.0
Guardian	108	82.7	17.3	65	75.5	24.5
Daily Express	32	89.2	10.8	18	81.2	18.8
Today	51	96.8	3.2	19	100.0	0.0
Daily Mail	40	90.0	10.0	32	96.5	3.5
Daily Mirror+	1	100.0	0.0	4	100.0	0.0
Sun+	9	97.4	2.6	4	89.4	10.6
Daily Star+	4	97.1	2.9	12	100.0	0.0

* Includes all business sections but excludes business matters which may be reported in other parts of the newspaper.
+ The percentages recorded here are relatively insignificant since the numbers of relevant column inches are so small.

Table 8A.6   News/features relevance in tabloids

	COLUMN INCHES		
	Total news features	Internal copy *	Internal copy as a percentage
Daily Express	376	89	24
Today	375	54	14
Daily Mail	371	31	8
Daily Mirror	286	106	37
The Sun	288	146	51
Daily Star	224	75	33

* 'Internal copy' is used here as a definition of material that appears to be entirely manufactured by the newspaper itself and does not seem to relate to any genuine event or trend in the outside world. Obvious examples would be the *Daily Star* or *Sun*'s copy for page three photographs: 'Gorgeous Gaynor Goodman's favourite picture ...', and so on. Other material in this category would include front page items such as 'Neighbours stars Alan Dale, Stefan Dennis and Fiona Corke launched fabulous *Sun* Lotto 4 last night ...'. In general, the author put material into this category where there did not seem to be a traditional legitimate press rationale behind it.

Appendix 9   Public opinion poll data

This presents a selection of public poll data on those issues examined in Chapter 6 on which it is possible to discern trends over a number of years.

GPI represents the monthly Gallup Political Index. All figures are expressed as percentages.

NATO

Q.   In case of war, to what extent do you think we could list the USA as an ally?

	Mar. 1984	Mar. 1986	Mar. 1989
A great deal	42	47	43
Up to a point	38	35	38
Not at all	14	13	11
Don't know	6	5	7

Source: GPI March 1984, March 1986, March 1989.

Q.   Do you think that the NATO alliance should be maintained or is the alliance not necessary any more?

	Oct. 1989
Should stay	71
Not necessary now	15
No opinion	14

Source: GPI October 1989.

Q.   Should Britain continue as a member of NATO?

	Sept. 1985
Yes	76
No	13
Don't know	12

329

INDEPENDENT DETERRENT

Q.   Should Great Britain get rid of all nuclear weapons even if other countries keep theirs?

	Yes	No	Don't know
Oct. 1981	23	69	8
Jan. 1983	23	72	5
Oct. 1983	25	73	2
Nov. 1986	31	63	6

Source: British Public Opinion (MORI), vol. 8 (10), November 1986.

Q.   It has been suggested that Great Britain should give up relying on nuclear weapons for defence whatever other countries decide. Do you think this is a good idea or a bad idea?

	Sep. 1980	Aug. 1986	Jan. 1987
Good idea	21	33	34
Bad idea	67	57	55
Don't know	11	9	11

Source: GPI September 1980, August 1986, January 1987.

TECHNOLOGY AND SCIENCE

Q.   Overall, do science and technology do more good than harm, or more harm than good?

	1985	1989
More good than harm	45	44
More harm than good	11	9
About equal	38	37
Don't know	6	10

Source: GPI May 1981, September 1989.

Q.   Leaving out military applications . . . do you think that scientific discovery can have a dangerous effect on war?

Yes	73
No	19
Don't know	9

Source: GPI May 1985.

Q.   How concerned are you that a similar nuclear accident to Chernobyl would occur in Britain?

Concerned	73
Not concerned	26

Source: GPI May 1986.

Q. What do you think should be the development of nuclear power generation in this country?

	May 1986	Jun. 1988	Mar. 1989
Should increase it	18	20	22
Should not develop more	39	41	37
Should stop generating it	36	33	33
Don't know	8	5	7

Source: GPI May 1986, June 1987, March 1989.

Q. What do you think about nuclear weapons in the long run?

Countries possess these weapons – whatever I personally do will make no difference	42
Some weapons are needed for deterrence but levels of weapons should be drastically reduced	48
One of the problems of nuclear weapons is the danger from accidental use	51

Note: These were easily the most popular three responses from a selection of 10 possible responses to the question.

Source: GPI June 1987.

EUROPEAN COMMUNITY

Q. People have been talking about something that is going to happen in 1992. Do you know what is going to happen in 1992?

	May 1988	Jun 1988
EEC as one with open trade	19	29
General mentions of EC	2	3
Full member of EC	1	2
Don't know	54	42

Source: GPI May 1988, June 1988.

Q. Generally speaking, do you think that Great Britain's membership of the European Community is a good thing, a bad thing, or neither?

	Jan. 1976	Jun. 1979	Jun. 1984	Oct. 1987	Aug. 1988	Mar. 1989
Good	50	37	34	36	36	36
Bad	24	34	36	35	36	30
Neither	17	19	26	21	18	27
Don't know	9	10	4	9	9	7

Source: GPI January 1976, June 1979, June 1984, October 1987, August 1988, March 1989.

SPECIFIC EUROPEAN COMMUNITY MATTERS

Q.   Here is a list of things that the European Community is urging Great Britain to do at the moment . . . Could you tell me, in each case, whether you think this is something Great Britain should do or not?

	Yes	*No*	*Don't know*
Agree to European beach cleanliness standards	92	4	4
Create a Euro-currency and scrap the £	31	56	12
Accept Euro-drinking water standards	82	10	8
Agree to abolish frontier controls between Community member-states	38	48	13

Source: GPI June 1988.

BRITAIN AS A WORLD POWER

Q.   Do you think that Britain's influence in the world has increased, decreased, or remained the same, over the past two years?

	1965	*1978*	*1981*
Increased	16	14	13
Decreased	40	48	59
Same	33	31	25
Don't know	11	6	3

Source: *Gallup Report 1981* (London: Sphere Books, 1982).

Q.   Do you think it is important for this country to try to be a leading power, or would you like to see us be more like Sweden and Switzerland?

	1965	*1985*
Be a world power	55	37
More like Sweden/Switzerland	26	55
Don't know	19	8

Source: *Gallup Survey of Britain 1985* (London: Croom Helm, 1986).

CONFIDENCE IN SUPERPOWER LEADERSHIP

Q. How much confidence do you have in the ability of the United States to deal wisely with present world problems – very great, considerable, little or very little? ('None at all', 'Don't know' are also available.)

	% of respondents answering 'very great' or 'considerable'	*% of respondents answering 'little' or 'very little'*
1977	48	36
1978	37	43
1979	28	50
1980	33	49
1981	30	49
1982	27	53
1983	24	58
Feb. 1984	27	47
Apr. 1984	19	58
Jun. 1984	22	55
Aug. 1984	20	57
Nov. 1984	27	52
Jan. 1985	20	58
Jul. 1985	26	57
Sep. 1985	23	55
Oct. 1985	28	50
Mar. 1986	30	53
Apr. 1 1986	21	53
Apr. 16 1986	29	50
Apr. 21 1986	27	50
Apr. 28 1986	29	49
Jun. 1986	20	57
Oct. 1986	28	54

Note: During the period from 1977–86, the number of people who answered 'None at all' rose from 7 per cent in 1977 to as high as 23 per cent in 1984. On average, however, from 1977–83 the figure was 11 per cent. From 1983 to 1986, it has averaged 17 per cent.

Source: GPI on the dates shown.

Q. All in all, do you have a good opinion of Mr Gorbachev, the Russian leader, or not such a good opinion?

	Feb. 1989
Good	79
Not so good	8
Don't know	14

Q.   All in all, do you have a good opinion of Mr Bush, the American leader, or not such a good opinion?

	Feb. 1989
Good	31
Not so good	20
Don't know	49

Q.   Do you think Mr Bush is or is not proving to be a good President of the USA?

	Nov. 1989	*Jan. 1990*
Is	39	44
Is not	18	17
Don't know	44	39

Source: GPI February 1989, November 1989, January 1990.

Q.   Do you think Mr Reagan is or is not proving to be a good president of the USA?

	Apr. 1986	*Aug. 1987*	*Jan. 1988*
Is	36	29	36
Is not	52	61	53
Don't know	12	9	12

Q.   Has your opinion of President Reagan changed recently?

	Apr. 1986	*Aug. 1987*	*Jan. 1988*
Gone up	11	2	8
Gone down	38	47	30
remained the same	48	49	59
Don't know	3	2	4

Q.   Do you think Mr Carter is proving a good President of the USA?

	Oct. 1978	*Jan. 1979*
Yes	48	42
No	32	37
Don't know	20	21

Q.   Has your opinion of President Carter changed recently?

	Oct. 1978	*Jan. 1979*
Gone up	23	8
Gone down	19	22
Remained the same	51	60
Don't know	6	10

Source: GPI   January   1979,   May   1986,   August   1987,   January 1988.

Q. Do you approve or disapprove of the role the United States is now playing in World Affairs? And what about the role of Russia?

Percentage of respondents answering 'Disapprove':

	Disapprove of United States	Disapprove of Russia
Nov. 1983	55	75
Feb. 1984	59	71
Jun. 1984	53	74
Aug. 1984	53	69
Nov. 1984	49	73
Jan. 1985	47	62
Jul. 1985	51	58
Sep. 1985	52	65
Oct. 1985	48	59
Mar. 1986	45	54
Apr. 1 1986	56	53
Apr. 16 1986	59	51
Apr. 21 1986	58	46
Apr. 28 1986	55	50
Jun. 1986	57	52
Oct. 1986	50	48
Aug. 1987	56	41
Sep. 1987	50	37
Oct. 1987	46	35
Nov. 1987	47	38
Jan. 1988	41	30

Note: The US attack on Libya took place on 14–15 April 1986.
Source: GPI on the dates shown.

SPECIFIC ISSUES CONCERNING THE SUPERPOWERS

Q. What is your opinion of the USA's/USSR's main objective at summit conferences? Are they more interested in maintaining a stronger military position than their 'opponents' or in reducing world tension?

	Aug. 1987		Dec. 1987	
	SU	US	SU	US
Strong military position	25	41	19	30
Reducing world tension	33	17	40	24

Source: GPI Dec 1987.

Q. Do you think the Russians/Americans can generally be trusted to keep to their agreement on nuclear arms or not?

	Russia	*USA*
Can be trusted	22	30
Cannot be trusted	64	56
Don't know	14	14

Source: *Gallup Survey of Britain 1985* (London: Croom Helm, 1986).

Q. If the United States and the Soviet Union reached an agreement on arms control, do you think the Soviet Union/United States would live up to the agreement or would it cheat?

	Soviet Union	*United States*
Live up to agreement	50	39
Would cheat	31	40
Don't know	18	21

Source: GPI October 1987.

Q. On the issue of limiting nuclear weapons, who do you find more believable – President Ronald Reagan or the Russian leader – Mr Gorbachev?

President Reagan	20
Mr Gorbachev	44
Neither	26
Don't know	10

Source: GPI April 1987.

Q. In your opinion which of the following best describes the Soviet Union's/United States' main objectives in world affairs?

	Sep. 1986		*Dec. 1987*	
	SU	*US*	*SU*	*US*
Russia/America seek to compete with America/Russia for more influence in different parts of the world	34	39	40	42

	Sep. 1986		Dec. 1987	
	SU	*US*	*SU*	*US*
Russia/America seeks global domination and will risk major war to achieve that domination if it can't be achieved by another means	9	11	6	7

Q. Do you approve or disapprove of the way the US/Russia is handling the problem in the Gulf between Iraq and Iran?

	Aug. 1987	
	US	*Russia*
Approve	33	25
Disapprove	46	33
Don't know	21	42

Source: GPI September 1987.

Q. Do you think that US/Russian actions in the Gulf will improve the situation or make it worse?

	July 1987	
	US	*Russia*
Improve	16	10
Worsen	57	36
No effect	6	13
Don't know	21	41

Source: GPI August 1987.

	Apr. 1987			*Jan. 1988*		
	Agree	*Disagree*	*DK*	*Agree*	*Disagree*	*DK*
Q. The US will never be first to use nuclear weapons	24	53	23	24	46	31
The Soviet Union will never be 1st to use nuclear weapons	29	45	25	25	42	34

Source: GPI January 1988.

Q.   Which is more likely to start a nuclear attack in Europe, the United
     States or the Soviet Union?

	Jan. 1983	Apr. 1987
US	28	45
SU	48	24
Don't know	24	31

Source: GPI April 1987.

Q.   Which superpower do you believe poses the greatest threat to peace in
     Europe, the United States or the Soviet Union?

	Dec. 1985
US	32
SU	33
Equal	28
Don't know	7

Source: GPI December 1985.

Index